THE MAKING OF STONEHENGE

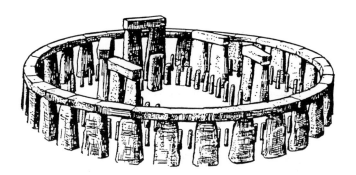

THE MAKING OF STONEHENGE

Rodney Castleden

Illustrated by the author

London and New York

First published 1993
by Routledge
11 New Fetter Lane, London EC4P 4EE

Simultaneously published in the USA and Canada
by Routledge
29 West 35th Street, New York, NY 10001

Typeset in Garamond by Florencetype Ltd, Kewstoke, Avon
Printed and bound in Great Britain by
Biddles Ltd, Guildford

British Library Cataloguing in Publication Data
A catalogue record for this book is available from the British Library

Library of Congress Cataloging in Publication Data
Castleden. Rodney.
The making of Stonehenge / Rodney Castleden.
p. cm.
Includes bibliographical references (p.) and index.
1. Stonehenge (England) 2. Megalithic monuments—England—Wiltshire. 3. Man,
Prehistoric—England–Wiltshire. 4. Wiltshire (England)—Antiquities. I. Title.
DA142.C37 1993
942.3′—dc20
93–12736

ISBN 0-415-08513-6

To Robin Ruffell, for old times' sake

And there is on this island a magnificent precinct sacred to Apollo and a notable spherical temple decorated with many votive offerings. There is also a community sacred to this god, where many of the inhabitants . . . worship the god with songs celebrating his deeds . . . It is said that the god returns to the island every 19 years, the period in which the return of the stars to the same place in the heavens is accomplished. At the time of the appearance, the god plays on the lyre and dances continuously by night from the spring equinox until the rising of the Pleiades.

Diodorus Siculus *Histories* Book V (50–30 BC),
paraphrasing Hecateus (330 BC), in what
may be the earliest documented description
of Stonehenge.

CONTENTS

ILLUSTRATIONS

FIGURES

PLATES

ACKNOWLEDGEMENTS

I am grateful to Carole Owen and Sue Marlow at English Heritage for making such smooth and easy arrangements for me to walk among the stones at the centre of Stonehenge and supplying me with a ladder so that I could reach the upper parts of the stones. I also have to thank Brian Davison, Inspector of Ancient Monuments, for giving his permission for me to take rubbings of the carvings on some of the stones. Shorrocks Security Guards watch over Stonehenge during the hours of darkness, when English Heritage go home to bed. The guards were both helpful and considerate, showing a sensitive concern for the monument and its past as well as caring for its present and future; I am grateful to them for keeping a discrete but benevolent distance while supervising my antics with compass, camera, measuring tape, ladder, rolls of paper and crayons: they must have wondered what I was at.

Brian McGregor, Librarian at the Ashmolean Library in Oxford, was once again kind enough to allow me the run of the archaeological books and journals in his care. I am grateful to John and Celia Clarke for their hospitality during my reading weeks in Oxford, as I am to Peter and Marilyn Swann for giving me a bed when I needed to undertake fieldwork in Wiltshire.

Conversations with Sir Michael Tippett led me to look at Stonehenge's location more carefully than I might otherwise have done. His deceptively simple interjection 'But why *there*?' led me to some unexpected conclusions: it was the right question at the right moment.

I owe a particular debt to Nigel Rose, a stone rubbing expert I met quite by chance at Stonehenge. While I made my rubbing of the 'box symbol' on stone 57, Nigel drove to Avebury to find, inspect and photograph the rubbings made forty years before by Robert Newall. The transparent vufoils Nigel later made of the Newall rubbing and my own have not only made detailed comparison much easier, but also made it possible to bring into sharper focus some major problems about the symbol's shape and meaning.

RC, Brighton, 1993.

1

INTRODUCTION

When, in 1986, I was writing an account of the society that produced Stonehenge, I emphasized that Stonehenge would only make sense when it was viewed within its cultural context. The way to the truth about Stonehenge seemed then to be to forget about Stonehenge in the first instance, to study the archaeology of other sites and then to piece the whole culture together like a jigsaw puzzle, starting with the edges and working in towards the centre. That centre was, of course, Stonehenge.[1] Even though that was not the prime intention, the writing of *The Stonehenge People* clarified my ideas about Stonehenge: I began to see it as through a dispersing early morning mist. More recently I compiled a gazetteer of the neolithic sites in Britain, mainly as a companion volume to *The Stonehenge People* to show the sort of archaeological site data that were available to justify and substantiate the more general statements in the earlier book, but something else happened.[2] I found that by looking closely at all the available evidence about all the British neolithic sites I was in effect assembling the pieces of an even bigger jigsaw puzzle than before. My image of Stonehenge became more sharply focused too, as if I was seeing it in the clear light of day for the first time. It is that sharper, clearer picture resulting from a second, longer and more arduous journey through the archaeological evidence that I want to share with readers.

In his thought-provoking book *Rethinking the Neolithic*, Julian Thomas expresses the view that searching for change through time in prehistory is in effect a means of disrupting the presumed continuities which are the foundation of the conventional wisdom.[3] I hope it will become apparent in *this* book that Stonehenge tells a different story altogether. When we look very closely at what appears to be a series of separate monuments built successively on or close to the same site, we will find a surprisingly large number of common threads and common themes that run through from stage to stage. In other words, *The Making of Stonehenge* reinforces, and perhaps plays its part in rediscovering, an idea of continuity at a time when many are ready to opt for discontinuity.

This may be an appropriate moment, before the story begins to unfold, to

1

reflect on our method and approach. How should we go about thinking about the remote past? Thinking about last week is easy: social customs, daily work routines, political contexts and perceptions of needs have not changed in that time so there is a continuum within which we can easily visualize what we, or others, were doing. But with the remote past it is different. There are dangers in regarding the distant past as essentially the same as the present or even the same as later periods of the past. There are problems in that, once we infer a structure such as the chiefdom society idea for bronze age Wessex, a part at least of our minds tends to succumb to all the associated assumptions and subordinate ideas that rightly belong to later examples of chiefdoms and we begin, willy-nilly, to impose mental stereo-types and to develop models of behaviour that may be totally anachronistic. Steering ourselves away from this 'Past-as-Present' way of thinking is difficult because modern analogues make the past more recognizable, more reassuring, more approachable. The Past-as-Other carries difficulties of its own: a culture that, when reconstructed, is totally alien is hard to imagine and also hard to test for internal consistency. Yet the Britain of the remote past may well have been like this: it may have been totally alien. As L. P. Hartley says, 'The past is a foreign country: they do things differently there.'[4]

If we seek to reconstruct the way Stonehenge came to be built we have another problem to contend with, and that is that archaeologists themselves shift their position from time to time. Traditionally, they have tended to view ancient cultures in terms of palaeotechnology: hence the stone age/ bronze age division. In the 1960s and 1970s there was a fruitful change towards the study of palaeoeconomics, and many useful studies have put the building of prehistoric monuments very successfully into a context of strained man–land relationships. This is an idea which reasserts itself during the course of this book, and seems to be an integral part of the Stonehenge saga.

In the 1980s a new approach emerged, one whose potential is only just beginning to be realized, and that is the study or rather the inference of palaeoideology. This is difficult, because it involves us in entering the often exotic thought-world of a remote and long-dead people. One useful idea which this approach has produced, to give an example, is that neolithic people were neolithic, rather than belonging to any other culture or value-system, because they recognized the potential of their raw materials and artefacts (or made objects) to symbolize and express the important division of the universe into Wild and Tame, Made and Unmade.[5]

Well, so it may be, and I believe the evidence does show this, but does it necessarily tell us the all-important thing: what did it mean to be a neolithic person? I think tracing the saga of the making of Stonehenge through the uncharted centuries of British prehistory may tell us at least part of the answer, and also tell us in what ways living in the bronze age (about

2100–750 BC) that followed the neolithic was different. Tracing the story of Stonehenge's rise and fall after all covers a very long period. If we take the history of the oldest cathedral in Christendom and double it we are still a thousand years short of the time Stonehenge took to evolve.

It was Colonel Hawley who, in the most literal sense, uncovered most of what we know about Stonehenge, and yet he understood very little of what he saw. His final verdict in 1928 as he came to the end of his excavations, the most extensive ever undertaken at Stonehenge, was pessimistic. 'So very little is known for certain about the place that what I say is mainly conjecture, and it is to be hoped that future excavators will be able to throw more light upon it than I have done.'[6]

Now, we have more to go on. There have, for example, been the important excavations of Stone, Piggott, Atkinson and Pitts: there are also radiocarbon dates for several phases of the monument's development. There have also been excavations at many of the monuments in the landscape round Stonehenge, which show an important continuity of tradition. There is a tendency, for example, for the neolithic and early bronze age monuments to 'point' towards the north-east: it is not just successive stages of Stonehenge which do this (Stonehenges I, II, IIIa and IIIc), but also the earlier earth circle up at Robin Hood's Ball on the shallow hill top to the north and the linear earthworks of the Great Cursus and Lesser Cursus close at hand. The monuments sprang from a very long-lasting fund of beliefs and customs held by the people of the area and presumably passed on by oral tradition. For this reason, I place Stonehenge repeatedly within its geographical frame, and the chronological series of maps in the text shows an area of 100 sq. km, a square 10 km by 10 km, with Stonehenge at its centre (see Figures 11, 16, 17, 20, 29, 41, 58, 92, 97). The people who conceived, built and used Stonehenge will have been very familiar with this area, where they built their houses, lived out their lives, gathered their firewood, hunted, grew their cereals and herded their cattle and pigs. As we shall see, putting Stonehenge into its geographical setting will help us to understand the whole ceremonial landscape, of which Stonehenge is but a part.

The Making of Stonehenge does not attempt to cover all aspects of the monument. Christopher Chippindale's excellent *Stonehenge Complete* deals with the social history of Stonehenge in modern times in vivid detail, whereas this book deals exclusively with the prehistoric Stonehenge.[7] Now seems like the right moment to attempt to collate all the scientific evidence, take account of modern archaeologists' interpretations, and attempt a synthesis that contains Stonehenge's meaning: it is very specifically Stonehenge's meaning to its makers that matters. This task is made easier for me by the existence of Atkinson's classic, though now rather dated, work written in the 1950s and the more recent books by Aubrey Burl and Julian Richards.[8]

It is difficult to fight one's way past the familiarity of the image of

Stonehenge from a thousand advertisements, posters, postcards, cartoons and book jackets. It has been dragged into many a book and film for its potency. In the film *Night of the Demon* it appears enwrapped in a pre-dawn mist and is associated unequivocally with calling up devils. In Thomas Hardy's *Tess of the D'Urbervilles*, the heroine becomes a modern and unconscious lunar sacrifice as she lies asleep on a stone shaped like an altar – a powerful and moving image.[9] There are, of course, many more. Some of the sense of wonder generated must have been intended by the original architects and the problem is to pare away the romantic, druidical and modern elements in our reaction to the monument. We have instead to try to experience the monument through the frame of reference of the prehistoric people who built and used it. I believe that as the chapters of *The Making of Stonehenge* unfold, the reader will discover that it *is* possible to recapture that prehistoric experience and understand what it was the makers of Stonehenge were striving to achieve.

Meanwhile, we can share with the eighteenth-century antiquary William Stukeley those curiously ambivalent feelings that Stonehenge contains and communicates, the sense of both crudity and sophisticated ingenuity, of ruin and architecture, of enormous weight gracefully borne. 'A serious view of this magnificent wonder is apt to put a thinking and judicious person into a kind of ecstasy. When he views the struggle between art and nature, the grandeur of that art that hides itself and seems unartful, for though the contrivance that put this massive frame together must have been exquisite, yet the founders endeavoured to hide it by the seeming rudeness of the work. It pleases like a magic spell, and the greatness of every part surprises.'[10]

2

'BEYOND ALL HISTORICAL RECALL'

It is remarkable that whoever has treated of this monument has
bestowed on it whatever class of antiquity he was particularly fond of.
Horace Walpole, *Anecdotes of Painting*, 1786

THE NOBLE RUIN

Stonehenge is the ruin of a single great prehistoric stone building. The huge
weathered blocks are simply shaped and arranged in deceptively simple
geometric shapes and, so far as we can tell, have always been undecorated.[1]
As it now stands, the monument is a physical wreck, a tight huddle of mid-
grey stones dwarfed by an expanse of open, rolling plain. Visitors are often
disappointed by their first sight of this wonder of the prehistoric past. 'It
looks so small' is what many of them say, but there is little to give any sense
of scale, the stones may not be approached, and there is nothing from the
remote past to explain it.

Of the most conspicuous element in the design, the Great Circle of
sarsens, only a half has survived (see Figure 70). Seventeen of the original
thirty uprights are still standing (stones 1–7, 10, 11, 16, 21–3, 27–30), three
lie fallen but intact (stones 12, 14 and 25) and five (stones 13, 17, 18, 20 and
24) have completely disappeared. The numbers of the stones are shown on
Figures 1 and 8. The thirty massive standing stones, 4 m, 2 m wide, 1 m
thick, were originally linked together by thirty running lintels forming a
continuous stone ring 4.3 m up in the air. Unfortunately, only six of these
(stones 101, 102, 105, 107, 122 and 130) are still in position.

The circle of smaller bluestones within the Great Sarsen Circle is even
more ruinous; the stones are more manageable in size, so more of them have
been carted away.[2] Only six out of an estimated original total of forty
bluestones still stand upright, while another five lean out of their sockets. Of
the five huge trilithons which rose up above the sarsen ring, only two are
complete and have always been so (stones 51–4). The lintel and one upright
of the fifth trilithon (stones 59–60) collapsed some time in antiquity: this
seems to be beyond restoration as each of the fallen stones is broken in three

5

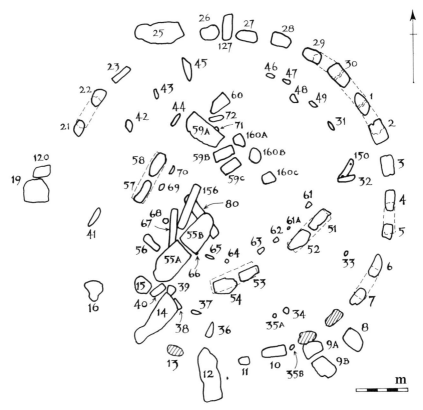

Figure 1 The central stone setting at Stonehenge in its present state. Dashed lines are lintels still in place. Shaded areas are empty stone-sockets.

and badly abraded by tourist erosion (stones 59a, b and c and 160a, b and c) (Plate 1). The fourth trilithon (stones 57–8) fell down on 3 May 1797 with such a crash that labourers working in the fields half a mile away felt the earth shake;[3] it was re-erected in 1958. The third and largest trilithon, sometimes called the Great Trilithon (stones 55–6), is ruined, with the lintel fallen and one upright fallen and broken in two (stones 156, 55a and 55b): the surviving upright, stone 56, is the tallest, finest, most graceful of the stones at Stonehenge (Plates 26 and 41).

Half of the original structure is either fallen or missing. Surrounding this wreckage is the very subdued circuit of bank and ditch that marks an earlier stage in Stonehenge's story. The bank has become degraded and the ditch filled in, to the extent that many visitors scarcely notice them, seeing only the stones at the centre (Figure 8). What is left is a badly damaged monument, mauled and preyed upon by man and weather – just the sort of noble ruin to appeal to lovers of the romantic and picturesque in the eighteenth

6

and nineteenth centuries. It is nevertheless important that we should see Stonehenge as a wrecked monument: we should not assume that our stone and bronze age ancestors deliberately created such a rough and chaotic jumble. The rich texture of the stones, patinated by weathering and scumbled with half a dozen different colours of lichen, must also be seen as a post-building feature; when newly dressed and ground, the stones would have been more uniform shades of blue-grey, green-grey and pearly pink, with the palest surfaces glinting in the sunshine like sugar. The patina of ageing has become, nevertheless, part of our image of Stonehenge.

It is in this sorry state that Stonehenge has become a powerful symbol of Britain's, and specifically England's, national heritage, a kind of time-mark for the dim, incoherent and baffling beginning of a long struggle towards national identity.[4] It has also become, for people all over the developed world, a symbol of a prehistoric past almost irretrievably lost. This book is about the making of Stonehenge, and about the methods, motives, values and ambitions of the people who were its original builders. If we are to arrive at an understanding of that remote past, a potentially alien world now fifty centuries dead, we will need to make allowance for the various ways in which we have been conditioned to 'see' Stonehenge. We tend, for example, because of the monument's status as a national identity symbol, to see it as very special, even unique, and this can blind us to the existence of hundreds of other stone rings and earth circles in the British Isles, monuments that can teach us a great deal about Stonehenge's original purpose.

Stonehenge is fundamentally a piece of architecture and therefore it contains within its design references outwards geographically and backwards in time to other monuments. The architectural cross-references (see Chapter 8 for a discussion of these) imply that the meaning of Stonehenge is also cross-referenced to that of other monuments in the neolithic and bronze age world. It will not do to attempt to explain Stonehenge on its own: no monument can be understood as an entirely closed-off system with all its meaning locked within itself; for this reason the book looks at Stonehenge within its landscape, as a word within a context, a word in the centre of its page. I have arbitrarily chosen an area of 100 sq. km with Stonehenge at its centre: surprisingly large numbers of satellite monuments and settlements have been discovered inside this area, and many of these will provide evidence of the other things people were doing – besides and between making Stonehenge.

There is also temporal chauvinism to contend with. The way people have responded to Stonehenge has often depended on their own social, economic and political predicament, on their vision of the society in which they live, and on their view of the dynamics of European history.[5] Reading a monument should be easy, if we have the right background information, but the problem lies in knowing what the significant background is. Since the monument *is* a monument and not a verbal text, its meaning is susceptible to

Time Bowling out the Druids.

Figure 2 Time Bowling out the Druids. *Source*: late nineteenth-century engraving.

varying interpretations. Each century tends to see both the present and the past in a different way. Even within the twentieth century AD, quite a short span of time, Stonehenge has been interpreted in several conspicuously different ways and it may be that disagreement about nuances of meaning occurred in the late neolithic and bronze age and became a focus of political and social struggle. One notable wrong turning has been the adoption of Stonehenge on the summer solstice by self-styled Druids. Although superficially harmless, the regular reappearance of these Druids until recent years has helped to perpetuate a popular delusion about Stonehenge, and the fewer misapprehensions there are about the monument's complicated past the better.[6]

The Ancient Order of Druids was founded only in 1781, and it was not until 24 August 1905 that its Grand Lodge visited Stonehenge for a banquet and mass initiation ceremony. The 258 novices were blindfolded and made to enter the stone circle along an avenue of sickle-wielding Brothers dressed up in white-cowled robes and Father Christmas beards – harmless enough mumbo-jumbo, so long as we recognize that it has absolutely nothing to do with the *prehistoric* Stonehenge.

The twentieth century has been a volatile and turbulent one in many ways, not least in terms of ideas about Stonehenge; extremes of mystical fantasy and cold scientific rationalism have been applied to it, and most ordinary people are as confused about its original function and how it came to be built

8

as they were a thousand years ago, long before anything at all had been written about Stonehenge.

THE MEDIEVAL VIEW

Henry of Huntingdon, who died in 1155, is sometimes credited with giving Stonehenge its first mention in documented history. In his *Historia Anglorum* (1154), Henry makes Stonehenge one of his four wonders of Britain, describing the monument as follows: 'Stones of wonderful size are set up in the manner of doorways . . . nor can anyone guess by what means so many stones were raised aloft, or why they were built there!'[7] Henry's account tells us little, but it is refreshingly honest and in its limited way very accurate. Historians and scientists of the middle ages were not equipped to deal with problems of that kind.

But Henry's text is not quite the earliest identifiable account. Geoffrey of Monmouth's *History of the Kings of Britain*, written in 1135, contains a lengthy passage about Stonehenge.[8] Geoffrey's largely folkloric account of the British dark ages tells us that large numbers of British chieftains were massacred by the Saxon Hengist in the time of King Vortigern. King Aurelius Ambrosius, visiting the grass-covered burial-place where their remains were buried, was moved to tears and decided that some memorial to their patriotism should be built. Aurelius gathered carpenters and stone-masons from all over his kingdom and commissioned them to design a building that would commemorate the dead heroes – one that would stand for ever – but, try as they might, they could not come up with a suitable design.

Tremorinus, Archbishop of the City of the Legions, suggested to the king that if any man could solve the problem it was Merlin, Vortigern's prophet. Messengers were sent out to find Merlin and when he was eventually brought before Aurelius, the king asked him to prophesy the future. Aurelius was keen to hear marvels, but Merlin swept the frivolous request aside: 'Mysteries of that sort cannot be revealed except where there is the most urgent need. If I were to utter them as an entertainment, then the spirit that controls me would forsake me in the moment of need.'

Then Merlin told Aurelius of a stone circle in Ireland called the Giants' Dance: that would be suitable to embellish the warrior-heroes' grave. Aurelius sent an expeditionary force to seize the circle. When the stone ring was on its way, spirited along by Merlin's magic, Aurelius Ambrosius summoned his priests and his people to a ceremonial rededication of the sacred site, crowning himself king there at Whitsuntide.[9]

This remarkable medieval view of Stonehenge contains a lot of material that may be very ancient in origin, and which we shall need to discuss in detail (see Chapter 5), but it also reflects the need that medieval kings felt to link their inheritance and their authority to an Arthurian past, the world of myth, magic and perfect kingship. It is no coincidence that, later in the twelfth century, Henry II ordered a search for the remains of Arthur and that Arthur's grave at Glastonbury was 'discovered'. Henry II acted from complex, mixed motives, but one reason for his quest for King Arthur was his desire to be seen as Arthur's heir and successor.[10]

A RENAISSANCE VIEW

A later king, James I, was intrigued by Stonehenge when he saw it in 1620, and his host at Wilton, the Duke of Buckingham, offered the owner of the site, one Robert Newdyk, 'any rate' if he would sell it, but Newdyk refused to part with it. The Duke nevertheless had a large hole dug at the centre of Stonehenge, to see what was buried there: unfortunately we cannot tell whether the antlers, bull-horns, stone mauls, arrowheads and charcoal later reported came from this excavation or some other. As John Aubrey said, *'something* was found, but what it was Mrs Mary Trotman hath forgot.'[11]

The king's curiosity was aroused and he commanded Inigo Jones, his Surveyor, to find out what he could about it. Even though Jones was intermittently at work on several projects in the area, including Wilton House, the Stonehenge commission remained uncompleted at the time of his death in 1652. John Webb put Jones's notes and drawings together to make what was to be the very first book about Stonehenge;[12] in fact it seems to have been the first book to be devoted to a single prehistoric monument.[13]

Jones argued that the native Britons, the people living in Britain when the Romans arrived, simply could not have built such a monument. He took at face value the Romans' derogatory account of the Celts as 'a savage and barbarous People, knowing no use at all of Garments . . . If destitute of the Knowledge, even to clothe themselves, much less any knowledge had they to erect stately structures.' Nor would it have been possible for the Britons to raise the stones of Stonehenge after the Romans withdrew from the islands: 'the Arts of Design, of which Architecture chief, were utterly lost even in Rome, much more in Britain.' The ensuing Saxon period was disturbed too much by 'the destructive Broils of War' for a major building project to have been undertaken then, and it was known that Stonehenge had been built by 1135, so as an acknowledged work of ancient architecture Stonehenge had to be the work of a Roman architect.

Jones felt that he had found a classical parallel to the design of Stonehenge in Daniele Barbaro's edition of Vitruvius and decided on the strength of this that Stonehenge was a Roman temple to the god Coelus.[14] Jones's plan and elevation of Stonehenge in its original state shows the irregular sarsen blocks tidied up and squared off a good deal, with an extra trilithon thrown in on the north-east side to make a symmetrical hexagonal arrangement (see Figure 3). The reconstructed plan resolves, Jones shows us, into four large equilateral triangles rotated inside the circumference of the Great Sarsen

Plate 1 Stonehenge III in ruins. Stone 60 to the right: the five fallen stones in the centre are the broken remains of 59 and 160. Trilithon 57–58 is in the centre at the back and stone 56 to the left. Three stones of the Bluestone Horseshoe are visible.

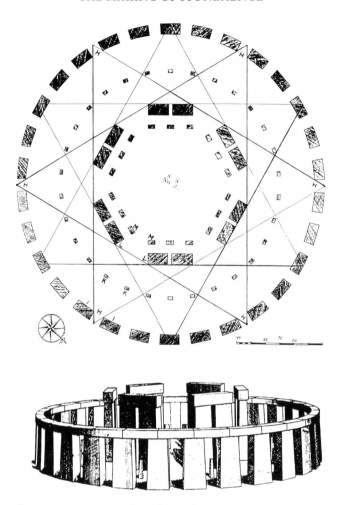

Figure 3 Inigo Jones's reconstruction of Stonehenge.

Circle. His reconstruction is a product of a Renaissance mind in which all great buildings had to be symmetrical, refined and in the classical tradition, but it takes many liberties with the archaeological remains. For a start, there was never a sixth trilithon. The Vitruvian plan of a Roman theatre – Jones's copy still exists[15] – shows a semicircular auditorium and a rectangular stage: it was nothing like a hexagon contained within a circle, and it was not a temple either.

The Inigo Jones hypothesis shows how the reality of prehistory can be bent beyond recognition to fit in with a cultural fashion. It was the Renaissance, so it was natural that someone should try to make Stonehenge Greek or Roman. It is a little like the fourteenth-century illustrated manu-

Figure 4 The earliest known likeness of Stonehenge. *Source*: Corpus Christi College Cambridge MS 194, fo. 57r.

script in Corpus Christi College, Cambridge, which shows the history of the world; the design is in boxes defined by lines and columns, so the drawing of Stonehenge squeezed into the text (Figure 4) inevitably shows it to be *rectangular*![16] The Jones theory was nevertheless unconvincingly presented and it was greeted with derision by Webb's contemporaries. One of the critics, Dr Glisson, rightly guessed that Stonehenge was 'at least 3 or 4 thousand years old before ye Romans came to Britain.'[17]

STONEHENGE AS A DANISH CROWNING-PLACE

One of John Webb's contemporaries, Dr Walter Charleton, persuaded himself that Stonehenge was, of all things, Danish. This was because of an imagined resemblance between Stonehenge and the megalithic tombs seen in Denmark, and it led Charleton to give Stonehenge one of the latest and most erroneous dates of all, the ninth century AD.[18]

Charleton was right to look for parallels between Stonehenge and other megalithic monuments, but it was perverse to compare it with *dysser*, the wrong type of monument in the wrong country, when there were plenty of stone circles and earth circles in England with which useful comparisons might have been drawn. He went on to suggest that Stonehenge was the ancient crowning-place of the Danish kings, the monument itself being shaped like a crown.

It was a tactful and elegantly apt proposal for a courtier to make – Charleton was Charles II's physician – and particularly so at the time of the Restoration of the Stuart monarchy. It illustrates tellingly how our interpretation of Stonehenge is coloured by the times in which we live. The point is underlined by Dryden's dedicatory poem for Charleton's book, in which the poet recalls the day (7 September 1651) when Charles II risked breaking cover during his escape from the battlefield of Worcester just to see 'the wonder of that country':[19]

STONE-HENGE, once thought a *Temple*, You have found
A Throne, where Kings, our Earthly Gods, were Crown'd.
Where by their wond'ring Subjects They were seen,
Chose by their Stature, and their Princely Mien.
Our *Sovereign* here above the rest might stand,
And here be chose again to sway the Land.

These Ruins sheltered once *His* Sacred Head,
Then when from Wor'ster's fatal Field *He* fled;
Watch'd by the Genius of this Kingly Place,
And mighty Visions of the Danish Race.
His *Refuge* then was for a *Temple* shown:
But, *He* Restor'd, 'tis now become a *Throne*.[20]

STONEHENGE AS A DRUID TEMPLE

It was John Aubrey the antiquary who first connected Stonehenge with the Druids (Figure 5). The first volume of his great work *Monumenta Britannica* is called *Templa Druidum*,[21] but it was his successor, William Stukeley, who popularized the Druidical connection. Stukeley first saw Stonehenge on 18 May 1719 and began serious fieldwork on the site shortly afterwards, discovering and naming the Cursus (now usually called the Great or Greater Cursus to distinguish it from the nearby Lesser Cursus) in August 1723. In 1740, Stukeley published his book about the monument, selecting a title that unambiguously nailed his colours to the Druid mast: *Stonehenge: A Temple Restor'd to the British Druids*.

Stukeley's friend Roger Gale had translated parts of Aubrey's work, and Stukeley will have seen Aubrey's firmly expressed opinions: 'Now my presumption is, that the Druids being the most eminent order of priests among the Britaines, 'tis odds, but that these monuments [Stonehenge and Avebury] were temples of the priests of the most eminent order, viz., Druids, and it is strongly to be presumed that they are as ancient as those days.'[22] The Druid connection was a red herring, but at least Aubrey admitted usefully that 'these Antiquities are so exceeding old that no Bookes doe reach them, so that there is no way to retrive them but by comparative antiquitie.' Aubrey also thought it self-evident that the great monuments of Stonehenge and Avebury were temples of the native British, and in this we can agree with him whole-heartedly: there was 'clear evidence that these monuments were Pagan-Temples.'[23]

The Druid connection had been reinforced for Stukeley by Aylett

Figure 5 John Aubrey. Portrait intended as frontispiece to *Monumenta Britannia* (1665).

Sammes's popular book, *Britannia Antiqua Illustrata* of 1676: this rather curiously proposed that the Druids had arrived in Britain in a Phoenician convoy under the leadership of Hercules, King of Tyra. Stukeley also read the work of an Anglesey vicar, the Revd Henry Rowlands[24] who proposed that the neolithic tombs of Anglesey were adapted by the Druids for their ceremonies and went on to speculate about other sites: 'Might not Stonehenge and Roll-rick Coronets be very well the Relics of antient Druidism?'[25]

But Stukeley's love affair with the Druids seems to have begun with what he had gleaned from Gale's copy of Aubrey's *Templa Druidum*, which sent him off to have a look at Avebury and led to the formation in 1722 of a Society of Roman Knights dedicated to the preservation of 'Roman' remains. Lord Winchelsea, Stukeley's patron, assumed the name of the Belgic prince Cingetorix, and Stukeley assumed that of a French Druid – he could not find an English one – Chyndonax. Faintly ridiculous though all this may now seem, it illustrates how Stukeley threw himself into his period, lived it, and even tried to imagine himself into the person of a prehistoric Druid. It was with this background of commitment and empathy that he began drawing and surveying neolithic monuments: later he was to graft his druidical fantasies onto these pieces of honest archaeology.[26]

Stukeley's imgination was given free rein by the sheer lack of documentary evidence for what the ancient British Druids were like. Tacitus, virtually the only contemporary source, describes them in terms that are less than admiring. He tells us that in AD 60, as Suetonius Paulinus advanced into Wales, the native British fell back into Anglesey. There, according to a translation available to Stukeley, 'the Enemy was ray'd upon the Shore, intermixed with Women, running to and fro, drest in the Habit of Furies, their Hair dischevel'd, Torches in their Hands, and encompast with Druids, who lifted up their Hands to Heaven, pouring forth most terrible Execrations. The Horrour of this Spectacle astonished our Men, and made them stand like Statues to receive the Enemies Assault . . . This Inhuman people were accustom'd to shed the Blood of their Prisoners on their Altars, and consult their Gods over the reeking Bowels of Men.'[27] Caesar and Diodorus Siculus described harrowing scenes of Druids' sacrifices on mainland Europe. In one rite, they were alleged to 'kill a man by a knife-stab in the region above the midriff and from his fall they foretell the future by the convulsions of his limbs, and the pouring of his blood.'[28]

This gory melodrama was tailor-made to appeal to eighteenth- and nineteenth-century readers of Gothick fiction and it goes a long way towards explaining the long-lived popular appeal of the Druids. Pliny provided another, more civilized side to the Druids in his *Natural History*, in which he focused on the importance of the oak and mistletoe in their rituals: 'they solemnize no sacrifice, nor perform any sacred ceremonies without branches and leaves thereof.' He also added some detail about priests wearing white vestments and the sacrifice of milk-white bullocks.[29]

The documentation was slight, but enough to ignite Stukeley's imagination.[30] There was, nevertheless, neither documentary nor archaeological evidence to connect Stonehenge with the Druids: there was only the assertion of John Aubrey. The aged and eccentric Aubrey went on ferreting among his Stonehenge notes into the 1690s, but his ideas were very mixed, some confused, almost feverish, some that would feed speculation during the three centuries following, and some that would not, such as the extraordinary idea that the Druids 'did converse with Eagles, and could understand their Language.' There is much that is fanciful, even deluded, but Aubrey had established one very important truth, that Stonehenge was an early temple built by native Britons, a 'Pagan-Temple'.[31]

The idea of Stonehenge as a ruined temple was naturally a very attractive one in the eighteenth and nineteenth centuries, harmonizing with the Romantic vision of man and landscape. Stonehenge was seen, especially with its overlay of horrible associations with druidical sacrifices, as sublime. Edmund Burke defined the sublime for us: 'whatever is fitted in any sort to excite ideas of pain, and danger, that is to say, whatever is in any sort terrible, or is analogous to terror is a source of the sublime: that is, it is

Figure 6 Stukeley's idea of a Druid. The drawing is signed 'Chindonax Britannicus'. *Source*: Stukeley 1740.

productive of the strongest emotions which the mind is capable of feeling . . . Stonehenge, neither for disposition nor ornament, has anything admirable; but those huge rude masses of stone, set on end, and piled on each other, turn the mind on the immense force necessary for such a work. Nay the rudeness of the work increases the cause of grandeur, as it excludes the idea of art and contrivance: for dexterity produces another sort of effect which is different enough from this.'[32]

Wordsworth saw Stonehenge and was impressed by the mystery of its origins:

> so proud to hint yet keep
> Thy secrets, thou that lov'st to stand and hear
> The Plain resounding to the whirlwind's sweep . . .[33]

Constable too came and saw and sketched it on 15 July 1820, working the pencil sketch through several versions until the final 1835 watercolour that has become so well known. In true Romantic style, this last shows the stones raised by man apparently laid low by nature; they are lit by a fitful, fleeting sunlight as a storm convulses the sky round about: a double rainbow arches symbolically down into the stone circle. Constable seems to have been content to set aside the Druids and see Stonehenge as a symbol of man's insignificance in the face of nature. He wrote in his caption for the painting, 'The mysterious monument of Stonehenge, standing remote on a bare and boundless heath, as much unconnected with the events of past ages as it is with the uses of the present, carries you back beyond all historical recall into the obscurity of a totally unknown period.'

STONEHENGE AS AN ASTRONOMICAL COMPUTER

Sublimity gave way to science.

The age of astro-archaeology had early beginnings. The Revd Edward Duke, who lived close to Stonehenge, had an idea that has been developed subsequently in many different ways – that Stonehenge was part of a much larger device that included significant astronomical alignments. 'Our ingenious ancestors', he wrote, 'portrayed on the Wiltshire Downs a Planetarium or stationary Orrery, located on a meridianal line, extending north and south the length of 16 miles; that the planetary temples thus located, seven in number, will, if put in motion, be supposed to revolve around Silbury Hill as centre.'[34] It is difficult to see what use a *fixed* model of this kind could be, although we could tiptoe one step further into madness and propose that the temples were once free to move round Silbury Hill. Duke's attractive, if rather alfresco, theory can be seen as the ancestor of an entire fringe literature in the twentieth century: some small bookshops are full of it.

Sir Norman Lockyer (1836–1920) was on the face of it a very different figure, although Stonehenge seems to cast its own brand of moonshine on even the best of minds. A respected scientist, Lockyer was editor of the journal *Nature* for many years and Director of the Solar Physics Laboratory in London. It was in 1906 that he published his startling book about the astronomical orientation of Stonehenge.[35] He retained the Druids, but argued that Stonehenge was a sun temple built for the purpose of observing the sunrise and pointed out the orientation of the main axis towards the first gleam of the midsummer sunrise in the second millennium BC, one of the great 'mainstream' Stonehenge ideas of the twentieth century.

There are oddities about Lockyer's work that are hard to explain. He established the precise orientation of Stonehenge's main axis as 49° 35′ 5″.[36] This azimuth or bearing passed close to Sidbury Hill about 13 km north-east of Stonehenge. There was no reason to connect Sidbury Hill or the later earthwork built on it with Stonehenge, yet Lockyer decided that a line from the centre of Stonehenge to the summit of Sidbury Hill was the key alignment after all, 49° 34′ 18″. This bearing, though different from the one he derived from the Avenue, was the one he used to calculate the date for the building of Stonehenge – 1680 BC. His method of arriving at it made it meaningless. This and other flaws in Lockyer's work made many archaeologists deeply suspicious of alleged astronomical alignments. Nevertheless, many of Lockyer's ideas were picked up again later and refined, and he is regarded by some as the father of British astro-archaeology.

The great boom in astro-archaeology did not come until over halfway through the twentieth century. It was in 1966 that the America-based astronomer Gerald Hawkins brought out his book *Stonehenge Decoded*, although his first results were published in *Nature* in 1963.[37] The 1963 article outlined his use of a computer to prove that the pattern of alignments from Stonehenge to twelve major solar and lunar events was very unlikely to have been the result of chance. The fully developed theory appeared in the United States in 1965 and in Britain in 1966.

Hawkins found that the alignments among 165 key points in the Stonehenge plan were not connected with the rising or setting positions of the planets or brighter stars, but very strongly correlated with rising and setting positions of the sun and moon. Then, more controversially, he went on to develop the idea that Stonehenge was a computer. These were early days in the computer revolution and Hawkins was excited by the results that the Harvard-Smithsonian IBM computer had produced for him; he was paying the makers of Stonehenge the highest available compliment in declaring that it too was a computer. It was cultural chauvinism again.

Hawkins's idea was that the circle of pits known as the Aubrey Holes (see Figure 8) was used as a tally for predicting eclipses of the moon. These occur every 18.61 years, and three times 18.61 is 55.83, or 56 years to the nearest whole number. There are fifty-six Aubrey Holes, now filled in but marked with concrete discs. Hawkins's hypothesis is that six alternately black and white marker stones spaced nine, nine, ten, nine, nine and ten Aubrey Holes apart were moved anticlockwise (or clockwise, it made no difference) round the circle at a rate of one hole per year; a seventh marker was moved round the sarsen circle by one stone per day.[38] Three of the Aubrey Holes, numbers 51, 56 and 5, were singled out as fixed markers (Figure 7).

If a white moving marker stone moved into Aubrey Hole 56, the full moon would rise over the Heel Stone in that year. In the following year, and Hawkins gives 1553 BC as his example, the white marker stone would have moved on to a safe position, hole 55, which meant that nothing spectacular would happen in the way of alignments that year. In fact nothing spectacular would happen for five years, until the white marker reached the northern fixed marker, hole 51. In that year, the winter moon at its extreme declination rose over the line between hole D and the centre, set along the line joining Station Stones 91 and 94 and was framed in one of the trilithon doorways. The summer moon rose along the line joining Station Stones 92

19

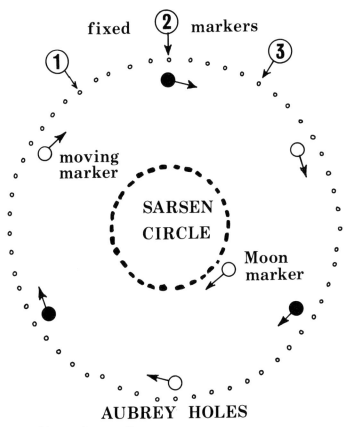

Figure 7 Hawkins's eclipse predictor.

and 93, again framed in a trilithon doorway. And so on. In other words a number of significant lunar alignments happened in 1549 BC and the Stonehenge astronomers were alerted to them by the arrival of the white marker stone in hole 51.

A black or white stone arrived at hole 56, in line with the Heel Stone, at intervals of nine, nine, ten, nine, nine, and ten years and this predicted moon events relating to the Heel Stone in those years. A white stone arrived at hole 51 at intervals of eighteen, nineteen and nineteen years and this predicted 'conditions of the high moon' at its extreme declination. Winter or summer eclipses occurred when any stone arrived at hole 56 or hole 28, that is, coinciding with the monument's main axis. Equinox eclipses happened whenever a white stone reached holes 5 or 51. Hawkins claimed that his eclipse predictor would have been capable of predicting accurately 'every important lunar event for hundreds of years'.

The seventh stone, moving nightly stone by stone round the Great Sarsen

Circle, completed a revolution of the circle in about a month, to keep track of the phases of the moon.

There was strong reaction from archaeologists against Hawkins's idea. Professor Richard Atkinson, a universally acknowledged expert on the archaeology of Stonehenge, denounced it in an *Antiquity* article entitled 'Moonshine on Stonehenge', in which he called Hawkins's work 'tendentious, slipshod and unconvincing'.[39] Atkinson felt that some of the holes used to generate sight-lines were natural cavities, not man-made features. He pointed out that there was too wide a margin of error – as much as 2° along the horizon for some of the alignments. Atkinson also argued that, given the large number of stones involved, and given that any stone or gap between stones might be a view-point, a very large number of possible sight-lines exists: that in turn means that the coincidence of sight-lines with astronomical events is very likely to happen just by chance.[40]

There was another major problem in treating the Aubrey Holes and the four Station Stones (stones 91–4) as part of the same observatory-computer system, in that the Station Stones in some cases are set over and erase Aubrey Holes. Any scheme which uses Aubrey Holes and Station Stones as part of a tally or tally-and-checking system, as Hawkins's idea does, must be incorrect.

Long after the heat had gone out of the controversy, in 1987, Aubrey Burl pointed out with his usual wisdom that the whole hypothesis depends on there being fifty-six Aubrey Holes. Yet if that number had been regarded as significant or even useful in antiquity, then it would recur in other comparable monuments – and it does not. There are other monuments with rings of pits of varying numbers and they were in general used as receptacles for cremations and related offerings. As Burl says, 'the Aubrey Holes were not components of a prehistoric computer.'[41]

The force of the clash between the two disciplines – astronomy and archaeology – led the editor of *Antiquity*, Glyn Daniel, to seek advice from Fred Hoyle, who was at that time Professor of Astronomy at Cambridge and well known for his adventurous lateral thinking. Hoyle examined Hawkins's work and then made his own analysis of the possible uses of Stonehenge as an astronomical observatory-computer.[42] Hoyle used three stones instead of Hawkins's seven to represent the sun, the moon and one node of the moon's orbit, and moved them round the circle of Aubrey Holes at approximately their real rates, treating Stonehenge as a geocentric model of the solar system. Eclipse seasons occurred only when the three marker stones lay close together or almost opposite each other: eclipses occurred within these seasons only when the moon stone came close to the sun stone or fell diametrically opposite to it. Hoyle's method is 'better' than Hawkins's in that it is simpler, alerts the observer to an impending eclipse season and also, in theory, predicts the actual day of the eclipse. It is not only simpler, it is also more sensitive.

Hoyle also proposed that the discrepancies between the sight-lines and the directions of astronomical events were not to be treated as errors in the design, but as deliberate offsets that would enable events to be dated by interpolation. The 'wrong' position for the Heel Stone in relation to the midsummer sunrise – one of the most important discoveries of recent decades – could be explained in this ingenious way; by watching the sun rise on several consecutive mornings it would be possible to note on which two days the sunrise was hidden behind the Heel Stone: the solstice could easily be calculated as the day midway between the two. Hoyle thought that Stonehenge I, in other words the monument as it stood in 3000 BC, was a very refined astronomical instrument but that Stonehenge III, that is, as it was in 2000 BC, was far less useful astronomically, even though architecturally impressive.

But others remained and still remain unconvinced.[43] It has been suggested that the Hawkins–Hoyle eclipse predictor would not have been accurate enough to be of any use, and that simpler ways of predicting eclipses are possible. For instance, one could observe whether the full moon at either midsummer or midwinter rises (or sets) directly opposite the point on the horizon where the sun sets (or rises): it must do this if an eclipse is to take place.

Hawkins's scheme in particular seemed, even if his claims were astronomically true, a hopelessly imprecise one. It is difficult to believe that anyone interested in astronomy, even in prehistoric times, would be content with such a coarse and unsatisfactory level of accuracy as identifying the *year* when an eclipse would happen. With hindsight, it seems strange that Hawkins's idea generated so much interest, but it was popular largely because it seemed that the oracle, in the shape of the IBM computer, had spoken and its verdict could not be gainsaid. Now we are more familiar with computers and what they can and cannot do for us, and 'rubbish in, rubbish out' has become one of the stock sayings of the late twentieth century. And, perhaps inevitably, we came to mistrust the prehistoric computer too.

While Hawkins was at work, another figure, less publicized and more painstaking, was also at work on the astronomical functions of Stonehenge and other megaliths. Professor of Engineering at Oxford until his retirement in 1961, Alexander Thom carefully and accurately surveyed and interpreted a large number of megalithic sites. In several important ways, Thom's work converged on that of Hawkins and Hoyle, emphasizing the Stonehenge builders' preoccupation with astronomy and mathematics. He contributed the important idea that British stone circles were built to common units of measurement which he called the Megalithic Fathom (1.6 m or 5.44 ft) and Megalithic Yard (0.83 m or 2.72 ft).[44] A second idea, which sprang directly from the surveys, was about the circles' geometry.[45] He found that megalithic 'circles' actually consisted of six different geometrical shapes: true circles, ellipses, two sorts of flattened circle and two sorts of egg shape.

22

Plate 2 The Stonehenge car park post-holes, view to the west. Hole C in the foreground.

Plate 3 The south entrance causeway and the Stonehenge I ditch.

23

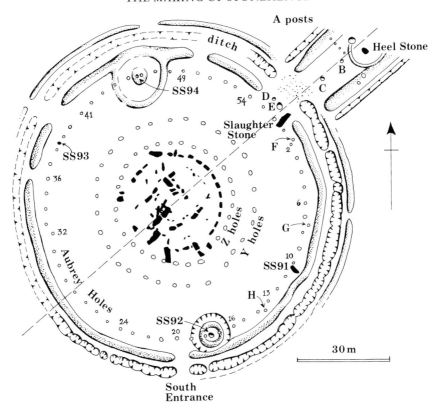

Figure 8 Plan of Stonehenge. SS: Station Stone. The numbers of the stones are shown on Figures 1 and 25.

Thom's third contribution concerned the astronomical alignments of the monuments, and this is where his work dovetails with the more sensational publications of Gerald Hawkins. In a whole string of publications, Thom explained the orientations of large numbers of megalithic sites to the sun and moon.[46]

As far as survey work went, Thom kept clear of Stonehenge and focused his attention on sites that he felt were important but neglected. There were, nevertheless, good, accurate surveys of Stonehenge available and he was prepared to suggest ways of interpreting them. He was, for instance, cautiously inclined to accept a lunar and solar observatory function for Stonehenge.[47] He also made an attempt at a geometrical analysis of the sarsen and bluestone structure. Four of the trilithons stand on an ellipse, but the fifth, the central one, stands well inside it, which strongly suggests to me that an ellipse was not in the builders' minds at all. Thom was unable to make the bluestone horseshoe fit round either a circle or an ellipse: it

24

followed no identifiable geometric shape. He had most success with the outer circle of sarsens, the Great Circle, which clearly had been laid out as a true circle.[48]

One great drawback with most of the 1960s Stonehenge astronomy was that most of the alignments inferred were marked by stones, pits, mounds or gaps between stones that were only 10–30 m apart. Lines drawn joining points that are close together and then extended out to the horizon are not likely to have been of any use for accurate observation. It was at Thom's suggestion that long-distance markers were added into the Stonehenge scheme to improve accuracy, although it could not be proved, as we saw with Lockyer's misuse of Sidbury Hill, that these markers were actually used in antiquity.[49] Peter's Mound, a knoll discovered by Peter Newham and named after him, stands some 3 km away to the north-east of Stonehenge and could have acted as a distant, skyline marker for the midsummer sunrise during the Stonehenge I phase. Thom proposed that other horizon markers, some as much as 13–15 km away, could have been used as well:

Coneybury Barrow	1.75 km	southernmost MR, minor standstill
Figsbury Rings	11 km	southernmost MR, major standstill
Chain Hill	6 km	southernmost MS, major standstill
Hanging Langford Camp	13 km	southernmost MS, minor standstill
Gibbet Knoll	15 km	northernmost MS, major standstill
(MR = moonrise, MS = moonset)		

The Thom family's ideas about megalithic science, both in general and in relation to Stonehenge, met with a favourable reaction from Richard Atkinson. Even though the new hypothesis cut across many of the received, established ideas about British prehistory, Atkinson was impressed by the evidence and prepared to consider that the Thoms were broadly right – and that the archaeological establishment needed to adjust to the new ideas.[50] Times were changing. The long-established view of neolithic and bronze age Britain as a barbarian backwater on the cultural edgeland of Europe was giving way to the view that megalith-building and many of the concepts that went with it had evolved independently and autonomously in north-west Europe.[51]

Atkinson's qualified acceptance of Thom's hypothesis was a courageous one, not least because of its many disorienting implications about the nature of British society at the time when the megaliths were built, broadly 3000–1500 BC. If standard measurements were in use, as Thom argued, there must have been measuring rods of fixed length, presumably calibrated from some master template in the hands of a central authority. There are problems here, because there is little corroborative evidence for regional, let alone pan-British socio-political organization: indeed much of the archaeological evidence points in the opposite direction, towards small-scale cellular societies.[52]

Our ancestors' knowledge of geometry, if what Thom says is true, was at a level that would not be attained again anywhere in Europe until the time of the mathematicians of ancient Greece. The neolithic Britons' knowledge of astronomy was similarly highly developed, based on many generations of observations. The lunar cycle of 18.6 years was rather longer than the likely working life of an ancient astronomer, and verifying the sight-lines by repeating observations does imply that detailed knowledge was passed on across two or three generations at least, possibly as many as seven or eight. This issue will emerge again when we look at the evidence of the stake-holes on the entrance causeway (see Chapter 3). There is very little evidence of writing as such from these early times – only a few simple symbols engraved on stone – and it is hard to see how detailed astronomical records could have been passed on without writing.[53]

And what of the intellectual implications? Fred Hoyle who, as we have seen, evolved his own interpretation of the way in which Stonehenge was used as a calculator, said that 'it demands a level of intellectual attainment orders of magnitude higher than the standard to be expected from a community of primitive farmers.' This means we have important choices to make as we evaluate the monument. Do we accept the Thom view and see late neolithic Britons as something other than primitive farmers?

On balance, I feel that the Thoms overstated their case. Some of the monuments do have solar and lunar orientations, but the evidence for an island-wide standard measuring system is weak, and the evidence for sophisticated geometry is susceptible of other and more sensible interpretations.[54] Many of the stone and earth rings that are not true circles were, to my mind, laid out as approximations to circles. So long as they looked like circles to people walking into or round them, that was good enough: we should not assume that any of the monuments was built to a plan drawn on paper first, still less to scale. In a way, discussing the monuments as we often do in books like this through the medium of scale plans is in itself an act of temporal and cultural chauvinism: we have little reason to believe that the Stonehenge people ever thought of their monuments in that way (for example, Figures 8 and 22), and we must beware of peopling prehistory with ourselves, thinly disguised.

The Thoms' work is impeccably good science and we can respect the thoroughness and intellectual rigour of their research, but in the end there is something about it that either misreads or misrepresents the neolithic and bronze age thought-world. The pseudo-exactness of the Thom megalithic yard sums up the problem. Ultimately, it may be an arbitrary matter exactly where the measurements are taken, especially if the stones or sockets are large and irregular. The megalithic yard only emerged as a statistical outcome, the mean of a whole mass of different numbers: it is by no means obvious in the actual measurements at individual sites. That in itself argues against the use of standard measuring rods. Since the 1960s, a softer approach has been applied to the problem, with far more plausible body-units such as the fathom, yard and cubit or the human pace being proposed.[55] Variations among these human units would certainly be enough to explain the apparent variations in unit sizes used at different sites.

The astronomy of Stonehenge has been seriously jolted by new knowledge about Stonehenge's date. This has happened partly because more radiocarbon dates have been obtained for the monument, and partly because the dates have been recalibrated, which has made them earlier. Hawkins, for example, discusses the way the eclipse predictors worked in 1554 BC, basing his analysis on Van den Bergh's *Eclipses -1600 to -1207*.[56] He was looking at second-millennium BC astronomical events when he should have been looking at the events of the late third millennium for Stonehenges II and III and the late fourth and early third millennia for Stonehenge I (see Appendix A for the Stonehenge chronology and Appendix C for radiocarbon dates). It now looks as if the Aubrey Holes were dug in about 2800 BC and filled in shortly afterwards, some of them being obscured by the later Station Stones. The sunrise positions, and still less the star-rise and star-set positions, calculated for 1554 BC would not have been valid for 2800 BC.

The complex of Thom's, Hawkins's and Hoyle's ideas seems somehow characteristic of the period in which they were floated, a period when it seemed that exact scientific measurement and computers would be able to do anything and when astronomy itself was breaking new theoretical ground.[57] The ideas of that time, just like all the others, bear the handprints of their age. The Thoms' hypothesis, however, should not be rejected out of hand. There is a very special baby that is in danger of being lost with the bath water, and that is the limited number of important orientations to the sun and moon that are enshrined – and that *is* the right word! – in the design of Stonehenge. They are there, for whatever reason, and the too-extreme claims made for Stonehenge as a high-accuracy observatory in the mid-twentieth century must not blind us to the very real existence of these solar and lunar alignments.

This outline of changing ideas about Stonehenge over the last 900 years is no more than a panoramic sketch. It is not intended to be complete or comprehensive, but rather to illustrate how each age reinterprets Stonehenge in a way that suits itself. Every age develops a view of Stonehenge that matches its own preoccupations in the present and its own conception of the past. It is vital, if we are to understand what really lay in the minds of its makers, that we are aware of this tendency, and that we guard against rebuilding Stonehenge, either in reality or in imagination, in a way that is alien to the actuality of the past. What if we find evidence that the people of the late neolithic and early bronze age were becoming increasingly aware of the damage they were causing to the environment, that they tried, perhaps too late, to reverse the process – that, in other words, their concerns closely parallel our own? If the evidence is there, we must accept its implications.

Above all, it is important to see Stonehenge as a key component of an evolving stone age and bronze age culture, and to try to discover what Stonehenge meant to the prehistoric people who built it.

3

THE FIRST STONEHENGE

The more we dig, the more the mystery appears to deepen.
Colonel Hawley, who excavated Stonehenge between
1919 and 1926, quoted in *The Times* 5 August 1927

THE OLDEST STONEHENGE OF ALL

Most visitors to Stonehenge are unaware that its development spanned a very long period of Britain's prehistory, beginning many centuries before the sarsen monument at the centre was built.[1] The softly weathered and grassed bank and ditch that unobtrusively ring the sarsen stones were created a thousand years before the sarsen building and there are suggestions that a structure of some sort existed there even earlier.[2]

When the present car park beside the A344 was laid out in 1966, the sockets of three large posts were discovered some 253 m to the north-west of the centre of Stonehenge (Figure 9).[3] The sockets were inconveniently located well in from the edges of the planned car park, so after they were excavated they were filled with concrete flush with the tarmac surface: their positions are still easy to see (Plate 2). These tree-trunk-sized totem poles were at first assumed to be contemporary with the main monument, though later it emerged that they are much older, and represent the earliest phase of Stonehenge that we know of. Since the posts, drily named A, B and C, are older than Stonehenge I by many centuries, we might call this earliest phase 'Stonehenge 0'. In fact, other prehistorians before me have argued the case for renumbering the building phases, and it is tempting to do so here, but I am afraid it would lead to unnecessary confusion and this account sticks almost entirely to the well-established conventional numbering.[4]

When Lance and Faith Vatcher excavated the sockets they found some fragments of the original timber posts still remaining in them, as well as some wedges that were clearly intended to keep the totem poles upright. This means that the posts must have been left to decay in position, not uprooted at the end of their period of use. This is not in itself surprising, because the posts of many of the later structures in Wessex were similarly

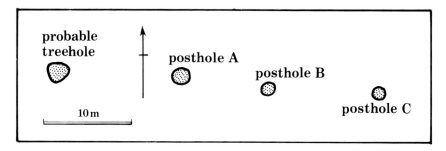

Figure 9 The Stonehenge car park post-holes.

left to rot and disintegrate in position.[5] The surprise comes from the radiocarbon dates. Samples of the wood from the bottom of two of the post-holes were dated, one – post A – to around 8000 BC, the other – post B – to about 7000 BC.[6] Both of these dates are disturbingly early, putting the erection of the totem poles well back into the mesolithic period rather than the neolithic, which did not begin in England until 4700 BC at the earliest.[7] In fact, the last ice age was only just ending and it is a sobering thought that, while there were still shrinking glaciers and snowpatches in the Scottish Highlands and a huge ice cap covered much of Norway, people were already at work shaping tree trunks to make some sort of religious, tribal or territorial focus at Stonehenge.[8]

Archaeologists have not really known what to make of these pine pillars or their phenomenally early date, often remaining silent and leaving them out of the Stonehenge story altogether.[9] Their bewildered excavators knew that the dated samples were pieces of the original posts and could only speculate that the samples were 'poor quality'.[10] Sometimes samples are contaminated and give false results: perhaps there was something wrong with the dating process, but it is odd that the two separate samples both produced exceptionally early dates, if a thousand years apart, and I think we should assume that they are correct. The fact that the wood was pine and not oak confirms the early date: the totem poles were raised at a time when Wessex was still cool in the aftermath of the ice age and yet to be colonized by oak trees.

How then should we interpret the three posts? There seem to be two possibilities. One which I find appealing is that the posts were raised one after the other, each replacing its disintegrating predecessor. At any one time a single totem pole stood as a sort of tribal focus, perhaps as an idol to be worshipped. There may even have been a lightly built cult-house or some other ancillary structure on the car park site. The other possibility is that the posts were raised as outlying markers for a structure already at this early stage standing 250 m away on the site of the sarsen monument. The central area of Stonehenge was so thoroughly and repeatedly redeveloped in antiquity and more recently dug over by antiquarians and treasure-seekers that it would be surprising if any trace of the earliest stages of the monument's evolution survived. We also have to allow for a subsequent lowering of the land surface by 0.3 m or so as a result of weathering: this will have removed altogether the remains of any shallow post-holes. So it has to remain an open question, but it is an exciting possibility that a lightly built wooden cult-house was standing at the centre of Stonehenge as early as 7000 BC, five thousand years before the sarsen monument was conceived.

If the posts were intended as foresights for an astronomical alignment, they must have indicated some event taking place on the north-western horizon. Peter Newham, a retired Gas Board manager and Stonehenge scholar, saw the posts as being 'in line with important setting phenomena of sun and moon when observed from the four Stations and Heel Stone positions'.[11] Newham identified alignments passing through the posts to the midsummer sunset, the major northerly moonset and the midpoint between the moon's northernmost settings (Figure 10). The Thoms thought the posts were all standing at the same time, supporting a platform to establish a very long sight-line from Stonehenge to Gibbet Knoll, far away to the north-west.[12] Christopher Chippindale dismisses these uses for the car park posts because they pre-date the known phases of the central monument and are therefore probably not connected with what happened much later at the main site.[13] It was Aubrey Burl who first pointed out that the radiocarbon dates were too early for the rest of the Stonehenge story, belonging 'in the Middle Stone Age, when Salisbury Plain was covered with coniferous forest'.[14]

It seems unwise to write the posts off as nothing to do with Stonehenge. Certainly the posts, if correctly dated to the mesolithic, cannot have been outliers or foresights for the much later Stonehenge I, so the Newham scheme must be wrong (see Appendix A for chronology). It may nevertheless be that a cult centre of some sort did stand on the site of Stonehenge as early as 7000 BC; alternatively it may be that the posts themselves alone served as the ancestral cult centre.

There is very little other evidence for what was happening in the Stonehenge area at this early stage. A few scattered stone tools are all there is in the way of direct evidence.[15] People at that time roamed the river valleys and forests, leaving virtually nothing behind that would survive in the archaeological record; their temporary camps are difficult to detect and in any case they had few belongings to leave on the landscape. It seems likely that they lived mainly in the Till and Avon valleys, where the widest variety of food was available, just as 20 km or so to the north they focused on the plentiful fish, fowl and game in the valley of the Kennet.[16]

The only sign that middle stone age people came anywhere near the totem poles is a solitary axe that someone dropped about 200 m to the south. A handful of stone flakes 1 km away to the east-south-east could represent a

Plate 4 The Heel Stone from the north-west: it leans towards the centre of Stonehenge.

Plate 5 Stonehenge from the Heel Stone. The Stonehenge I ditch can be seen, back left.

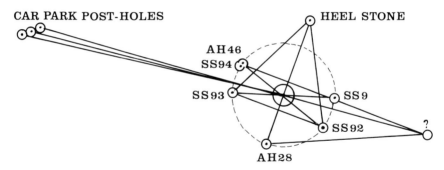

Figure 10 The relationship between Stonehenge and the car park post-holes according to Newham. SS: Station Stone. AH: Aubrey Hole.

campsite: the nearest unambiguous evidence of a camp is on the Avon valley floor close to the site of Durrington Walls. It is very difficult, in this virtual vacuum, to explain why people repeatedly set up their totem pole in the wilderness so far from the valleys that were their main focus. Possibilities can nevertheless be suggested.

We know very few people were living in England and, although we cannot define the territory of any particular group, people may have roamed freely across large territories without meeting anyone else. In an empty landscape, places where other bands might be met would have a special significance: such meetings may have been necessary from time to time to arrange marriages, confirm territorial boundaries and exchange gifts. If trade at this early time seems unlikely, we have the evidence of tools made of Portland chert which are concentrated round their source in Dorset but have been found over a wide area of southern England from Cornwall to Sussex.[17] Perhaps the totem pole was raised halfway between the valleys of the Avon and the Till, in the wooded no man's land, on an otherwise invisible boundary. Was it instead placed centrally, as a declaration of ownership: 'This sanctuary and all the territory hereabouts belong to us'? Or was it instead a landmark to help hunters find their way round the still uncleared forest? A shrine to the wilderness itself?

We can get an impression of what this ancient forest was like by visiting the Fargo Plantation, just 1 km to the north-west of the Stonehenge car park. There are deciduous trees in parts of the wood, especially near the road, but as we walk towards the Cursus it is as if we travel back from neolithic to mesolithic: there are pines, hazels and birches just as there would have been on the Stonehenge site in 7000 BC. Where the path opens into a ragged clearing, it is possible to imagine a group of middle stone age hunters raising a carved post as a waymark.

We have to look further afield for positive evidence of the kind of lives people led in the mesolithic, lives dominated by the hazel, pine and birch

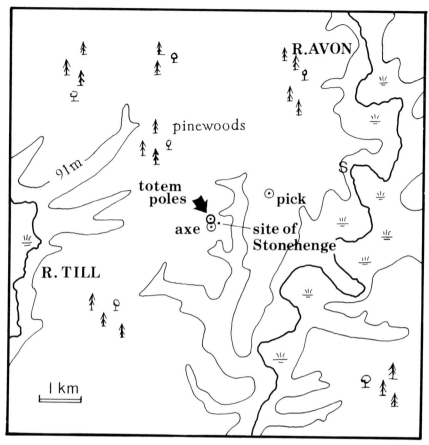

Figure 11 The Stonehenge area in 7000 BC. S: settlement.

woods that smothered the North European Plain, of which Salisbury Plain
was just a small corner: the southern North Sea was still dry land. People
lived by hunting, fowling, fishing and collecting fruit, berries and nuts. A
semi-nomadic life style seems likely, with each band of people using several
contrasting environments relatively close together in a more or less systematic rotation. In the Stonehenge area, they probably walked from campsite to
campsite, exploiting in turn the riverbanks, marshes and water meadows on
the valley floors, the scrublands of the valley sides, the closed pine and birch
forests and woodland clearings up on the rolling plain, and then returned to
their base camps near the river to begin all over again. There are signs that in
the late mesolithic people had already started cutting down trees and we can
only speculate about the reason. Obviously they were not clearing land for
farming because farming had not yet begun, but they may have been creating
grassy woodland clearings that would attract game animals for grazing.[18]

33

From Star Carr in Yorkshire, perhaps five hundred years before the older of the dated totem poles, comes evidence that people were interested in ritual. The Star Carr people trimmed, lightened and smoothed antlers so that they could be mounted on a leather cap and worn as a headdress. They probably wore antler frontlets as an aid to stalking, but for this purpose the lighter skulls of young stags could easily have been selected. In fact, larger skulls were chosen at Star Carr and they involved a lot of extra work, so we have to assume that some special effect was wanted. It is likely that the Star Carr frontlets were made as animal masks for a ritual dance, a deer-hunting dance just like the Abbots Bromley Horn Dance; in this remarkable survival six deer-men dance with horns on their shoulders while a bowman called Robin Hood pretends to stalk and shoot them – a straightforward piece of sympathetic magic. This type of ceremony was probably widespread in northern Europe in the middle stone age, when deer meat was an important part of the diet. Antler frontlets have been found not only in England but also in Germany, at Hohen Viecheln near Berlin, so deer rituals were not just a local phenomenon. In Brittany at this time boulder-covered graves were made, some of them containing clothed and ochre-painted bodies trussed tightly into a contracted position as if they were parcelled up for return to the womb. Significantly, seashells were arranged around their heads with what seem to have been antler crowns, as if to say that the dead commanded the resources of both land and water.[19]

Northern England, Germany and Brittany (Figure 12): in all of these places there were rituals using deer antlers, and it is likely that similar and related rituals took place in the deer-stocked woodlands in between, including the Stonehenge area. Wessex people probably danced the horn dance round the Stonehenge totem pole; they would certainly have used the pinewoods for deer-stalking, perhaps enticing the deer with heaps of ivy, as at Star Carr, then hunting them down with dogs, bows and arrows. There were wild oxen in the forest too, and we can be sure these were also hunted.

It is a strange exercise, knowing as we do now that Stonehenge has existed time out of mind, to try to visualize a time when it was not there, when the rolling plain west of the Avon was a blank page, a tract of pine forest with virtually nothing man-made to be seen anywhere. Building a monument was a way of showing that a place was to be special. Perhaps it had become special even before it was marked out because of some event, material or spiritual, that had happened there, but something that the Stonehenge people (and other monument-builders too) learned was that the monument, once built, physically transformed and magnetized the landscape: it could never again be the same in human perception. Gradually, during the fourth and third millennia BC, the 100 sq. km surrounding Stonehenge were inscribed with more and more of these monumental landmarks: henges, circles of earth, stone and wood, offering pits, long barrows, avenues; they became stations in people's movement through the landscape, constraining, defining,

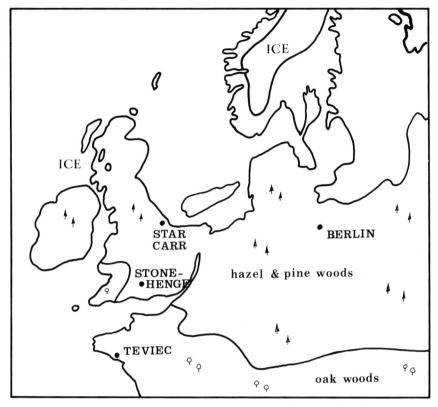

Figure 12 North-west Europe in 7000 BC.

focusing and intensifying their perception of the landscape.[20] But before that happened the mesolithic forest was a natural, untouched, unaltered landscape alive with birds, deer, red squirrels, bears and wild oxen. When people ventured in, possibly from the campsite close to Durrington Walls, they chose a site – was it at random? – to make a forest shrine. Halfway between the two river valleys, they raised the first timber of a monument that would gradually grow in importance and complexity as a territorial marker and ritual focus, develop over a period of five thousand years and become, nine thousand years on, the most celebrated ancient monument in the world.

LONG BARROWS AND RITUAL FEASTING

After the totem poles were raised, nothing else in the way of monument-building happened for three thousand years. Whatever the mesolithic people were doing in the area during that time has left no detectable archaeological trace, apart from a very thin scatter of tiny stone tools, the microliths they bound into wooden hafts to make saws and knives. But by 4500 BC major changes in the way people lived were under way.[21] At first small clearings were made in the forest with fire and axe, used for pasture or crops and then the forest was allowed to creep back and reclaim the land, but as time went by the clearings became larger and more permanent. By 4000 BC a large part of the area round Stonehenge seems to have been opened up, mainly for pasture where cattle and pigs were raised: cultivation of cereals was not a major objective at this stage.[22] With the beginning of farming came a more settled and organized way of life; people needed to stay in one place to tend crops or livestock, and because they stayed in one place for a long time they left us much clearer evidence of their presence than before. We can see more clearly where they were – and what they were doing.

The early neolithic cattle-herders and pig-farmers very soon laid out a distinct and recognizable ritual landscape, which they completed between 4000 and 3400 BC. They built the earth circle of Robin Hood's Ball on a low summit 4 km to the north-north-west of Stonehenge, and it is tempting to see it as a dry run for the earth circle later laid out at Stonehenge itself; significantly, it went out of use just before Stonehenge I was built.[23] With this idea in mind, we should take a closer look at the earlier circle. It is sited just to the south of a 140 m high hilltop, so it is slightly false-crested. This tendency to build a little to one side of a summit or ridge-crest was very widespread in the early and middle neolithic: hundreds of long barrows and chambered tombs are located in this way and it is easy to understand why. Most English hills have upper slopes that are convex, so it is not usually possible to see from the surrounding valleys structures that are 2–3 m high built on hill tops. Where they *are* visible, it is only the upper parts that we can see, so they look rather small and insignificant. The neolithic builders understood this and, to make their burial mounds look as imposing as possible, they placed them off the summits.[24]

The fact that many neolithic monuments are false-crested tells us a lot about the makers of Stonehenge, their intelligence and their awareness of the physical landscape and its properties; they were not putting up monuments at random but on carefully selected sites. It also tells us that it mattered to them that these monuments should be seen from afar. That in turn is significant, because it means that the landscape cannot then have been closed woodland; a long-distance view would only have been possible if much of the woodland round the monument and also round the spectators had been cleared, and that fits the other evidence (largely pollen evidence) for forest clearance. The false-cresting also indicates that the builders intended their monument to be seen from a particular direction, a particular area of lowland, and that gives us a useful indication of where the territories lay. Robin Hood's Ball is slightly to the south-east of a hill crest, which means that it was designed to be seen by people living and working in the meadows to the south-east: in other words it was to be seen by people on the gentle

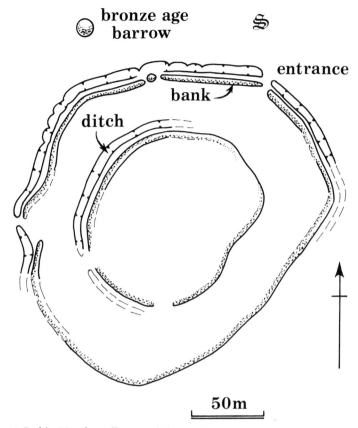

bronze age barrow

S

entrance

bank

ditch

50m

Figure 13 Robin Hood's Ball. S: neolithic settlement.

grassy slopes leading down towards Stonehenge 4 km away.

Like other causewayed enclosures in lowland England, the plan of Robin Hood's Ball is irregular, consisting of two circuits of banks and broken ditches enclosing an area of 3 ha altogether, in other words about the area of the Inner Circle in Regent's Park in London, or three times the size of the Theatre of Dionysus in Athens.

The inner bank has been more completely levelled by later erosion than the outer: it is scarcely visible at all. The second ditch and bank are about 30 m outside the first (Figure 13). Both ditches have the steep sides and flat floors that all neolithic communities in Britain preferred – no one knows why. As Sir Richard Colt Hoare said in 1812 when describing this monument, 'We have to regret the great injury these circles have sustained by the plough, as in their original state they must have been highly curious.'[25] The inner bank surrounds an oval precinct of about 1 ha, with its long axis lying south-west to north-east. It may be that this was a response to the physical geography of the site, the axis lying along the slope, or it may have a greater significance: the main axes of Woodhenge, Coneybury Henge and all the phases of Stonehenge were later to be oriented in the same way, from south-west to north-east. One of the themes of this book is that in spite of the many transformations in the ritual landscape of Stonehenge there was far more continuity and conscious back-reference to the past than has hitherto been recognized.

A point that is often overlooked is that, in spite of its insignificant appearance, the enclosure at Robin Hood's Ball was the major building project of its day, and very much the forerunner of the spectacular developments at Stonehenge. The enclosure would have taken twenty people working full time every day of the week, every week of the year, three years to complete. It may be that twice or three times as many people were actually involved, and there is no reason to suppose that they worked continuously, but the figures give a good indication of the amount of work involved (see Appendix B).

The earth circle on the hill was built for ceremonial purposes: a settlement site of the same period was built immediately beside it just 30 m away from its north-east entrance. The two roughly concentric magic circles inscribed on the earth were meant to mark out the site as a special place, the space within as separate and other than the space without: as such they fore-shadowed the whole sequence of monuments that would follow, including Stonehenge itself. It seems not even to have mattered that the perimeter of the ragged circle became blurred with time: the richest deposits of objects were actually found on top of the collapsed banks, where they must have been laid after much of the bank material had slid, or been pushed, back into the ditches. The finds of scrapers and arrowheads, pig, sheep and cattle bones, round-bottomed pots and traces of a hearth imply that early farmers either lived at the settlement site and built the enclosure next to it specially for ceremonial purposes or, more likely, came to live beside the magic circle after it was made. Probably people from all the farmsteads scattered across the slopes to the south-east gathered from time to time in the ritual enclosure.[26]

The settlement on the hill was occupied from at least as early as 3500 BC until 3200 or 3100 BC.[27] The enclosure next to it probably dates from 3500 or earlier. The people who built Maiden Castle earth circle away to the south were using types of pottery very similar to those used at Robin Hood's Ball,[28] even to the presence of imported Cornish pottery,[29] and the Maiden Castle earth circle was in use from about 3900 to 3200 BC, so the trend of the evidence is towards Robin Hood's Ball being built some time between 3900 and 3500 BC; in fact, most of the thirteen causewayed enclosures in southern England that have been radiocarbon dated at the time of writing fall between those dates, with an average at 3700 BC.

The map of Wessex at this time (Figure 14) shows that what was to

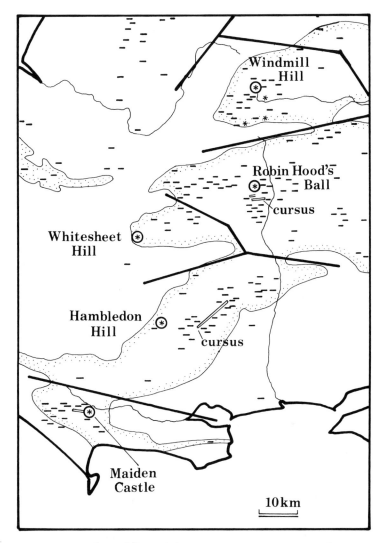

Figure 14 Wessex in the middle neolithic (3500–3000 BC). The named sites are major causewayed enclosures. Dash: long barrow. Solid black lines: suggested boundaries between tribal territories (it is likely these were ill-defined). Small dotted area in the west: Carboniferous Limestone. Large dotted area in the centre: Chalk. By the mid-neolithic the Wessex chalklands had evolved into five large tribal territories.

become the Stonehenge territory was just one of five similar territories, each with a high density of long barrows and a large causewayed enclosure at its heart: three of them were to acquire large-scale processional ways shortly afterwards. The monuments of the Stonehenge territory were evolving

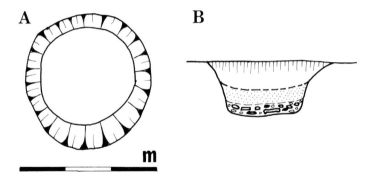

Figure 15 The Coneybury pit: plan (A) and section (B). The dashed line shows the likely level of the filling at the time when the adjacent henge was created.

precisely in step with those of the rest of Wessex. Robin Hood's Ball was a perfectly normal, standard, unexceptional ceremonial enclosure, as ordinary in its day as the average parish church built in the middle ages.

Round about the same time 5^1/$_2$ km to the south-east, about as far as from Regent's Park to the Tower of London, and 1^1/$_2$ km beyond Stonehenge, which using the same analogue would stand on the site of St Paul's Cathedral, a different group of people dug a pit 1 m in diameter and threw into it the remains of a huge feast (Figure 15). At first sight it may look like rubbish disposal, but it is more likely to have been an offering of some kind. There were cooking pots and small cups – over forty vessels in all – and the remains of cattle, roe and red deer, piglets, fish and two young beavers. The people who made this lavish feast offering in 3850 BC were apparently still leading a pre-neolithic existence, living mainly by exploiting the wilderness of forest and river valley, so we should visualize two different ways of life going on in the Stonehenge area: new pastoralists living side by side with old hunters.[30]

It is possible that the slowly evolving farming communities in the north and west of the area devised the rough earth circle at Robin Hood's Ball for their own ceremonies relating exclusively to their agricultural system: religion and economy are always closely bound together in archaic societies. The farmers must have felt an urgent need to enlist supernatural help in their agricultural adventure: they were after all harnessing natural forces in a much more ambitious way than ever before. Excluded from the earth circle and its rites, the hunters and gatherers living in the Avon valley fell back on older rituals and made offerings at their own forest shrine: the pit seems to have been dug in scrubland, a wilder area than the open pastures to the north and west. The backwoodsmen had no access to the fine pottery which the farmers at Robin Hood's Ball were importing, and this suggests that the hunters had to depend on what they could get locally, while the farmers were developing trading contacts far afield. The signs are that British society was neither consistent nor uniform: even at this early time there were groups of people living side by side with different ways of life, different customs, and each with its own shrine.

Crude and minimal though the Coneybury offering pit may look to us now, it seems to have been remembered long afterwards by the local people. Just as the site of the mesolithic totem poles seems to have influenced the choice of location for Stonehenge I, a smaller henge was later to be created right beside the Coneybury pit. They had very long memories, the Stonehenge people.

Meanwhile, the bands of farmers in their scattered farmsteads elaborated markers that established their claims to specific areas of the plain. Unlike their mesolithic predecessors, they made the places where they buried their dead into lasting monuments. It was a new departure, with new implications. Archaeologists have explored many neolithic burial monuments and pieced together some of the elaborate rituals that the living carried out with the remains of the dead. Corpses were often exposed immediately after death and it has been suggested that some of the causewayed enclosures were used mainly or exclusively for this purpose.[31]

In the Stonehenge territory, it looks as if bodies were exposed in rectangular mortuary enclosures or, especially later on, in small wooden mortuary houses.[32] Few modern scientific investigations of the Stonehenge long barrows – that is to say, the barrows in the 100 sq. km centring on Stonehenge – have been undertaken, but their shape shows that they belong to that large family of neolithic long barrows found across a large swathe of southern and eastern England.[33] Nutbane, only 20 km from Stonehenge, was an earth and chalk rubble mound covering the ruined remains of a wooden mortuary enclosure and cult-house. The cult-house was perhaps in use for a long time: it was rebuilt and enlarged to a substantial 8 m by 6 m, and its front wall was turned into a formal facade for a forecourt by adding a pair of large posts – perhaps totem poles – at each end. The Nutbane people placed the body of a man inside the cult-house and then, in 3400 BC, decided that the time had come to convert the shrine into a barrow. The enclosure where the dead were laid out was filled with soil, the cult-house was set on fire and, while it was still aflame, the mound of the long barrow was thrown over it, putting out the fire and completely burying the whole structure.[34]

The interior of Nutbane gives us valuable evidence of the rituals that were conducted at the long barrows, whole sequences of complicated and carefully planned ceremonies involving fresh corpses, bundles of old bones, wooden buildings, fences, pits, lines of totem poles – and the spectacle of purifying fire. None of this is apparent now from the smooth bland exterior of the barrow, which is often 40 or 50 m long with more or less parallel sides and parallel flanking quarry ditches, the whole mound softened by rain, frost and plough and often overgrown by grass. Frequently the barrow is

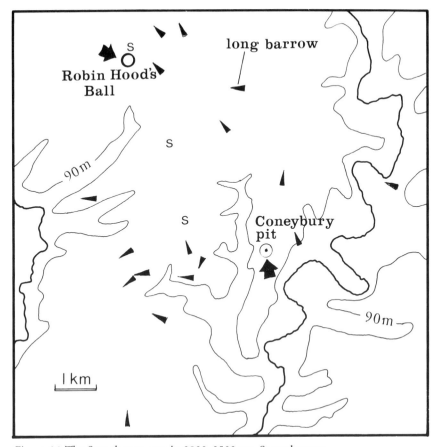

Figure 16 The Stonehenge area in 3900–3500 BC. S: settlement.

tapered so that the eastern end, where the burials and timber structures were usually placed, is wider and higher.

As with Stonehenge, orientation was all-important. Eighty per cent of the long barrows on Salisbury Plain point to the north-east, east or south-east, towards the horizon where the sun rises, a pathetic gesture of faith that the rays of the rising, life-giving sun would re-animate the dead bones of the ancestors.[35]

In times before the true nature of the long barrows was understood, it was often assumed that these enormous mounds, twenty times longer than a modern grave, must be the graves of great men – giants, even.[36] Yet they were rarely graves for individual people, and some barrows contained the remains of as many as forty people. On another level, we can argue that the barrows were not primarily graves at all. Only a small fraction of the long mounds was needed to cover the burials and the remains of the mortuary

Plate 6 View along the midsummer sunrise axis from the centre of Stonehenge. Stones 49 and 31 of the Bluestone Circle, 29, 30, 1 and 2 of the Great Sarsen Circle can be seen in the foreground, the Slaughter and Heel Stones in the middle distance.

Plate 7 Stonehenge from the north-east entrance causeway, Slaughter Stone in the left foreground. The view is to the south-west, along the midsummer sunrise axis.

buildings: the rest, the 'tail' of the mound, was for display, to turn the tomb into a major landmark. Each band of farmers was probably a family group,[37] and it wanted to mark its territory in a distinctive and permanent way. It seems likely from a number of studies that they built their barrows on the edges of their territories, well away from their huts.[38] Often they deliberately positioned the barrow on rising ground and false-crested it so that they could easily see it from the patch of farmland below, and in this respect it had a close kinship with the causewayed enclosure that they could see up on the hill.

The barrow was an expression of a family's claim, through the ancestors who had first cleared the forest, to a particular patch of land. This claim nested within the larger claim expressed by the causewayed enclosure, which brought together all these farming families for tribal gatherings.

PROCESSIONAL WAYS

As the ritual landscape of the early farmers evolved, a new type of monument emerged, one that speaks of a highly organized society driven by some powerful religious or ceremonial need. As I write, there is a world-wide surge of popular guilt at the despoliation of the environment, a communal heart-searching over ozone holes, the greenhouse effect, global warming and rising sea level, the destruction of rain forests and the wholesale pollution of the seas. Since we tend to cast our ancestors in our own image, it is inevitably a fashionable theme among archaeologists to portray our neolithic ancestors as environmental destroyers. Yet, even after allowing for an element of temporal bias, it does look as though the wholesale clearance of the forests by neolithic farmers led to a deterioration in the soils and to widespread soil erosion. The first farmers would not have understood what was happening in ecological terms and understandably resorted to religion to help them out; the increasing scale and elaborateness of their ceremonial monuments may be interpreted as signs of mounting desperation. Each successive monument in the Stonehenge landscape can be seen as a new cry for help, a step nearer despair, as the monument-builders tried to reverse the processes that were decimating their food supplies. We cannot *know* what was in their minds, but the environmental evidence is there.[39]

Gaining in confidence or sliding into despair, depending on one's point of view, the family groups of the Stonehenge territory joined forces to make a large and ambitious communal monument. Its shape, a very long and relatively narrow enclosure, naturally suggests people moving along inside it rather like communicants walking up the aisle of a church, though we have no way of knowing whether they walked, ran or danced along it, no way of knowing how formal this movement was, and no way of knowing how many people were involved or how frequently. How the cursus monument was used is surrounded in mystery. One thing we do know is that the

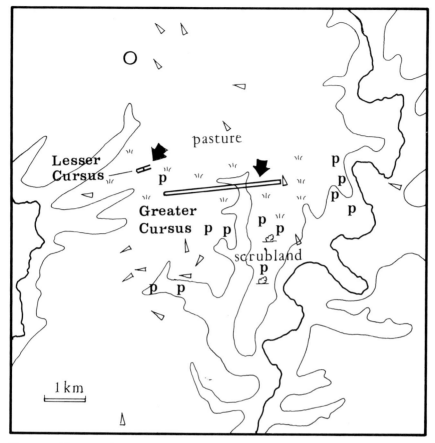

Figure 17 The Stonehenge area in 3500–3350 BC. P: pottery and flintwork, showing the intensively domesticated zone south of the cursus monuments.

mobilization of labour at this time at Stonehenge was paralleled by similar stirrings in other territories. Huge earthworks were similarly laid out in about 3500–3200 BC at Hambledon Hill and the Dorset Cursus.

Its banks degraded and its ditches filled by long-continued ploughing, the Great Cursus now looks very insignificant (Figure 17). It is quite hard to see except from the air. But when it was new, in around 3500 BC, it must have been startlingly impressive: in a world without motorways or railways, the double earthwork slicing across the territory in two white slashes of chalk caught and surprised the cowherd's eye. The twenty-one medieval cathedrals of central and southern England might be fitted end to end between its banks, and walking along it would have been like walking the length of those twenty-one aisles one after another, a certain affirmation of faith.[40]

Technically, the earthwork was simple, involving no techniques that had

45

not already been used at Robin Hood's Ball, but it was very large and digging out its ditches and building the adjacent banks took almost as much time as creating the spectacular sarsen monument that was later raised just to the south at Stonehenge. The bounding ditch of the cursus was 3 m wide 1 m deep and flat-floored: the bank inside it may originally have stood 1 m high.

Laid out on undulating land, the Great Cursus starts and ends on higher ground, in between passing down into the shallow dry valley of Stonehenge Bottom: this shape means that even though the two ends are 2,800 m apart they are clearly intervisible and would be even if there were many people in the enclosure. The woodland that used to cover its western end has recently been cleared so that once again, as in antiquity, there is a clear view across unkempt pasture along the full length of the cursus. The ends are carefully squared off, and all the evidence suggests that what took place at both ends was of significance. The western end is on fairly level ground and a diagonal earthwork, apparently part of the original design, separated an area at the terminus from the rest of the cursus.[41]

The sides are almost exactly parallel and a maximum of 150 m apart; the builders for some reason went to some trouble to correct their surveying errors, drawing the width in to about 90 m at each end. Covering an area of 280,000 sq.m, almost the size of the Sumerian city of Ur at its peak a thousand years later, and three times as long as the Athenians' Panathenaic Way, the Great Cursus was the greatest monument the Stonehenge people had attempted so far. It cost them an enormous amount in the only real currency they possessed, their labour – some 1,250,000 man-hours (see Appendix B).

Just beyond its eastern end is a long barrow oriented north–south,[42] and it is sometimes said that this forms the eastern terminus, but it does not: there is a clear gap of 20 m between the eastern end of the cursus and the long barrow. Nevertheless, we can see from the way the cursus was laid out that it was designed to lead towards it. The barrow stands on a subdued ridge and because the middle of the cursus sags into a shallow valley observers could see the barrow clearly from the western end of the cursus, almost 3 km away.[43]

Later, perhaps not much later, the Great Cursus was modified. The original ditch was dug out at the eastern end to a depth of only 1.5 m. Then its depth was doubled. This would have added to the height and brightness of the bank. The intention was clearly to make the eastern end of the cursus more imposing and dramatic, a major visual focus. A drive to make monuments bigger, grander, more spectacular was clearly part of the Stonehenge people's make-up from early on. We see it at this stage, in about 3450–3400 BC. We see it again twelve hundred years later when the stonework was built and rebuilt at the centre of Stonehenge.[44]

A much smaller cursus was begun but never finished about 600 m north-west of the Great Cursus. It looks insignificant on maps mainly because it is

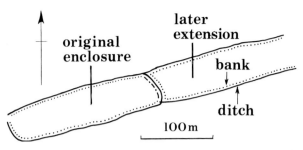

Figure 18 The Lesser Cursus. The dot-and-dash line represents the (internal) cross bank of the original enclosure.

dwarfed by the neighbouring Great Cursus, but the Lesser Cursus is a major monument in its own right; it is sobering to realize that twelve Parthenons could be fitted into its roughly rectangular shape.[45] Measuring 400 m long and 60 m wide, the Lesser Cursus runs from west-south-west to east-north-east along the top of a broad, flat-topped ridge. This monument was levelled by ploughing in the 1940s and nothing is visible in the landscape now. Halfway along the Lesser Cursus the sides pinch in slightly and a cross bank and ditch run across; this is reminiscent of the angled cross ditch near the western end of the Great Cursus and the implication that the western half of the Lesser Cursus was created first and the eastern half was a later and uncompleted extension is hard to resist. The fact that the cross bank is on the east side of the ditch creates a problem here, though, because the other three sides of the coffin-shaped western enclosure are made by a ditch surrounding an internal bank: if the cross bank was part of this design, making the fourth side, it should be to the *west* of its ditch (see Figure 18).

This problem has recently been resolved by excavation.[46] The original, rather shallow cross ditch may have had its bank to the west (the dot-and-dash line on Figure 18), but the second phase ditch was dug significantly deeper and wider, and it was during this recutting at the time of the eastward extension that the surviving traces of bank material were thrown to the east. It is very clear now that the eastern half of the monument really was a later addition.[47]

As the eastern ditches were dug out antler picks were laid carefully and deliberately along their flat floors, roughly a step apart, a routine neolithic foundation offering and a natural reference to the way the monument was made. The second phase has been dated from one of the antlers to 3400 BC.[48] For some reason this cursus was only extended by 200 m, exactly doubling its original size, and never finished off with an eastern terminal bank and ditch. Even more surprisingly, the new ditches were deliberately filled in again almost straight away. Yet similar things happened at causewayed enclosures, where burials or other offerings were tucked into the ditches and parts of the adjacent bank were pushed in to cover them. It was the rituals of

Figure 19 Excavating a ditch and building a bank in the neolithic. This is how the cursus monuments and the Stonehenge earth circle were probably made.

making – in this case digging, depositing and filling – that were of prime importance rather than the appearance of the finished structure. This is a very different approach to architecture from our own, and one to bear in mind when we try to interpret Stonehenge itself.

George Meaden's (1992) idea that each cursus marks the track of a prehistoric tornado is interesting, plausibly assuming that a tornado may well have been seen by an archaic community as a visitation by the sky-god. Meaden argues that swathes of woodland were cleared by the tornadoes, so that nature itself laid out the cursus site, but tornadoes are less than systematic in their destruction and, as likely as not, two-thirds of the trees remain standing after a tornado has passed. The idea comes apart with the proposition that long barrows point towards the terminals of the cursus: this is not so at the Dorset Cursus, where Gussage St Michael I and II point away from the Thickthorn (southern) terminal: at the northern terminal, two long barrows point towards the terminal and four do not. There are admittedly clusters of long barrows at each end of the Dorset Cursus: either the cursus was designed to travel between them or, more likely, additional barrows were built to reinforce the terminals after the cursus was completed. As far as the Great Cursus at Stonehenge is concerned, nine out of the seventeen long barrows in our 100 sq. km territory do not point to either of the cursus terminals, so it would be unwise to assume any significant association.

The sequence of monuments built in the early neolithic is the warp and weft of the ritual landscape of the Stonehenge territory, the half-finished tapestry into which Stonehenge was to be sewn. By understanding how people gradually built up this ritual landscape, we can begin to see how Stonehenge fitted into it. It is almost as if the Stonehenge people, like the other peoples of neolithic Britain, were experimenting with inscriptions on the earth: seen from the air their monuments are like a giant's alphabet: pictograms consisting of lines, circles, double lines, circles with lines, circles within circles, and so on. Coincidentally, on the other fringe of Europe, while the Stonehenge people were inventing geoglyphs, the Egyptians were at about the same time (3300 BC) inventing hieroglyphs.

The cursus monuments were probably the last components to be added to the ritual landscape before the earth circle at Stonehenge was built. The early farmers shifted their cult focus from Robin Hood's Ball across towards the centre of the undulating basin, perhaps as a gesture of compromise building their cursus monuments roughly halfway between their old earth circle and the hunters' ritual pit – or perhaps halfway between the circle and the Avon valley where the hunters were based. The next phase, the creation of a monument at the Stonehenge site, may have been prompted by any one of three thoughts. It may have been the need to renew a tryst with the old mesolithic shrine-site: it was quite common for old sites to be commemorated or revived with new monuments. The new site of Stonehenge was also exactly halfway between the Coneybury feast pit and the enclosure marking the western end of the Greater Cursus, and once again compromise or reconciliation may have been the motive. The new site was also roughly in the centre of an east–west zone alive with activity immediately to the south of the Great Cursus, a 'domestic' zone that was rich in finds of early neolithic pottery and flintwork (see Figure 17). Which of these considerations was uppermost in the minds of the builders of Stonehenge I we cannot tell: perhaps some other thought entirely.

STONEHENGE I: THE EARTH CIRCLE

It was around 3100 BC that the Stonehenge people constructed the oldest part of the great monument to survive visibly into modern times.[49] Although it is tempting always to portray Stonehenge as exceptional, it is worth remembering that this phase, Stonehenge I, involved the same amount of work, around 100,000 man-hours, as all the long barrows in the Stonehenge area put together. In fact the Stonehenge project probably represents the pooled labour of the same family groups who built the long barrows. On an open mead close to the site of the early totem poles they built a rather unusual henge monument, a circular bank with two, or possibly three, breaks in it and a surrounding ditch about 115 m in

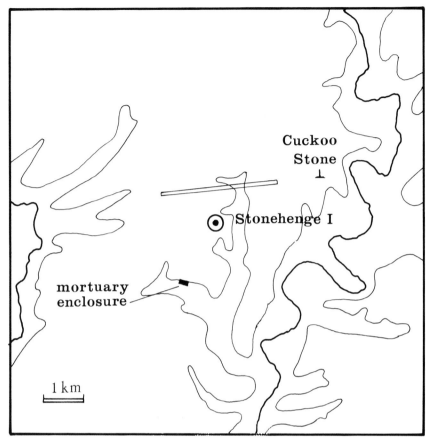

Figure 20 The Stonehenge area in 3250–3100 BC. The Cuckoo Stone may have been raised later, at the time when Woodhenge was built.

diameter.[50] Hereford Cathedral could be fitted within the encircling ditch.

The first radiocarbon dates for Avebury have recently been released, and they reveal something quite unexpected. Instead of belonging to the same period as those of Durrington Walls, Mount Pleasant and Marden – the other Wessex superhenges – the huge bank and ditch at Avebury were created several centuries earlier, between 3200 and 2900 BC. In other words, the very large henge at Avebury was laid out at the same time as the much smaller one at Stonehenge: Avebury is four times larger in diameter than Stonehenge. We can safely assume from this that Stonehenge I was *not* the pre-eminent ceremonial building project of its day, that greater things were happening at Avebury.

The Stonehenge people laid out their earth circle with characteristically simple technology. First, they marked a large circle on the gently sloping

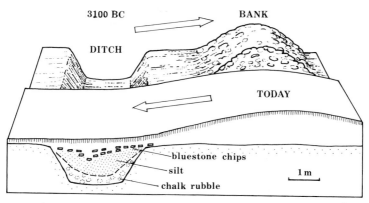

Figure 21 The Stonehenge I earthwork when newly built (back) and after five thousand years of weathering.

turf, probably with a rope 55 m long tied to a central post and a set of perhaps fifty or sixty sharpened pegs hammered into the ground at intervals round the circumference: this was to be the inner edge of the ditch.[51] Then they lengthened the rope to 60.5 m to knock a second circle of pegs into the turf where the ditch's outer edge would be. They peeled off the turf between the two circles, possibly using simply made wooden spades, and stacked it up neatly along the outer rim of the ditch: then the topsoil was dug out and dumped over the turves to make a low outer bank.[52] This very low earthwork is now barely perceptible and can only have been about 0.5 m high in 3100 BC, when it was made.

Work on Stonehenge had to be fitted in round agricultural work, housebuilding and repair, cooking, hunting and gathering. This was a society of participation rather than a society of specialists, with whole communities of men, women and children involved in producing food and building monuments. Work on Stonehenge, like the work already done on the Great Cursus, Lesser Cursus and the long barrows, was probably intermittent and spread across many years. There was no hurry to get things finished.[53]

It may be that once the circles were marked and the turf and soil stripped out from between them work stopped for the season. Thereafter, groups of people came along from time to time to work on a section of the ditch, possibly in a fairly informal way, although the ditch-ends next to the two entrance gaps must have been established very early on with well-marked craters (Figure 24). Workers dug with antler picks, which are surprisingly effective on chalk, quarrying away at the inner edge of the ditch and facing the centre of the circle. After a short time each worker or pair of workers was standing on the flat floor of a steep-sided pit. Each pit was enlarged back to the line of the outer circle and sideways until it joined the next pit.[54] People were used to quarrying the chalk like this; they had had generations of experience in clearing tree-roots from their farmland and making post-holes for their houses: even the simplest rectangular hut with a ridge-roof needed at least two earth-fast posts to support the ridge-pole. One person was probably able to quarry a tonne of chalk in a day and think nothing of it.

Other workers carried the chalk rubble in baskets, trays or leather sacks across to the bank they were building just inside the ditch (Figure 19). When the bank was complete it stood 6 m wide and a little taller than a man. Because the covering turf and topsoil had been deliberately built into a separate low bank outside the ditch, the inner bank, like the ditch, was a shining pure white. In fact the sequence of events makes it clear that the makers of Stonehenge wanted the inner bank to be made of chalk and nothing but chalk. There is good reason to believe, because of discoveries at other ritual centres, that the whiteness of the bank was very significant.[55] Perhaps white had special associations for them, associations with purity, goodness, spirituality, godhead, just as it still does for us today. Perhaps it was in the first place simply an accident of the building method that the earlier Wessex monuments, like the long barrows and causewayed enclosures, had turned out white, and the colour, or lack of it, became indelibly associated with important ceremonial buildings. The people of the Stonehenge territory must also have noticed that making monuments of white chalk was a sure way of making them conspicuous in the landscape. Wordsworth pointed out in his 1822 *Description of the Scenery of the Lakes* that whitewashing houses makes them visible from a great distance: he disapproved strongly because the dazzle destroyed the natural aerial perspective.

Painstakingly dug out over several years, the Stonehenge ditch ended up as an approximation to a true circle with wobbling, wavy edges, its form clearly showing its origin as something approaching a hundred oval pits.[56] Although now it is scarcely noticeable, some 6,000 tonnes of turf, soil and chalk were removed to create it. It could have been made in a single autumn by a workforce of two hundred people,[57] but there is no reason to suppose that the monument was at this stage the work of such a large community. Here, as at other neolithic sites, it would be wiser to assume that fairly small numbers of people were involved, and usually for short periods at a time. Since there is no reason to suppose that the Stonehenge earth circle was made in a single season, we may as well assume it took a decade.

When the work was finally done, as at the Lesser Cursus two hundred years before, the workers deliberately laid their antler picks down on the floor of the ditch. Some of these have been used for radiocarbon dating and they tell us the ditch was completed in about 3050 BC.[58] It nevertheless looks as if there was some cult activity on the site before this. The position of the mesolithic totem poles, as we saw, implies at least the possibility of a cult-house at Stonehenge, a marker from which the midsummer sunset might have been observed.

Plate 8 Part of the Bluestone Circle at Stonehenge under excavation in 1954: stones 150, 32 and 33 are visible. The complexity of this zone is obvious, with post- and stone-holes of several building phases intersecting. The stumps of three broken bluestones can just be made out.

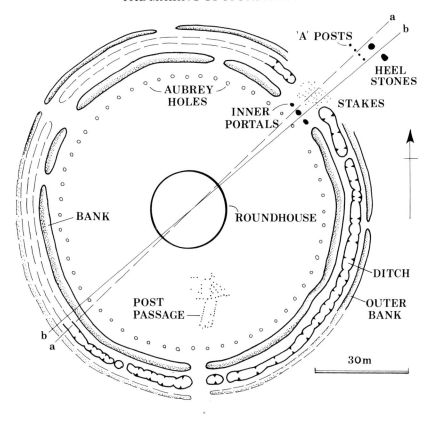

Figure 22 Plan of Stonehenge I. The initial axis (a) passed through the centre of the entrance causeway according to Burl; the later axis (b) passed between the Heel Stones.

There is also the more positive evidence of the stakes marking lunar observations: these must have been planted *before* the ditch was cut because although they lie mainly on the north-east entrance causeway the ends of the ditch cut into some of them. The stakes nevertheless imply that observers stood at the centre of the earth circle when making their observations, and the general location of the scatter of stakes determined where the north-east entrance of the henge would be, so it is likely that the century of lunar observations and the stake-planting that marked their results came immediately before the Stonehenge ditch was cut, in other words between 3200 and 3100 BC.

In the ditch and bank a broad gap as wide as a tennis court was left on the north-east side to make the circle's main entrance, and this was probably intended for ceremonial use.[59] There was a much narrower gap, about 3.5 m across, on the south side: this is convincingly identified as a second entrance

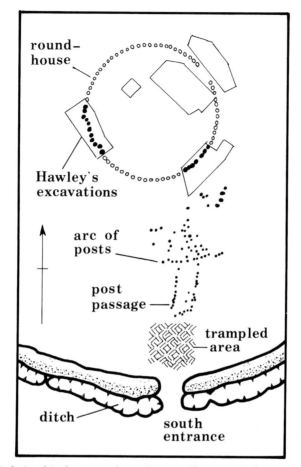

Figure 23 Relationship between the early roundhouse and the south entrance at Stonehenge.

by Aubrey Burl.[60] It is strange that this south entrance has been overlooked or forgotten by many writers on the subject, and indeed the cartographers who draw plans of the monument, because it was identified by Colonel Hawley when he excavated it early in the twentieth century and it is still clearly visible (Plate 3).[61] It seems likely from its size and from the lack of ceremonial structures that this south entrance was the normal everyday entrance used by prehistoric visitors. Just inside it the soil was 'very flinty and hard' across an area about 7 m in diameter, and it can only have become compacted by people continually tramping across, presumably dispersing from or converging on the south entrance (Figure 23).

Across the causeway at the north-east entrance there was a maze of stake-holes, generally about 0.5 m across and 0.6 m deep, that are far less straightforward to interpret. When Hawley examined them in 1922 he thought they might have formed a palisade, but there would have been little sense in raising six closely spaced parallel fences across the entrance gap, whether to keep out people or animals, when one would have sufficed. Each one of these 'fences' has to be seen as a separate row of stakes and it is now clear that each stake marked the northernmost position of the rising moon in a particular year.[62] The moonrise, then as now, shifted along the horizon, so the Stonehenge observers had to plant another stake each year; the most northerly stake in the row would then mark the major northern moonrise, the turning-point in the lunar cycle which took 18.6 years to complete. That the observers were following the moon's movements in this methodical way is revealing enough in itself, but that they *went on* following them through another cycle and then another shows a thoroughness that is quite startling. The existence of *six* rows of stakes shows that they were determined to establish beyond any doubt that there was a pattern in the moon's fickle movements, one that would be repeated time out of mind, and one that would be predictable.

There is nothing to see of these posts or their sockets today, yet they are as dramatic a testament to the Stonehenge people's purpose as the later sarsen monument. They tell us that observers systematically visited Stonehenge at night from midsummer onwards to watch the rising moon from the circle's centre, perhaps at this time marked by little more than a lean-to hut or a post; they also tell us that this went on for a period of at least 112 years – six complete lunar cycles – so that they could check and re-check the northernmost position for each year until they were absolutely certain they had found the overall northernmost moonrise position. That they went on watching until that overall northernmost moonrise had recurred five times tells us, more than any other single feature of the monument, how determined and obsessive they were.

Few people lived beyond their thirties in neolithic Britain, and if we allow that an apprentice observer might have begun at 15 and died at 30 the full set of observations must have spanned seven or eight generations.[63] The watchers must either have recorded their observations on stone, wood or hide or, more likely, they used oral tradition to pass on their knowledge. They must have had a fairly complex language too, or the purpose could not have been transmitted, but unfortunately nothing is known of their language.

The southernmost stakes line up on the midsummer sunrise, perhaps coincidentally, but it must have been round about that time of year that the observations of the moonrises began. A possible early link between solar and lunar observations is hinted at here. There are no stake-holes south of this line, even though there is space for them on part of the causeway, so we know the observers were not interested in the 'minor' moonrises. The southernmost stakes marked the moonrise at what is called 'mid-swing'.

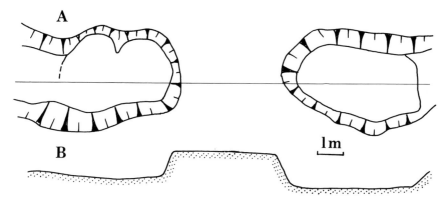

Figure 24 The south entrance of Stonehenge I, plan (A) and section (B) (after Hawley). Two well-made oval pits or craters mark the ditch terminals.

Scholars have disagreed about the causeway stake-holes. In the 1920s Hawley vaguely suggested a palisade and never returned to discuss them any further, and it was not until 1972 that Peter Newham proposed that they were markers for northern moonrises. Heggie dismissed Newham's explanation as 'a poor one', while Richard Atkinson was guarded, saying it was 'possible, but clearly the observations thus marked were not made systematically with respect to time.' Wood felt that 'the evidence on balance supports the view that Stonehenge was a lunar observatory from its earliest times.' Burl feels that the evidence is 'imperfect and ambiguous, but several additional features support Newham's theory.' In particular, Burl sees the four large posts 25 m outside the entrance causeway and discovered by Hawley in 1924 as proof that Newham was on the right trail.[64]

These 'A posts' (Figure 25) were massive tree-trunks about 1 m in diameter and spaced an orderly 1.8 m (three steps) apart: their huge girth implies that they were tall, possibly 4 m or more high. They served as summaries of the stake-hole observations. When the new stone age moon rose in the space between the right-hand post and the one next to it, it was a quarter of the way between the midpoint of the lunar cycle and the northern extreme. When it rose in the gap between posts two and three, reading from the south, it was one-third of the distance.[65] In this way the A posts signalled a sort of count-down to the northernmost moonset. Here the moonrise explanation seems to be weakened beyond repair, because two more posts are needed to the north of the four surviving post-holes: the gap between the imagined fifth and sixth posts would indicate the major moonrise. If the stakes and posts were really raised to find and mark out the lunar cycle, why is the climax of the cycle left unmarked? The answer may be that it *was* marked and that there were originally two more posts. When we look closely at Hawley's plan we can see that his excavation stopped just short of the place where a fifth post-hole might lie. The location of the sixth post-hole has been lost beyond recovery because it was destroyed when the Avenue was created a thousand years later: it lay on the mid-point of the north-western ditch. There is a chance that small-scale excavation in the Avenue bank might uncover the fifth post-hole: if and when it does, the moonrise interpretation will be vindicated.

The enclosing ditch comes up very close to the array of stake-holes on both sides, actually cutting across the tops of one or two of them and proving that the century of lunar observations came first. In fact, it may well be that the stake-holes, A posts and portal stones were all in place before the ditch and bank were created.

THE HEEL STONE

Several metres out from the A posts, the builders raised the first two megaliths of Stonehenge, stones 96 and 97 (Figures 22 and 25). The two large sarsen stones were perhaps found close to Stonehenge, but very few sarsens can be seen there now, apart from the stones incorporated in Stonehenge, so it seems more probable that like the large consignment of stones brought in for Stonehenge III they were imported from the Marlborough Downs near Avebury – and this as early as 3100 BC.[66] Stone 97 was removed long ago, but stone 96 still stands and, in lone state as the one conspicuous outlier, it is one of the features of the monument that everyone knows. In the popular imagination of the last two hundred years the Heel Stone, stone 96, indicates the direction of the midsummer sunrise, although this was emphatically not its purpose in antiquity.[67]

It stands 77 m from the centre of Stonehenge and leans 27° from the vertical as if bowing reverently towards the sarsen ring (Plates 4 and 5); it may be that weathering of the chalk socket has made it lean so, or the decay of the timbers that originally lined the socket: it was almost certainly vertical when it was set up five thousand years ago. It is a crude, unshaped, eroded cylinder of sarsen 2.4 m thick with its tip 4.7 m above the ground. In its original upright position it would have been 5.2 m tall, with another 1.2 m of its length buried in the ground.[68] Weighing over 35 tonnes, more than four elephants, it would have taken 150 people or – more likely in my view – 16 oxen to haul it upright.[69]

As a solitary outlier it has naturally attracted attention, folklore and many misconceptions. Over the years it has been known as the Friar's Heel, Crwm Leche or the Bowing Stone, the Marker, Pointer Stone, Index Stone, Sun Stone, Hele Stone and, especially since about 1960, the Heel Stone. Aubrey Burl has written a delightful account of the stone's modern history, but more important to us here is the stone's role in prehistory.[70]

The position of the sunrise shifts seasonally along the horizon, from south-east in December to east in March and north-east in June. The sunrise

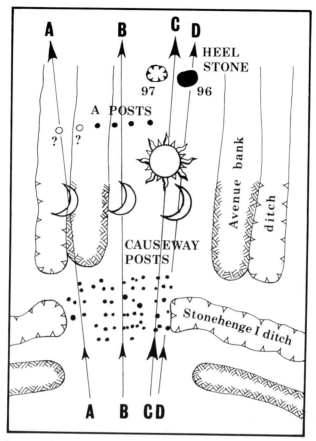

Figure 25 The Stonehenge I north-east entrance, showing major lunar and solar alignments. A: northernmost moonrise. B: one-third of the way between northernmost moonrise and midpoint of lunar cycle (and initial axis of Stonehenge I). C: floating-free position of sun at midsummer sunrise D: moonrise at midpoint of lunar cycle.

reaches this northernmost position, about 50° from true north, on 21 June, hovering there for three or four days before crawling back southwards again. Many people take for granted that this phenomenon was of great interest and importance to the builders of Stonehenge and that they raised the Heel Stone and possibly the monument as a whole specially to mark it, but we must not be too hasty in our assumptions. William Stukeley seems to have been the first to express the belief that Stonehenge was astronomically aligned: 'The Avenue . . . answers to the principal line of the whole work, the north-east, where abouts the sun rises, when the days are longest.'[71] Interestingly, Stukeley makes it clear that he is referring to the Avenue and the monument's south-west to north-east axis, not to the Heel Stone. A little later in the same book Stukeley returns to the idea: 'The interest of the founders of Stonehenge was to set the entrance full north-east, being the point where the sun rises, or nearly, at the summer solstice.'[72] Stukeley's 'nearly' is revealing, as is his continued reticence about the Heel Stone, which he clearly did not think pointed to the midsummer sunrise.

It was left to John Wood a few years later to suggest that the Heel Stone was a prehistoric astronomical marker, but he thought of it as a lunar pointer: 'the great pillar before the front of STONEHENGE is situated North Eastward from that Edifice; and in each case [he draws a comparison with Stanton Drew] a phase of the New Moon is pointed out.' Wood thought the Heel Stone was 'in line to that Quarter of the Heavens where the New Moon first appears on that Day of her Age when the Druids began their Times and Festivals.'[73]

Dr John Smith was the next to interpret the Heel Stone, this time making the historic connection with the summer solstice sunrise. Dr Smith was driven from his practice by hostile villagers as a result of his experiments with smallpox inoculations and took refuge, like Charles II before him, in speculation at Stonehenge. His survey methods were less than scientific. 'Without an Instrument, or any assistance whatever, but White's Ephemeris, I began my survey. I suspected the Stone, called the Friar's Heel, to be the Index that would disclose the uses of this Structure; nor was I deceived', he boasted. 'The stone number one [the Heel Stone], in the middle of the grand avenue to the Temple, is the Key or Gnomon, by which I propose to unlock this Ambre, or Repository of Druidical Secrets . . . At the summer solstice [the sun] seems to rise in the same point of the horizon, three days together. The Arch Druid standing against his stall, and looking down the right line of the temple, over stones II. and I. [II = the Slaughter Stone] his eye is bounded by Durrington field (a charming horizon about two miles distant), he there sees the sun rise from behind the hill; the apex of the stone number I. points directly to the place.'[74]

Given Smith's background, unscientific method and rather sweeping presentation, it is surprising that his proposal met with ready acceptance, yet the great majority of subsequent writers about Stonehenge have gone along with Smith's summer solstice interpretation. It is nevertheless incorrect.

In 1924 Stone drily wrote, 'Midsummer sunrise has never yet taken place over the Heel Stone, and will not do so until more than a thousand years have passed away.'[75] Richard Atkinson tried again in 1979 to dispel the illusion: 'The Heel Stone is the subject of one of the most popular and persistent misconceptions concerning Stonehenge, namely that it marks the point of sunrise on Midsummer Day . . . Actually, it does nothing of the sort.'[76]

The best-informed archaeologists and prehistorians have known for a long time that the Heel Stone does not mark the midsummer sunrise and – which is more important – never did. We know that the earthwork was laid out in about 3100 BC and that the Heel Stone was probably raised then or shortly afterwards in line with the right-hand, southern side of the north-east entrance (Plate 6).

Burl reminds us that it was common practice in prehistoric monuments to direct an alignment to the marked edge of an entrance rather than to an unmarked axis, quoting similar features at Long Meg, Swinside and the Rollright Stones. Since the Heel Stone is just 40 cm to the south of a lunar alignment, Burl argues that the monolith was intended to mark this – the moonrise at mid-swing. This is very plausible, and certainly more sensible than proposing that the stone's tip marked the midsummer sunrise when that event, in 3100 BC, must have taken place nearly 2 m away to the north. Burl's explanation of the Heel Stone as a moon-mark has added force when we remember that the stake-holes and the A posts were also moon-marks.[77]

Nevertheless, the discovery in 1979 of a large hollow to the north-west of the Heel stone opened the door to a new possibility.[78] Although Burl likes to see it as an addition in the bluestone phase a thousand years later, 'when the axis was converted to a solar alignment', there is no reason to suppose that a stone did not stand there back in Stonehenge I.[79] In fact, the small protective earth circle built round the Heel Stone while work on the Avenue was going on strongly implies that stone 97 was either taken out at this time or had already been removed long before: the socket for 97 has no protective circle round it.

Stones 97 and 96 should be seen as a pair. Standing side by side they created an astronomical doorway within which the rising midsummer sun was framed. In 3100 BC the midsummer sun rose well to the left, that is north, of the Heel stone but the full disc just detaching itself from the earth would have been framed between the two Heel Stones – and this, I believe, was the builders' intention. Another exciting possibility is that the stone portal was designed to fulfil three functions, the doorway itself marking the floating-free position of the rising midsummer sun, the right-hand pillar marking the moonrise at mid-swing and the left-hand pillar emphasizing or even replacing in stone the first of the lunar A posts. Seen in this way, the sarsen portal was a salutation to both sun and moon, a stone epigram. It is certain from what we are learning about the complexity of Stonehenge that its makers were both intelligent and subtle enough to have arrived at this.

At later cult sites too the enclosure entrances were often developed in a special way, often going through as many changes as the central structure. At Gournay, 70 km north of Paris, an iron age sanctuary was laid out as part of the capital of a pagus of the Bellovaci tribe in about 350 BC. Like Stonehenge, Gournay was in use for a long time (until about AD 350) and its central temple went through several rebuilding phases; its entrance also underwent several transformations, starting as a mere gap in the enclosure ditch and evolving gradually into a monumental portico flanked by sacrificial remains. Closer to home, the bronze age enclosure at Rams Hill shows a similar preoccupation with elaborating and altering the entrance; from about 1280 BC onwards, the Rams Hill entrance was changed at least five times.[80]

THE INNER PORTALS

Returning from the Heel Stones towards the north-east entrance we come once again to the broad causeway with its scatter of stake-holes. Immediately inside those are three large stone sockets, one of them once occupied by the fallen Slaughter Stone, stone 95, the other two completely empty (Plate 7). It is uncertain when the Slaughter Stone was first raised in its socket. The fact that it has been tooled into shape, unlike the Heel Stone, and is the same length as the stones of the Great Sarsen Circle may tell us that it was raised late, at the time of Stonehenge III, but it may belong to Stonehenge II. An axial line passing between stones 96 and 97 up the centre of the Avenue (which belongs to the Stonehenge II phase) also passes halfway between the Slaughter Stone's socket and its neighbour, stone-hole E; that suggests that portal stones belonging to Stonehenge II could have stood in sockets E and 95. On the other hand, a straight line drawn from the centre of Stonehenge out through the centre of the Stonehenge I causeway (and also, incidentally, halfway between A posts 2 and 3) passes between stone-holes D and E; that suggests that the Stonehenge I inner portals could have stood in sockets D and E (see Figure 8).

There is no simple solution to this complicated problem. It may be that portal stones were set up first in sockets D and E to mark the entrance into the precinct: the left-hand, northern edge of stone D could have been used as a marker for the northernmost moonrise. Then, later, the stones may have been repositioned in sockets E and 95 so that they reinforced the sight-line passing out between stones 96 and 97.

John Webb's seventeenth-century sketch of Stonehenge shows four stones at the north-east entrance as obelisks, which he called 'pyramids', two inside the ditch, two outside. Fifty years later, John Aubrey saw the two inner stones, E and 95, but one stone from the outer pair had gone: all three of the survivors were then standing, it seems. By William Stukeley's time only the Slaughter Stone remained, and that 'flat on the ground'.[81] It is possible that there were originally four stones standing on the entrance causeway: many other neolithic sites had impressive portals of this kind.[82] On the other hand, it is odd that no sockets for an outer pair have been reported and the area of the causeway has been excavated (by Hawley).

THE AUBREY HOLES

While making his survey of Stonehenge for Charles II, John Aubrey noticed five shallow depressions irregularly spaced round the precinct, just within the bank. These 'little cavities in the ground, from whence one may well conjecture the stones were taken', are known as Aubrey Holes after their discoverer. Some have doubted whether Aubrey could really have detected the Aubrey Holes, but the summer of 1666 was the second very hot, dry summer in succession; as a result the grass would have been parched and brown over wide areas, while the grass over the deeper soil in the Aubrey Holes may have remained green, and that could have made them visible.

It was not until 1920 that Aubrey's pits were rediscovered. Hawley first consulted Aubrey's plan in the Bodleian Library at Oxford and then probed the Stonehenge soil for them: he found one, then more, and finally discovered an entire sequence of regularly spaced pits about 5 m apart. Hawley emptied thirty-two of the pits, numbers 1–30, 55 and 56: in other words all the pits on the eastern and southern sides. Later, in 1950, Richard Atkinson and Stuart Piggott opened pits 31 and 32 and obtained some charcoal for radiocarbon dating. This showed that pit 32 was dug between 2700 and 1950 BC: the dating method was very new then and the margin of error was wide. Given that the ditch was dug in about 3100 BC, the earlier end of this time band, around 2700 BC, would appear more likely for the Aubrey Holes. Fragments of bluestone, which we know was on the site only from 2150 BC onwards, are found only at the very top of the Aubrey Hole filling, showing that the pits had probably been dug long before 2150 BC.

The Aubrey Holes were laid out on a true circle, which means that a circle was struck with a rope from the centre of the monument. The circle was concentric with the circles of the ditch and bank, so all three must have been drawn out when the central area was clear of sarsens or bluestones, or any pre-existing timber building which had presumably by then collapsed or been dismantled. These features again tell us that the Aubrey Holes must be earlier than Stonehenge II or III. The pits lie on the circumference of a regular circle with a 43.3 m radius, yet are themselves quite irregular, some 0.8 m across, others 1 m more, and varying in depth from 0.6 m to 1.1 m. But that only tells us that the pits were not measured, merely dug out. They are not exactly 5 m apart, either: that again is not surprising because they were very likely spaced out by pacing seven steps, and length of step varies slightly.[83]

Many theories have been devised to explain the Aubrey Holes. Apart from Hawkins's and Hoyle's eclipse predictions,[84] the pits have been seen as sockets for posts or stones.[85] Although the bases of the holes show no sign that they have ever borne heavy stones, it is possible that they carried small ones, say, 1 m high; small boulders would be easy to cart off for building or road-mending, so evidence for such a stone circle would not have survived into modern times. It is a possibility, but no more than that.

It is more likely that the steep-sided, flat-floored (typically neolithic) pits were dug for a different purpose, for offerings to the deities of the underworld. Many neolithic sanctuaries had offering pits of this kind, and the practice of making offerings to the earth deities was widespread and long-lived in the ancient world. On the far side of Europe, there were square libation pits in the paved floors of Minoan pillar crypts that were in use before 1500 BC.[86] Homer's Odysseus, from a later Aegean world, described how he communicated with the spirits of the dead:

> . . . with my sword
> I dug out a pit a cubit round and deep,
> And poured three libations to the unnumbered dead,
> First honey mixed with milk, then wine and water,
> And scattered barley on these gifts
> Before calling to the blurred spirits of the unbreathing dead.[87]

In this archaic world, digging a pit in the ground with the appropriate ceremonies was a way of opening a door to the gods of the underworld. The best-known and most dramatic account of this ritual is found in the *Aeneid*, when Aeneas descends into Hades to consult the spirit of his father, Anchises. Following the Sibyl's directions, Aeneas hastens to the cave of Avernus, the 'birdless place' deep in the forest. The Sibyl pours a libation of wine on the foreheads of four black bullocks, offering them as a preliminary sacrifice to Hecate, goddess of the underworld.

> While others laid their knives to the victims' throats and caught
> The fresh warm blood in bowls, Aeneas sacrificed
> A black-fleeced lamb to Night, mother of the Furies,
> And her great sister, Earth, and a virgin heifer to Persephone.
> Then he set up altars at night to the god of the Underworld,
> Committing to the flames whole carcases of bulls
> And pouring rich oil over their burning entrails.
> But listen! – at the first crack of dawn, the ground
> Beneath began to mutter, the forested hills to shake,
> And a baying of hounds was heard through the half-light:
> The goddess was on her way,
> Hecate. The Sibyl cried: 'Away! Now stand apart
> You uninitiated ones, depart from the wood!
> But you, Aeneas, draw your sword from its scabbard and go forth!
> Now you need all your courage and steadfastness of heart.'
> This she spoke and plunged ecstatic into the opened cave:
> Step for step Aeneas went, unshrinking, with his guide.[88]

The Stonehenge people too communicated with the underworld by leaving a variety of offerings to Night, Earth and their presiding goddess. They left offerings of soil, charcoal, cremated human bones in the Aubrey Holes, each a symbolic Avernus. Some holes were dug and backfilled straight away: some were dug, filled and later reopened and filled again with chalk, burnt soil and pieces of wood. Long bone pins were sometimes used to fix together

Plate 9 Cwm-garw standing stones: a bluestone monument near the source of the bluestones.

Plate 10 Cwm-garw. The clubbed foot of this naturally shaped stone has been used to give it a more stable base. Stone 55 at Stonehenge was given a deliberately shaped clubbed foot. At both sites packing stones were used to secure the megaliths in their sockets.

cloth bags holding bundles of cremated bones: very similar bone pins were found at Dorchester-on-Thames holding together leather bags full of cremated bones. There were also rod-like pieces of flint of unknown purpose; they may have been special, non-functional offerings or they may have been everyday objects that the dead happened to possess and would want to have with them in the afterlife: it has been suggested that they were strike-a-lights.[89] There were also flint flakes, a stone mace-head, an earthenware cup and ashes.

Offering pits like these were not just made at Stonehenge: they were a routine part of neolithic ritual. Just to the south of Durrington Walls, about 3 km from Stonehenge, four pits were dug, then promptly filled in with basketfuls of new, unused flint tools, bones of pig, ox, roe deer and fox together with the remains of seafood that had been ferried up the Avon from Christchurch Harbour, 50 km away – chub, scallops, mussels and oysters. At Ratfyn, 1 km or so down the Avon from Durrington Walls, two pits contained some big cattle bones and the bones of a brown bear, one of the most fearsome creatures of the neolithic forest, as well as some fine arrowheads. Another pit on the King Barrows Ridge immediately to the east of Stonehenge was filled with piglets' trotters. Although at first sight they may look like rubbish pits, the particular combinations of objects in each pit do imply selection and deliberation, depositing rather than throwing away.

The evidence points to Stonehenge being used, at least at the time when the Aubrey Holes were dug, for the final burial of the dead – possibly for the burial of sacrificial victims who died in ceremonies at Stonehenge. The central burial at Woodhenge was very clearly a child sacrifice (see Chapter 4). Disposing of the dead was a complex and long drawn out business. It may be that somewhere nearby, not necessarily in the circle itself, the bodies of the Stonehenge people were exposed for a year or two until the flesh was gone; it is commonly believed in archaic communities that the spirit will not leave a corpse until the flesh and all the moisture have gone. What remained of the bodies was gathered up and buried, either informally in the earth or formally in a barrow, or alternatively cremated. The scorching in the cremation pyre made certain that the process of desiccation was finally complete. The spirits were freed and would no longer trouble the living; fear of the un-dead – those unfortunate, tortured souls trapped between life and death – is also common in archaic societies.

Cremation was the regular method for drying dead bones in the east of England and the practice was taken up, possibly because it was more efficient and effective than air- and sun-drying, by some groups of people living on Salisbury Plain, the Stonehenge people among them.[90] It is understandable that people who worshipped the sun or some principle or spirit symbolized by the sun were eager to use fire in their ceremonies. Symbolic gesture was of enormous importance to the makers of Stonehenge, and using fire as a symbol of the burning summer sun must have held a strong appeal for them.

The cremations in the Aubrey Holes were among the earliest in Wessex.[91] The first cremations they contained were untidy – incompetently carried out, even – whereas the later cremations tucked in above them were neater and more orderly.[92] Only one of the first phase of cremations, found in hole 55, was accompanied by any other kind of offering or grave-good: two antlers were deposited underneath a thick layer of bone and ash. It is probably significant that the antlers were placed here rather than in any other hole, because it was right beside the axis of Stonehenge, next to the entrance causeway – a special place in the circle (see Chapter 8).

Many more grave-goods, if simple ones, were deposited with the secondary (i.e., later) cremations, including flints, antlers, a chalk ball and animal bones. There was also a pattern in the way these offerings were distributed: there were more on the east than on the west, the cardinal compass points were marked, and the two entrances were marked with deposits not found elsewhere. The cremations are so regular on the east side – every single hole from hole 2 to hole 18 – that it may be that the Stonehenge people buried their dead in a planned and systematic way starting near the north-east entrance and worked their way clockwise round the circle, stopping at the south entrance. Whether these burials were deposited in quick succession, perhaps all in the space of a year or two, or were spread out over decades or centuries cannot be determined. After they reached the south entrance the ritual seems to have petered out into something more erratic, but the pattern is not yet completely known: the holes on the north-west have not been opened, and more radiocarbon dates are needed to fill out the story.

THE ROUNDHOUSE

The builders of Stonehenge I completed their design by raising a large timber building at the centre.[93] They must have done this before building Stonehenge II, the stone-holes of which cut into and destroy many of its post-holes, but after they made the ditch, bank and Aubrey Holes of Stonehenge I; the true circles formed by these large-scale features of the first Stonehenge can only have been marked out at a time when the central precinct was completely clear except perhaps for a post or totem pole at the very centre. The roundhouse could, however, have been raised once the Aubrey Holes circle was marked out. Probably while it was actually being built the Aubrey Holes were being dug, one by one at peg-marked sites round the precinct's edge. The roundhouse has not been precisely dated but, as with some other components of Stonehenge's complicated structure, it can at least be put into its relative position in the sequence of events (as shown in Appendix A).

It is difficult to imagine a wooden roundhouse on the site now, as all

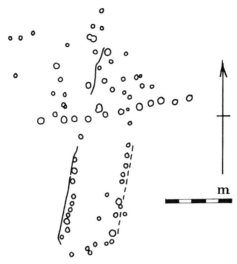

Figure 26 The remains of the Stonehenge I post-passage. The lines are changes in ground level, probably marking the positions of plank-built walls.

surface traces of it have been obliterated and it has been supplanted by stones; the lines of its walls were later closely followed by the Double Bluestone Circle, then that too was destroyed and after an interval replaced by the late Bluestone Circle of Stonehenge IIIc (Plate 8). Some may think that these repetitions of older forms are just coincidental, but the Stonehenge people had long memories and it is likely that they deliberately repeated and reinforced the wall line of the ancient circle, as shown in Figure 72. It was quite common for neolithic and bronze age monument-builders to commemorate old, destroyed buildings with stone structures.[94] The early wooden building at Stonehenge enclosed the central area just within the massive stones of the Great Sarsen Circle. A few of the post-sockets of its walls were discovered during the Hawley excavations of the 1920s. One hole was 1.2 m deep and 0.8 m across and it had been packed tightly with chalk when its post was pulled out in antiquity: in this instance the ground surface had to be made good for a major new building project, the raising of Stonehenge II.[95]

It is too pessimistic to say, as Richard Atkinson did, that 'nothing more can be done than to record the fact that these post-holes exist. Upon the evidence available, it is useless to try to interpret them.'[96] Despairing words indeed. Since two substantial arcs of post-sockets have survived, on the south-east and west sides (see Figure 23), it is possible to reconstruct the whole circle, which would have been 25 m (82 ft) in diameter.[97]

A few centuries later, ambitious circular wooden buildings of some sophistication were to be built nearby, at Durrington Walls, and the

Stonehenge roundhouse was probably similar in design: possibly it was a prototype which the Durrington roundhouses imitated. We can tentatively reconstruct how it was built. The outer wall, made of perhaps seventy closely spaced oak posts 2–3 m tall, supported the lower ends of the radial roof timbers. There may have been some taller posts further in, supporting the mid-points of the rafters on a ring-beam, but no trace of these has survived. There may also have been a tall central pillar supporting the inner (upper) ends of the radial timbers, but not necessarily: the slanting timbers may simply have been lashed together, wigwam-style, at the apex of a shallow conical roof some 8 m above the ground.

How solid the roundhouse walls were is not known. If observations were still being carried out from the centre of Stonehenge at this time – perhaps 2900 BC – gaps must have been left between the posts to ensure an unobstructed view to the horizon. On the other hand, if only certain sectors of the horizon were of interest to the builders, they may have left window gaps open at certain points while the rest of the wall circuit was boarded up. They must have left open the view towards the north-east, where we know they watched northern moonrises and midsummer sunrises. The gaps between the posts were no more than 3 m wide, so it would have been an easy task to peg or tie planks horizontally from post to post to make a continuous, solid wall round the rest of the circuit.

There was probably an entrance gap of some kind on the building's south side. A scatter of post-holes to the south shows that a timber avenue led northwards towards the roundhouse from the well-trodden reception area just inside the henge's south entrance (Figure 26). The avenue consisted of regularly spaced posts set in two parallel bedding trenches about 3.7 m (12 ft) apart: the grooves in the earth suggest that the posts supported walls made of horizontal planks. It may have been, as Burl suggests, a roofed ceremonial approach corridor.[98] About halfway to the roundhouse, the avenue or corridor was crossed at an angle by a 9 m long arc of posts, three to the west, three to the east and three standing in it like the doorjambs of a double door. The course of the avenue or passage beyond this is frustratingly hard to interpret, and I think the detail of its arrival at the roundhouse may be beyond reconstruction.[99]

Nevertheless, similar post-passages with post-arcs were to be fitted 300–600 years later to the roundhouses at Durrington Walls (Figure 36). That these architectural motifs were repeated nearby shows that what happened at Stonehenge and the other sites in the area was by no means random or spontaneous: it also shows beyond any doubt that the building of the post-passage was connected with the building of the roundhouse. When the northern roundhouse at Durrington Walls was rebuilt in around 2400 BC, its post-passage was also rebuilt, on a slightly different alignment from the original passage but still, like the one at Stonehenge, oriented roughly north–south. There is also a suggestion, both at Durrington and at

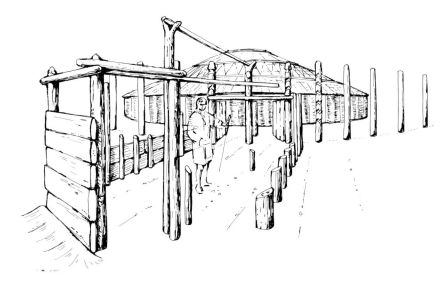

Figure 27 The post-passage and roundhouse of Stonehenge I: a partial reconstruction.

Stonehenge, that a double door may have divided the passage about halfway along, and I have incorporated this feature in my two reconstructions (Figures 27 and 36).

We have come to think of Stonehenge as being made of stone and earth, and may find it difficult to think in terms of timber being a major component in the design. But it must be remembered that timber was a material of which the Stonehenge people had plenty, and were very used to handling. They were evidently master-carpenters. Most of their work has unfortunately perished, but in the Lake District a few fragments have survived; at Storrs Moss a grooved and tenoned post was found, apparently having functioned as an upright post slotted into a floorboard in a wooden house, demonstrating that neolithic carpenters were capable of making useful joints. They showed similar skill in designing and building the trackways across the Somerset Levels, taking care to choose appropriate types of wood for different tasks. We can be sure that they would have shown a similar sympathy for materials when they built their 'big top', the wooden marquee at the centre of Stonehenge.

There may have been textile hangings decorating the walls. Tantalizingly small fragments of cloth have survived from the neolithic and early bronze age, like the piece found sticking to the Bush Barrow chieftain's axe (see Chapter 6), and they are often fine, well-made fabrics. The rich patterns carved on two chalk talismans found just 1 km east of Stonehenge give an idea of the sort of designs they may have woven into their fabrics (Figure

Figure 28 Carved plaques found in a pit not far to the east of Stonehenge.

28). Sadly, we shall never know what refinements of decorative detail they lavished on the Stonehenge roundhouse. Perhaps they left it as a simple, clean-cut, functional shape: I think it more likely that they embellished the walls with birch-bark, wove symbolic patterns in the thatch, hung the eaves with talismans and the doorposts with flowers, investing the building with all the mystic trappings of a great temple.

4

STONEHENGE ABANDONED?

O Solitude! if I must with thee dwell,
Let it not be among the jumbled heap
Of murky buildings; climb with me the steep, –
Nature's observatory – whence the dell,
Its flowery slopes, its river's crystal swell,
May seem a span; let me thy vigils keep
'Mongst boughs pavilion'd, where the deer's swift leap
Startles the wild bee from the foxglove bell.

Keats, *Sonnet on Solitude*

A TIME OF SHADOWS

Until quite recently it has been assumed that although Stonehenge went through several phases of construction and modification it still remained in continuous use; this is implicit, even if not actually stated, in much of the Stonehenge literature.[1] Refined radiocarbon dates nevertheless show that Stonehenge I, the Stonehenge discussed in the previous chapter, was built a very long time – nearly a thousand years – before Stonehenge II (discussed in Chapter 5). Evidence from the layers of sediment lining the earth circle's ditch shows that there was a period in between, perhaps lasting several hundred years, when Stonehenge was abandoned. As long ago as 1921 Colonel Hawley sensed that something peculiar had happened: 'At some time in the history of Stonehenge, and perhaps for a long period, there must have been a considerable amount of vegetation covering the site.'[2]

Hawley came to this important conclusion from the large number of small snail-shells on the site, and his interpretation was confirmed by a more detailed and scientific study in the 1970s, when a cutting through the bank and ditch revealed hundreds more of Hawley's prehistoric snails. The 1978 cutting exposed ten separate layers from the bedrock at the bottom of the ditch up to the modern turf, each layer revealing a phase in the ditch's history. There were few snail-shells in the lowest layer of the chalky fill, showing that after the ditch was first cut, around 3100 BC, the site was not only open but also dry and grassless, as we might expect if all the building activity was followed by intensive ceremonial activity: the comings and goings of many moccasined feet padding across the site would have kept it clear of vegetation, and it may even have been systematically weeded. The next layer shows that weeds and other vegetation gradually invaded, together with a type of snail, *Vallonia costata*, that preferred open terrain, so the landscape was still open, but grass-covered. This is presumably the phase when the Aubrey Holes were dug, sometimes known as Stonehenge Ib. But the next layer of ditch silt shows a significant change: light-loving varieties of snail became rarer and a new species became common, *Zontidiae*, a type usually found in rough pasture and the leaf-litter of woodlands.[3]

With this evidence in mind, it is possible to explain the irregular pits on the site (holes F, G and H near the Aubrey Holes and the two holes under the Avenue bank close to the Heel Stone) as craters made by tree-roots (Figure 8). If shrubs and a few trees were allowed to encroach, their root systems might well leave holes. The even spacing of F, G and H just outside the circle of Aubrey Holes at first suggests that they are the sockets of a large circle of stones spaced about 30 m apart, something like the Great Circle just inside the bounding ditch at Avebury, but no further sockets from this large circle have been discovered and the holes are too irregular in shape to have been stone-sockets. Colonel Hawley thought they had been made by bushes and we can agree with him.[4]

It is hard to assess what this period of neglect means. Its modern dis-coverer, J. G. Evans, felt that it proved an important cultural discontinuity in Stonehenge's development.[5] If Stonehenge fell into disuse for a few hundred years, a period that may have been longer than the Roman occu-pation of Britain, does it mean that the builders' descendants packed up and went away, or that they lost faith in their temple, or that they were massacred by some neighbouring tribe? It looks, on the face of it, as if Stonehenge II was an entirely separate project from Stonehenge I, but may the fact that the new monument was built plumb in the centre of the old mean that an invading tribe decided to build their own temple on the derelict remains as a calculated gesture of contempt or conquest? Documentary evidence from five hundred years later tells us that in about 1630 BC the Hittite King Hattusili captured the statue of a weather-god from his power-ful adversaries in Syria, the people of Haleb, modern Aleppo. In the ancient world, capturing temples and idols was a common way of humiliating and demoralizing your enemy and increasing your spiritual and secular power.[6] It may be that something like this happened at Stonehenge – a prehistoric propaganda *coup*. Another possibility is that the religious faith of the original community was in some way renewed, born again, after a lapse.

The implications are many, and it is very difficult to read the human story behind the archaeology, but the evidence suggests that the whole early and middle neolithic monument complex surrounding Stonehenge, including the cursus monuments and long barrows, fell into neglect at about the same time. It was not just Stonehenge that was neglected.

From 2550 until 2150 BC the area was sufficiently deserted for grass, scrub and trees to steal across it. The white chalk bank became degraded, weathering back into the ditch: both became softened in outline by a covering of soil and vegetation. Why should the Stonehenge people have given up work on this area, roughly 1 km in all directions from Stonehenge? One widespread problem in the middle neolithic, and one that must have affected this area, was soil exhaustion. The first farmers of the new stone age made gardens in small clearings that were fed by leaf-fall from the surrounding forest and in any case were not kept open for many years. New clearings were made to replace the old and the general level of soil fertility was kept up. But by the middle neolithic, when Stonehenge I was created, the clearings on Salisbury Plain had become very large and the farmers kept them open for decades on end. By 3100 BC, when the earth circle was created, soils were already declining in fertility.[7]

Maybe it was for this reason that the area immediately round Stonehenge was left for a time to be reclaimed by scrub. A radiocarbon date of 2550 BC for the silting of the western ditches of the Lesser Cursus seems to show that this monument was decommissioned or fell into disuse at about the same time that Stonehenge was abandoned. As we saw in the last chapter, the eastward extension of the Lesser Cursus was destroyed immediately after it was made, but the original western enclosure was evidently left operational for another eight hundred years. But then the old monuments were closed down and people moved eastwards, clearing the woodlands that lay towards the Avon valley. In the new area they built six farmsteads, apparently round the edges of a 2 km by 1 km oval of newly cleared land.

Associated with the new land were two foci of ceremonial activity: one, Coneybury henge, at the south-western end and the other, Durrington Walls, at the north-eastern end. These are known to have been created in the late neolithic, Coneybury in 2750 BC and Durrington in 2550 BC, and it looks very much as if the whole complex – fields, livestock, settlements and henges – was part of an overall population and activity shift towards the Avon (Figure 57).

THE NEW HENGES

In 2750 BC, about a hundred years before the Pharaoh Khufu ordered the building of the Great Pyramid at Giza, a modest new henge was laid out within sight of Stonehenge: it stood on Coneybury Hill about 1.3 km south-east of the old monument. The new henge took the form of a roughly egg-shaped earth circle with its long axis aligned south-west to north-east – just like Stonehenge – and a single entrance at the north-east end.[8] The overall size of the henge along its long diameter was about 44 m; its ditch was 2 m

Plate 11 Carnmenyn, in the Preseli Hills.

Plate 12 One of the tor-like summits of Carnmenyn. Bizarre rock formations give the hill its distinctive personality.

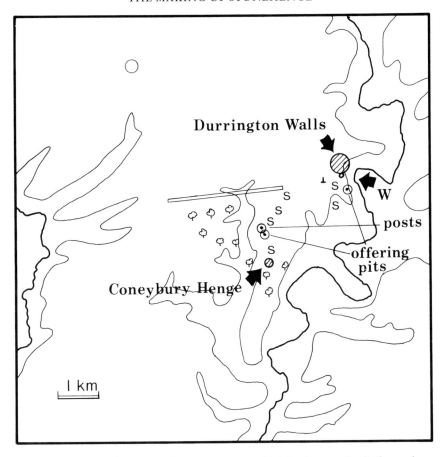

Figure 29 The Stonehenge area in 2750–2300 BC. Activity is now clearly focused on the ridge to the east of Stonehenge.

deep and steep-sided, enclosing a precinct that had been carefully cut across the gentle hill slope to make it level. At the bottom of the ditch were the bones of a dog and a white-tailed sea eagle, a rare bird this far inland: it may have been caught on the coast and brought up the Avon as a special sacrificial offering, perhaps even as a foundation offering. Inside the precinct there was a cluster of offering pits, some containing the special, elaborately decorated pottery known as Grooved Ware and over seven hundred post-and stake-holes. Unfortunately the 1980 excavation did not uncover enough of the interior to reveal any overall pattern in these holes, so it is not yet possible to say whether they represent a building or some other structures that perhaps imitated Stonehenge I. An arc of post-holes on the south-west side implies that there may have been an oval post-ring with a maximum diameter of about 25 m running round within the ditch. The posts were

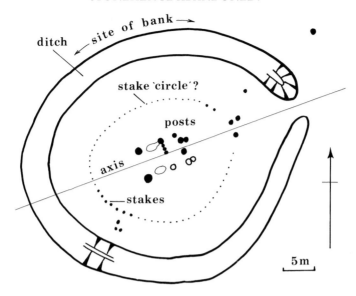

Figure 30 Coneybury henge. The many small stake-holes (of unknown purpose) have been omitted.

spaced about 1.5 m apart, suggesting a fairly light fence: although this would have been a lightweight affair compared with the one at Stonehenge, its overall dimensions were very similar and a conscious reference across to the roundhouse, by now in a ruinous state, at the centre of Stonehenge may have been intended. Fires were lit within the Coneybury post-setting.

The surrounding ditch was dug deep and with sides so steep that the ancient ditch-diggers had to cut chalk steps into the ditch wall close to the entrance to enable them to climb out more easily. Although the scale is very different, the *form* of the ditch is reminiscent of the deep, steep-sided ditch excavated at Avebury over two hundred years earlier, and it is possible that this and some of the other developments in the Stonehenge area may have been stimulated by what went on at the cult centres of neighbouring territories.

Some of the larger pits near the centre of the Coneybury henge may have held a construction made of upright timbers or even stones, but the dense and patternless profusion of stake-holes covering most of the henge interior is very puzzling (Figure 30).

In spite of this flurry of activity, the Coneybury henge was used for ritual for only a short time before it too was abandoned. Once again it is as if the *making* of the monument was the most important act, rather than its use when finished. The deep ditch began to fill with soil washed in by rain from the adjacent bank and the gradually thickening silt layers show that people made no attempt to interrupt this process by clearing it out or recutting it.

77

The silt contains pollen showing that the henge was quickly overwhelmed by scrub and woodland.[9]

There is no surface trace of Coneybury henge now and it has never been described as a standing earthwork, so it can only be assumed that the site was levelled by ploughing in the middle ages or earlier.

At the north-eastern end of the 'new land' the Stonehenge people built a more spectacular and more enduring monument on the site of one of their earlier, unenclosed settlements, a place where they had been living since 3300 BC – Durrington Walls.[10] On the western side of the Avon valley, it is still possible to make out a severely ploughed-down bank encircling a shallow dry coombe that runs down towards the river's broad floodplain. This loop of degraded bank is all that remains to be seen of one of the greatest achievements of neolithic Wessex, a colossal henge 500 m across enclosing an area of 12 ha. Although now only 1 m high, it must once have been at least 4 m and probably as much as 6 m high; excavation shows that it was originally 27 m wide and separated from the ditch that snaked round inside it by a berm varying from 6 to 36 m in width. The silted-up ditch was originally 6 m deep with a flat bottom and 13 m wide at the top.[11]

It is debatable whether these huge earthworks were intended to be defensive. They were certainly meant to be impressive, but surely an *external* ditch would have made a far more effective defence against marauders? There has been a great deal of speculation about the reasons for the many large-scale changes that came about in late neolithic Britain: political instability of some kind is usually blamed.[12] It is certainly true that the earthworks built at this time were larger in scale than before, more continuous, and frequently palisaded.[13] The earthworks may nevertheless have had some purpose other than defence, such as keeping in livestock, keeping out wild animals, or expressing newly acquired higher social or territorial status. It may be that these showy earthworks were rather like the prestigious high-rise blocks built in the City of London in the late twentieth century AD: Canary Wharf similarly conveys a grim assertiveness that smacks of quasi-military power, although it simply provides office-space. Gigantic earthworks at Mount Pleasant, Knowlton and Marden were raised at about the same time as those at Durrington Walls and their spacing suggests that each of these major projects was in some sense the 'capital' of a large territory of 400–500 sq. km (see Figure 31).[14]

If we could travel back through time and visit Durrington Walls in its heyday, we would see it perhaps as no more than a substantial village, but if we could look through the eyes and minds of the small-scale communities of the neolithic we would see it as a major settlement of metropolitan status. Durrington Walls was four times bigger than the bronze age walled town of Mycenae, which gives an indication of its likely importance in the ancient world.

Durrington's irregular girdle of earthworks (Figure 32) is broken by just

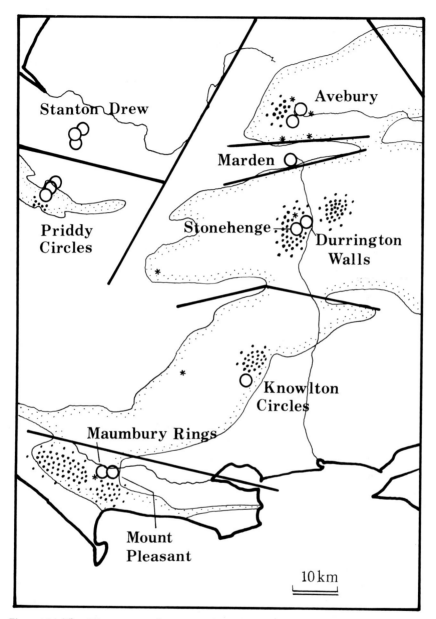

Figure 31 The Wessex superhenge territories of the later neolithic. The circles represent large henges or stone circles. The dots represent clusters of round barrows.

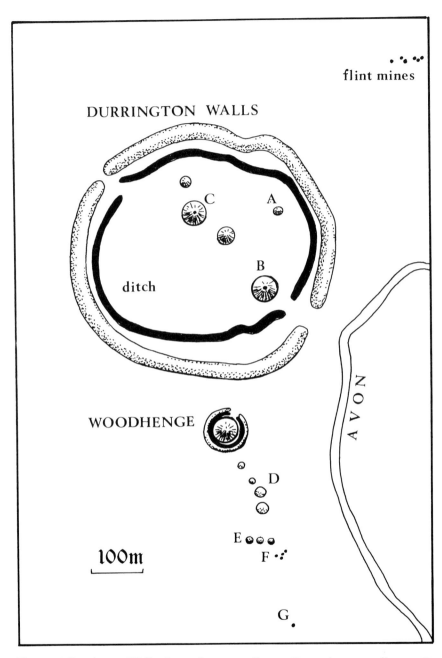

Figure 32 Durrington Walls. A: northern roundhouse. B: southern roundhouse. C: further roundhouses detected by geophysical survey or on air photographs, but not yet excavated. D: round barrows. E: round barrows formerly interpreted as a long barrow. F & G: offering pits.

two entrances, to the north-west and south-east: this opposed-entrances arrangement is seen in a great many henges, large and small, throughout Britain.[15] The south-east entrance, 22 m wide, is at the lower end of the coombe and seems to have been designed to face the river bank of the Avon, which is only 60 m away: as a result, it is the one major monument in the Stonehenge complex that was *not* oriented to the north-east or east-north-east. This may mean that the huge henge was a ceremonial centre dedicated at least in part to a water cult,[16] or that Durrington was a secular enclosure, in effect a late neolithic river port. This last alternative is more likely than it might at first appear. We know that Christchurch Harbour at the mouth of the Avon was in regular use as a neolithic seaport and transhipment point, and that stone axes, pottery and probably other commodities as well were sent from there up the Avon to the Stonehenge area, so an unloading point on the river bank at Amesbury or Durrington is actually very likely.[17] Then as now the Avon would have been navigable for dug-out canoes, composite boats made out of two or three canoes lashed together, and light-weight skin-frame boats such as coracles.

When the Stonehenge people built their huge earthwork at Durrington, they shifted 50,000 cu. m of chalk – probably over 100,000 man-days of work – making it one of the largest communal work projects in Wessex. The site they built it on had originally been woodland, like the rest of Salisbury Plain, and this they cleared in 3300 BC to make way for an open settlement, at exactly the time when the recently discovered 'Iceman' met his death from hypothermia on the Similaun Glacier high in the Italian Alps. The synchronicity of the Iceman's death and the founding of Durrington Walls is just a coincidence, but what is significant is that Durrington was founded shortly before Stonehenge I was built. It is likely that, of the many small farmsteads and hamlets in the area, it was the people living at Durrington who initiated, designed and controlled the building of Stonehenge. As we saw in Chapter 3, the observations of moonrises must have begun at Stonehenge in about 3200 BC, in other words as soon as the new settlement at Durrington had been established: the close matching of the dates implies a connection between the moon-watchers and the builders of Durrington. They may have been the same people. Certainly it was they who gained ascendancy as the forest clearance crept back from Stonehenge towards the Avon, and certainly they were living at Durrington in 3100 BC at the time when Stonehenge I was being built. It was in about 2550 BC that they laid out the superhenge earthwork round their settlement amid a short-turfed, pastoral landscape.[18] Just as at the other superhenge sites of Marden and Avebury to the north, there was at Durrington a substantial time-lag between the initial forest clearance and the creation of the large earthworks. Although at Durrington that delay may have been partly due to preoccupation with the work that was going forward at Stonehenge from 3150 BC onwards, Stonehenge cannot be held responsible for such a long delay: it is much more likely that the idea

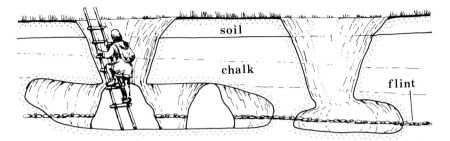

Figure 33 The shallow flint mines at Durrington. These were dug in response to a huge demand for tools at Durrington Walls, but were found to be inadequate: tool-flint must have been imported from elsewhere.

of raising the status of settlements by dignifying them with huge earthworks was simply not in the air until around 2550 BC.

In 1966–8 Geoffrey Wainwright excavated the eastern part of the Durrington superhenge.[19] It was a rescue dig in advance of road straightening, and the area Wainwright excavated is now unfortunately covered by the realigned A345 which runs across the site on top of an embankment. Immediately inside the south-east entrance he found the post-holes of a complicated round structure consisting of six concentric rings of thick wooden posts. The posts increased in girth towards the centre, which implies that they also increased in height. The structure may have been open to the sky, looking like a gigantic pincushion, but it seems more natural to interpret it as a roofed rotunda 38 m in diameter.[20]

People shoved flint tools, pottery and the remains of joints of meat against the bases of the posts, which some have thought implies offerings, but this is not necessarily so: there is a purely secular explanation. People walked about inside the roundhouse following the centres of the corridor-spaces; in fact it is possible to map very precisely the routes they commonly followed by mapping the areas of the old ground surface that were most compacted (see Figure 34). People left the spaces nearest the posts as natural accumulation or deliberate storage areas, in much the same way that in a modern house we tend to put much of the furniture against the walls to leave the 'movement-space' unobstructed. Only the spatially illiterate would leave a pile of belongings in a doorway, and we know that the people of late neolithic Wessex knew about space and were keen to define and control it: great buildings like Stonehenge and the Durrington roundhouses tell us this.

The southern roundhouse, which was first built in 2460 BC, was rebuilt at least once before it fell into final decay: a second phase dates to around 2330 BC.[21] What went on inside this cavernous building is a mystery, but we do at least know from the patterns of trampled earth that people moved around inside it in a fairly systematic and ordered way, dispersing from the doorway

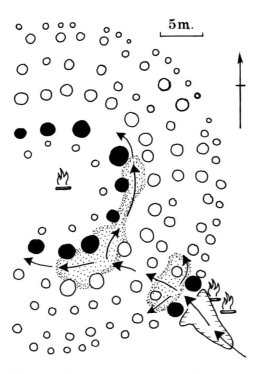

Figure 34 The southern roundhouse at Durrington Walls, showing archaeologically proved patterns of activity. People entered via the south-east doorway (pair of black spots) across a chalk platform (horizontal shading) with fires burning on their right. Trampled surfaces (stippled) show lines of movement within the roundhouse, avoiding the open central area inside the second circle of posts (solid black).

on the south-east side and apparently avoiding a taboo area in the centre where a fire burned: that may have been avoided simply because it was open to the sky. There were also fires immediately outside the doorway. To the north-east, behind the site of the roundhouse, there was an oval midden 12 m long held in place by arcs of stakes. Amongst the rubbish there were bones, antlers, stone and flint tools, together with large amounts of Grooved Ware pottery. Some archaeologists have been surprised at the presence here of this large quantity of domestic refuse, because they assume that the henge was purely ceremonial and that the roundhouses were used only for ritual, but there is no reason to see Durrington Walls as anything other than a settlement, albeit one with the possible ritual protection of a surrounding henge. The midden in any case seems to date from 2910 BC, from the open settlement phase before the earthworks of the henge were thrown round the site.[22] Here, in the southern roundhouse, the descendants of the designers of Stonehenge I and the builders of Stonehenges II and III relaxed, drank from

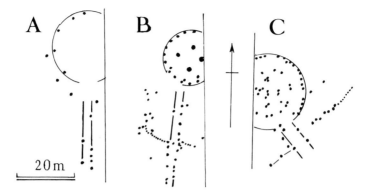

Figure 35 Durrington Walls roundhouse plans. A: northern roundhouse phase 1.
B: northern roundhouse phase 2. C: southern roundhouse phase 1.

bowls that hung from the cross beams in nets of knotted string, and feasted
on pork, watched by dogs alert for meat scraps.[23]

At a distance of 120 m to the north was a second, smaller, circular building
consisting initially of two concentric post-rings 27 and 19 m in diameter. It
was approached from the south-south-west by an avenue of posts passing
through a curving screen of totem poles. This feature is strongly reminiscent
of the timber corridor and post-arc that led from just inside Stonehenge's
south entrance to the central roundhouse way back in 3000 BC: even the
orientation is similar. Later, presumably when the northern roundhouse had
rotted, disintegrated and collapsed, it was replaced by another, smaller in
diameter but built of stouter posts; it had an arrangement of four huge posts
in the middle suggesting either a raised central square lantern or a square
skylight (Figures 35B and 36). There was also a replacement timber avenue
built on a slightly different alignment from the first.

Wainwright's excavation corridor exposed the remains of two roundhouses and there is every reason to suppose that there were several more
large round buildings within the extensive unexplored part of the henge.
Woodhenge, a very similar building that stood just outside the precinct, has
been known about for many years.

Woodhenge was one of the earliest archaeological discoveries to be made
as a direct result of aerial survey and is for this reason a landmark in British
archaeology. The site looks very unimpressive on the ground, with a scatter
of unsatisfactory squat concrete drums marking the positions of its post-
holes. At the time when it was first photographed from the air by Squadron
Leader Insall in 1925 it had been ploughed flat and there was nothing to be
seen, but its local nickname, the Dough Cover, suggests that the ditches
were visible within the last century or two, giving the oval precinct a
subdued convex shape. The Insall photograph showed a revealing pattern of

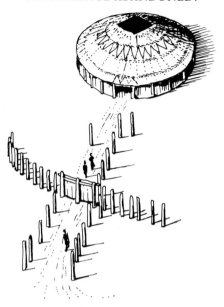

Figure 36 Durrington Walls northern roundhouse phase 2: a reconstruction. Compare Figures 26, 27, 38, 39, 40.

post-sockets arranged in rings and excavation by Mr and Mrs Cunnington quickly followed in 1926–7.[24]

The monument originally consisted of six concentric near-circles, or 'eggs' surrounded by a substantial ditch with an outer bank. It was in effect a henge with its single entrance oriented, like Coneybury's and Stonehenge's, roughly towards the north-east. The Woodhenge ditch was dug in about 2300 BC.[25] The original timber building, probably raised immediately afterwards, may have been roofed or it may have stood open to the sky, a timber equivalent to Stonehenge, as the Cunningtons' tenacious nickname for the site implies. On the whole, it is more likely that it was a roofed rotunda, probably with an open atrium at the centre. It would have been a very large building, too: its long diameter is the same as that of the dome of the Pantheon, built in Rome in AD 125.[26]

In a pit almost at the centre of Woodhenge, the builders buried the body of a 3-year-old girl. She had been brutally killed with a blow on the head that split her skull in two. It is the clearest evidence of child sacrifice, and the little girl may have been killed as a foundation offering at the time when the monument was built. A small cairn of cemented flints marks the site of this sad little grave pit.[27]

The range of pottery found at Woodhenge suggests that the site was in use for about three hundred years, in other words from 2300 to 2000 BC. This was a very significant period in the Stonehenge story, because during these

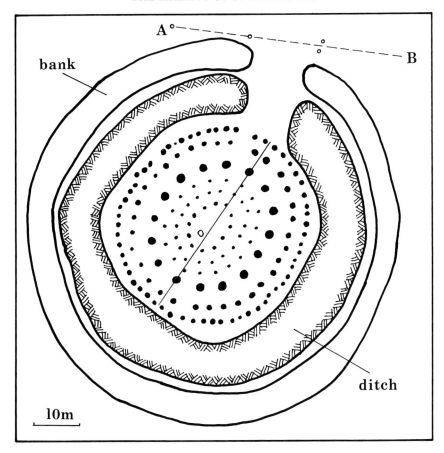

Figure 37 Plan of Woodhenge. The totem poles outside the entrance may have marked an alignment of some kind (A–B). The roundhouse axis (marked) is *not* aligned on the midsummer sunrise.

three hundred years the period of neglect came to an end, the bluestone monument was built and dismantled, and the great sarsen monument was put in its place.

The measurements of the Woodhenge post-rings are of particular interest, implying that the Stonehenge people were using a specific unit of measurement and a system of counting. Cunnington proposed that they used a 'Short Foot' of 29.2 cm (11½ in.), which would make the long diameters of the four innermost rings 40.1, 60.1, 80.2 and 100.2 Short Feet. This in turn implies, as Cunnington proposed, that they were counting in tens. The numbers of posts in each ring, however, are not in multiples of ten; the rings had twelve, eighteen, sixteen, thirty-two and sixty posts. Aubrey Burl has suggested a different and more convincing interpretation – a counting-base

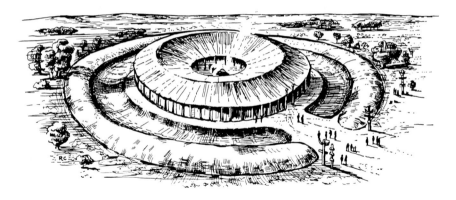

Figure 38 Woodhenge: a reconstruction.

of four and measurement in Beaker Yards of 73 cm which would also bring the long diameters into multiples of four:[28]

Long diameters in:	Outermost	Post-rings at Woodhenge				Innermost
	A	B	C	D	E	F
feet	144	125	96	76.8	57.6	38.4
metres	43.9	38.1	29.3	23.4	17.6	11.7
Short Feet	150.3	130.5	100.2	80.2	60.1	40.1
Beaker Yards	60	52.1	40	32	24	16
Number of posts	60	32	16	18	18	12
Number of posts/4	15	8	4	4.5	4.5	3

It may not be a coincidence that the overall size of the Coneybury henge was 44 m, the same as the largest post-oval at Woodhenge. The results are persuasive, but whether this means that the Stonehenge people really did measure in Beaker Yards or count in fours is entirely another matter. It has to be admitted that there is no evidence that Stonehenge I was laid out according to this system: only one dimension there fits neatly into it – the radius of the Aubrey Holes circle. This is 43.3 m, which is 59.3 Beaker Yards, very close to 60, a plausibly round number which can be divided by four: it also recurs as the number of posts in the largest circle at Woodhenge.

It is not just the measurements that imply order at Woodhenge. The way in which objects were distributed round the site was also startlingly orderly, with large numbers of pig bones near the outermost circle of posts, decreasing regularly towards the centre: conversely there were large numbers of cattle bones near the centre, decreasing towards the edge (Figure 91). The surrounding ditch contained the bones of wild animals and a small number of human bones. The implication is that the exterior of Woodhenge was made to represent the wildwood, where wild animals and the spirits of the dead roamed: pigs too were run into the woods to forage, so they made a link between home and wilderness. Cattle were domestic animals, grazing on man-made, man-maintained pasture, and the interior of Woodhenge represented that tamed world. It may be possible to penetrate one step further into the thought-world of late neolithic people. Can we see the little murdered girl at the centre of Woodhenge as epitomizing the tame, the ultimate in human control of the universe, the symbolic and actual surrender of their own young and their own strongest emotions? Certainly the pattern of bones here suggests that the girl's death was not seen as an ordinary death. It also shows an exceptionally high degree of order in the way people used space.[29]

THE MEANING OF DURRINGTON

Air photography revealed something of the nature of Woodhenge in the 1920s. Later air photographs have shown tonal variations in the grass inside the precinct of Durrington Walls, showing us where more as yet unexcavated buildings may have stood. A geophysical survey confirms that at least one large circular building 35 m across existed very close to the centre of the superhenge.[30] How many roundhouses were standing and functioning at any one time we can only speculate, but it seems likely that they belong to several different phases of use. Each roundhouse must have taken vast amounts of timber and time to build.

The size alone of Durrington Walls tells us that it was important. To give an idea of its scale, Winchester Cathedral, the longest Gothic cathedral in Europe, would fit lengthwise two-and-a-half times over into the precinct's long axis; the Roman Colosseum would fit inside the ditched precinct twice over with room to spare; the Minoan palace-temple at Knossos would fit into it four times over; the early city of Troy, Troy II, which was contemporary with Durrington Walls, would have fitted inside it *eight* times over. There can be no doubt that this was an important place in the ancient world.

Nevertheless, a quarter of a century after it was excavated, Durrington remains enigmatic and controversial. It may have been a primarily religious, ritual centre, possibly entirely supplanting Stonehenge as a religious centre during the period 2550–2150 BC: the Woodhenge evidence is certainly explicable in terms of religious observances of some kind. But it is equally possible that it was a thoroughgoing town: ritual elements like totem poles and placed deposits might well be dotted around a settlement. This may seem too early for towns to be appearing, but in Sumeria ancient settlements like Uruk, Lagash, Nippur and Ur were evolving into towns in 3500 BC: by the time Durrington was walled a thousand years later those towns were well-established cities already with long histories behind them. So, what were the large rotundas for? On the European mainland some very big longhouses were built and they clearly were used as communal homes shared by several families.[31] The big southern roundhouse at Durrington might well have been used in a similar way as a communal dwelling for, say, thirty families.[32]

Plate 13 Carnmenyn. These bluestones loosened from the bedrock by frost would be easy to lift out; they are similar in size to those used at Stonehenge.

Plate 14 The Eastern Cleddau at Gelli. The bluestones may have been loaded onto boats here.

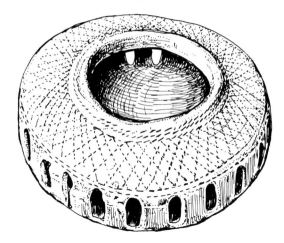

Figure 39 An offering or incense cup found with a burial on Normanton Down. The gaps in the walls (windows? doors?) and the thatch design on the roof suggest that this may be a representation, 4 cm high, of a timber roundhouse.

Some have speculated that it might have been a military kraal, a monastery, or even a university.[33] What is certain is that the elaborately decorated Grooved Ware pottery which the inhabitants of Durrington used puts them into a special class. This type of pottery was the 'Sunday-best' pottery of the later neolithic, and it was used at high-status places in several parts of Britain, not just in Wessex. That the Durrington people were using it may mean that they adopted a Sunday-best style of behaviour, possibly dressing in a special way when they visited Durrington Walls as their ceremonial centre in much the same way that the traditional church-goer 'dresses up' to go to church. Alternatively it may be that as a group they held some special status in the eyes of their contemporaries. That special status may have been associated with political supremacy; maybe a tribal chieftain or even a paramount chief and his family lived there; maybe the elders of the group living there acted as a steering committee for the big communal projects involving all the small rural communities of the Stonehenge territory. It may be that this special group consisted of a non-farming intellectual elite of the area: its wise men, magicians, priests, witch-doctors, surveyors and engineers.[34] It must be significant that the remains of seafood have been found at three places within 1 km of Durrington Walls, but nowhere else in the Stonehenge territory; exotic and therefore expensive food was being imported from Christchurch Harbour up the River Avon for consumption at or near Durrington Walls.[35]

My feeling is that it was the ambitious, high-status people living at Durrington who instigated and co-ordinated the very ambitious, high-status developments at Stonehenge from 2150 BC onwards – the bluestone and

Figure 40 The Durrington Walls southern roundhouse: a reconstruction.

sarsen structures – and it is likely, given the close matching of the dates that we saw earlier, that they were involved in designing and creating Stonehenge I as well.[36]

As the late neolithic roundhouses fell into disuse and ruin they were replaced but not demolished. The huge posts were left to decay slowly in their sockets, the thatch and lighter roof timbers disintegrating first, leaving the uprights and a few cross beams or lintels. This process would have left the structure looking very much like the sarsen monument at Stonehenge, which dates from the period when the southern roundhouse was in a state of decay, so it may well be that Stonehenge III was consciously and deliberately designed as a symbolic roundhouse in ruins.[37]

If the large scale and virtuosity of Stonehenge III impress us, we must remember that its builders first created the earthworks and rotundas of Durrington Walls, and that in its different way Durrington would have been profoundly impressive as well. The bank, as high as a two-storey house, was an imposing structure and although its summit has been weathered out of existence it is very likely that there was a stoutly built palisade mounted on top. Within the south-east entrance and dominating it the huge thatched cone of the southern roundhouse rose 9, 10 or 12 m into the air. Its single doorway, flanked by two massive and probably very tall doorposts, faced visitors as they came in through the henge entrance: the idea of the monumental portal, already created in stone at Stonehenge, was here created in wood (Figure 40). Inside, a maze of great wooden columns made of full-grown tree-trunks soared leaflessly into the gloomy roof, doubtless a masterpiece of prehistoric carpentry, creating something of the atmosphere of a cathedral, with the central light-well reminding us of the lantern at Ely. The roundhouse was 7 m (23 ft) larger in diameter than the dome of St Paul's. The interior must also have had something of the atmosphere of a circus tent. But for its neolithic inhabitants, who knew nothing of circuses or cathedrals, it must have had other resonances; it will have reminded them nostalgically of the great mother forest that once, long before, had hemmed in the newly settled clearing but which was now shrinking back to the horizon. The rotunda was an ordered microcosm of their natural world, with a symbolic clearing at the centre letting in slanting shafts of sunlight.[38]

Before Durrington's colossal earthwork was laid out, all the settlements in the Stonehenge area were open, and this may mean that until 2600 BC the settlers were keeping their options open too. In a landscape where there were still tracts of virgin or secondary forest close by, the scope for new clearances still existed. But by the time the Durrington settlement was enclosed, the Stonehenge people may have recognized that there was nowhere new left for them to colonize because they had cut down all the larger expanses of forest. This may in turn have led them to make a commitment to Durrington Walls as their permanent, 'central' settlement, the focus for the territory's communal activities.

But meanwhile what of Stonehenge itself? From around 2600 BC, when work on the superhenge at Durrington began, Stonehenge was neglected. The site was left untended, unweeded and the ditches were left uncleared of accumulating silt. But it is easy to see why. It was not a loss of faith or a change of social structure: it was a major distraction in the form of a huge new work project which absorbed all the surplus labour in the area. We should also bear in mind that the lack of new work on Stonehenge does not in itself mean that people from Durrington never visited the site: it is possible for people in quite large numbers to walk around in scrubland or even woodland without changing the overall composition of the vegetation significantly. I think it both possible and likely that, in spite of the major eastward shift of interest to the Coneybury-Durrington area and the extra work entailed, the people of the area went on visiting Stonehenge. It may be that cremations were still being secreted in the Aubrey Holes right through this shadowy period; many of them remain to be excavated and dated.

More important still, the Stonehenge people went on thinking of Stonehenge as their centre, their temple, their trysting place: it occupied the same position in their belief system. This, I believe, is proved by the way in which the people living at Durrington and the other groups living in the area came back to Stonehenge and redeveloped the site in about 2150 BC; when they did so, it was with a full knowledge of the architecture, orientation and functions of the old monument, as we shall see, and that could only have been so within a continuous tradition. Stonehenge was perhaps neglected and poorly maintained for a few centuries, from 2550 until 2150 BC, but not abandoned and certainly not forgotten.

5

STONES FROM AFAR: THE BLUESTONE ENIGMA

The ignorant Rustic will with a vacant stare attribute it to the Giants, or the mighty Archfiend; and the Antiquary, equally uninformed as to its origins, will regret that its history is veiled in perpetual obscurity. The Artist, on viewing these enormous masses, will wonder that art could thus rival nature in magnificence and picturesque effect . . . and all with one accord will exclaim, How grand! How wonderful! How incomprehensible!

Sir Richard Colt Hoare, *The Ancient History of South Wiltshire*, 1812

A NEW BEGINNING

It is the year 2150 BC. In Egypt the Old Kingdom has come to an end and central government has collapsed; on Crete the small Minoan town of Knossos grows apace, but the building of its spectacular red-pillared palace-temple still lies two hundred years into the future.[1] In Britain the site of Stonehenge has lain neglected for four hundred years while its people have been preoccupied with building huge earthworks and rotundas at Durrington Walls, projects that must have taken getting on for a million man-hours to complete.

The neglect of Stonehenge is not in itself difficult to explain, since every monument must sooner or later fall into disuse and decay, and it is easy to see that the builders and users of Stonehenge were preoccupied with Durrington Walls: what is surprising is that after such a long period of neglect the Stonehenge people showed a sudden renewed interest in the old monument, returned to the site and cleared it of shrubs and trees before rebuilding in a new style. Why did this happen? The classic explanation, and one that would have satisfied most prehistorians until the last few decades, is 'new people': incomers colonized or conquered the Stonehenge territory and then established their own new temple on the ancient sacred site. The date seems to suit this hypothesis quite well, in that the enigmatic Beaker people with their flat-based pottery were settling in England at that time. But that explanation is a little too neat: there were small numbers of Beaker

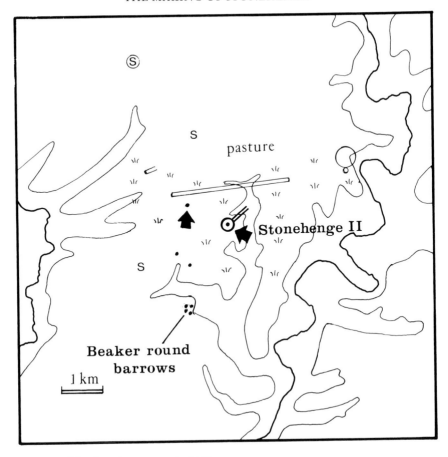

Figure 41 The Stonehenge area in 2150 BC.

people (possibly of Dutch origin) in Wessex for several centuries before 2150 BC.[2] On the whole, the dawning of new ideas – whether native or imported – seems a more likely explanation.

The Double Bluestone Circle, often known as Stonehenge II, may have been built because the distinctive blue-grey, green-grey stones became available. It is possible that in 2200 BC, having just completed the ambitious complex at Durrington Walls, the Stonehenge people had no current plans at all to develop the site of the decaying Stonehenge I. But there were changes in the air, and new fashions: stone circles had been built with spectacular success in other territories not far away, notably at Avebury to the north and Stanton Drew to the north-west. They may have been jolted into redeveloping the old monument because a consignment of stones was wished on them as a diplomatic gift – one that custom forced them to accept. Or it may be that the Stonehenge people, who were great consumers of trade-goods, wanted to establish a political or diplomatic bond with the people of Dyfed (Pembrokeshire), in order to secure their trade route north into the Irish Sea.[3] Standing out like a huge natural pier at the entrance to the Irish Sea, halfway between Stonehenge and the Boyne valley in Ireland, Dyfed was an obvious choice for a staging-post to the peoples of the Boyne valley, Cumbria, the Western Isles and Orkney. An exchange of prestige gifts with this key group could have resulted in the presentation of the bluestones to the Stonehenge people.

In terms of their mineralogy, the bluestones are not a single rock type. At Stonehenge they include spotted dolerite, unspotted dolerite, rhyolite and a rather brittle, laminated stone composed of volcanic ash. What they have in common is that when freshly broken they are blue or blue-green in colour and they originated as loose boulders at the eastern end of the Preseli Hills. Much has been made of the spotted dolerite, because with its large pink or white crystals of felspar it is easily the most distinctive of the rocks, but it accounts for only about half of the Stonehenge bluestones. A recent and detailed mineralogical study shows that most of the stones did, as both Thomas and Atkinson proposed, come from within 1 km of the summit of Carnmenyn. Some came from an outcrop 11 km away to the west-north-west, at Carn Clust-y-ci and Carn Llwyd, but the direction of ice flow across the Preseli Hills in the earlier cold stages of the ice age is known from trails of dolerite fragments to the south-east of Carnmenyn to have been from west-north-west to east-south-east. This is enough to explain how Carn Llwyd bluestone boulders found their way onto Carnmenyn, where further boulders of the local spotted dolerite were loosened on the spot by freeze-thaw in the Devensian: the Preselis were not overrun by an ice sheet in the Devensian, the final cold stage of the ice age.

This curiously mixed bag of stones of different types, but all blue (or green), found its way onto a mountain side in the eastern Preselis and there, somehow, the Stonehenge people got hold of it. Precisely how eighty-five bluestones became available to people living far away on Salisbury Plain in 2150 BC is just one of the great unsolved mysteries of the Stonehenge story. A gift-exchange to facilitate access to the Irish Sea is one possibility, but there are other possible scenarios that can be imagined. Perhaps the Stonehenge people were aggressive and wanted to assert their political ascendancy over south-west Wales, possibly with a view to absolute control over the trade routes passing through the Irish Sea, and seized the bluestones from the slopes of the Preseli Hills to prove their power. Of all the Preseli tops, Carnmenyn is the most distinctive, with a peculiarly wild and jagged shape that contrasts strongly with the smooth whalebacks of all the surrounding hills. It is peculiar, almost setting itself apart as an alien and special place: it is instantly identifiable as a landmark from many kilometres away, a magnet for modern and prehistoric travellers alike, it would seem. From close up, it is strange, melodramatic, awe-inspiring – a place where gods might once have lived (Plates 11, 12, 13). Perhaps, if Carnmenyn was sacred, the frost-loosened blocks bristling from its summit were turned into holy stones: a circle made out of such stones would have a special sanctity.[4] Perhaps, taking this idea a step further, the circle of sacred stones was designed to trap the Preseli mountain-gods in Wessex, and even this action might have had either a religious or a political motive.

Some have suggested that the bluestones were already assembled into a circle in Wales, possibly somewhere on the southern slopes of the Preselis, and that an entire monument was uprooted and taken away by force. There is archaeological evidence that the slopes of the Preselis were, at the end of the neolithic and the beginning of the bronze age, attracting attention from the local people.[5] There were ceremonial centres at Meini–gwyr, Letterston, Gors Fawr and Dyffryn Syfynwy, all marked out by circles of standing stones.[6] In addition to these there are several standing stones, either single or in pairs, and it may be that some of these too represent the remains of stone circles; the pair 1.5 km east of Efailwen and the pair at Cwm-garw 3 km to the south-west of Carnmenyn are the likeliest candidates (Plate 9). All the megalithic monuments close to Carnmenyn are made of unshaped blue-stones that seem to have been selected for their natural shape and lifted straight out of the mountain. In other words the megalith-builders living within 10 km of the bluestone outcrop used bluestones, but this does not tell us whether they were simply using a locally available raw material for purely practical reasons or felt that that stone in particular held some special magical quality.[7] There is no evidence that Welsh megalith-builders further afield were particularly interested in bluestones, but that does not mean that the people living in Wessex did not covet them, or attach a very high value to them. The fact that the stones were far away and therefore exceedingly difficult to get hold of will actually have made them more valuable, more desirable. The people of bronze age Wessex also wanted amber, for making prestige objects like buttons, beads and cups – amber that came ultimately from Denmark. Amber was sometimes included in Wessex burials of the very highest status, alongside beautiful gold objects: exotic, rare, difficult to obtain, it was evidently a highly prized substance. Yet in Denmark, where it was easily available, it was considered to be of no special importance.[8] As with amber, so perhaps with bluestones?

Significantly, several funnel-necked pots decorated with bars of zig-zags have been found in the Preseli area and at Stonehenge, and they date from the centuries around 2000 BC.[9] So there was contact between the peoples of the two areas at about the right time and both groups were interested in building circles of standing stones. It may be going a little too far to suggest that it was the Preseli people who introduced the idea of building stone circles to the people of Wessex, having themselves borrowed it from the Irish, but it is possible.[10] Although the Preseli monuments are badly damaged, the evidence is still plainly visible that people living in that area were not only interested in raising megaliths, but also in raising *large* megaliths – see Cwm-garw, for example – and arranging them in circles.[11] To judge from the meagre remains of Meini-gwyr, they also liked to alternate circle stones of contrasting shapes, deliberately placing tall rectangular slabs next to shorter triangular ones: this is the same pattern that was built into the bluestone horseshoe at Stonehenge, where carefully shaped parallel-sided pillars alternate with tapered pillars, male and female partners in the Giants' Dance. There was another link, too, not directly to do with the monuments, perhaps, but certainly to do with the stones. Maces and battle-axes made of bluestone (spotted dolerite) from Preseli were much prized by the Wessex chieftains at about the same time. Unfortunately we shall probably never know whether it was the high status accorded by the bluestone battle-axes that made the Stonehenge people seek out more of the same type of stone to build a monument or the sanctity of the bluestones incorporated into Stonehenge that made them covet ceremonial maces made out of the same material – the radiocarbon dates do not allow us to infer which came first, but there seems to have been a connection of some kind. The important thing is that archaeology proves the parallels, links and contacts in the late neolithic and early bronze age.

Still other scenarios can be developed on this skeletal information. The Preseli people may not have been forced to hand over the stones; they may have freely and generously offered the bluestone monument or its constituent stones, perhaps as an acknowledgement of the Stonehenge people's high status, as an act of friendship, or in exchange for some gift that has since disappeared from the landscape. Gift-giving of this kind is very common in archaic societies. In the tribal villages of New Guinea, the bigman organizes large-scale ceremonial feasts, or mokas, at which he offers lavish gifts to all his guests: and all the gifts must be taken. The North American Indians of the nineteenth century held similar feasts, called potlatches. It looks as if, even in materially poor societies – and late neolithic and early bronze age Wessex was on the whole of this type – gifts have always been a way of strengthening social bonds, between individuals and between whole tribes.[12] And, once offered, such friendship gifts cannot be refused.

THE MEDIEVAL PERSPECTIVE

Somehow, at least 85 and possibly as many as 125 of these mysterious gifts found their way from Wales to Wessex, 217 km (135 miles) as the crow flies, the distance between London and Cardiff, Baltimore and New York, or Paris and Boulogne. How was it done?[13] More to the point, how was it done 2150 years before Christ, at a time of political fragmentation when Britain was not a single united country, and without the aid of modern technology?

Unlikely though it may seem, there are accounts written in the twelfth century AD which may throw light on the mystery. The story told by the medieval historian Geoffrey of Monmouth has Merlin *floating* the stones to Stonehenge, transporting a ready-made stone circle from a place called Killaraus in Ireland.[14] The place cannot be traced with any certainty, though perhaps Kildare was intended. Clearly Geoffrey was not recording history accurately, as will be obvious from some of his other detail, and Killaraus could have been transposed from south-west Wales, from some unknown site in the Preselis: to the people of Stonehenge both Preseli and Ireland lay far to the west, and Preseli was very much on the route to Ireland. Late neolithic and early bronze age ideas of geography must have been very different from our own, most probably based on itineraries and memorized lists of landmarks and seamarks: it is unlikely that maps existed either on paper or in the mind. Transposing a place in south-west Wales to southern Ireland could easily have happened while the story of the stones' journey was endlessly retold from century to century between 2150 BC and AD 1135.[15]

Now that we know the bluestones came from Wales, Geoffrey's mention of a transfer of stones from the west has lost its impact. But we have only known that the bluestones came from Wales since an epoch-making geological analysis in 1923: before that there had been no indication that they were far-travelled.[16] Professor Stuart Piggott quite rightly said that 'twelfth-century science was hardly sufficiently advanced to question the presence of spotted dolerite in a cretaceous landscape . . . While the building itself might well be regarded as the work of giants or of wizardry, it would be unnecessary to invoke the transportation of its stones from afar.'[17] In other words, the arrangement of stones in a ring might call for some sort of explanation – and giants, wizards, witches or the Devil were often given the credit for these undertakings – but medieval people saw the stones themselves as just stones that might be found anywhere.

An interesting situation arises. Modern awareness takes the long journey of the bluestones in its stride and does not appreciate how strange the idea would have been to medieval people, for whom the sciences of geology, geomorphology and archaeology did not exist. It may be a coincidence that Geoffrey proposed a long journey by water from the west for the stones – just a wild fancy that would lend colour and excitement to his story – but it seems more likely to me, as it did to Professor Piggott, that Geoffrey was drawing on a body of knowledge about Stonehenge that had been passed down by word of mouth from the bronze age.[18]

Stuart Piggott points out that the ancient Britons may have used their open-air temples continuously from the neolithic right through the bronze age and iron age until the Roman occupation; possibly that temple-using tradition survived in some places into the pagan dark ages, the twilit Arthurian period. If the stone circles and other sacred sites were in use throughout that long period, there may have been a continuous tradition of priestcraft. That in its turn would have provided the medium needed to

Plate 15 Christchurch Harbour, a hive of neolithic and bronze age activity. The entrance to the harbour is in the right background. In the centre foreground is a bronze age barrow, part of a barrow cemetery on Hengistbury Head. A late neolithic settlement once flourished among the trees halfway between the barrow and the harbour.

Plate 16 The River Avon at West Amesbury, view upstream. The bluestones were probably landed on the river-bank to the left.

transmit the legend from age to age. It may be hard to imagine priestly elders passing the bluestones story on to their novices and acolytes across 130 generations without a break: it is nevertheless possibly what happened. It may sound as far-fetched as the stones themselves, but it really is possible that Geoffrey of Monmouth drew on a celtic dark age tradition which had been passed down from the bronze age priests of Stonehenge. A similar process after all operated on a lesser scale in ancient Greece, where oral traditions permitted Homer to write down for the first time in the eighth century BC stories that contained Mycenean elements from five hundred years and more before.

Certainly there is some distortion and garbling in Geoffrey's version of Stonehenge's prehistory, just as there is in Homer's account of the fall of Troy. The introduction of King Arthur's uncle Ambrosius as the dark age king who commissioned the building of Stonehenge has led many to dismiss Geoffrey's work as a piece of serious history. If Arthur lived at all, it must have been in the sixth century AD, and we know from the radiocarbon dates that Stonehenge is much older than that. Yet a mixing of anachronisms is exactly the type of thing we should look for in an authentic ancient tradition, which picks up contemporary overlays and glosses each time it is retold. The most extraordinary thing is that a part of the tradition turns out to be recognizable – the acquisition of the bluestone circle from 'the west' and its re-erection at Stonehenge – and archaeologically datable, to the years around 2150 BC.

Another medieval writer, Gerald of Wales, visited Ireland with Prince John in 1185, fifty years after Geoffrey wrote his account. Gerald recorded that he saw many standing stones: 'In Ireland in ancient times there was a collection of stones called the Giants' Dance, that demanded admiration . . . On the plains of Kildare, not far from Naas, [giants] set them up as much by skill as by strength. Moreover, stones just like them, and raised in the same way, are to be seen there to the present day.'[19] And Gerald was right. There are indeed megaliths still standing there. The tallest of them, the Punchestown Pillar, is a colossal 8 m high, which makes it the tallest standing stone in the British Isles after the Rudston Monolith. Nevertheless, this seeming evidence that the Stonehenge stones came after all from Ireland rather than from Wales should be treated with caution. The survival of the big Irish stones may go some way towards explaining the change of the story's setting to Ireland from south-west Wales, where the megalithic heritage is far less conspicuous. The Irish stones are nevertheless the wrong stones: they are made of Wicklow granite and the Stonehenge bluestones are not.

It is worth looking closely at Geoffrey's earlier account of the acquisition of the Double Bluestone Circle, not least because his full text is rarely seen. This is what he wrote:

The King (Aurelius Ambrosius) spoke to Merlin about the monument he was planning. Merlin replied, 'If you want to grace the burial place of those men with a work that will endure for ever, send for the Dance of the Giants which is on Mount Killaraus in Ireland. For there stands a stone structure that no man of this age could ever raise, unless he were able to add great cunning to his artistry. The stones are enormous, and there is no stone anywhere of greater virtue. If they were set up in a circle round this site, in the same way that they are arranged over there, they would stand here for ever.'

At these words of Merlin's, Aurelius burst out laughing. 'How can such large stones be moved from so distant a country? It is hardly as if Britain itself is lacking in stones big enough for the task!'

'Try not to give way to foolish laughter, your majesty', Merlin answered. 'There is nothing absurd in what I am suggesting. These stones contain a mystery and a healing virtue against many ailments. Giants of old carried them from the furthest ends of Africa and set them up in Ireland at the time when they lived there. Whenever they felt ill, it was their custom to prepare baths at the foot of the stones; they used to pour water over the stones into baths in which the sick were cured. They also used to mix the water with herbal concoctions to heal their wounds. There is not a single stone among them which has not some medicinal property.'

When the Britons heard all this, they made up their minds to send for the stones and to make war on the people of Ireland if they tried to withhold them. In the end the King's brother, Uther Pendragon, and 15,000 men were sent to accomplish the task. Merlin, too, was sent so that all the problems that had to be overcome could have the benefit of his knowledge and advice. They made ready their ships and put to sea. The winds were favourable and they arrived in Ireland.

[The Irish under a brave young man called Gillomanius assembled an army to oppose Uther's army, but they were defeated quickly and easily.]

The Britons made their way to Mount Killaraus. When they came to the stone structure, they were filled with joy and wonder. Merlin came up to them as they stood round in a group. 'Try your strength', he said, 'and see whether skill can do more than strength, or brute strength more than skill, when it comes to taking down these stones!'

At his bidding they all set to with every conceivable kind of device and tried their hardest to take the ring down. They rigged up hawsers and ropes and propped up scaling ladders, each trying what he thought would be most effective, but none of these things advanced them one inch. When he saw what a mess they were making of it, Merlin burst out laughing; he placed in position all the gear he considered necessary and took down the stones more easily than you could ever believe.

Once he had pulled them down, he had them carried to the ships and stored on board, and they all set sail once more for Britain with joy in their hearts.

The winds were fair. They came to the shore and set off with the stones for the place where the heroes had been buried. The moment this was reported to him, Aurelius dispatched messengers to all the different regions of Britain, ordering the clergy and the people to assemble at Mount Ambrius, where with due ceremony and rejoicing they were to re-dedicate the burial-place I have described.

[After crowning himself at Whitsuntide at the Mount of Amesbury, i.e. the site of Stonehenge] Ambrosius Aurelius ordered Merlin to raise round the burial place the stones he had brought from Ireland. Merlin obeyed the King's command and set the stones in a circle round the burial ground – in exactly the same arrangement as on Mount Killaraus.

A TALE FROM THE BRONZE AGE?

Geoffrey of Monmouth's account is full of arresting details that may be pointers to what really happened in 2150 BC. He has the circle brought to Stonehenge to mark the sacred precinct of a burial ground: Aubrey Burl has recently argued that Stonehenge was used primarily for funeral rites.[20] Geoffrey has the circle dismantled, transported and re-erected with the use of craft rather than strength; we know from their skeletons that late neolithic people were lightly built and from their settlements and burial places that their communities were small, mostly isolated farmsteads and hamlets, so they would have been obliged to use skill in preference to strength. New estimates of the work they put into the building of Stonehenge are still high (see Appendix B), but only one-tenth of the thirty million man-hours some prehistorians have estimated.

Geoffrey describes the stones as enormous. It is the sarsen stones that are enormous, not the bluestones.[21] The Geoffrey of Monmouth account understandably muddles the earlier and smaller bluestones with the later and larger sarsens; medieval people would have assumed the saga referred to the larger stones at Stonehenge, although, as we saw earlier, there are large bluestones raised as megaliths in the Preseli area. This does not mean that the bronze age tradition held that the sarsens came from Ireland or Wales, only that like many an old story it had become distorted through time.

Aurelius laughs at the absurdity of bringing stones from so far away, when there are stones enough in Wessex. It was perfectly true that there were plenty of sarsen stones closer at hand in the Avebury area, and they were in fact used shortly afterwards, for Stonehenge IIIa, yet in 2150 BC the bluestones in far-off Wales were for some reason seen as more attractive. Geoffrey tells us that the stones contain 'a mystery'. Merlin's insistence that they were well worth fetching because they contained magical healing properties as well as 'a mystery' gives us a glimpse of a prehistoric motive; it gives us the hint we need that the stones came from some holy place and were believed to possess mystic, supernatural properties. Geoffrey's comment that giants of old brought the circle from the furthest ends of Africa tells us that the bluestones, whether or not already assembled into a circle, were regarded as imbued with some ancient magic even before the time came for them to be transferred to Stonehenge.

The folk tradition has it that the Stonehenge people decided to take the Giants' Dance whether its owners would give it to them or not. This suggests, but does not prove, that the Stonehenge people seized the stones by an act of aggression. The stones were floated to Amesbury by Merlin's magic; this fits well with the idea of the bluestones being transported on log-boats from Milford Haven to Amesbury, an achievement that must have seemed as utterly remarkable to awestruck bronze age listeners round the camp fire as it does to us now, who have seen men walk on the Moon. Geoffrey tells us that Mount Ambrius was selected as the new site for the Giants' Dance. This place is probably, as I have already suggested, the higher ground above Amesbury, or 'Ambr's Burg', which is where the remains of Stonehenge still stand. Finally, there is the great public ceremony ordered by Aurelius Ambrosius for the stone circle's rededication. This strongly suggests just the sort of whole-community foundation ceremony that was probably held at Stonehenge when the first bluestones were raised there.

The seventeenth-century antiquary John Aubrey made his own copy of another version of the story that he found in William Caxton's *Chronicles*. It contains some interesting variations. Whereas Geoffrey gives a Latinized form of the Irish king's name, Gillomanius, Aubrey and Caxton give what seems likely to be its original form, and '*Gwillom*' sounds distinctly Welsh. He also gives a different version of the original location of the Giants' Dance: instead of Killaraus it is 'Kyan'; it may be significant that nearly all the summits in the Preselis where the bluestones come from have as part of their names the prefix 'carn', meaning 'hill': Carngyfrwy, Carn Ddafad Ias, Carnbreseb, Carn Llwyd, Carnmenyn.[22]

Where does all this lead us? The Geoffrey of Monmouth story can be interpreted in several ways – as fact, fiction, or pure fantasy – but it seems to me that it has many of the characteristics of an ancient oral tradition; seen in this way, it offers glimpses of the complicated events that led to the arrival of the bluestones at Stonehenge, even, perhaps, something of the motivation behind them.

THE SOURCE OF THE BLUESTONES

But Stonehenge scholars differ on this. E. H. Stone and Stuart Piggott agree with the ancient tradition idea: Aubrey Burl, a writer of equal authority, disagrees.[23] Ultimately, it is the solid archaeological evidence that counts, and it is on this question that the sciences of geology and geomorphology have made the most dramatic contribution. Samples of the bluestones were tested in 1923 by the geologist H. H. Thomas.[24] He discovered that the Stonehenge bluestones are not one type but several types of rock, which means that they must have come from different places. The commonest type of stone is a green-blue spotted dolerite: there are also a few stones made of a dark blue-green rhyolite and four broken stumps of dark green baked volcanic ash. Thomas traced these three rock types to the Preseli Hills in south-west Wales and found that there was just one area, between the summits of Carnmenyn and Foel Trigarn, where all three can be picked out of natural rock outcrops within the space of a square mile (2.6 sq. km). Freezing and thawing in the ice age loosened the stones, breaking them away along the networks of natural cracks that ran through the rock, so that megaliths seem to explode ready-made from the tor-like summits (Plates 11–13). Slabs or pillars 2, 3 or even 4 m long could and still can simply be dragged from the mountain top. Some loosened stones rolled or slid down the slopes, so they could be gathered from the boulder fields lower down. The seventeen small bluestone boulders of the Gors Fawr stone circle, just 3 km south of Carnmenyn, were probably gathered with very little trouble from among the boulders that lay around on the common.[25] Carnmenyn seemed to Thomas, and still seems to me, by far the most likely source (bedrock source, that is) of the majority of the Stonehenge bluestones: boulders of the main types of rock can still be seen lying around on the hilltop. The fact that no bluestone quarry can be identified from tool-marks or other archaeological evidence is disappointing but not altogether unexpected. The bluestones selected were already loose and had only to be lifted away, so the best we could expect to find would be an area cleared of loose stones and that would only be apparent if all eighty-five stones were lifted from the same spot, which is on the whole unlikely as the stones must have been selected on size. There is nevertheless a rectangular area that seems unnaturally clear of stones amongst the cluster of tors that makes Carnmenyn's summit: it forms a kind of platform open to the south.

As well as the three main types of bluestone, there are three less important types. There are three stones at Stonehenge (44, 45 and 62) made of unspotted dolerite, and Richard Atkinson has discovered that this too outcrops in the Preselis.[26] One stump is made of calcareous ash. Two further stumps and the important Altar Stone are made of Cosheston sandstone, which outcrops below the main source area on the gentle hill slopes close to Milford Haven.[27] But the commonest type of stone on Carnmenyn, and among the local megaliths, and among the bluestones at Stonehenge, is the distinctive spotted dolerite, a greenish-blue stone with pale pink crystals of felspar.

Suddenly, the ultimate origin of the bluestones comes into focus out of the mists of bardic tale-spinning, tracked to earth by geology. One of the most important mysteries of the bluestones has been solved. But experts still disagree about the way the bluestones travelled from Preseli to Stonehenge. I firmly believe that the Stonehenge people, the native people of the territory centring on Durrington Walls, went to Wales to collect them. In the 1970s, the geologist G. A. Kellaway developed the idea that the bluestones were erratics that had been carried to Salisbury Plain by an ice sheet; the glacial theory still has its supporters, so we need to examine it carefully.[28]

STONEHENGE IN THE ICE AGE

The last large-scale (late Devensian) glaciation happened around 25,000–12,000 years ago. Huge snow-fed ice caps built up over the mountains in Scotland, England and Wales, spread out and merged with each other, leaving the lowlands of East Anglia, the Midlands, Wessex and south-west England uncovered. Even at the ice maximum 18,000 years ago ice could not have carried stones from Wales into Salisbury Plain. In earlier glaciations that we know of during the last half million years, conditions were rather colder, with ice sheets extending to cover the whole of Britain as far south as a line running from the Bristol Channel to the Thames estuary (Figure 43).

The spreading ice could quarry well-jointed rocks, however hard, simply by freezing onto them and tugging them away, and then carrying them maybe tens of miles towards the ice front. These blocks of rock, or erratics as geologists call them, could not have reached Salisbury Plain during the earlier glaciations of which we have clear evidence.

The evidence for what happened in Britain during earlier stages of the ice age diminishes as we go backwards in time, but there were many more cold phases than the ones that produced the four or five recent glaciations. It is almost certain that several of these little-known phases of prehistory produced huge ice sheets covering northern and central Britain. Kellaway's theory is that in one or more of these early glaciations Britain was entirely covered by ice; in this situation an ice sheet crossing south-west Wales could have picked up a selection of bluestones and carried them south-eastwards across the floor of the Bristol Channel – then dry land – and deposited them at or near the site of Stonehenge (Figure 42).

Kellaway was not the first to suggest that the bluestones at Stonehenge are glacial erratics: Judd proposed it as early as 1903.[29] The long distance involved itself persuasively supports the glacial drift theory. As Aubrey Burl has pointed out, there is no other stone circle known in Britain to which stones were dragged more than 8–10 km (5–6 miles); the gritstone block used to make the Rudston Monolith was dragged a little further, the 16 km (10 miles) from Cayton Bay, but this is nothing compared with the 217 km, crow-flight, travelled by the Stonehenge bluestones. They are an anomaly. Even so, this is not in itself a proof that the glacial theory is right. It may well be that in this as in certain other ways Stonehenge is exceptional.

It has been claimed that one stone found at Stonehenge, admittedly not one of the bluestones, may have come from the area round Snowdon in north Wales, but, if so, the known patterns of ice flow within Wales are enough to explain how this came to be deposited among the Preseli blue-stones in south-west Wales (Figure 43). We can believe in this amount of glacial help without going so far as proposing that ice carried all the stones all the way to Salisbury Plain. The report of this extra, north Welsh stone by supporters of the glacial theory is itself rather erratic.[30] The Open University geologists report that G. A. Kellaway told them in a letter what the late Robert Newall had told him about a stone allegedly found at Stonehenge during the 1920s excavations, in which Newall took part; according to this, by now fourth-hand, report Colonel Hawley saw no significance in the stone and ignored it. To make matters even less scientific, the stone itself, supposedly in the hands of the British Geological Survey, has not been produced for mineralogical examination. The stone may exist, and it may have come from a prehistoric context within the ruins of Stonehenge, though neither is certain: it may have come originally from a bedrock source in Snowdonia too. Even if all that is so, we can *still* explain its presence on Salisbury Plain without believing that ice carried it all the way there. Equally unconvincing is the listing of 'other erratic material' at Stonehenge, apparently with the intention of proving that there was a lot of different glacial debris in the area. The oolitic ragstone probably came from Chilmark, not far from Stonehenge, and was almost certainly brought in by prehistoric people as part of their toolkits when they walked over to help build Stonehenge. The Niedermendig lava, which is also mentioned, can only have come from the Rhineland, 700 km to the east of Stonehenge, and this must have arrived by human agency: not even the most enthusiastic glaciophiles have proposed that ice swept into Salisbury Plain from Germany. The existence at Stonehenge and its satellite sites of substances like the German lava and Danish amber is, in fact, excellent evidence that the early bronze age people living in Wessex were ready to travel any distance to procure exactly the types of raw materials they wanted.

The main argument against Kellaway's glacial theory is the general lack of evidence for a 'southern England' glaciation: there are no distinctively glacial landforms and no glacial deposits beyond the well-attested sites in north Devon. Geologists and geomorphologists have reached a consensus that in the last (Devensian) glaciation an ice sheet covered most of Wales, though not the Preselis and it did not cross the Bristol Channel. There is evidence that in an earlier glaciation the ice extended a little further south, to the coast of north Devon. There are glacial erratics at Croyde Bay (dolerite, sandstone and gneiss) which were carried there from Scotland and Wales; there is another glacial deposit, the Fremington till, near Barnstaple.[31] There are also traces of till near the north Somerset coast. There is no conclusive evidence that the ice front, where the ice sheet would in any case have been thin and

Plate 17 Station Stone 91 at Stonehenge.

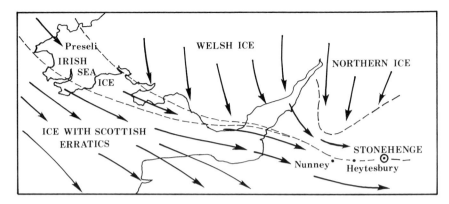

Figure 42 Ice brings the bluestones to Stonehenge: Kellaway's interpretation. Arrows show the direction of ice flow.

weak, rode up into any of the southern English hill areas: the Mendips, Cotswolds and Chilterns almost certainly stood up like islands above the thinning ice, and it is unlikely in this situation that the ice reached Salisbury Plain.

Kellaway proposed that the ice sheet extended much further south than this, with the southern counties of England completely swamped by ice. Even though we cannot be sure what happened in the early cold stages of the ice age, what Kellaway proposed does not seem physically possible. It is difficult to imagine a mechanism that could form the ice and send it eastwards along the Channel coast. Kellaway himself proposed that ice accumulated in the Western Approaches and surged from this centre towards Brighton and Dover, but there are serious problems with this. The other, known centres of ice accumulation are hill and mountain areas, areas that now have heavy relief rainfall and would in cold stages have experienced heavy snowfall. The Western Approaches were either shallow sea or lowlands during the cold stages of the ice age, so an ice cap is very unlikely to have built up there. Even if it had, it could only have spread downhill, and there is a gradual shallowing of the sea between the Atlantic and Dover: in other words, the ice would have been travelling uphill all the way. Although ice *can* flow uphill, it can only do so under special conditions, for short distances and with a massive head of ice behind it – and these conditions were absent. The Kellaway scenario is utterly at odds with what is known of ice sheet behaviour.

We also know that glacial erratics are deposited by ice in trails that tend to fan out from the source outcrop. It would be quite extraordinary for an ice sheet to gather the Stonehenge bluestones from a small area in Wales and deposit them in another small area on Salisbury Plain: stones from Preseli of all the types found at Stonehenge ought to be littered all over Somerset and

Wiltshire. As far as I am aware, the only non-Stonehenge bluestone that has been found in southern England is the one discovered in Boles Barrow, and that, very significantly, was built into the fabric of a neolithic barrow by neolithic people.[32] Searches have been made, yet the only other stray pieces in the region are a few bluestone artefacts and chippings tightly clustering on Stonehenge and a couple close to Avebury: there are none in the area in between or surrounding these key sites. Instead there is a clear association between the occurrence of bluestone and major foci of neolithic and bronze age ceremonial activity.[33]

The Open University team misquote an early nineteenth-century geologist in support of their idea that there were once many glacial erratics lying around on Salisbury Plain: J. A. de Luc claimed to have seen 'blocks of granite and trap [an old term for dense igneous rock]' there and that these were later buried by improving farmers.[34] It is well known from contemporary accounts that this happened at Avebury, and Alexander Keiller successfully exhumed and re-erected several megaliths that he discovered still lying in grave-pits. The Open University team's case is seriously weakened by the lack of positive evidence for what they claim: they have not identified any farmer-buried erratics on the Plain, nor, significantly, have they yet identified any undisturbed glacial debris on the Plain. One of the few tangible pieces of evidence for the invasion of ice beyond the north Devon and north Somerset coastal area is a drift deposit at Nunney. This reddish-brown sandy clay contains chalk and flint and is therefore not local in origin. There is nevertheless a chalk escarpment a few miles to the east and it is well known that chalk blocks and chalk mud were commonly transported in mudflows during cold phases of the ice age, and it would have been quite possible for chalk debris, including flints, to flow well beyond the western edge of the chalk outcrop. In other words, the commonsense explanation for a deposit containing chalk and flints just to the west of a chalk escarpment would be that it arrived from the east; Kellaway opts for what seems to me a perverse explanation that it originated in some chalk outcrop far away to the north-west, no one knows where.

Professor Richard Atkinson has recently proposed that people collected some of the bluestones from the Preselis and some – the inferior, softer ones – from a site, as yet undiscovered, in west Wiltshire. Yet this hypothetical Wessex bluestone source still cannot be identified, more than twenty years after Kellaway floated the idea, which strongly suggests that it does not exist. The alternative – which is to propose that the imagined ice sheet brought precisely the right number, and no more, of bluestone blocks for the building of Stonehenge II – defies credibility. There is in any case Christopher Green's study of the river gravels of Salisbury Plain. Rivers inevitably pick up samples of all the rocks and sediments exposed in their catchment areas and deposit them downstream, so that looking at the contents of river gravels is a good way of testing for the presence of foreign

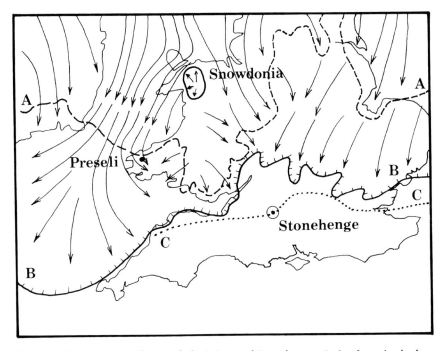

Figure 43 Southernmost limits of glaciation and Stonehenge. A: ice front in the late Devensian (Devensian maximum), 18,000 years ago. B: ice front in the Anglian, consensus view among geomorphologists. C: ice front in an unspecified glaciation according to Thorpe et al. Note that radial ice flow in Snowdonia could easily have delivered north Welsh rocks to Irish Sea ice and thereby be transferred to the Preseli Hills. Arrows show the repeating patterns of ice flow, reaching their maximum known extent in the Anglian.

material in the landscape at different times.[35] Green's tests convincingly show that although gravels were deposited in the Avon basin in many different phases of the ice age, it is the highest and oldest ones that contain the most 'foreign' material, and that consists of small amounts of rocks more recent than the chalk which have now been largely eroded away. The younger gravels contain less and less of this foreign material, which shows that there was no glacial intervention: there could have been no sudden introduction of erratics by an ice sheet in the middle or later part of the ice age. Green has undoubtedly proved that no ice sheet reached the present catchment area of the Wiltshire Avon, and that to hope for natural occurrences of bluestones as glacial erratics anywhere on Salisbury Plain is futile.

The bluestone in the Boles Barrow was discovered by William Cunnington when his workmen were digging into the eastern end of the long barrow in 1801. It is not clear why the stone was originally included in the barrow, although it does seem to have been placed at a symbolic point, close to a collection of fourteen human skulls and the skulls of at least seven oxen. Cunnington had to stop his excavation when the collapsing mound made it dangerous for him to continue, but he took the block of bluestone home with him, recognizing it as the same sort of stone as the smaller pillars at Stonehenge, and made it a feature of his garden at Heytesbury.[36] Now it stands guard, spot-lit and rather sinister, at the entrance to the Stonehenge exhibition at Salisbury Museum.

The Boles Barrow bluestone presents us with another problem. At first sight the presence of a bluestone in a neolithic barrow may seem to add support to the case for the neolithic Wessex people as importers of stones for cult purposes, but the problem is the time-gap between the building of the Boles Barrow and the building of the Double Bluestone Circle. Long barrows were no longer being built by the time the Stonehenge bluestones were imported in 2150 BC: in fact, the building of long barrows ceased not long after 3000 BC. It looks, in other words, as if the bluestones were imported into Wessex at different times.

It is quite likely that diplomatic and trading contacts between Wessex and Preseli were kept up over many centuries, and we could see the large consignment of circle-stones as the climax, the crowning glory, of a long succession of imports from Wales. Exactly why the Boles Barrow bluestone was imported, and why it was built into the barrow rather than displayed, are unlikely ever to be discovered.

There is another possible explanation, and that is the importation of both the Boles Barrow bluestone and the Stonehenge bluestones in around 3000 BC. It would have been quite possible for the technology of the middle neolithic to have coped with this undertaking, and certainly no less possible than for the early bronze age technology of 2150 BC. We also know that the Stonehenge bluestones were moved around into different arrangements at Stonehenge itself, and that for a time they were actually taken away again (see Chapters 6 and 7). Serious consideration should be given to the possibility that in 2150 BC the bluestones were brought to Stonehenge, not directly from Wales but from another ceremonial site on Salisbury Plain, possibly in the vicinity of Boles Barrow, and that a bluestone monument of some sort may have existed somewhere in the 15 km of downland to the west of Stonehenge between 3000 and 2150 BC. There is no definite evidence of this, but it is another possible scenario to bear in mind, and it may be that one day the stone-holes of this early monument will come to light. For the time being, I am nevertheless going to assume that the Boles Barrow bluestone was fetched on a middle neolithic trip to Wales and that the Stonehenge bluestones were collected in a series of expeditions to Wales in the twenty-second century BC.

The stones came from Wales: that much at least is certain. But how exactly were they gathered? There are three possibilities and there is no pressing reason to prefer one to another. It may be that the Stonehenge people

111

voyaged to Wales, making landfall at the eastern head of Milford Haven, a perfect natural harbour, and then struck north-eastwards 24 km overland across rolling hill country, to gather the stones strewn along the sacred mountain side of Carnmenyn. Alternatively, the Preseli people, themselves megalith-builders, may have gathered together a consignment of suitably shaped natural boulders ready for the visitors to collect, possibly even a ready-to-assemble stone circle kit. A third possibility is that the Stonehenge people took or were offered as a gift an existing stone circle, of which there were several in the area.[37] This brings us back to the epic adventure of the oral tradition, the voyage to the west to seize the Giants' Dance.

THE BLUESTONE VOYAGES

The bluestones were easy to quarry, as the action of frost long before in the ice age had loosened the blocks so that they had only to be lifted away from the bedrock among the spikes and spires of the Preseli mountain tops. Nor would they have been difficult to transport. A family car with two people on board weighs 1 tonne: a typical bluestone weighs just four times as much. Significantly, there are many blocks on Carnmenyn that are larger than the stones selected for Stonehenge: it seems that the prospectors had a clear idea of what was wanted – and what was practicable. Four-tonne bluestones would have been fairly easy to drag on sledges south–westwards down the gentle slope followed today by the A478, passing the stone circles of Gors Fawr and Meini-gwyr, towards the head of the Eastern Cleddau (Figure 44). A route north-westwards towards Cardigan Bay would have been shorter, but the risks involved in rounding St David's Head and the tidal races in the channels between the mainland and the islands of Ramsey, Skomer and Skokholm would have made this a less sensible choice. The longer land route south-westwards was far safer.

Where the stones were loaded onto the boats is not known. It would have been very easy to moor and load substantial log-boats at the site of Blackpool Mill or Minwear Wood and begin the voyage from there, but the Eastern Cleddau is navigable further upstream and there would have been significant advantages in getting the stones afloat earlier if it was possible. The north–south ridge slopes very gently southwards as far as Clunderwen, but between there and Minwear the landscape is dissected by several streams and it would be more difficult to haul the stone sledges up and down these many short but steep slopes. The Eastern Cleddau, which has its source on the side of Carnmenyn, is navigable as far inland as Gelli. In high summer the river there is about 5 m wide and knee-deep, which Atkinson's experiments suggest would be quite deep enough to float a craft laden with a bluestone (Plate 14). This launching-place makes a great deal of sense in relation to the sledge route; from Llandissilio to Gelli a tributary valley of the Eastern Cleddau leads down from the ridge, providing a gentle ramp

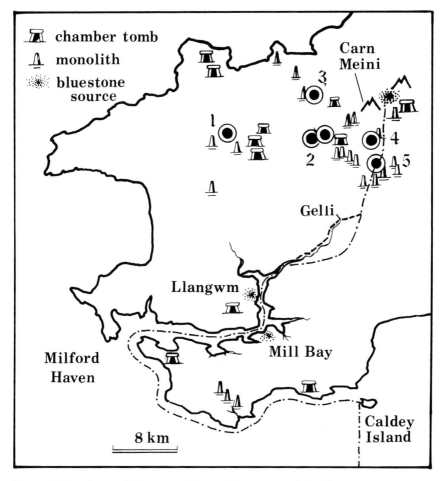

Figure 44 South-west Wales: megaliths and the source of the bluestones. 1–5: stone circles. The Stonehenge bluestone journeys probably followed the dot-and-dash line. Alternative route via Gelli shown dashed.

down to the river bank, ideal for dragging the stone sledges. The Gelli site seems the best option, reducing the length of the sledge haul to only 15 km.[38]

Given the known technology of the period, the most likely craft to be used is a composite boat made of three dug-out canoes lashed together side by side. If these were 7.6 m (25 ft) long, 1 m wide and 0.6 m deep, they could easily have carried the weight of a bluestone with 0.3 m (1 ft) or so of freeboard. The weight of the stone had to be spread so that it would not break the gunwales, and the obvious way of achieving this was to lay a deck amidships right across the vessel so that each of the three canoes took a share

113

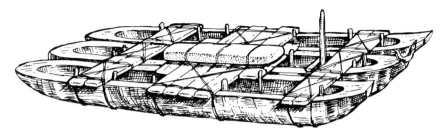

Figure 45 A bluestone boat reconstructed as a decked trimaran.

of the weight (Figure 45). A craft like this would have been stable and steerable and could have been paddled by a crew of perhaps eight or ten people quite safely in calm waters. Trouble would have been encountered in rough seas, since the low freeboard would have allowed a 4 ft wave, not uncommon in the Bristol Channel, to swamp the vessel. Maybe there were losses that inevitably have gone unrecorded and a bluestone that is reputed to lie on the bed of the Cleddau may represent just one of many mishaps. Maybe instead the bluestone adventurers were cautious enough to wait patiently for the right weather conditions and only sailed in a flat calm.

There is another possibility, which would have been within the scope of early bronze age technology, and that is the addition of stout planks slotted onto dowels or pegs along the gunwales. In The Gambia, dug-out canoes are made for fishing in calm backwaters and mangrove swamps: the same dug-out hulls can easily be converted into pirogues for sea-fishing in the Atlantic by adding planks along the sides. The 0.5 m of extra freeboard allows the pirogue to be used even in the heavy surf of an exposed Atlantic coastline.[39] If this is possible using traditional low technology in The Gambia today, it must also have been possible in bronze age Britain.[40] The extra freeboard of the pirogue would allow just two hulls to bear a bluestone, but the weight of the stone resting on their adjacent gunwales would probably have made a catamaran break up; on balance, the most likely craft given the available technology and the specific problems involved is a decked trimaran or, put another way, a triple-hulled pirogue.

One of the many unknown elements in this exciting episode in the Stonehenge story is the scale of the expedition or expeditions. We have no way of knowing how many people or vessels were involved. My instinct, given the small scale of the communities and the very long time-scales involved not just at Stonehenge but also in many other neolithic and bronze age projects, is to suppose that the bluestones were not collected all at once but in pairs or fours, each consignment accompanied by a small auxiliary flotilla of log-boats.

It is not known whether the Stonehenge people paid for their bluestones, but given the 'archaic' nature of their society it is likely that they did.

Probably some exchange of goods or gifts took place, although it may be that the exchange-goods were perishables or consumables that have left no trace.

Let us try to re-create, in our mind's eye, what happened in the twenty-second century BC. Each summer – since success depended on calm, fair-weather conditions it had to be high summer – a flotilla of perhaps six log-boats in all, four of them floating a little lower in the water with their blue-grey, coffin-like burdens and two escort vessels floating higher, stole slowly and carefully down Daucleddau, the upper reach of Milford Haven. On the way they passed Llangwm on the west bank. This was the place where the Altar Stone was collected, a piece of unusual pale green sandstone flecked with mica and studded with tiny pink garnets: there is nothing like it anywhere else and it must have looked startlingly beautiful when freshly ground and polished. Six km further on they passed on the left or south Mill Bay, a site represented at Stonehenge by just one chip of stone: they must have stopped here too to collect a stone for some reason. Little by little the small flotilla crept the 27 slow km (17 miles) to Thorn Island at the entrance to Milford Haven, each stone-laden boat like a megalithic hearse bound for some distant funeral.

From Thorn Island the flotilla sailed east along the sea-coast, exploiting the tidal current to carry the stones the 37 km (23 miles) to the distinctive seamark of Caldey Island. And there the sea mist rolls in on us and the prehistoric voyagers and their wave-lapped log-boats are lost to view. We do not know which way they went on from there. They may have sailed either east or south. Professor Richard Atkinson assumes that they continued eastwards as far as Newport and Caldicot Level, hugging the coastline all the way, and then crossed the Severn estuary to gain the mouth of the Bristol Avon, where another choice presented itself.[41] Atkinson has little hesitation in opting for the shorter, safer inland route.[42] This would have taken the log-boats up the Bristol Avon through the site of Bristol itself to a point about 11 km above Bath and from there up the River Frome. From the site of the modern town of Frome the expedition would have needed to cross overland a distance of some 9 km to reach the headstream of the River Wylye at Warminster. From there the river current of the Wylye took the floating stones down to its confluence with the Wiltshire–Hampshire Avon at Salisbury; a northward turn here took the log-boat navigators against the current of the Avon 11 km (7 miles) up to Amesbury – although of course none of these towns then existed.

Atkinson feels that the Bristol route is 'for every reason' the most likely. It is certainly the shortest, and some 640 km (400 miles) shorter than his alternative coastwise route, but it is beset by a serious problem: it involves dragging the stones overland for 9 km in addition to the overland hauls at the beginning and end of the journey. For this the stones would have needed to be unloaded from the log-boats and lashed to sledges, and then both stones and boats required portage across country; then the stones would have had to be lifted back onto the log-boats and secured. These transhipments would have necessitated a lot of extra effort and organization. There are logistical problems too. Where would the stone sledges have come from? Were they specially made in advance and left at Frome for the purpose? If so, were they dragged back to Frome from Warminster once the stones were transferred, ready for the next consignment? If not, were they instead carried somehow on board the log-boats?

The practical logistics seem difficult especially when we consider that the overland transfer was happening 32 km (20 miles) west of Stonehenge and therefore presumably well outside the relatively small territory over which the Stonehenge people had direct control. The lowest profile that I can visualize for the bluestone transfer is about four stones per summer, and that pattern of activity would have required the collaboration or at least friendly acquiescence of the people living in the Frome–Warminster area for a period of thirty years. The complete Double Bluestone Circle design seems to have required 125 stones, and there may well have been years when bad weather at sea, crop failures, bad omens, epidemics, or some other intervention prevented the Stonehenge people from making an expedition to Wales: the enterprise may have stretched across fifty years rather than thirty.

The spacing of the major ceremonial centres in Wessex suggests that in the late neolithic larger territories were evolving, each perhaps with a paramount chief.[43] If, as seems likely, they were 50 km or so across by the early bronze age then it is possible that the reach of the Stonehenge people extended as far west as Warminster, but their 'frontier', if it could be called that, probably lay between Warminster and Frome, at a point equidistant between Stonehenge in the east and Priddy Circles and Stanton Drew in the west: this is a likely location as it was also a watershed, a natural physical boundary. So, even within the framework of a small number of larger territories in Wessex, it looks as if the overland transfer of bluestones from Frome to Warminster would have straddled a territorial boundary. The pattern of settlements in late neolithic and early bronze age Wessex is known in some detail (Figure 46a). Since these fall into evenly spaced clusters it is likely that the clusters represent tribal groupings of some kind and were located somewhere near the centres of territories. Although the boundaries that we can draw midway between the settlement clusters are generally in different places from the boundaries implied by the ceremonial centres, which raises interesting questions in its turn, the boundary between Stonehenge and Priddy falls in the same place (Figure 46b).

All things considered, keeping the bluestones lashed to the log-boats and the boats themselves on the water seems far more likely. The detour round the West Country may have taken much longer, but it would in several ways have been easier to manage. We also know that time as such was fairly unimportant to the Stonehenge people. It seems not to have mattered to

Plate 18 Stonehenge: stone 55, filling most of the picture, rests on the Altar Stone. To the right is the fallen lintel of the Great Trilithon.

Plate 19 Bush Barrow. The pit marking the chieftain's grave can be seen left of centre. Stonehenge may just be made out in the left distance.

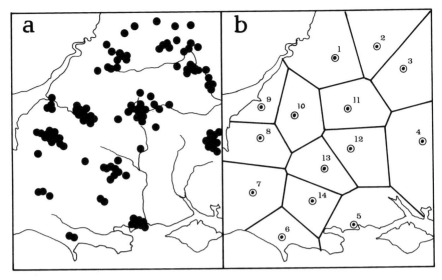

Figure 46 Late neolithic Wessex. Distribution of settlements: (a) implies roughly equal-sized tribal territories; (b) each with a settlement cluster at its centre. It is assumed that Stonehenge was a territorial centre. The settlement clusters centre on Cirencester (1), Burford (2), Abingdon (3), Basingstoke (4), Christchurch (5), Dorchester (6), Montacute (7), Mendip (8), Avonmouth (9), Bristol (10), Avebury (11), Stonehenge (12), Wardour Castle (13), Hambledon Hill (14).

them that building a monument took several generations: it was the doing, the making, that was important, rather than getting the structure finished. As we shall see later, Stonehenge was in a sense never finished in the modern meaning of the word, in spite of the many centuries spent on it. The Stonehenge people would not have minded how many years or decades it would take them to bring the Giants' Dance to its new home.

Richard Atkinson allows that there is an alternative to his Bristol route, a sea route continuing from the Severn crossing along the Somerset and North Devon coasts towards Cornwall.[44] He cautiously diverts his bluestone flotilla across the neck of the Penwith peninsula to avoid the dangerous waters of Land's End, and there is in fact a very attractive low-level route across, with a maximum height of only 26 m (85 ft) and gentle gradients, from the mouth of the River Hayle to Mount's Bay, close to St Michael's Mount. Although the overland haul is a mere 6 km, even this short distance would have meant unloading the bluestones from their log-boats, lashing them to sledges, dragging both stones and log-boats overland and then reloading the stones onto the refloated boats at Marazion. There is also the implied storage of sledges from year to year at Hayle or Marazion and the implied co-operation of the local Cornish people over a period of thirty to fifty years.

118

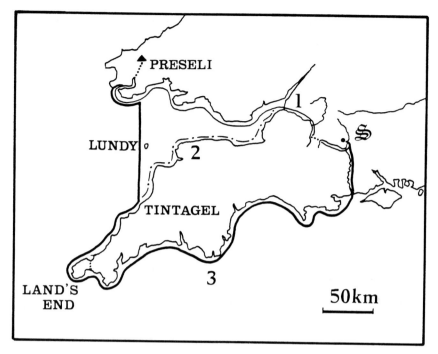

Figure 47 The bluestone routes. 1: Atkinson's (shorter) route. 2: Atkinson's (longer) coastwise route including crossing the Penwith peninsula. 3: The 'open-water' route via Lundy and Land's End. S: Stonehenge.

The simplest way round these practical and political problems would have been to keep the stones on the water and float them with care round Land's End. This would have been extremely dangerous, but the risks might be reduced by waiting, perhaps laying up for days on a beach near St Just until the sea was flat calm. Under high summer anticyclonic conditions there are usually a couple of weeks of such weather, when Land's End might be rounded in relative safety.

This, I believe, is how the bluestones were brought, with perhaps one additional piece of daring, a short-cut across the Bristol Channel. Although a coastwise voyage right round the head of the Severn estuary would have been safer, it is possible that the bluestone voyagers struck out due south when they reached Caldey Island, following the midday sun and using Lundy Island as a halfway seamark, to meet the north Cornish coast somewhere near Crackington Haven or Tintagel.[45] It may not be a coincidence that in a ravine leading down to the sea close to Tintagel there are two prehistoric rock carvings of a spiral maze, widely recognized as a symbol of a voyage or spiritual quest. The mazes may even have been carved by the bluestone adventurers themselves to ensure a safe landfall; we can be certain that they used all kinds of magic charms to make their expeditions success-ful. A little further up the same ravine is St Nectan's Kieve, a double waterfall that drops through a man-sized and entirely natural stone ring. This is known to have been a prehistoric cult site, and it even has its own folklore; it is said to have been a trysting-place where knights took solemn vows before embarking on a quest for the Grail, and to which they returned when they failed.[46]

From Mount's Bay to Stonehenge we are on a well-established and often-used neolithic and bronze age trade route, so this section of the journey is far less controversial than the rest. We know from the scatter of Cornish greenstone axes found along the Hampshire Avon valley and focusing on Christchurch Harbour in the south and the Stonehenge area in the north that traders bay-hopped along the Channel coast, carrying their goods eastwards to the fine natural harbour at Christchurch and from there paddled north-wards up the slow, twisting Avon. Axes and pottery are known to have travelled this way: possibly perishables such as salt were traded along the same route.[47] Axes made in north wales – Group VII axes were manufac-tured in the Conwy area – were also exported to the consumers by sea. The significant concentrations of foreign north Welsh axes round the shores of neolithic natural harbours like Christchurch Harbour, Pevensey Bay in Sussex and the Blackwater estuary in Essex prove this, so even longer sea journeys than the bluestone voyages were undertaken by the ancestors of the bluestone navigators.[48] It is also well established that there were specific customer-areas for particular types of axe. People in the Yorkshire Wolds liked to import Cumbrian axes, whereas those living in the Peak District preferred axes from Conwy: the preference for Cornish axes among the people of the Stonehenge and Avebury territories was thus part of a wider pattern (Figure 48). The special mystique that surrounded these coveted foreign axes persisted for a very long time. A bronze age family building a house at Thorny Down, 10 km south-east of Stonehenge, deliberately buried a piece of a Cornish greenstone axe at the bottom of one of their post-holes, and this foundation offering was made hundreds of years after the axe had been imported.[49] Another greenstone axe was buried, significantly, at the bottom of the Altar Stone's socket when it was erected in 2150 BC as part of the Double Bluestone Circle. Local people still believed in the protective power of these ancient 'thunderstones' as late as the nineteenth century AD, a late manifestation of the continuity of custom and belief that is one of the themes of this book.

The bluestone voyages were most likely following the middle part of a familiar and well-used trade route, and scattered along this trade route, along the south coast of England between Sidmouth and Christchurch, dolerite axes that can only have come from Preseli have been found.[50] Looking back in the opposite direction, we can see that axes made in Cornwall were traded by sea from south to north across the Bristol Channel; there are unusually

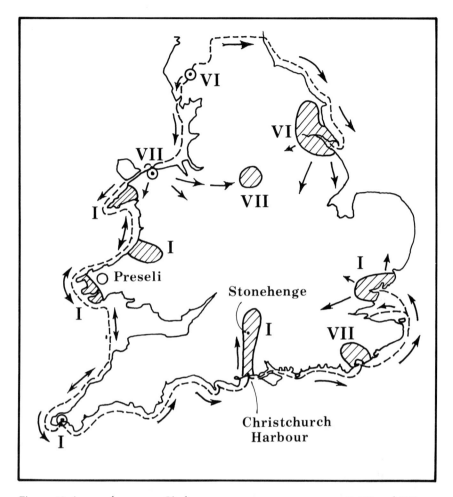

Figure 48 Axe trade routes. Circles represent axe-stone sources (I, VI and VII are types of axe-stone). Shading shows main customer areas for the three types of axe. Arrows and dashed lines show inferred axe trade routes. *Source*: Cummins 1980.

high concentrations of Cornish axes at the head of the Severn estuary, in Dyfed around Milford Haven and St Bride's Bay, at Aberystwyth in Cardigan Bay and on the Lleyn Peninsula: clearly the trade was two-way, as we might have expected.[51]

At a much earlier time, the time of the pine totem poles, there were middle stone age people living at Christchurch. They made themselves hearths out of great slabs of Purbeck Limestone which they must have carried, whether by land, river or sea, from the Isle of Purbeck. Swanage Bay, the nearest place that could have supplied the stone, was 19 km (12 miles) away to the west, although not at that time a bay: sea level was many metres lower than now. Even at that early stage, many centuries before the bluestone adventure, the people of the Avon valley were very selective about the sorts of stones they would use.[52] It is also worth remembering that the neolithic people borrowed many economic practices from their mesolithic predecessors and probably formed social relationships along similar lines.[53]

The people who built the Newgrange passage grave in Ireland in around 3100 BC, at about the same time that Stonehenge I was laid out, were also careful in their selection of stone. For the angular cobbles of white quartz which they wanted to embellish the retaining wall of the huge circular mound they were prepared to travel 80 km to the Wicklow Mountains, and this was a thousand years before the bluestone voyages.[54] People in antiquity were travelling surprisingly long distances, sometimes overland but more especially by sea, where territorial boundaries presented no problems. There are traces of sea trade routes connecting southern England and Brittany in the late neolithic and early bronze age; four Breton dolerite axes have been found in England, all, significantly, within 1 km or so of a harbour or estuary: Southampton Water, Poole Harbour and the Severn estuary. Voyages to Denmark to fetch amber must have followed the Channel coast of England as far as Dover, then the southern coast of the North Sea as far as Jutland: prehistoric amber beads have been found in Holland, halfway along this 'amber trail'.[55]

By the late neolithic there was a cluster of four settlements round the shores of Christchurch Harbour (Figure 49). The harbour was a hive of activity, probably a thoroughgoing port dealing with traders passing eastwards and westwards along the coast as well as with the transhipment of goods for Stonehenge and Avebury to the north (Plate 15). A barrow burial at one of the settlements on Hengistbury Head shows that a 20-year-old bigman there considered himself the equal in status of the chiefs of the Stonehenge and Avebury territories, wearing the same badges of status made of gold, copper and amber, the same prestigious clothing. The close similarity of these objects, even to the halberd pendants (Figure 50), proves that there was close contact, perhaps even kinship, among these three groups of people.[56]

Long after the bluestones had been unloaded on the north bank of the Avon at West Amesbury (Plate 16) and dragged up to Stonehenge, the last 3 km overland to the monument were to be marked out by the curving arc of the Stonehenge Avenue (see Chapter 8).[57] This processional way follows some of the easiest gradients out of the Avon valley and then arrives, with a sublimely appropriate gesture, along the main midsummer sunrise axis of Stonehenge. It is close to the most likely path that the bluestone-laden sledges followed as they were dragged slowly up, inch by inch, probably by teams of oxen, ready to be made into a remarkable new monument.

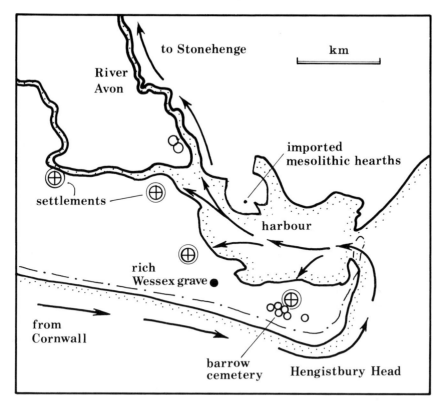

Figure 49 Christchurch Harbour in 2200 BC. Arrows show trade route from Cornwall to Stonehenge. People living in the cluster of settlements round the harbour probably handled the transhipment of goods and raw materials for Stonehenge. Dot-and-dash line represents present shoreline (rate of erosion of 0.35 m per year inferred from mean rates for the twentieth century AD). *Sources*: May 1966; Cunliffe 1987.

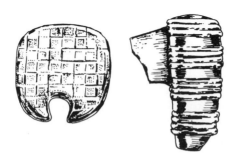

Figure 50 A gold talisman and a halberd pendant from a high-status woman's grave (Wilsford G8) in the Normanton Down cemetery.

123

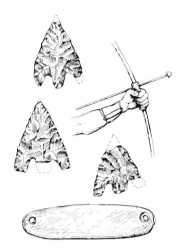

Figure 51 The three arrowheads that killed the Stonehenge archer. Below is his stone wristguard, originally worn laced to his wrist as shown top right.

A HUMAN SACRIFICE?

Once at Stonehenge, the bluestones were painstakingly battered and ground into shape and then, one by one, set up on end in paired sockets. While this slow and laborious work was going on, something strange and sinister happened. We even know the date, to within a little – 2130 BC. The evidence came to light in 1978 as archaeologists dug a trench across the silted ditch about 9 m west of the Stonehenge I entrance causeway. It was the skeleton of a healthy young man aged 25–30, who had been murdered in antiquity by being shot with arrows and then dumped in the ditch (Plate 44). In some ways he was a typical man of his time: although in generally good health he had some minor deformities, a rather twisted spine and slightly bowed legs, which together would have given him a distinctive posture and gait. If we could meet these people now, we would think them old before their time, and in fact few lived to be 40: in some areas the life expectancy was significantly shorter than that. The wear on the murdered man's ankle-bones showed that, like many of his contemporaries, he habitually squatted on his heels rather than sat when eating, chatting or relaxing.[58]

We know that the man was an archer, as a polished slate wristguard lay against his forearm where it would have protected his skin from the sting of the bowstring (Figure 51). Nothing except perhaps the power of sanctuary could have protected him from the murderous shots that killed him. Unusually for skeletons of this ancient period, there is enough forensic evidence for us to be able to reconstruct fairly precisely how he died. Three broken stone arrowheads lay beside the skeleton but, since the wristguard tells us he was an archer, they might have been part of his own equipment, perhaps ritually broken in order to make sure that they too died and travelled with him to the next world: the deliberate breaking of grave-goods in this way is common in prehistoric burials of many cultures. But the broken-off points of the three arrowheads were found embedded in his ribs. Arrows were evidently fired at close range, one from the side, one from the right into the chest and the third from behind to the left: this third shot was probably the one that actually killed him by penetrating his heart.

It was a peculiar killing. It was not a hunting accident, or a normal death in battle or skirmish. The archer was isolated, surrounded and then shot dead at short range: none of the arrows was falling. It was more like an execution than anything else and it may be that he had offended the guardians of Stonehenge by breaking one of their taboos. It is easy to imagine a great ceremonial centre like Stonehenge becoming wreathed in mystery and mystique, with special rules of conduct, with certain areas excluded from general public view and a whole battery of prohibitions relating to behaviour and possibly even dress. It would have been easy for a visiting stranger to break these taboos unwittingly. As an unusually tall stranger, 178 cm (5 ft 10 in.) tall, he would have been very conspicuous among the Stonehenge people.

Alternatively it may be that there was more than one social or ethnic group on Salisbury Plain at the time and that there was tension between them. The appearance of Beaker objects from about 2500 BC onwards suggests that at least some 'foreigners' were present in Wessex. There is no proof, no direct evidence of conflict between old and new cultures, but there is a suggestion of tension and insecurity in the region at exactly this time. The enormous ditched earthwork built 65 km (40 miles) to the south of Stonehenge at Mount Pleasant in about 2160 BC could imply the expectation of warfare, if not warfare itself. The big earthwork may have had a purely ritual purpose, like the Avebury henge, but a defensive role is implied in that shortly afterwards, in about 2020 BC, it was reinforced with a massive timber palisade. Two of the murder arrows were of a local 'Coneygar' style, so it is possible that an incomer committed some intolerable and wilful act of sacrilege and was instantly set upon by the Stonehenge people and killed. A slightly different scenario would be that he managed to elude his killers for a time, was pursued by them and ran to Stonehenge in the vain hope of finding sanctuary there: we know that he had the unusually strong leg muscles of an experienced runner.[59]

Another possibility is that the execution of this healthy, well-built 25-year-old man had a religious motive, that it was a cold-blooded human sacrifice. We know from evidence at other sacred sites that our neolithic ancestors did sacrifice people at their shrines. Not far away at Woodhenge, which was completed only shortly before, in about 2300 BC, a 3½-year-old girl was cruelly put to death with a massive axe blow on the head, a blow that split her skull in two. Her body was buried in a shallow grave close to the centre of Woodhenge. The skull was sent to the Royal College of Surgeons in 1934 for further examination and unfortunately destroyed by fire during the Second World War. The little girl's death was nevertheless obviously a human sacrifice, a dedication offering made at the time when Woodhenge was founded.[60]

Other monuments were offered human sacrifices, and it is a distinct possibility that the execution and burial of the young archer at Stonehenge was also a foundation offering.[61] The date of the sacrifice corroborates this interpretation. A corrected radiocarbon date for the victim's left thigh bone gives us the approximate calendar date of his death – 2130 BC. The radiocarbon dates for the antler picks found in the Avenue ditch give us the most likely date for the Double Bluestone Circle, 2170–2130 BC. Not far from Stonehenge there is corroboration of this date for the Bluestone Circle. A bowl barrow just to the south of the Great Cursus and excavated by William Cunnington in the nineteenth century was reopened by Paul Ashbee in 1960. In a large central grave there was a mortuary house made of jointed timbers. It contained the skeleton of a man folded up in the usual crouched position, and he had been buried with a disc of bone that had been removed from his skull: evidently he was the victim of unsuccessful early bronze age surgery.[62] After this initial burial, a round barrow was raised over the wooden house and secondary burials were added. A wooden tool buried with one of these later burials was radiocarbon dated to 2130 BC. Chips of bluestone – rhyolite in this case – were scattered throughout the mound, showing without any doubt that Stonehenge bluestones were being shaped nearby at the time when the barrow was raised.[63] In the dates 2130 BC, 2170–2130 BC and 2130 BC we have strong, convergent evidence that the young man was sacrificed at the very time when Stonehenge II was being built.

At the timber circle at Sarn-y-Bryn-Caled in Powys a strikingly similar human sacrifice was carried out. Cremated human remains were found in a pit right at the centre of the circle, together with four prestigious arrowheads that had not been burnt as severely as might have been expected, presumably because they were embedded in flesh at the time of the cremation. *Four* shots seem too many for a hunting accident: it also seems unlikely that this was an executed criminal because the burial was located in a place of honour. Sacrifice seems the most natural explanation and it is significant that it took place, to judge from the style of the arrowheads, at about the same period as the Stonehenge sacrifice.[64]

The Stonehenge builders may have needed to carry out a reconsecration sacrifice because the creation of the Double Bluestone Circle was such a significant alteration to the monument, and possibly also because they had neglected the site for so long. As if confirming the connection between the young archer's death and the raising of the bluestone ring, a few bluestone chips from the masons' workings were kicked into his grave by his killers.

THE DOUBLE RING AND THE AVENUE

Meanwhile the bluestones were slowly being dressed to shape, using techniques very similar to those used later on the sarsens from Avebury. This detail suggests that it was the same people, the Stonehenge people, who shaped both lots of stones. Three of the bluestones show traces of the shallow transverse grooving which was a kind of preliminary dressing, but most of the surfaces were later worked to a smooth finish, probably by people pecking over them with hammer stones and then rubbing them with grinders. Even though the tools were of the simplest type imaginable – unshaped stones – the workmanship is of an extraordinarily high standard. Perhaps even more extraordinary is that, given the virtuoso handling of stone displayed here, it seems never to have been used, copied or imitated in any way in a later monument, except at Stonehenge itself. In this respect Stonehenge really was unique.

We know from the pattern of the surviving sockets that the complete bluestone circle design required eighty-two uprights.[65] But we also know that lintels were used in the design, because one or two were later reused as uprights when they were incorporated into the design of Stonehenge III. Since the Stonehenge II pillars were arranged in pairs, it seems likely that each pair was intended to carry a lintel. If the groups of three and four uprights at the entrance were capped by running lintels, as their running sockets imply, a total of forty-two lintels would have been needed; to this we must add the Altar Stone, which stood upright on its own on the southwest side of the double circle, making an overall total of 125 stones (Figures 52 and 55).

Uprights	82
Lintels	42
Altar Stone	1
TOTAL	125

There may have been additional lintels crossing the entrance colonnade, to accentuate the illusion of entering a once-roofed but now ruined building.

Where the paired stone-holes are rather far apart, larger than normal bluestones would have been required. Although these would have been available in the Preseli Hills, perhaps it would be more cautious to propose as an alternative lintels made of timber. A timber-and-stone monument is a real possibility and one that has not been given sufficient consideration. Obviously no traces of above-ground timber components have survived, but that does not mean that they did not once exist. It is known that wooden monuments were often replaced or commemorated by stone ones, for

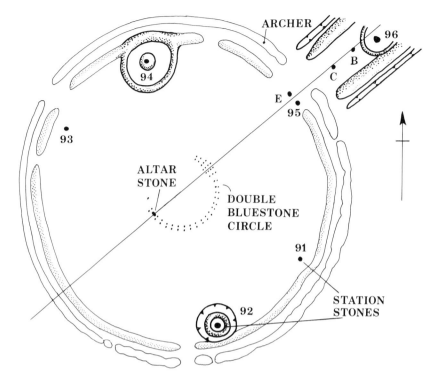

Figure 52 Plan of Stonehenge II.

example at the Sanctuary near Avebury and the Lochhill Long Cairn. The timber circle at Street House in Cleveland from around 2150 BC, the same time as Stonehenge II, combined timber and stone with a boulder set strategically in the centre of each of its four palisaded entrances.[66] Stone 150 is the only stone lintel to have survived into the later Bluestone Circle, recycled as an upright, and it can still be seen on the site today. With a length of 2.5 m it was certainly long enough to have acted as a lintel for the paired uprights of the Q and R holes, but its mortices are only 1.04 m apart, centre to centre, when they would have needed to be 1.28 m apart to span the Q and R holes. This stone must therefore have served as a lintel on a bluestone trilithon in some intermediate stage instead.

The double circle with its north-east entrance was laid out on the same midsummer sunrise axis as Stonehenge I, which proves that the ancient purpose and design of the monument had not been forgotten: indeed it argues strongly for a continuity of tradition and use during the time when we may have thought the site was abandoned.[67] The Stonehenge II builders gave the ancient magical alignment extra emphasis by building a straight length of avenue out from the earth circle's entrance towards the north-east.

Plate 20 The Great Sarsen Circle at Stonehenge, from left to right stones 7, 6, 5, 4, 3 and 2.

The Avenue cannot have been part of the Stonehenge I design because the end of the Avenue is much wider than the Stonehenge I entrance causeway: they were not part of the same design at all. Colonel Hawley found that nearly 8 m (26 ft) of the Stonehenge I ditch on the south-east side of the entrance had been filled in during the making of Stonehenge II, and this would have had the effect of broadening the entrance to match the width of the Avenue.[68] The clean chalk that fills the ditch to a depth of 0.9 m (3 ft) shows that the ditch was open to that depth when the rubble was thrown in, and that level also corresponds to the level where the earliest chips of bluestone and pieces of Beaker pottery have been found.[69]

All the archaeological evidence points to the same thing: the north-east entrance to Stonehenge, its ritual entrance, was remodelled and embellished with a straight stretch of avenue at the same time that the Double Bluestone Circle was built (Figure 52). As suggested earlier, one motive for laying out the Avenue was to mark and commemorate the processional way used for hauling the bluestones up from the bank of the River Avon, but it is really only the much later section of the Avenue that can be matched persuasively with this route: the first (Stonehenge II) section was oriented unequivocally on the midsummer sunrise. Curiously, this initial stretch is also aligned on a point in the cursus bank where there is an entrance gap in it, although this alignment may have been quite unintentional.

The width of the Avenue seems to have been fixed partly by the position of the earlier entrance. The Avenue's north-west ditch was lined up on the north-west edge of the Stonehenge I entrance causeway. The centre-line of the Avenue was fixed by the main axis of the monument as a whole, and the south-east Avenue ditch had to be an equal distance from that centre-line. This gives a total width of 21 m (70 ft). While the work on the Avenue was going on one of the Heel Stones, stone 97, was taken down and the survivor, stone 96, was given ritual protection by a circular ditch. I can offer no explanation at all for the removal of stone 97: as far as I know, no one has yet offered a plausible explanation. The pair of Heel Stones made a perfect ritual doorway for the midsummer sun, and it is clear from the creation of the Avenue and the elaborate entrance to the Double Bluestone Circle that that alignment was still of paramount importance in Stonehenge II. If marking the midsummer sunrise had lost its importance by then, or if it was to be marked instead by the erection of stones B and C on the axial line itself, then it would have made more sense to take down *both* Heel Stones, not just one.

The soil and chalk rubble dug out of the two Avenue ditches were piled up to make two internal banks. The ditches have been ploughed over so that they are now barely perceptible: the lines of the banks can sometimes be made out by the thicker growth of thistles on them. Unfortunately what must originally have been quite an imposing feature in its own right has all but vanished from the landscape.[70] The processional way enclosed between the Avenue banks was about 12 m (39 ft or 16 Beaker Yards) wide.

The idea of adding an avenue to a circular temple was not unique to Stonehenge. The huge megalithic henge at Avebury originally had two ceremonial approaches marked out by paired standing stones. Two of the Stanton Drew stone circles near Bristol have short megalithic avenues too. Callanish on the Isle of Lewis had four such avenues. The kinship between Stonehenge II and these other late neolithic or early bronze age monuments may have been even closer, since there were probably stones placed at intervals along the Stonehenge Avenue's earth banks. There was a short stone avenue leading into the west side of the Meini-gwyr stone circle, close to the source of the bluestones, on the bluestone route, and made originally of seventeen bluestones. The Stonehenge people would have seen this struc-ture as they collected their stones, and may have collected the embanked stone avenue idea too. The avenue bank at least at Meini-gwyr was disused by the middle bronze age, implying that this monument, like Stonehenge II, may have had but a short life.[71] Gors Fawr, a circle of seventeen bluestones even closer to the bluestone source, has two outlying standing stones about 130 m away to the north of the circle; a line running from south-west to north-east and joining the two outliers may possibly have indicated the direction of the midsummer sunrise: if so, here too is an idea in common with Stonehenge.[72]

No stones at all remain of the Stonehenge Avenue and we must assume that they were grubbed out long ago by farmers who found them in their way. Even in William Stukeley's day there were no stones to be seen, but he provides us with the evidence we need: 'It may be reckoned bold to assert an Avenue at Stonehenge when there is not one stone left, but I did not invent it, having been able to measure the very intervals of almost every Stone, from the manifest hollows left in their stations and probably they were taken away when Christianity first prevaild here.'[73] Stukeley's friend Roger Gale wrote to him in 1740, after Stukeley's book about Stonehenge had been published, rebuking him for not mentioning the Avenue stones: 'I think you have omitted a remarkable particular, which is that the avenue up to the chief entrance was formerly planted with great stones, opposite to each other on the side banks of it.'[74]

Geophysical soundings taken through the soil for the first 240 m of the Avenue indicate spot-disturbances in the Avenue bank which represent the probable positions of some of the Avenue stone-sockets.[75] My interpret-ation of the data reveals a pattern of eight pairs of stone–holes spaced about 28.5 m (39 Beaker Yards) apart, starting 28.5 m outside the Heel Stone; interestingly, the Heel Stones were set up 28.5 m outside the earth circle, so the Stonehenge II design was in a very real way a sensitive development of the Stonehenge I design – yet another indication of continuity (Figure 53). It is not known whether the Avenue stones were bluestones or sarsens. Excavation might resolve this question: if the floors of the sockets have survived, some broken-off pieces of the uprooted stones may still rest there.

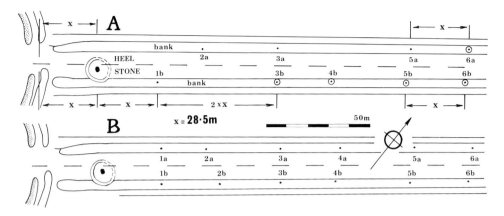

Figure 53 The Stonehenge Avenue rediscovered. A: stone-sockets detected in resistivity (dots) and magnetometer (circled dots) surveys. B: the completed pattern – 2b and 4a are added from slight indications on the survey data, 28.5 m out from 1b and 3a.

The Avenue idea was repeated at other sites. The Double Bluestone Circle design was original and not, as far as I know, imitated or foreshadowed anywhere else. The paired stones were set in unusual dumb-bell-shaped sockets with each pair of stones probably carrying a radial lintel. These are known as the Q and R holes, R being the inner ring, Q the outer.[76] Given the spacing of the sockets and the shapes of the surviving recycled stones, each of these megalithic structures would have made a doorway rather wider and lower than a modern house door, typically 1.6 m high and 2 m or so wide overall. It is nevertheless not likely that the builders intended the resulting trilithon (literally 'three stones') to be or even symbolize a doorway, not least because their doorways were small and often very constricted indeed.

In plan, seen from the air, the design fitted with lintels looked like the rays of the sun drawn the way children and 'primitives' often draw them; in fact this same symbol can be seen pecked out of stone on a much smaller scale in both neolithic and bronze age rock art at other sites. There are several neolithic sun symbols carved on the stones of Newgrange, the Irish temple-tomb which housed the dead and also celebrated the midwinter sunrise (Figure 73). One Newgrange sun symbol was actually pecked onto the decorated lintel of the roof-box that was specially made to let the rays of the rising sun into the centre of the tomb on the winter solstice (Figure 54). So there can be no doubt that a circle with short radial rays, or a set of radial rays on their own, symbolized the sun in the minds of neolithic people. We know from the design and orientation of Stonehenge I, which was built at about the same time as Newgrange, that it was a sun-temple. This deliberate

Figure 54 Symbols carved on the roofbox at Newgrange. The hidden sunburst symbol secretly celebrates the midwinter dawn.

and self-conscious addition of a stone sun symbol in Stonehenge II confirms it.

Curiously, the internal diameter of the Bluestone Circle, 22 m, or 30 Beaker Yards, is the same as the diameters of two of the Preseli stone circles. Gors Fawr has a diameter of 22.3 m, Dyffryn Syfynwy 22 m. Meini-gwyr is a little smaller, with a diameter of 18.3 m, or 25 Beaker Yards. Was the Stonehenge circle a deliberate copy of one of the Preseli circles, or was some magic number perhaps incorporated in its dimensions? The coincidence is unlikely to be accidental. It was probably also deliberate that the 22 m and 26 m diameter double ring of stones at Stonehenge more or less coincided with the site of the old 25 m diameter wooden building that had stood at the centre of Stonehenge I centuries before.[77] In the south-east quadrant of Stonehenge the arc of R holes coincides almost exactly with that of the early wooden building: the arc of the later bluestone circle, built in Stonehenge III, follows the same path again. The circles had different centres so their circumferences do not coincide all the way round: they are nevertheless close enough to suggest that a deliberate commemoration of the early timber rotunda was intended. The late neolithic and early bronze age monument-builders often commemorated older, ruined timber structures by building stone ones on the same sites (Figure 72). This point also reinforces the idea of a continuous tradition from Stonehenge I to Stonehenge II, across the period of neglect.

Adding a stone circle to an older earth circle may be a reflection of Stonehenge's frontier location, on the boundary of two cultural provinces. The earth circle had its origins in the English lowlands where the soil, then as now, was soft and deep and it was easy to dig a ditch and raise an earth bank. In the highlands of the west the soil was, then just as it is now, thin and stony and the underlying rock was hard to excavate. Generally the neolithic highlanders found it easier to mark out their sacred precincts with boulders or slabs planted in a ring. The two temple-building traditions seem to have developed in parallel for a time, but in the later neolithic a cross-fertilization took place. So, at Avebury some four hundred years after the henge was laid out a great circle of sarsen stones was added. After a longer delay, the double stone circle was added at Stonehenge too. The Stonehenge that we see now is a classic case of an idea invented, exported, developed and then reimported in its transformed state – a little like the English pop singers who sing even their own songs with American accents.

It would be all too easy to overlook the insignificant-looking Station Stones. Although they are sarsens, these four stones (stones 91–4) seem to have been put in position during the bluestone phase. They were placed just inside the henge bank at the corners of a large rectangle 80 m by 35 m, the shorter sides of which were oriented south-west to north-east, parallel to the main axis of the bluestone circle. Stones 92 and 94 have long since gone and their positions concealed by low mounds; stone 93 is a reshaped stump only 1 m high and stone 91 is 3 m long and prostrate (Plate 17). The socket of the missing stone 94 was not discovered until 1978: it was cut through an Aubrey Hole, which shows that it belongs to a later stage than Stonehenge I, and this is why we place it and the other Station Stones in Stonehenge II. Another reason for putting the Station Stones in Stonehenge II is that the rectangle's diagonals intersect at a point which coincides with the centres of Stonehenges II and III, 1 m north of the centre of Stonehenge I; this implies that the Station Stones were not part of the Stonehenge I design but were added afterwards.

It is often assumed, although not proved, that the low Station Stones were used as astronomical sights. If that is so, the view along the diagonals would have been clear in Stonehenge II because the bluestones were quite low, but obstructed in Stonehenge III once the tall sarsens were in place. This again points to their belonging to Stonehenge II. There is another possibility which is attractive and that is that the Station Stones belong to an in-between stage, after Stonehenge I but before Stonehenge II: really there is not enough evidence to be sure. If the Station Stone setting seems odd in relation to the rest of the Stonehenge design, it was by no means unique in the megalithic vocabulary. In Brittany, there is a similar setting known as the Crucuno rectangle, not far from Carnac. This is smaller than the British setting, about 33 m from east to west and 25 m from north to south, but clearly belongs to the same belief system. The east–west orientation of the long sides of the Crucuno rectangle implies that they were designed to indicate the equinox sunrises or sunsets.[78] As we shall see later, this is by no means the only parallel between developments at Stonehenge and developments in Brittany.

THE CENTRE-PIECE

The entrance to the Double Bluestone Circle was emphasized by adding extra stones, the pairs becoming triplets and then double-pairs. The builders did this partly to increase the magical strength of the monument and partly to emphasize its orientation towards the midsummer sunrise. The eight pillars of the entrance passage made a double colonnade, foreshadowing an idea that would be taken up again much later, in classical architecture (Figure

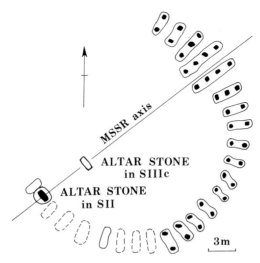

Figure 55 Plan of the Double Bluestone Circle at Stonehenge. Note the curious double sockets. MSSR: midsummer sunrise.

56). The rays of the newly risen sun on midsummer morning shone directly over the tops of stones B and C, which were the old inner portal stones repositioned on the monument's main axis, passed along the bluestone colonnade, crossed the open space at the centre and lit up the pale green face of the Altar Stone on the circle's far side.

The Altar Stone must therefore have been regarded as the centre-piece of the whole design, and almost certainly as some kind of idol. The stone is big – 4.9 m (16 ft) long, 1 m wide and 0.5 m thick, rectangular in cross-section – and must once have stood some 4.3 m (14 ft) tall. This once-revered goddess-stone now lies ignominiously fallen across its later socket, crushed and degraded under a sprawl of other fallen stones, one of its grey-green surfaces just showing at ground level (Plate 18). There is, nevertheless, every reason to see it as the one-time focus of attention and worship in Stonehenge II.

A large circular pit was found where the main axis crosses the south-west sector of the Q and R circles: this pit was obviously intended for a stone that was much larger than the rest of the bluestones, a description that fits only the Altar Stone, and it was placed very significantly facing the entrance colonnade. When the pit was excavated a stone axe was found at the bottom, with its cutting edge (deliberately?) battered off. The axe was *Cornish* and may even have been picked up at Mount's Bay at the time when the Altar Stone itself was being ferried to Stonehenge: it was deliberately placed in the stone-socket as a foundation offering. If this large pit did indeed house the Altar Stone in Stonehenge II, as my plan and reconstruction show (Figures 55 and 56), it must have been moved off-site with the rest of the bluestones

135

for a time while the big sarsen stones were dragged into position and hauled upright. When the Altar Stone was brought back again and raised in its new position closer to the centre of Stonehenge is not known, but it seems likely from its size and focal position that it was the first bluestone to return. My feeling is that it was part of the Stonehenge IIIa design – probably the last piece to be added to it – and that it was only removed from the central precinct for the shortest possible time to make space to raise the trilithons. Like the Cornish axe that marked its first dedication, the Altar Stone was a green stone, the irregular waving layers within it giving its surface a swirling, marbled effect when it was first dressed and polished, like the grain of an exotic timber.

Pillars like the Altar Stone stand in places of honour at other late neolithic and bronze age sites, such as the roughly contemporary temple of Hagar Qim on Malta or, closer to home, the Bryn Celli Ddu passage grave on Anglesey. We can, if we want to, see them as phallic fertility symbols, and it may be that our ancestors saw them in that way too. Or we can see them as representatives of a deity, perhaps of the sun-god himself or, more likely, of the earth-goddess he was visiting on the solstice. A few of the megalithic idols that have survived are primitively shaped, with suggestions of shoulders and breasts, and this proves that they are intended as representations of the goddess. Those lone standing stones that do not have the tell-tale breasts or other anatomical hints may nevertheless also be idols, but of a type that is sometimes called 'aniconic', meaning a non-representational substitute for the goddess, or even a dwelling-place that she may in some sense inhabit.

With all these ideas in mind, there can be little doubt that the Altar Stone – a large slab-like pillar set apart from the other stones – was intended either as a representation of the goddess or as a dwelling-place for her. The goddess-stone at Stonehenge is made of Cosheston sandstone, a rock that can only have been gathered at Llangwm near the shore of Milford Haven, so it is likely to have been gathered at the same time and by the same route as the other stones. When in its original position and standing 4 m or so tall, it dominated the 22 m (72 ft) diameter holy of holies, commanding the centre space of Stonehenge.

All this is hard to visualize at the site today, now that the Stonehenge II structure has been completely demolished and replaced and the Altar Stone lies crushed underneath a collapsing later structure, so I have sketched a reconstruction which gives an impression of the appearance of the Double Bluestone Circle as it *would* have looked if completed (Figure 56). Original and startling though the bluestone design was, work on it stopped when the building was about two-thirds finished. The bluestone adventure would have been an extraordinary episode in Britain's prehistory even if the monument had been completed to that design and left unaltered for ever after. But for it to be scrapped a little over halfway through in favour of

Figure 56 How the Double Bluestone Circle at Stonehenge might have looked had it been completed.

another large-scale project, using another lot of stones, makes us gasp in wonder at our ancestors' ambition and extravagance.

The Stonehenge people went to colossal lengths to build the Double Bluestone Circle, and yet they rejected it. The fact that they did this shows that they did not regard themselves as functioning at a subsistence level, as savages desperately scratching a meagre existence in a hostile landscape, as victims of their environment. They saw themselves as masters of their landscape, capable of organizing enormous projects, and flexible enough to change them even when a huge commitment of time and resources had been made. They did in fact command surprisingly large resources, not the least of which was determination. We might have thought that gathering between 80 and 125 4-tonne megaliths from Wales would of itself have exhausted a small-scale archaic society, even if the bands living in a score of neighbouring territories joined forces. Not a bit of it. Far from exhausting themselves on the bluestone enterprise and then basking in the sunshine of its accomplishment, they threw the design to the winds in favour of an even grander scheme using much larger stones.

If we find it hard to understand why they went to the trouble of hauling bluestones from Wales to embellish their monument, it is even harder to understand why they cast them aside, virtually on arrival. There is a multiple mystery here, and we need to imagine what reasoning may have lain behind these critical changes of mind. Why did the Stonehenge people stop work on their bluestone project? What attracted them to the idea of using much larger stones from the Avebury area instead, an area where stone circles had already been raised and where the people had apparently gone over to building huge round enclosures in timber rather than stone?[79] And – something which is often overlooked – what happened to the bluestones, brought from Wales with such care and at such great human cost, after the Stonehenge II design was scrapped?

6

CULMINATION: THE SARSEN MONUMENT

When you enter the building, whether on foot or horseback, and cast your eyes around the yawning ruins, you are struck into an extatic reverie, which none can describe, and they only can be sensible of it, that feel it. Other buildings fall by piece-meal: but here a single stone is a ruin, and lies like the haughty carcase of Goliath . . . When we advance farther, the dark part of the ponderous imposts over our heads, the chasm of sky between the jambs of the cell, the odd construction of the whole, and the greatness of every part surprises.

William Stukeley, *Stonehenge*, 1743

RICH BURIALS AND SOCIAL TRANSFORMATION

It was in about 2100 BC that Stonehenge began its most remarkable transformation. The half-finished Double Bluestone Circle was taken down and, apparently straight away, the sarsen monument was built in its place. Many questions are raised by this turn of events. Why was the bluestone monument abandoned before it was even finished? Why did the builders feel a need to attempt a much more ambitious design in its place? Why were sarsens used for the new monument rather than bluestones? Where did the sarsens come from and how were these very hard and heavy stones transported, shaped and raised?

In order to answer these questions convincingly we need to put the events into a social and cultural context and for Stonehenge IIIa, which is what archaeologists call the sarsen monument, that evidence comes largely from contemporary burials near Stonehenge. It has often been commented that the plain round Stonehenge is spattered with round barrows of every conceivable type, many of them dating from the late phase of the monument's development that began with the raising of the sarsens. Within a radius of 6 km of Stonehenge there are at least ten cemeteries or barrow clusters as well as over a hundred isolated barrows (Figure 58).[1]

There had been long barrow burials here a thousand years earlier, and the late neolithic and early bronze age barrows were often built close to these

Plate 21 Stone 60 at Stonehenge, expertly shaped into a rectangular pillar.

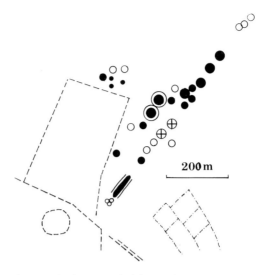

Figure 57 Winterbourne Stoke: a typical linear barrow cemetery near Stonehenge. The axis of the long barrow controlled later developments, even the location of three bronze age houses at its south-west end. Dashed lines are ancient boundary ditches. Dot-and-dash lines show a bronze age field system. Black-filled circle: bowl barrow. Crossed circle: bell barrow. Open circle: pond barrow, saucer barrow or levelled barrow. Black-filled circle inside open circle: disc barrow.

ancestral tombs. People were remembering and confirming their ties with the land. Sometimes, as at Winterbourne Stoke crossroads, new barrows and even new houses were built on the same alignment as the old long barrow's axis, as if the builders were conscientiously honouring an ancient tryst (Figure 57). Aubrey Burl has developed the idea that Stonehenge was a mortuary house, a place where the dead were laid out before burial, and he implies that its position at the heart of the massive concentration of burials confirms this interpretation.[2] Certainly the association is strong, and yet there is a marked *absence* of barrows very close to Stonehenge. Sir William Flinders Petrie, who carried out the first accurate survey of Stonehenge itself, compiled a table showing the numbers of barrows lying within certain distances of Stonehenge.[3]

Distance from Stonehenge (miles)	Number of barrows	Number per sq. mile
0–1/2	17	22
1/2–1	89	38
1–1 1/2	92	23
1 1/2–2	66	12
2–3	74	5
3–5	87	2

Petrie's table neatly makes the point that although the density of barrows is indeed high in the Stonehenge area it is actually highest in the zone 1/2–1

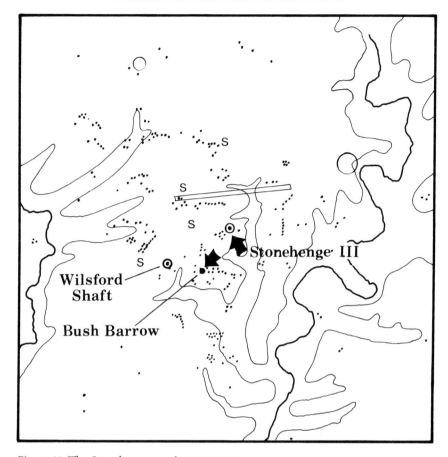

Figure 58 The Stonehenge area in 2100–1600 BC.

mile away from the monument: there are no barrows at all within 150 m of Stonehenge. This implies that whilst higher status was conferred on a burial by placing it within sight of Stonehenge there was some taboo on barrow burial at the monument itself, which was set aside for some other purpose. Nor could we argue that Stonehenge was designed exclusively or primarily for funeral rituals on the strength of the non-barrow burials on the site. We would not contemplate arguing that because Westminster Abbey houses many burials it was purpose-built as a charnel house; the great have been buried there because it has a special numen, special associations acquired over the course of centuries. So too, in all probability, had Stonehenge – and that is why Wessex chieftains and their families wanted to be buried within sight of it.

The contents of these high-status burials are very different in conception and implication from the earlier long barrow burials. The early burials were frankly poor, often with minimal or no grave-goods, and they imply a society in which all (adults at least) were equal. Such organization as there was – and the building of large monuments like causewayed enclosures and cursus monuments tells us that some form of social organization existed – presumably sprang from a village bigman or headman. He would have acted, like his present-day New Guinea counterparts, as a discussion chairman, work co-ordinator and foreman, although he may not have been held in any special awe or have been given any special rights, an equal among equals.[4] There is an occasional glimpse of a middle or late neolithic bigman in the first burial marking the beginning of a communal tomb's history, but this is rare.[5] It becomes commoner in the late neolithic for grave-goods to be added, particularly to male burials. Indeed, it looks as if from 3000 BC onwards, men began to achieve a much higher social status than women. As part of this 'status-split', which began with the building of Stonehenge I, it is likely that other differences emerged, with some men acquiring significantly higher status than others by the late neolithic.[6] The appearance of chieftains round about 2100 BC led to more changes: they seem to have exalted not only themselves but also their families, unless some of the chieftains were women, which is not impossible.[7]

With these major social changes in mind, we can explore the contents of some of the barrows near Stonehenge and piece together something of the society that produced Stonehenge IIIa. The Normanton Down Barrows form a straggling linear cemetery along the ridge 1 km to the south of Stonehenge, and visible as a clear skyline feature from Stonehenge. Amongst the spatter of low rounded bumps and discs is the Bush Barrow, which is thought to be contemporary with the building of Stonehenge IIIa (Plate 19).[8]

When Cunnington excavated the barrow in 1808 he found, lying on its back on the old ground surface, the skeleton of 'a stout and tall man lying from south to north: the extreme length of his thigh was 20 inches'. Close to his head were pieces of wood and bronze together with some rivets, perhaps the disintegrated remains of a wooden-framed leather helmet. Next to his left shoulder was a bronze axe that had rested on some woollen cloth, possibly a fold of his cloak. Next to his right forearm there were two daggers side by side, one made of copper and housed in a leather-lined sheath, the other heavier and made of bronze with a central midrib. Part of one of the wooden pommels survived, decorated with zig-zag patterns 'with a labour and exactness almost unaccountable, by thousands of gold rivets, smaller than the smallest pin'.[9] The work was so fine that it is hard to see how it could have been done without the use of a piece of polished crystal or quartz as a magnifying glass. If this seems too unlikely to be worth considering, much of the miniature artwork done by Minoan craftsmen at Knossos in about 1700 BC must have been done with the aid of magnifying glasses of some kind. One miniature painting of a bull depicted on the flat side of a

142

crystal plaque found at Knossos was not only painted with the help of a quartz magnifier, but it also actually exploits the magnifying property of the crystal on which it is painted. If such things were possible on Crete in 1700 BC, then they were just possible in early bronze age Wessex too.[10]

Near the daggers Cunnington found a finely made gold belt-buckle delicately engraved with curving lines following, with machine-like accuracy, the curved edge of the plate. There had perhaps been a third dagger in the man's right hand, but it was badly corroded and fell to pieces when Cunnington tried to remove it. On the man's chest, originally sewn with thread onto a woven tunic, was a wafer-thin sheet of gold as big as a hand and shaped like a diamond: it was engraved with four more sets of lozenges, nested one within another, a zig-zag round the outside and a cross-hatched diamond in the centre. Near his right hand were the remains of a sceptre, a ceremonial mace: its head was a rare, flecked limestone that had come from Devon, polished into an egg shape and drilled through to house a wooden handle. The shaft had rotted away, but what may have been its decorative mountings – six short cylinders of bone delicately carved into zig-zags – survived.[11]

A sharply focused picture emerges from the detail: the large barrow, the woven cloth, the axe, the sceptre, the two or three rich metal daggers and the beautiful gold work all point to the princely rank of the man buried in the Bush Barrow (Figure 59). Nor was this the only rich burial in the cemetery. 150 m away to the east stands a bowl barrow which is thought to be the grave of a high-status woman. It yielded a shale bead wrapped in gold, shale and amber pendants, fragments of gold sheet and two tubular fossils perforated to turn them into beads. North-north-east of this at a distance of 100 m is a bell barrow (Wilsford South 8) which may also have contained a high-status female. A gold-covered shale button, a bone pendant, six amber pendants, a gold-bound amber pendant and two gold-bound amber discs perforated perhaps for use as earrings were found in this rich barrow; there were also a bronze pendant like a miniature neck-ring sheathed in gold foil, a halberd pendant with an amber and gold handle, and a low 'incense' pot with open ribbed sides. Sir Richard Colt Hoare wrote, 'No barrow that we have yet opened has ever produced such a variety of singular and elegant articles'.[12]

Gold burials are uncommon. To find more than one gold burial within a cemetery does seem to indicate unusual wealth and status, and it may be that there were more than the three described: three more bowl barrows have been plundered without any record or even rumour of their contents surviving. The fact that these barrows and their neighbours are visible on the ridge-crest south of Stonehenge carries with it a powerful implication. Were these rich people members of the 'ruling family' (whatever that may have meant four thousand years ago) at Stonehenge in the years around 2100 BC? Was the Bush Barrow chieftain the bigman who ordered and organized the building of Stonehenge III? It has seemed to several scholars a strong possibility.[13] Professor Lord Renfrew has said in a television programme that he thinks the Bush Barrow chieftain must have been the Lord of Stonehenge and, given the royal paraphernalia, possibly even Paramount Chief of Southern England.[14] Certainly the Bush Barrow chieftain was a high-status figure of considerable power and wealth.

On the other hand, he was not the only high-status figure in the Stonehenge area. We have already seen that two princesses were buried within 180 m of the Bush Barrow. They may have been warrior-queens – and there were other barrow cemeteries close to Stonehenge that had royal burials too. Due south of the Bush Barrow at a distance of 1 1/2 km is a bell barrow known as Wilsford South 58. This is the westernmost barrow in the Wilsford group, standing on the north flank of Lake Down, the next ridge to the south of Normanton Down. When Cunnington opened this bell barrow in 1807 he found the skeleton of a tall, well-built man lying on his right side with his head to the south-east: this unusual position enabled the dead chieftain to cast his eyes northwards towards Stonehenge. His high status is shown by his grave-goods – a flanged bronze axe, a dolerite battle-axe, a huge boar's tusk, a grooved whetstone made of Forest Marble and a strange bronze object like a two-pronged toasting fork. This object may have been a royal standard, a mounting for a swinging pendant or a narrow woven pennant; the three rivet-holes show that it was originally mounted on a wooden shaft and three bronze rings nearby may have been fittings for the pennant.[15]

All the evidence indicates that this goldless burial was also that of a great chief. There are, in other words, several candidates that we can point to in the Stonehenge cemeteries for the title 'Lord of Stonehenge' and we should not be too hasty in identifying the Bush Barrow chieftain as the man who ordered the building of the sarsen monument. It is a great pity that there are no absolute dates for any of these royal burials. A calibrated radiocarbon date of 2100 BC for the Bush Barrow chieftain, for example, would strongly support, though still not prove, the widely felt view that he was the chief responsible for Stonehenge IIIa. On the other hand, a date three hundred years later, which would be equally consistent with the finds, would put him out of the running.[16]

The bronze age idea of rich grave-goods was a novel one, newer and more revolutionary than we can now visualize. For perhaps the first time in Britain's story, people began to think of expressing their individuality and social status in terms of prestige possession. Now, perhaps, we take personal ownership too much for granted: it is a commonplace of everyday life. Then, it was revolutionary. The status-split and the use of personal possessions as status symbols led to a demand for those possessions – and to begin with at any rate they were in short supply. A powerful stimulus to trade, gift-exchange and very likely ultimately warfare was unleashed in Britain: hence

Figure 59 The Lord of Stonehenge? The Bush Barrow chieftain may have looked like this. The helmet is speculatively reconstructed from an area 30 cm across, close to the head, with thin sheets of bronze, traces of wood and thirty-three bronze rivets.

the conspicuousness of axes and daggers in the chieftains' graves. It was the beginning, among other things, of the English class war.[17]

These were the causes and the symptoms of a large-scale social transformation in the Stonehenge area; these lay behind the Stonehenge people's decision to rebuild Stonehenge in a more grandiose and flamboyant way than before. How far these ideas were stimulated from outside Wessex we cannot tell, but large-scale monument-building occurred in Brittany too and there are significant parallels between the way the rich and powerful were buried in Brittany and Wessex: in both, for example, there are daggers with hilts decorated with tiny gold pins. Whether the cross-Channel contact was entirely a trading one, or whether there was a social, spiritual or political bond of some kind linking the two regions is not yet clear. Breton monuments in use in 3000 BC had been decommissioned by 2300 BC, implying a parallel with Stonehenge I, and Mark Patton suggests that the social elite responsible for raising the Carnac stone rows simply collapsed, to be replaced later by entirely separate bronze age chiefdoms.[18]

THE AVEBURY CONNECTION

Why was the bluestone design abandoned? One possibility is that the source of supply for the bluestones dried up. If the bluestone voyages were spread over two or more decades, as would be the case if only four stones were fetched each summer, it is possible that the relationship between Wessex and Preseli shifted significantly during that time. Perhaps there was some failure of diplomacy, an incident of some kind. Perhaps the Welsh suppliers became uncooperative for some reason and refused access to the hillside where the stones lay. Cut off from their supplies and with an ambitious monument half-built, the Stonehenge people had to look elsewhere. But the social and cultural transformation that was under way in Wessex in 2100 BC is sufficient to explain why the Stonehenge people wanted to remodel Stonehenge in bigger stones. The difficulty was that no large stones were available on Salisbury Plain. No one any longer seriously believes that the seventy-five new sarsens needed to build Stonehenge III were found lying on the ground close to the site: the arguments against this are too strong. Where, for instance, are the spare, rejected and undersized sarsens to be found? If there had once been sarsens scattered across the Stonehenge site, we would expect some of them to have been used to build megalithic tombs like the West Kennet Long Barrow or the Devil's Den near Avebury, yet there are none in the vicinity of Stonehenge, only earthen long barrows: the nearest megalithic tomb is 22 km away at Tidcombe. There is corroboration too from the traditional domestic architecture of the area; sarsen is not seen in the walls of houses and churches on Salisbury Plain and we do not come across it until we reach the villages round Avebury: it is from there that Stonehenge's sarsens must have been brought.[19] Once again the builders brought raw materials in from a significant distance away, from outside their territory, and we should see this as a normal early bronze age phenomenon. Bronze age Scandinavians, for instance, made and used metal objects, yet without touching any local sources of copper, tin or gold, even though Scandinavian copper ores at least were available. Instead the metal ores were brought in from the Harz Mountains and Bohemia, 300 km away, implying a large-scale organizational structure and exchanges of some kind, perhaps of amber and furs.[20] Seen in this context, the acquisition for Stonehenge of sarsens from 30 km away and bluestones from about 220 km away was really a normal part of the early bronze age way of doing things: all that was unusual was the weight of the individual items traded.

Before we consider the technical problems involved in transporting the sarsen stones from Avebury, it is worth looking at the social and political implications. We can interpret this project in more than one way. It was at least in part a display of man-power, wealth and strength. The smallest possible overall cost of transporting, shaping and raising the stones would be 1½ million man-hours. The scale was colossal: ten times as much as the cost of building a causewayed enclosure, fifteen times as much as Stonehenge I. Following the idea that people – the bigmen and their families in particular – were seeking personal possessions as symbols of power, we can speculate that the stronger bigmen and their supporters will have conquered or bloodlessly annexed neighbouring territories in order to increase their wealth and status. Avebury is the next conspicuous late neolithic ceremonial centre to the north and, given this aggression hypothesis, it would have been logical for an ambitious 'Lord of Stonehenge' to reach out and take Avebury, where the Great Stone Circle laid out around 2800–2600 BC and now already ancient showed what it was possible to achieve and what had to be bettered. As part of that gesture he might have ordered the seizure and transfer of seventy-five great stones from the hillsides east of Avebury in order to make a monument at Stonehenge that would surpass the spectacular stone rings already standing at Avebury. This gesture would have been a signal to all the peoples of Wessex that the Avebury territory was subservient to the Stonehenge people. Taking the Avebury people's resources and using them to overtop the design of their ceremonial centre would have been as effective and public a signal as the hammering of African tribes by the British soldiery in the nineteenth century. In a similar symbolic gesture, King Edgar signalled his supremacy as Emperor of Britain by a solemn coronation at Bath in May 973, and then had eight British sub-kings row him on the River Dee while he himself held the rudder.[21]

But there is another interpretation which is softer and subtler. Just as the consignment of bluestones for Stonehenge II may have been a gift from a Welsh tribe well disposed towards the Stonehenge people, the sarsen stones may have been presented as a gift by the Avebury people, in friendship and without duress. At an earlier phase in Stonehenge's development, in 3100 BC, at least two of the four portal stones were given to the people of Stonehenge by the people of Avebury, proving not only friendship between the two tribal groups but also a particularly close and enduring one, one that lasted over a thousand years. In the centuries following 3100 BC doubtless many more gifts, mostly of a perishable nature, passed between the two and we can see the seventy-five huge sarsens that made Stonehenge as the climactic and most conspicuous and ostentatious gift from Avebury.

What the Stonehenge people might have given to Avebury we can only guess, but it was possibly an archaeologically invisible gift such as food or teams of volunteers or conscripts to help build one of the great monuments raised by the Avebury people. The building sequence at Avebury is not yet entirely understood, but it seems to have been as in the table on p. 148.

The Stonehenge people may have contributed labour to build Silbury Hill, the stone avenues and post-circles, or sent food to sustain the work force or even supplied timber for the post-circles. Archaeology simply does not give us enough information to infer what happened, although it does imply that

Avebury		Parallels at Stonehenge	
Obelisk?	initial	Totem pole	initial
Windmill Hill enclosure	3350 BC	Robin Hood's Ball	3900 BC?
Central structure: North			
& South Circles	3300 BC	Central structure: timber	
		cult-house	3200 BC?
Henge ditch & bank	3300–		
	3000 BC	Henge bank & ditch	3100 BC
Henge bank raised in			
height	2780 BC	Aubrey Holes	3000–2800 BC
Silbury Hill	2750 BC	Coneybury henge	2750 BC
Great Circle: large stone			
ring	2750–		
	2300 BC	Durrington Walls: large	
		earth ring	2550 BC
Beckhampton &			
W. Kennet Avenues	2300–2100		
	BC?	Stonehenge II & Avenue	2150 BC
Dwarf burial in		Archer burial in second-	
secondary fill of ditch		ary fill of ditch to RH	
to RH of henge entrance	2100 BC	of henge entrance	2130 BC
W. Kennet post-circles	2100 BC	Stonehenge IIIa	2100 BC

cross-references of some kind, including exchanges of commodities and ideas, took place between the two peoples.

The Manton Barrow, which lies about 6 km east of Avebury, contained the rich accoutrements of a barbarian princess. She had with her a bronze dagger with an amber pommel, two miniature cups, three bronze awls for leather-working, a pottery stud which was probably a cloak fastener, a shale bead encased in gold wire and a 150-bead necklace made of jet, shale and small fossils. There was also a finely made disc of red amber set in a gold ring embossed with six concentric circles of neatly made dots. This last object is so similar to the two amber discs found in the Wilsford South 8 Barrow at Stonehenge that it can safely be assumed that they were all made by the same person. There was also a little pendant in the shape of a halberd in both burials. This evidence shows freedom of movement between the two terri- tories and that gifts were being exchanged between them, but it is important to recognize that this could have happened without the whole area being under one rule.

Whether the Stonehenge people were pleased or embarrassed by the gift of sarsens from the Avebury people we cannot tell, but they would have regarded it as binding. In an archaic society, declining a gift is far more than a mere breach of etiquette: it may lead to a disastrous breakdown in diplomatic relations, even to warfare. They had to accept the sarsens, even though the bluestones were sacred and had been acquired at such cost, in order to preserve the friendship bond with Avebury. That is the 'soft'

Plate 22 Broad tooling on the back (outer face) of stone 59 at Stonehenge.

Plate 23 Trilithon 53–54 at Stonehenge. Stone 54 (left) shows the ripple marks of broad tooling: the builders did not think it worth smoothing off the stone's back.

scenario, which I prefer. In reality, the acquisition of the sarsen stones may have had elements of both scenarios. The gift of sarsen stones may, for instance, have been offered as an act of friendly submission to the Stonehenge people in acknowledgement of their superior status; whether any intimidation or implicit threat was involved, whether the stones were in effect extorted from the Avebury people as protection money, is simply unknowable.[22]

The great size and majesty of the sarsen stones perfectly matched the newly enhanced self-esteem of the Stonehenge people (Plate 20). The longest of the new stones was a full 9 m (29 ft 8 in.) long – as long as a bus – and stones as big as this could be made to soar in a way that the man-sized bluestones never would. In addition, the symbolism that the Stonehenge builders were groping their way towards required the stones to rise higher and higher towards the centre. The sarsen circle was to stand 4.9 m high to its lintel-tops; within it the trilithons were to rise to 6.1 m, 6.4 m and – the Great Trilithon – 7.3 m into the air.

TRANSPORTING THE SARSEN STONES

The sarsens came from Overton Down, the low bleak hills immediately to the east of Avebury, and close to the Avebury people's great monument complex. As discussion has already made clear, these sarsens could not have been taken without dealing with the Avebury people first, whether in a friendly and diplomatic way or by the use of force. Clearly a raid is out of the question because of the time-scales involved. Whether transferring the stones the 29 km (18 miles as the crow flies) southwards to Stonehenge necessitated dealing with any other communities in the territories in between is not clear, and this issue has been avoided by most writers on the subject.

Between Durrington Walls and Avebury there was nevertheless another superhenge. Its grassed and tree-grown remains may still be seen at Marden, and in the late neolithic it presumably commanded a territory of its own, though possibly a smaller and less well-established one.[23] If Marden emerged as a major territorial focus late in the neolithic, as the absence of a long barrow cluster suggests, it may have been possible for the Stonehenge people to cross its territory fairly informally. Nevertheless the radiocarbon dates imply that developments at Marden itself were very much in phase with those at Durrington Walls; the Marden site was cleared of woodland and settled in about 3250 BC, the same as Durrington, and it was enclosed with a huge wandering loop of bank and ditch to make it into a superhenge in about 2460 BC, less than a hundred years after Durrington Walls. The three territorial 'capitals' may have been developing roughly in step with one another in the later neolithic and the peoples of their three territories may have been on friendly terms with one another. Contrary to popular belief, it is quite usual for good diplomatic relations to be maintained among archaic communities, largely by carefully organized and often highly ritualized exchanges of gifts.

It is not known for certain how the sarsens were transported to Stonehenge: archaeology has so far been unable to tell us either the route or the method of transport. We can nevertheless make educated guesses about what happened. Let us take the means of transport first. No river or sea route connects Avebury and Stonehenge: the upper reach of the Avon, which covers about half of the distance, is mostly too shallow and winding to have been of any use. The route must therefore have been overland, and the balance of evidence suggests that sledges were used. The Stonehenge people at this time almost certainly had knowledge of the wheel, but it is unlikely that they would have considered using a wheeled cart for a job like this. The remains of solid wooden wheels made without any metal parts have been found on mainland Europe: without bronze or iron bearings such wheels would have broken apart under the huge weight of the sarsen stones. Nevertheless, it is interesting to speculate that the makers of Stonehenge may have investigated the possibility of using a huge multi-wheeled carriage, and rejected it: we are dealing with a more sophisticated community than is often realized. The popular image of loose stones being dragged over wooden rollers is unlikely to be true, simply because it would be all too easy for the stones to slide sideways or diagonally off the rollers and become grounded. Lashed to a stout wooden sledge, a stone would be much more manageable over a variety of terrains and easier to steer: the runners would have helped to make the stone run straight. We also know that the Stonehenge people and their contemporaries built wooden sledges: an example was found in the ceremonial complex at Dorchester-on-Thames, where it was apparently used as a hearse.

The route is more problematic. It can be assumed that major obstacles like deep rivers and steep slopes would have been avoided. In fact, it would have been worth making detours of several kilometres to avoid hauling a 26 tonne stone up a steep hill. Although the slopes due south from Overton Down are fairly gentle, fording the River Kennet there might have presented some difficulty. Avebury stands at the lowest safe fording place on the Kennet, so it seems probable that the stones were taken there to cross the stream: south from Overton Down, first following the gentle downhill gradient as far as the site of the Sanctuary, one of Avebury's roundhouses,[24] and then west and north-west, going down a moderately steep slope for a short distance before crossing to Avebury. The stones would, in doing this, have passed along the West Kennet Avenue and their passage through the great henge of Avebury at the beginning of their epic journey was probably the occasion of important ceremonies. We can imagine the witch-doctors of Avebury charming the stones to sanctify them and ensure their safety on the long and perilous journey ahead.

The Avebury henge was by now already a thousand years old, and a good deal of the rubble that was piled onto the high bank had been washed by rain back down into the ditch. Beside the south entrance, where the West Kennet Avenue entered the henge, a female dwarf was buried in those ditch silts. Whether this strange, freakish burial was an offering by the Stonehenge people as they passed through with their stones is not known, but it is possible: the corrected radiocarbon date of 2100 BC fits this interpretation.

Outside Avebury's west entrance, the stones were dragged on their sledges along the Beckhampton Avenue to the Kennet ford and away to the south-west; the avenue marked the first 2 km of the journey from Avebury to Stonehenge and its megaliths may even have been raised as a guard of honour to celebrate the sending of the Stonehenge sarsens, one of the big moments of British prehistory.[25] With its three stone circles and its enormous ditched and banked enclosure, Avebury was at that time the most impressive and possibly the most famous monument in Wessex. Stonehenge in all probability had yet to make its name – whatever that name was in prehistory; it consisted of a modest circular earthwork that was now silted up and almost invisible, and a half-built double circle of man-sized stones that were even now being uprooted one by one. Yet the people of Avebury acquiesced in the aggrandisement of Stonehenge and watched the huge stones crawl, one by one, through their henge and down the Beckhampton Avenue.

From the point where the Beckhampton Avenue petered out, the stones were most likely dragged along the line of the A361, the road to Devizes. Professor Richard Atkinson thinks the route turned south at Bishops Cannings, past Etchilhampton, to run up the chalk escarpment at Redhorn Hill.[26] He argues that this was necessary because the escarpment stretches for 6 km to both east and west and could not have been avoided if the Stonehenge people were to exploit the easy downhill gradients on the chalk backslope to the south. Atkinson may well be right, but the alternatives should be considered (Figure 60).

The first is a detour to the east, by way of the modern villages of Chirton, Charlton, Upavon and Figheldean. This avoids the steep escarpment altogether, but runs into trouble in the Avon valley, which is narrow, meandering and fairly steep-sided: it is difficult to see how the sarsens on their big, slow-turning sledges could have been dragged through it without repeatedly going up and over the low but steep-sided spurs projecting from the valley sides. The second alternative is more attractive, offering easy gradients all the way. This route in effect follows the line of the modern A361 all the way to Devizes, and from there the line of the A360 south through West Lavington and Tilshead to Shrewton. The route exploits an important windgap in the chalk escarpment south of West Lavington, and this means that the stones need not have been dragged to such a high altitude; they only had to be taken to a height of 126 m at Gore Cross, and even that ascent was eased by following a valley naturally eroded back into

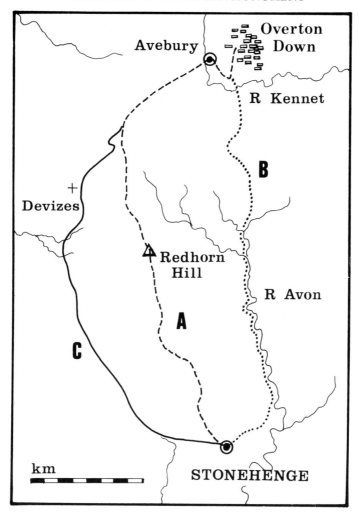

Figure 60 Alternative sarsen routes. A: Atkinson's favoured route. B: eastern route via Avon valley. C: western route via Tilshead valley.

the escarpment.[27] This summit compares very favourably with Redhorn Hill, Atkinson's route, which would have meant taking the stones up a 20° slope to a height of 212 m: Gore Cross meant a 5° climb to half that height. From Gore Cross there was a very easy, gradual descent to the south-east, following the floor of the broad, shallow Tilshead dry valley as far as Shrewton. Here we are only 5 km from Stonehenge and we can visualize the stones being hauled eastwards up one of the low, gently sloping valley sides onto Winterbourne Stoke Down to approach Stonehenge from the west.

Atkinson's route from Overton Down to Stonehenge is about 39 km

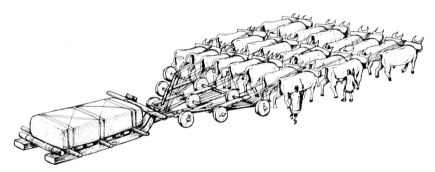

Figure 61 Transporting the sarsens. A wooden trolley or bogie would have been needed to stop the ropes snagging the oxen's legs; it would also have ensured that the oxen's pull was systematically distributed.

(24½ miles) long. The route to the west via Devizes, Tilshead and Shrewton is 43 km (27 miles) long. On balance, I think this alternative route to the west is the most likely. Although it is 4 km further, it offers easier gradients, and there is another reason for thinking that the Stonehenge people might have favoured it. The detour to the west would have enabled them to give the Marden superhenge the widest possible berth; the sarsen sledges would have come no closer to it than 9.5 km (6 miles), and it may have been considered tactical to steer clear of Marden henge, which incidentally never acquired any megaliths.

The great stones were probably transported, just one or two at a time, at seasons when there was little work to do on the land, perhaps in the autumn when the harvest was in, or winter when the wet clay lowlands were frozen: a cover of snow would have made hauling the sledges easier still. Each journey from Overton Down to Stonehenge would have taken perhaps seven weeks. Richard Atkinson and most other writers on the subject have assumed that men pulled the stones along, but we know that oxen were available. If we tend to dismiss oxen as slow, we should remember that there is no reason whatever to suppose that the builders of Stonehenge were in a hurry, and oxen are in any case only 4 per cent slower than people when hauling. What is more, an ox is nine times stronger than a man, so only a hundred oxen would have been needed to drag the largest of the Stonehenge stones up the steepest slope from West Lavington to Gore. Assembling a team of oxen of that size would have made great demands on a small community, but I think it would have been easier than calling up perhaps 1,200 healthy adolescents, which was the alternative.[28] People would still have been needed to tend the stones and guide and encourage the oxen, but possibly as few as twenty (Figure 61).

SHAPING THE STONES

One by one or two by two, the colossal stones edged their way over the horizon west of Stonehenge and gathered at the site of the new monument. A minor mystery has been made out of the penetration of the sarsens into the henge, as there is no sign of a temporary breach in the henge bank and no trace of any infilling of the Avenue ditch.[29] In fact, some of the stones at least could have been dragged in through the 3.5 m wide south entrance. If this did not allow enough room for manoeuvre, it would have been easy to fill a stretch of the north-western Avenue ditch with round timber and drag the sarsens in through the main north-east entrance: a temporary filling will have left no archaeological trace. The inner portal stones, stones E and 95, were taken down at this time for resiting, so the whole width of the entrance causeway was available.[30]

As the stones arrived, the laborious job of dressing them to the required shape began. Probably some preliminary shaping was carried out before the journey started, as this will have reduced the stones' weight. The sarsen stone originated as a continuous layer of sandstone up to 1 m thick and, although this layer was greatly broken up and weathered in antiquity, the natural stones that resulted were often slab-like, with two broadly flat faces parallel to one another. Many of the stones in the Avebury circles are tabular slabs of this kind. The Avebury stones display another characteristic of sarsen stone, which is that it tends to break up into rough diamond shapes: stones with parallel *sides* seem to have been very rare. So, although the masons were able to rely on the faces being parallel, they would have had to put a lot of work into reducing the natural form of the slab edges to create pillars (Plate 21). It is likely that some work was done on this at the Avebury end, with craftsmen on Overton Down working to detailed specifications brought with them from Durrington Walls.

The sarsen stones split most easily in a plane at right-angles to their broad faces, and the largest projections were probably broken off along these fracture planes in various ways. A natural crack close to the required line might be opened by hammering wooden pegs into it and soaking them with water to make them expand. Alternatively, fires might be lit along the required line; when the stone was hot, water could be poured onto it to cool it and crack it. Failing that, or in combination with either of the other techniques, a row of people might simultaneously bring huge stone mauls the size of footballs crashing down on the required line. There is archaeological proof that at least two of these methods were used. Excavation at Stonehenge in 1901 exposed a lot of sarsen mauls, some the size of tennis balls, others weighing as much as 30 kg.[31] In 1923, Colonel Hawley found a lot of sarsen chips resting on a spread of sarsen sand close to or underneath the north-west Avenue bank near the north-east entrance, clear evidence that a sarsen had been shaped at that spot. Some of the chips were parts of the naturally weathered crust of the stone, others were reddened by burning: he found five small hammer stones at the same site. Unfortunately Hawley's account does not make it clear whether he found these remains underneath the Avenue bank or beside it: if underneath, they must represent the shaping of the Heel Stones or inner portal stones of Stonehenge I, but we can be sure that the technique would have been the same in Stonehenge IIIa.[32]

Gradually the sarsen was reduced to an approximation of the correct shape by masons repeatedly dashing large mauls against it. The second stage in the stone dressing was done with small mauls. Groups of teenagers stood or crouched along the sides of the stone and rubbed mauls backwards and forwards. This produced a pattern of broad ripples 20 cm wide and 5 cm deep, which can still be seen on stones (Plates 22 and 23) that were for some reason left unfinished.[33] As chance would have it, the Stonehenge people had chosen to make their monument out of one of the hardest rocks in Britain, and this dressing must have taken them a very long time. One of the most surprising things about Stonehenge III is that it was completed; the project took a long time and there was every practical reason for giving it up. It says a great deal about the tenacity and determination of the Stonehenge people that they saw it through. If just 5 cm had to be removed from the face of an average Stonehenge upright, it would have taken some 380 man-hours.[34] Put differently, if eight people worked five hours a day on the stone, it would have taken them ten days to dress one face; then the stone had to be levered over onto its side to have its edge dressed – perhaps five days' work – and onto its back to have the second face dressed. The coarse dressing of a single stone would have taken over a month.

This was usually followed by a finer dressing consisting of the creation of narrower and shallower grooves 20 cm long, 5 cm wide and only 0.5 cm deep; this type of tooling can be seen on stones 16 and 52, and high up on the eastern side of stone 53 (Plate 24). Next the grooves and ridges were obliterated by pounding the surface with mauls, this time all over. This gave the surface a characteristic 'orange-peel' texture, at least when it was new: later weathering has smoothed it off wherever the stone is exposed.[35] Finally the pecked surface was ground and polished, although it is not known how; this polishing was evidently difficult to do and it was only applied to the inner faces of some of the stones, such as stone 10. It is difficult to tell how extensive this polishing may once have been, because some at least must have been damaged by later weathering and the souvenir hunters of the last few centuries. Even so, it is clear that the makers of Stonehenge went to a lot of trouble to give the inner surfaces of the stones the best possible finish (Plate 25); the edges were less well finished and the outer surfaces – the backs – were often left fairly rough. The implication is that the monument was meant to be seen from inside: the visual impression it made on people standing outside was of less importance. Indeed, it may well be that the man-high bank raised round the precinct in Stonehenge I was designed to prevent people outside the magic circle from seeing the secret ceremonies being performed within and the approach in Stonehenge III was broadly similar.

One notable exception is the Great Trilithon (stones 55 and 56), whose sides and outer faces are as finely finished as the inner faces. This confirms what we might already have guessed from its height and central position, that the Great Trilithon was the most important component of the sarsen monument (Plate 26). It may also mean that it was intended to be seen from both sides and that the spot immediately behind the trilithon had some ceremonial significance, although it is not clear precisely what that might have been.[36]

A colossal amount of work was involved. If we assume that a team of twenty-five people worked continuously for five hours a day, seven days a week, all the year round, it would have taken them about fifteen years to complete the dressing and polishing. That is not to say that fifteen years is how long it took: we have no way of knowing how many people were working at Stonehenge at any one time, nor do we know how continuously they worked. My feeling is that the work was so tedious and repetitive that it might have spread across a much longer period, and that it went on in intervals between agricultural work. It is likely that the job extended across two, three or four generations of the work-force, possibly more.

THE BUILDING

The main feature of the new monument was to be a stone circle with an inner diameter of almost 30 m, or 40 Beaker Yards, the same size as the massive rotunda supporting the dome of St Paul's Cathedral. It was slightly larger, by 3 m, than the 26 m diameter Double Bluestone Circle, just as that in its turn had been built slightly larger than the 25 m diameter roundhouse. To lay the circle out accurately, the builders must first have cleared the central area of any pre-existing structures. The bluestones were pulled up and taken away to enable surveyors to draw the new circle: even the Altar Stone, which was to be part of the new design, was probably temporarily removed to enable the Great Trilithon to be raised. The builders may have found the centre by trial and error, by stretching a measuring-string out from the assumed centre to the Aubrey Holes, which at that time would still have been perceptible as shallow pits; the central stake could have been moved about until the arcs struck from the measuring-string coincided with the circle of Aubrey Holes. It looks as if a trial-and-error method was used, because the centre from which the Great Sarsen Circle was eventually struck was slightly different from the centre of Stonehenge I. It was 0.6 m (2 ft) out: in other words, the builders of Stonehenge III did not accurately find what they were looking for, though it was near enough.

It is possible that geometry was used instead. The four Station Stones left over from the earlier design could have been used to rediscover the centre.

They mark the corners of a rectangle and if lengths of string were stretched diagonally across it from corner to corner the crossing-place would mark its centre. The Station Stones could also have been used to re-establish the midsummer sunrise axis, and so fix the main axis of the new monument, by stretching ropes from stones 92 to 93 and 91 to 94, and then stretching a third rope in such a way that it crossed their mid-points.

Once the centre had been determined and fixed with a stake, the two circles marking the inner and outer faces of the sarsen circle could be struck from it. Alexander Thom suggested that these two circles had circumferences of 48 and 45 of his Megalithic Rods (i.e. 99.5 and 93.3 m).[37] It is not clear to me how the builders would have arrived at this kind of geometry, but the sarsen uprights do fit very neatly into circles of these sizes: the average width of the gaps, 1 m or half a Megalithic Rod, is just half the average width of the stones, 2.1 m or 1 Megalithic Rod. We should not, however, make too much out of these measurements, because the widths of both stones and gaps vary considerably. To get an overall orderly and rhythmic effect, the builders set the centres of the inner faces at equal intervals of 3.2 m (1½ Megalithic Rods or, more likely, 6 steps) round the circle. These points were probably marked by large pegs hammered down flush with the ground: there they could remain, if necessary, for decades while the stones were dragged onto the site and erected one by one.

The next step was to mark out, probably also with pegs, the five trilithons in a horseshoe arrangement symmetrically about the axis. Fourteen points 2.7 m or 5 steps apart were marked out round a horseshoe that was 5 of these units of 5 steps across. Every third peg was then pulled out to make a space: each of the remaining pegs marked the mid-point of the inner face of a trilithon upright. A trilithon consists of three stones, two uprights and a lintel, built in the form of a gigantic doorway.[38] The outermost trilithons are 6.1 m high from the ground to their lintel-tops, the inner ones 0.5 m taller. The central trilithon, which must have been an awe-inspiring sight when complete, rose to a height of 7.3 m. Even the lower trilithons are 2 m taller than the Lion Gate at Mycenae, built nearly a millennium later in about 1250 BC, and the central trilithon is almost twice as high as the Lion Gate.[39] These megalithic structures were wonders of the ancient world in their own right. The ten largest stones in the consignment were set aside to be the uprights for these trilithons: indeed it is likely that they were earmarked right from the beginning, on the hillside east of Avebury. The Stonehenge builders decided early on that the lintels of the trilithons and the sarsen circle were to be exactly horizontal, and also that they were to rise in tiers towards the monument's focus, the area marked by the Altar Stone and the Great Trilithon. It is not known for certain how this was achieved, but it has been suggested that some kind of mock-up of timber scaffolding may have been erected before any of the stones was raised.[40]

Posts may have been raised on the site of the Great Trilithon, their tops

Plate 24 Fine tooling on the side of stone 16 at Stonehenge.

Plate 25 The smoothly ground inner face of stone 30 at Stonehenge. The ancient crack which runs to the stone's root represents a near-disaster at the time when the stone was raised.

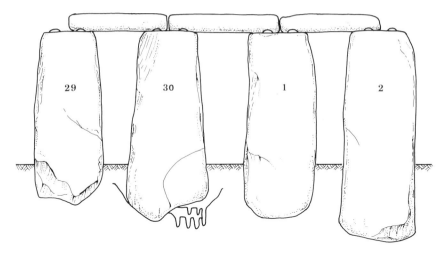

Figure 62 Part of the Great Sarsen Circle at Stonehenge, showing varying socket depth. Note the major crack at the base of stone 30 and the 'emergency' post-holes below it. *Source*: Hawley

marking the eventual position of the tops of the upright stones. A cross beam was fitted to the post-tops and a long, narrow trough filled with water was rested on it to check that it was level. If the water did not fill the trough evenly to the brim, the level and cross beam were removed and one of the posts hammered further into the ground. The cross beam was refitted and checked again until it was level. The bottoms of the posts were then notched with a flint axe to mark the length of stone that would show above ground. The posts were lifted from their sockets and laid against the supine dressed stones, and the desired ground level was either lightly chiselled or painted round the base of the stones: from this the length of stone that would be buried could be measured exactly, and therefore the precise depth of the socket. When two stones of unequal length were paired, as was the case with the Great Trilithon, the sockets had to be dug to differing depths. Stone 56 has a socket 2.5 m (over 8 ft) deep. Since stone 55 was shorter, it had to perch in a dangerously shallow socket. To compensate for the reduced stability, the masons gave stone 55 a broader base, but this was not enough to save it and it now lies fallen, broken, across the Altar Stone.[41] The dressed, above-ground part of stone 55A measures 2.75 m and the separated fragment, stone 55B, measures 3.95 m. The overall height of 55 when standing and complete was therefore 6.7 m, which is the height of stone 56: this means that although the tip of 55B may look battered and damaged, in fact only its tenon is missing. Figure 62, compiled from several of Hawley's drawings, shows how much variation there was from one stone-socket to another in the Great Circle.

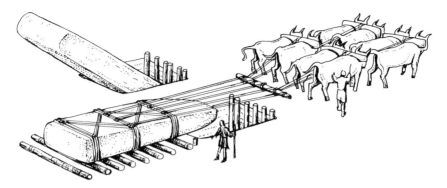

Figure 63 Hauling a sarsen into its socket.

Since the Great Sarsen Circle completely encloses the five trilithons and the gaps between its uprights are very narrow, the trilithons must have been raised first. The sockets for the trilithon uprights were carefully prepared with three vertical walls and a sloping entry ramp down which the stone was tipped as it was erected. The long stones of the Great Trilithon were dragged into position on huge log rollers and pushed forwards until their toes overhung the entry ramps. As the centre of gravity passed over the leading roller, the stone tipped forwards, its toe dropping squarely into the hole but crashing into the far wall of the socket with some force: to reduce the damage to both stone and socket, the socket wall was lined with timber (Figure 63). All the known entry ramps for the circle stones approach from outside except the one leading to stone 21, which for some reason was raised from the centre outwards. The ramp for stone 56 is even more extraordinary. It enters from the side, beneath the fallen stone 55. Was stone 56, the largest stone in the monument, really raised on one edge – a very precarious undertaking indeed – or on its face and then swivelled through 90° once it was vertical? Either way it was a very peculiar manoeuvre for the builders to attempt, unless there was some obstacle either to the south-west or to the north-east of the deep socket they had prepared for the stone. One possible explanation is that because stone 56 was so long and thin the builders were afraid it would snap in two if they raised it on its face: edgewise it would be less likely to break. Accidents did happen when stones were being raised. The Breton megalith-builders had a catastrophic accident with the Pierre de la Fée at Locmariaquer, which is believed to have broken into four pieces while they were trying to raise it. That was 20 m long and substantially thicker: although stone 56 at Stonehenge is only half that length, it is wafer-shaped.

Once planted diagonally in its socket, the stone may have been pushed upright from behind with wooden levers, or hauled from in front with ropes: possibly both methods were used. It would have been easier if a pair

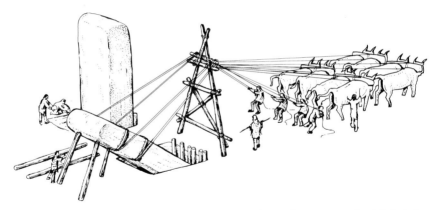

Figure 64 Raising a sarsen with oxen and shear-legs. The stone to the left is being secured with packing stones.

of shear-legs was used, and these could easily have been built using the technology of the age. By hauling ropes slung over the apex of the shear-legs a team of people or oxen could exert the most efficient force.[42] In fact experiments with scale models suggest that a trilithon could have been raised by as few as twenty-five oxen (Figure 64).[43]

Even when standing in its socket, the stone needed adjustment to ensure that it was truly vertical. Although there is no proof that the builders used plumb-lines any more than there is proof that they used levels, it is difficult to see how they could have achieved all the horizontals and verticals of the sarsen monument without them. To help with this final adjustment, the bases of the uprights were roughly pointed. Probably the newly planted stone was edged slightly in its socket one way and then another with guy ropes or timber props until the worker with the plumb-line called out that it was finally there. Then the gaps between the stone and the sides of the hole were packed tightly with discarded mauls. Some of the stones found here had come from as far away as Chilmark, some 17 km (11 miles) away to the south-west. This has been explained in terms of a shortage of hard stone in the Stonehenge area,[44] or some special ritual or magical connection.[45] It may simply be that some of the workers lived at Chilmark and quite naturally took some of their local tool-stone with them to do the job: in this case, we have incidentally acquired a useful indication that Stonehenge commanded a territory of at least 200–250 sq. km.

Some settlement must have taken place, given the great weight of the uprights and the weakness of the chalk, so each upright was probably left alone for a year or more before any new work, such as mounting the lintel, was attempted. It may be that the trilithon uprights were left unlintelled until the sarsen circle had been virtually completed round them: probably the trilithon lintels were hoisted into place just before the last two circle

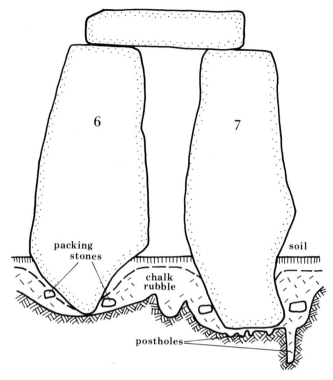

Figure 65 Two stones of the Great Sarsen Circle at Stonehenge.

uprights were raised.[46] The circle uprights could not be raised until the level that their tops would reach had been accurately established. The invisible circle floating horizontally 4 m up in the air was probably fixed by planting posts on the sites of the uprights and moving the level and 3.2 m long cross beam carefully round the post-ring. The technique was the same as that suggested for getting the Great Trilithon's lintel level, but extended on from post to post right round in a circle, establishing the exact positions, 3.2 m apart, of the tops of the thirty circle stones.

Then, when nearly all the uprights of the new monument had been erected and given a year to settle, work began on the lintels. The lintels do not merely rest on the uprights: they are held on by mortice-and-tenon joints, a technique borrowed from carpentry. Each circle upright had two roughly hemispherical knobs carved into its upper surface: these tenons are 15 cm in diameter and about 8 cm high, and it is likely that they were made first, before the mortices. Each lintel had to be tailored to bridge a particular gap, because the gaps between the stones varied significantly, and the mortices on the lintels' undersides had to be made to match their particular tenons. To make sure the lintels seated securely and would not rock, the masons made

Figure 66 The tenon on the top of stone 56 at Stonehenge.

the top surfaces of the uprights slightly dished and the undersides of the lintels chamfered to correspond. The detailed work is actually quite large in scale. The fallen lintel of the Great Trilithon gives a good indication, with its two huge oval mortices as much as 70 cm by 45 cm and a maximum of 39 cm deep. These are very large holes that would hold 69 litres (15 gallons) of water, and every cubic centimetre had to be chipped or ground out by hand. The trilithon lintels were tailor-made with the same precision as the circle lintels. Add the width of stones 55 and 56 and the width of the gap between them, and the result, 4.55 m, is the precise length of the lintel, stone 156.

The stone joints, which most modern visitors are unaware of, involved the builders in an enormous amount of extra work, but they evidently considered it worthwhile to make *this* monument, the third Stonehenge, strong enough and secure enough to stand for all time. To make the circle of running lintels, the only air-borne ring of stone to be attempted, even more secure each lintel was jointed to its neighbour by a tongue-and-groove joint. Some lintels have a groove at one end and a tongue at the other, like lintels 101 and 102, but oddly enough not all of them, which would have seemed a natural and orderly way of doing things. Perhaps someone made a mistake. Some lintels, such as 122 and 130, have a pair of tongues: it follows that other, now vanished, lintels must have had a groove at each end.

The lintels were fitted with enormous care onto the uprights so that they seated properly onto the tenons, and also slotted exactly into the tongued-and-grooved lintels on each side. Each lintel was given slightly curving faces to conform to the curvature of the circle. The result was a remarkable and unique monument – a continuous ring of stone 30 m in diameter and poised 4.3 m (14 ft) off the ground. The stones were as beautifully dressed and well fitted as the much softer stones of the Maltese temples which were already standing at this time.[47]

The question that remains is the one that has challenged one Stonehenge scholar after another, and caused the medieval mind to turn to thoughts of Merlin and magic for an answer. How did the megalith-builders raise the lintels onto the uprights? The lintels are smaller and lighter stones than the uprights, to be sure, and from that point of view present less of a technical problem, but they still weigh 6 tonnes – which is heavier by a tonne than a fully grown hippopotamus – and they had to be hoisted bodily 4 m up into the air (Plates 27 and 28).

As we saw in Chapter 3, the Stonehenge people knew a great deal about raising large timber buildings from their experience in building roundhouses at Durrington Walls from 2550 BC onwards. We also saw in Chapter 2 that they had several generations earlier built a similar rotunda at the centre of Stonehenge, perhaps some time between 3100 and 2900 BC. The skills needed to haul huge posts upright and hoist heavy ring beams several metres off the ground were already there: they had been deployed for many centuries before they were applied to masonry, and were available, fully developed, to raise the Stonehenge III lintels.

Elsewhere in Wessex megalithic masons had been practising their craft for a long time. The impressive later phase of Wayland's Smithy, a large long barrow in Oxfordshire with stone-built chambers and a megalithic facade, was built in 3500 BC. The capstones that roof the chambers and passages of these megalithic tombs were evidently dragged into position up the sides of the half-built barrow mounds. There is every reason to believe that the Stonehenge people were pooling all the accumulated wisdom and skill of the whole Wessex region, and they would have drawn on experience gained during the building of these tombs. Some have suggested that earth ramps similar to the megalithic barrow mounds might have been used at Stonehenge but there are arguments against this. No signs of such ramps have been detected on the site, although that is understandable since they could have been built and removed without leaving any archaeological trace; a stronger argument hinges on the impracticability and clumsiness of moving a large earth ramp repeatedly, to serve each successive pair of uprights, including the five trilithons in the middle.[48]

An alternative to this is a ramp built of timber scaffolding. This seems unlikely as it would have required the sinking of a significant number of post-holes to hold it still. Whilst there are some post-holes, there is no repeating pattern of holes. For some years now it has been generally accepted that the most likely method was the building of a platform of big squared logs of uniform size, perhaps 15 cm thick. The platform was probably built underneath the stone lintel, layer by layer, by levering up one end of the stone, sliding a beam under it, then levering up the other end and inserting several more beams underneath parallel to the first. To raise the stone another 15 cm, the process could be repeated, with a second layer of logs added at right-angles to the first. As the crib increased in height, it would have been advisable to secure the logs to stop them slipping sideways:

165

Figure 67 Raising a lintel on a wooden crib (after Atkinson 1979).

this could have been done relatively easily with wooden pegs or simply by tying them together. The only serious problem with this method would have been the large amount of timber needed – perhaps 2 km of mature tree-trunks – but at least it would have been reusable. The platform would also have been easy to dismantle and reassemble. A small team of perhaps thirty people could have inched the lintels up to the height of the tenons on the uprights, then levered them sideways into place: slow, painstaking work (Figure 67).[49]

There may have been an easier way of raising the lintels. Experiments with a full-sized trilithon made of concrete have shown that it can be done by between ten and twenty people using only four large timbers and several lengths of rope. The principle is very simple. Two 10 m long oak beams form a ramp, upper ends resting on the tops of the uprights, lower ends on the ground. The lintel is hauled up the ramp beams by one or two teams of workers on the far side of the uprights using two light pine timbers 4.5 m long as levers: it is possible to raise a lintel in this way with as few as ten people, although it takes several days (Figure 68). The area within the horseshoe of trilithons is about 13 m, which is just enough space for dragging the lintels from the centre outwards up 10 m long beams. The simplicity and economy of the method makes it a clear favourite.[50]

The overall investment of time and commitment was nevertheless colossal. The work directly involved in transporting, preparing and raising the stones

166

Figure 68 Raising a lintel up two oak beams (after Pavel 1992).

may have taken the Stonehenge people 1.5 million working hours, and to this we need to add a significant amount of pre-planning, since it is clear that only stones close to the right length, width and shape were brought from Avebury. The enterprise also demanded a great deal of back-up work in providing tools, levers, beams, ropes, oxen, mauls and support for the work-force in the form of food, firewood and shelter.

Before we leave the great sarsen monument in its state of pristine completeness, sparkling brightly in the bronze age sun, mention must be made of one peculiarity of the sarsen circle, and that is stone 11 (Plate 29). Measuring 2.4 m high and 1.1 m wide, it is significantly shorter and thinner than the other circle stones, the runt of the litter. Many attempts have been made to explain this; perhaps it was softer stone than the rest and disintegrated under long-continued weathering; perhaps it was the last stone to be raised and there was not enough room left for a full-sized pillar; perhaps it was broken by a lightning strike; perhaps there were not enough big stones left. The reason is almost certainly that it marks the position of an entrance and that a slim pillar was required for this purpose. When we look at the north-east entrance, we can see that the gap between the stones there was deliberately made slightly wider. Stone 11 stands on the southern limb of the circle, exactly opposite the causewayed south entrance into the henge through the phase I ditch and bank. A slim stone at this point would have created wider gaps, in effect a double door, at what seems to have been the secular entrance, the entrance for mortals: there was a double door in the early post-passage too.

Stone 11 was probably originally the same height as the other uprights and supported two lintels. Some time after Stonehenge III was finished, to focus greater attention on the south entrance, these two lintels were taken off and the central doorjamb was reduced. Alternatively, the stone may have been shortened accidentally as the lintels were being removed; it is easy to imagine one of the lintels slipping off the crib and breaking off the top of stone 11. Accidents like this must have been common enough during the building of Stonehenge III.[51] Either way, the south entrance, breaking the ring of stone, would have become a more conspicuous feature.

'LILACS OUT OF THE DEAD LAND'

What was it for? We take for granted now, through long familiarity, that Stonehenge is made of stone, but it would not have been the natural and most obvious choice of material at the time when the monument was built. Neither chalk nor flint could be made into a stone circle: the chalk-flint environment of Salisbury Plain is one where timber would have been the natural choice of building material, and indeed we know that at this time the Avebury people living in a sarsen-rich landscape to the north had completed their stone monuments and were building large ceremonial circles out of timber. The Stonehenge people had already attempted large-scale structures in wood, but these had collapsed after a couple of centuries. The stones were hauled in, into a stoneless land, because they were imperishable, immortal, everlasting. It is a sobering thought that if they had built Stonehenge III out of timber, it would have disintegrated without trace thousands of years ago, that its silted sockets might have gone unnoticed until aerial photography picked them out as faint cropmarks in the twentieth century AD: a few archaeologists would show interest, but as a nation we would think little of such a site. The Stonehenge builders' hunch was right: building in stone would speak clearly down the ages of their power, faith, tenacity, skill and daring. They bred lilacs out of the dead land.[52]

The big stones, soaring ever-higher towards the centre, suggested and commemorated the timbers of the great roundhouse in decay, a nostalgic and romantic image of the community's heritage, a symbol of the past inherent in the present. Like a cadaver on a medieval prince's tomb, it froze the image of decay for all time as a *memento mori*. The monument was grand beyond anything else that had so far been achieved in stone in Britain, or would be achieved again for at least two thousand years; it must have filled the people who built it with pride and their neighbours with awe and envy.

An element of social competition must have been involved, too; it is surely not by chance that adjacent communities in Wiltshire and Dorset produced huge monuments such as Avebury, Silbury, Marden, Stonehenge, Durrington Walls, the Dorset Cursus and Mount Pleasant. We can sense, even at this distance of time, that the people of neolithic and early bronze age Wessex were competing with one another, trying to outdo one another in their zeal to produce more and more spectacular monuments. It is possible also to sense a deep religious commitment. Stonehenge was, after all, a temple as well as a tribal status symbol. A chief who was only interested in

Plate 26 The smoothly ground edge (sunlit side) of stone 56 at Stonehenge. Only stones 55 and 56 were given this special treatment.

Plate 27 The smooth inner faces of stones 53 and 54 at Stonehenge.

169

self-glorification might have built himself a great hall, a palace, or a castle, as would happen in later cultures, but here the communal effort was invested – and on a huge scale – in building a sacred precinct for religious ceremonies. Clearly these were people gripped by an ideology, so caught up with thoughts about sun-, moon- and earth-deities that they felt driven to express their thoughts in a way that would last for ever. It may nevertheless be that the spectacular scale of the monument and the impression of power and confidence which it conveys are deceptive. Sometimes great monuments are a last throw, an attempt to conceal or maybe even avert a cultural collapse. We can see parallel situations in the twentieth century AD. As I write, the imposing monolithic tower at Canary Wharf in London's Dockland stands empty: designed to symbolize the long-awaited rebirth of the Dockland's communal life and commercial strength, it instead has become an emblem of large-scale weak organization, of a gamble that misfired. That this impressive building was raised in the depths of a recession intensifies the irony. Perhaps Stonehenge III was the Canary Wharf of early bronze age Wessex.

R. S. Newall saw Stonehenge as a temple for the dead and the Great Trilithon as a representation of a tomb entrance.[53] As such, the Great Trilithon symbolized the entrance to the Netherworld, the land of the Dead. The sun's rays would have passed through this door at sunset on the winter solstice and struck the back of the Altar Stone just beyond. It may or may not be that this was intended, but it is an attractive idea, and it neatly matches the ideas that we know were built into the earlier Stonehenge designs, which were oriented towards the 'life force' of the rising sun at midsummer. The fact that, unusually, both outer and inner faces of the Great Trilithon uprights were finely finished does rather confirm that the structure was intended to face both ways, so maybe it really was a Janus doorway designed to join together the great polarities of summer and winter, the rising and setting of the sun, the life and death of the community that built it.

7

STONEHENGE COMPLETED: THE RETURN OF THE BLUESTONES

Let us now approach this mysterious Building, and enter within its hallowed precincts. At first sight all is amazement and confusion; the eye is surprised, the mind bewildered. The stones begin now, and not before, to assume their proper grandeur; and the interior of the Temple, hitherto blinded by an uniform exterior, displays a most singular variety and gigantic magnificence.

Sir Richard Colt Hoare, 1812

STONEHENGE IIIb OR 'BLUESTONEHENGE'

When the Stonehenge people built their sarsen monument they had first to destroy the half-completed Double Bluestone Circle that was already taking shape on the site. The bluestones that had been put in position were taken out, including the Altar Stone. They nevertheless found their way back into the final monument as a circle of between forty and sixty stones set within the Great Sarsen Circle and a horseshoe of nineteen stones set within the horseshoe of trilithons. It is tempting to take a simple view of the building sequence: that the builders moved the bluestones offsite just long enough for them to raise the sarsens, and then immediately afterwards arranged them in their present settings. Most archaeologists believe that the bronze age reality was far more complicated, with at least one intermediate stage.

One reason why people have thought there was a stage in between IIIa and IIIc is the existence of a ragged double circle of empty pits, now filled and invisible, well outside the Great Sarsen Circle – the Y and Z holes (see Figure 8).[1] It is generally assumed that these were dug as sockets for bluestones, although they were never actually used as such: as we shall see, they belong to a later phase anyway. Another reason for believing in an interim stage is that a few of the bluestones appear to have been recycled from an earlier monument other than Stonehenge II, most conspicuously two stones that had been fitted with mortices and had therefore been used as trilithon lintels.[2] We have to consider the strength of the evidence. It is certain that the builders moved the bluestones out of the central precinct of

171

the monument to allow them to work on the sarsen structure, and it is likely that that work took something like fifty years. So the bluestones remained, somewhere offsite, for at least that length of time. It is possible that this offsite location was nothing more exciting than a purely functional stone-stack, like a pile of bricks in a builder's yard.

The evidence of the two morticed bluestones is ambiguous: they could have been lintels in an offsite stone ring or in Stonehenge II. One reason for supposing they might belong to a structure other than Stonehenge II is that each has at least one curved edge, and there would have been no point in curving the edges of the radial lintels we presume were planned for Stonehenge II. The mortices of stone 150 are too close together for Stonehenge II. The tongued-and-grooved bluestones are clearer evidence: they had no place in Stonehenge II or IIIc and must belong to another, missing design. So, the likelihood is that the stones were built into a new monument somewhere else, perhaps close by. It is possible that in 2000 BC the builders had no intention at all of bringing the bluestones back to Stonehenge. Meaden's recent suggestion that the bluestones were simply planted out along the Avenue banks is ingenious: there are, after all, no stones in the Avenue banks now that the bluestones are back at the centre of Stonehenge, so perhaps they were temporarily arranged as a guard of honour for the arrival of the sarsen stones.[3] But this will not work. Given that the stretch of Avenue built in Stonehenge II was only 520 m long and the spacing of the stones is known (28.5 m apart), only thirty-four stones could have been used in this way: there would have been another fifty stones to dispose of somewhere else.

The hypothetical offsite monument, which we can call 'Bluestonehenge', may have stood just to the south of the Greater Cursus, near its western end. A concentration of bluestone chippings exists there, which could be explained as the debris from a reshaping and dressing process in preparation for the raising of a monument on that site. Yet the cursus location may equally have been used for dressing the stones for Stonehenge II, and there is some evidence that this is so. The bowl barrow known as barrow 51 contained a plank-built mortuary house and some of the wood from this was radiocarbon dated to 2150 BC, when we know Stonehenge II was being built.[4] Since bluestone chips were found in the barrow, they too must date from 2150 or earlier, so other bluestone chips found nearby may also belong to this earlier date. The location of 'Bluestonehenge', the missing IIIb monument, is therefore still a mystery.

As far as I know, no systematic search has been made for a pattern of stone-holes belonging to this hypothetical monument, and it may be that a circle, oval or horseshoe of pits may one day show up as a pattern of crop marks.

Stonehenge IIIb may therefore have consisted of a sarsen monument (Stonehenge IIIa) with a separate bluestone monument some 1200 m away to

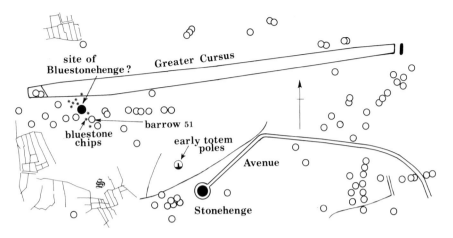

Figure 69 Stonehenge in its local setting, with monuments of various phases of prehistory. The field systems and ranch boundaries are bronze age. S: the farmstead nearest Stonehenge, which was occupied throughout the neolithic and bronze age. Note how the late bronze age ranch boundary respects both Stonehenge and its Avenue.

the north-west.[5] Adjacent stone circles are not unknown. Avebury began as two stone circles side by side, and a third was probably begun; Stanton Drew developed as a cluster of three stone circles.

THE MYSTERY OF THE Y AND Z HOLES

Another view of this phase is that the Y and Z holes were dug after the sarsens were raised as a way of bringing the bluestones back into the main precinct and then abandoned in favour of settings inside the sarsen monument, but this interpretation presents several problems. The Y and Z holes are laid out in two very badly made circles, Z about 38 m in diameter, Y about 53 m. It looks as if there were to have been thirty holes in each circle. One major difficulty is the surprisingly inaccurate geometry of the two circles, given the very high standards applied in the sarsen building. The builders seem to have begun opposite stone 9 of the sarsen circle, digging hole Z9 3.7 m out from it and hole Y9 7.3 m further out. The second measurement is twice as large as the first, and it may be that, once again, the builders were using Beaker Yards: Z9 is 5 Beaker Yards out from stone 9 and Y9 is 15 Beaker Yards out.[6] The Y and Z holes seem to have been matched radially to the stones of the sarsen circle, which is how there come to be thirty of each, but the distances were not measured properly.[7] By the time the builders had gone right round the sarsen circle, instead of finishing up where they had started, they were 3 m out. In fact, they were so far out that they

173

gave up. Y7 was only half finished and Z8 was not even begun.

It was a failure. Perhaps, even more significantly, it was an unnecessary failure. The Great Sarsen Circle had been successfully laid out as a true circle, like the Aubrey Hole circle of Ib and the inner stone circle of Stonehenge II. Careful measurement out from each sarsen upright with a length of knotted string would have produced a close approximation to concentric circles. Either it did not matter to the builders whether they made true circles or not, or they had forgotten how to make them: either way, it suggests that the people who made the Y and Z holes were applying different standards from those applied to the sarsen monument. It would seem likely that there was a significant time gap between the two phases.

The Y and Z holes are hard to date. They were dug out 1 m across, 1.8 m long and 0.9 m deep and, unlike the Stonehenge II stone-holes, they were never backfilled. They were left open to the sky and filled up slowly with the natural debris that people trod and the wind blew around the site: bits of sarsen and bluestone, soil, chalk, flints and dust. Is it possible that the pits were never intended to be sockets for bluestones? The shallow depth and unnecessary length of the pits suggest they would have been unsuitable as bluestone sockets. Their size and shape actually make them more suitable to receive crouched burials, ritual deposits or libations, and we should not rule out the possibility that these late pit-rings may after all have much in common with the Aubrey Holes of more than a thousand years before, which were used for offerings to the spirits of the underworld. Another parallel may be significant: the Aubrey Holes were used in a clockwise direction, starting at the north-east entrance, and the Y and Z holes were probably created in a similar way, clockwise, though starting from the south-east.

The main reason why some people have earmarked the Y and Z holes for bluestones is the numbers involved.[8] On the face of it there seems to be a neat correspondence between the sixty sockets of the Y and Z holes and the sixty stones of the final bluestone circle, but it is not certain exactly how many stones there were in that final circle. Although Atkinson's recent reconstruction plan shows sixty stones, it is also clear that only ten of these are still standing and a further eight lie fallen.[9] The sockets of the late circle lie in a very disturbed zone of the monument where entry ramps for sarsen circle stones, phase II bluestone sockets, phase I post-holes and phase IIIc sockets collide to produce an almost indecipherable jumble of pits (Plate 8). We cannot really be certain that there were sixty bluestones in that IIIc circle. Since the earlier phase II structure was never finished, we cannot be certain that it was to have consisted of eighty-two uprights – eighty-three if the Altar Stone is included – even though it looks likely. We cannot even be sure that any more stones were imported from Wales than the fifty-four or fifty-five that fitted into the fifty-four or fifty-five sockets that were dug before the scheme was abandoned.

It has to be left as an open question. We can, if we wish, float the working hypothesis that the Y and Z holes were dug as sockets for sixty bluestone uprights.[10] Nevertheless, there are no bluestone stumps remaining in them, nor are there any bluestone chippings resting in the floors of the holes. Nor is there any sign that stones of any kind stood in them. Nor, significantly, is there any evidence that they were dug *before* the final setting of bluestones was created: they could as easily have been dug afterwards. Indeed, the discrepancy in the standards of accuracy discussed earlier points to their being late, and for that reason it would be safer to put them into a later stage, following the final bluestone design. We could call it Stonehenge IIId.[11] From this later time, not far from Stonehenge, comes more evidence that people were worshipping the dark gods of the under-world. At Wilsford, just 1½ km away to the south-west, they dug a shaft almost 30 m deep, perhaps as a well, as pieces of rope and the remains of wooden casks or buckets were found in it, or as something more. Organic remains, including an ox skull and pieces of pottery, suggest that it may have been an offering pit where gifts or sacrifices may have been dropped to please the spirits of the deep. The organic material was dated to 1640 BC, a century or so before the Y and Z holes. The Wilsford Shaft evidence is ambiguous, but a similar shaft of similar age at Swanwick near Fareham in Hampshire was clearly used for animal sacrifices: a stake was set upright at its base, presumably for impaling the unfortunate animals, and round it were traces of decomposed flesh.

The Y and Z holes were made after IIIa, because hole Z7 is cut through the filling of one of the sarsen uprights' entry ramps (stone 7). What happened in phase IIIb remains one of Stonehenge's mysteries. The 1954 and 1956 excavations revealed some evidence of an oval setting closely following the line of the horseshoe of bluestone uprights.[12] This may, as was assumed at the time, be the solution to the IIIb mystery. It may be that IIIb was really two phases, not one, with the bluestones first dragged off on sledges to the Greater Cursus or some other site to be made into a satellite stone circle and then later, when the sarsen monument was complete, dragged back to make an oval setting. The oval ring is alleged to have consisted of twenty-two stones.[13] The logic now becomes clear. The eighty-three stones of Stonehenge II become the Altar Stone plus the sixty-stone setting that was to stand in the Y and Z holes plus the twenty-two stones of the oval ring.[14] This interpretation is supported by the number of dressed bluestones that exist in the final setting: the nineteen stones of the horseshoe, the two dressed lintels used as uprights in the circle and the Altar Stone added together come to twenty-two stones, the twenty-two stones of the oval ring of dressed stones recycled.[15] This scheme assumes that two of the uprights in the oval setting were old lintels, which presupposes an earlier bluestone setting that included trilithons: even if the oval setting existed, *another* bluestone setting must have preceded it. But the evidence for the oval setting is itself ambiguous.[16] There is a major problem here, and new evidence is needed to unravel it.

It nevertheless becomes clearer with time that the Y and Z holes are nothing to do with the IIIb phase, but belong to a later one. The casual, desultory nature of the pits tells us that they belong to a period of decadence and decline, and an antler found at the bottom of one of the Y holes giving a calibrated radiocarbon date of 1500 BC confirms this view.[17] The filling of the holes contains many fragments of a coarse type of pottery that also belongs to this later period, the middle bronze age.[18]

It was possible to propose reasons why first bluestones and then sarsens were added to the earth circle, and we can search for specific reasons for the later alterations too, but it is as well to see *change* as a commonplace of prehistoric temples. People not infrequently added tails to long barrows to make them longer, masonry shells to round cairns to make them larger, or long mounds to small round cairns to make them more fashionable: there was a general trend during the neolithic and early bronze age towards more and more impressive monuments. These actions were part of a dialogue with the past and a way of saying something new about that past: they were statements that everyone would have understood, including people of neighbouring communities. In a very real sense, each change was a redefinition of the place and the ideas it contained, and also a redefinition of the makers' own identity.[19]

THE FINAL DESIGN

The final bluestone design for the centre of Stonehenge was to consist of a horseshoe setting and a circle. The circle of unshaped bluestone uprights was set just inside the Great Sarsen Circle: as we have already seen, it is not certain how many stones there were – perhaps as few as thirty or as many as sixty. Charrière suggests that the number was fifty-seven, three times nineteen, there being nineteen bluestones in the bluestone horseshoe: this would have made a neat and symmetrical parallel with the sarsen structure, which had thirty uprights in a circle and ten in a horseshoe (the trilithons), in each case the outer setting having exactly three times the number of stones in the inner.[20] The circle was laid out fairly roughly (Figure 70). Obviously, a true circle could no longer be struck from the centre because the sarsen trilithons were in the way, but the circle is unduly inaccurate: stone 33 is as much as 60 cm off the line of the true circle.[21] A better approximation to a circle could have been achieved quite simply by measuring in 3 m (4 Beaker Yards) from the inner face of each of the sarsen circle stones, yet the makers of Stonehenge IIIc did not do this. Bronze age Britain was not as dominated by astronomer-priests, meticulous surveyors and philosopher-mathematicians as some would have us believe.[22]

The bluestones skulk among the sarsens, like dwarfs among giants, in an

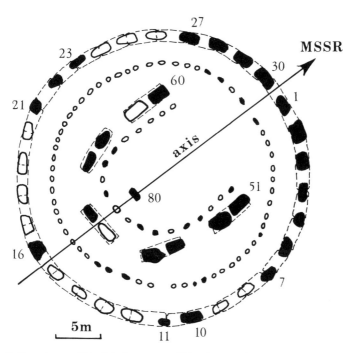

Figure 70 Stonehenge IIIc. Black: stone still in place. White: stone fallen or missing. MSSR: midsummer sunrise. Note the small size of stone 11 and the focal position of stone 80.

irregular ring 23–24 m in diameter. They proved easier to uproot and cart away than the sarsens, and only six of them remain standing in an upright position: five more lean and the rest lie fallen or have been completely removed from the site.[23] Some were evidently pulled out with some force, leaving broken stumps in the sockets. Since the ring is in such a bad state it is difficult to see any overall shape or design. Luckily an arc on the north-east side is fairly well preserved and we can see that the builders deliberately left an unusually wide gap between stones 31 and 49 (Plates 6 and 31): this perfectly matches the broader gap between stones 1 and 30 in the Great Sarsen Circle, and confirms that in phase IIIc the major ceremonial entrance to the monument was still the old north-east entrance. The original orientation was still to be honoured. The persistence of the underlying idea of Stonehenge – a round temple with a ceremonial orientation towards the north-east – may seem remarkable, and yet it is quite common to find something like this at sacred sites. At the iron age sanctuary of Gournay in northern France the wooden temple at the centre of the enclosure was rebuilt over and over again through a period lasting perhaps a thousand years, and always on the same axis.[24]

177

It is not clear how many stones stood between bluestones 35 and 36.[25] There is now a broad gap here and it may be that a gap was originally intended, in line with the south entrance. If so, we have another pointer to a very long-enduring tradition. The north-east and south entrances were fixed in the original design of Stonehenge I, way back in 3100 BC. After all the vicissitudes of the intervening centuries, all the changes of plan, the detail, significance and symbolism of that original design were still perceived and acknowledged. It is not known precisely when Stonehenge IIIc was created, but it must have been at some time between 2000 and 1600 BC, possibly at the halfway point around 1800 BC.[26] This means that at least some of the Stonehenge I tradition endured for not less than 1,300 years, probably seventy-seven generations, a major feat of lore-transmission in a pre-literate society.

The circle of bluestones was obviously intended to echo or emphasize the circle of sarsens, which shows a clear tradition link between phases IIIc and IIIa. The horseshoe of sarsen trilithons was similarly reinforced in IIIc by the addition of a bluestone horseshoe just 1 m inside it. Whereas the circle uprights were left rough and unshaped, the horseshoe stones were smoothed into alternating tall pillars and tapering triangles, rather in the spirit of the alternating shapes of Avebury's West Kennet Avenue. The polishing of the inner faces of the horseshoe stones was a direct IIIc parallel to the smoothing of the inner faces of the sarsen stones in IIIa. The alternating shapes suggest another and perhaps more significant parallel with a monument-building tradition in the Preseli area. Although the Meini-gwyr stone circle is badly damaged – all but three of the circle stones have gone and all of its avenue stones – there is just enough left to make a link across to the bluestone design at Stonehenge. The two stones left upright at Meini-gwyr stand side by side, a tall, straight-sided block and a shorter, emphatically triangular stone, the same male and female shapes that appear at Stonehenge. This may be another clue to the prehistoric connection between Preseli and Stonehenge (Plate 32). Geoffrey of Monmouth emphasized that Merlin placed the stones near Amesbury *'in the same order* as they had stood on the mountain in Ireland' (my italic), which suggests that the precise positions and patterns of the stones, such as alternating shapes, mattered a great deal.

The bluestone horseshoe stones were graded in height, like the stones of the sarsen trilithons, the lowest at the north-east ends and the tallest close to the Great Trilithon. Once again, the builders deliberately echoed the height-grading of the trilithons, which step up towards the south-west.

BLUESTONE TRILITHONS

Whether the dressed stones were specially shaped for the horseshoe setting, or selected from among the stones of an earlier monument is difficult to assess. Certainly *some* of the dressed stones must have been recycled. Stone

Plate 28 A finely preserved Stonehenge lintel (154) showing its slight taper and gentle curvature.

Plate 29 Stone 11 (centre) compared with stone 10 (left). This was the south entrance to the Great Sarsen Circle at Stonehenge.

36, an upright in the IIIc horseshoe, has two beautifully made mortices on one of its flat faces, showing that it had earlier been a trilithon lintel; this was discovered when Atkinson and Piggott lifted the stone in 1954 (Plate 34). Stone 150, another 2.5 m long upright now lying on the ground (Plate 35), also has two well-defined mortice-holes on its upper surface, so an earlier bluestone monument included at least two bluestone trilithons; this may have been the IIIb monument that stood somewhere offsite. The pits for phase II were paired, which suggests that the paired uprights were topped by lintels. The spacing of the mortices in stones 36 and 150 is 1.04 m centre to centre, too close together to have been used in Stonehenge II, so it is more likely that they were recycled from 'Bluestonehenge'.

The underside of stone 36 gives us more evidence of its history. Richard Atkinson found signs of significant wear between the stone and its support-ing uprights.[27] Grooves close to the joints can only have been produced by the expansion and contraction of the stones resulting from daily or seasonal heating and cooling or from rocking in high winds: the sharp ridge edging the top of stone 69 is just the sort of seating to create the grooving. Unfortunately it is not possible to assign a particular length of time to this amount of wear: nevertheless, it would seem likely that it could represent between fifty and two hundred years. This tells us that the recycled stones stood as trilithons for that length of time before being built into Stonehenge IIIc as uprights, rather too long for Stonehenge II, which was dismantled while being built. The polished interiors of stone 150's exposed mortices also suggest a long period of wear: it is hard to imagine the builders deliberately putting this sort of finish on a surface that would never be seen.

The recycled stones were arranged so that their better faces turned inwards: damaged, holed faces were turned outwards so that they would not be visible from the holy of holies. As before, it was the visual effect from the centre that counted most, and this is another link back to the values and beliefs of phase IIIa.

Two more stones in the Bluestone Horseshoe are known to have had tenons on their tops, indicating that they were trilithon uprights in an earlier design. The tenon on stone 67 has been removed, but the one on stone 70 can still be seen although not from ground level. Stone 69 has a rim round its top, rather like the dishing of the sarsen uprights, so that too may have formed part of a trilithon. The evidence that has survived indicates that in some earlier design than Stonehenge IIIc there were two trilithons – but no more. There is no sign that any of the other surviving bluestones was used as a lintel or a supporting upright, and mortices at least would have been impossible to erase.

A possibility is that Stonehenge II was originally intended to have lintels all the way round the double circle, but that insufficient bluestones were available to make them. Instead, only two or three bluestone lintels were fitted perhaps at the north-east entrance, where they would be noticed, and the other lintels were made of wood. As such they will have been taken for firewood without leaving any trace.

One other peculiarity of the Bluestone Horseshoe is the vestiges of earlier work on stones 66 and 68. A peculiar tongue runs vertically up one edge of the stump of stone 66: presumably this continued to the top before the stone was broken. The tongue is matched by a corresponding groove on stone 68, which is complete and still standing. The two stones are recycled from an earlier design in which a broader slab was needed, and the only way of achieving this with the bluestones was to fit two together side by side. The use of tongue-and-groove might seem more appropriate to woodwork, but there was a clear precedent in the way the builders tongued-and-grooved the sarsen lintels. Why, in phase IIIb, they felt they needed a broader slab we can only speculate, although it may be that it occupied some focal point in the design, just as the Altar Stone did in the main monument. This is to an extent confirmed by the position chosen for the dismantled stones in IIIc: one stands on each side of the Altar Stone immediately inside the Great Trilithon. That they were chosen for this place of honour, close to the focus of Stonehenge does imply that they had acquired some special sanctity as a focus for 'Bluestonehenge'.

We can see emerging from this detail a convergence on the finished design. It was not all planned from the start – it could not have been, or we would not have seen the Double Bluestone Circle begun and abandoned – but it was adapted and developed with a kind of intuitive creativity that groped its way towards the final design of Stonehenge IIIc. Faint traces of the early earth circle still showed as a soft green perimeter. Just one of the outer portal stones from Stonehenge I, the Heel Stone, was kept as a bond with the past and a reminder of the solar orientation, and the Altar Stone was retained from Stonehenge II as the monument's central idol, the dwelling place of its goddess, though moved in closer to the centre. All the sarsens of Stonehenge IIIa were kept: they were to remain for all time – the stone crown of the neolithic, even if raised after the new stone age had really come to a close. Rather like the royal crown placed on Oliver Cromwell's effigy for his state funeral, the crown he had refused in life, it was a posthumous accolade to a whole phase of the past. Or, to draw a comparison from modern times, it was like the Anglican Cathedral of Liverpool, a Victorian Gothic master-piece in spirit and conception, although designed after Victoria's death and not completed until near the close of the twentieth century, by which time architectural tastes had changed considerably. The bluestones, reincorpor-ated into Stonehenge, accentuated the monument's far-reaching links with other territories as well as bonding several phases of endeavour together. They also increased the likeness of the monument to a ruined roundhouse, a maze of timbers large and small arrayed in concentric circles.

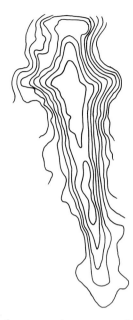

Figure 71 Contours of the dagger carving on stone 53 at Stonehenge.

FACE TO FACE WITH THE GODDESS

What went on at this extraordinary place, this super-status symbol, we can only guess. A place for ceremony, certainly, and religious ceremony at that. It was in about 2000 BC that carvings were added to some of the stones, carvings that may, if we can interpret them, tell us much about the monument's significance.

The most celebrated carvings are those on the inner face of stone 53, next to the Great Trilithon. There is a dagger 30 cm long pointing at the ground, with a double-axe apparently carved at the same time beside it (Figure 71). These were probably the weapons and symbols of deities.[28] Parallels between the axe carving at Stonehenge and the role of the double-axe in the contemporary Minoan belief system spring to mind. At just this time at the other end of Europe, an elaborate religion focusing on a pantheon of gods and goddesses was fully developed on Crete. In particular, there were goddesses, or several aspects of a principal goddess called Potnia, and her symbol, which is shown in many images, was the double-axe. Sometimes she is shown with the double-axe; sometimes her priestesses are shown conducting ceremonies while the double-axe hovers in the air as a manifestation of the goddess; sometimes the double-axe is honoured in her place.[29]

Similarly, we should see the weapons on the stones of Stonehenge as the attributes or badges of a deity.[30] When the carvings were first discovered in

182

1953 a connection was quickly, perhaps too hastily, made with the Aegean cultures.[31] The dagger in the carving was square-shouldered just like a dagger from shaft-grave VI at Mycenae, and another that was carved over shaft-grave V was dated to about 1550 BC; for a time it was thought that maybe Stonehenge had been built by a Mycenean architect.[32] Stonehenge as an 'import' from the civilized Mediterranean was, in the 1950s and 1960s, an attractive way round a serious mental obstacle;[33] the academic community did not want to think of north-west Europe as in any sense a centre of cultural innovation producing its own sophisticated architecture – although that is what it has turned out to be. Attractive though the idea was in its way, the dates are wrong. The Mycenean daggers date from around 1600–1500 BC, whereas the Stonehenge trilithons were raised in about 2100 BC, too early to have been built by Myceneans.[34] A halfway house could be that the stones were erected in 2100 BC and decorated by visiting Myceneans in 1550 BC, but even this does not convince. The Stonehenge carvings could only be seen as tourist graffiti if they were unique to Stonehenge, whereas similar carvings have been found on other monuments of the same culture. A sandstone slab found inside the Badbury Barrow in Dorset has very clear carvings of hafted daggers and flat axe blades of exactly the same type.[35] The largest dagger on the Badbury Barrow slab is even the same length, 30 cm, as the one at Stonehenge (Plate 36).

Both the carvings and the ideas they expressed were part of the native culture. In France, at Collorgues near Nimes, a neolithic statue-menhir has been well preserved by being reused as a capstone in a megalithic tomb. It clearly shows a goddess. Her face, owlish eyes, breasts and arms are depicted in stone and, near her arms, a stone axe. This confirms the association of the axe with a goddess. There is a beautifully detailed carving of a hafted stone axe pecked out of the capstone in the burial chamber of the Table des Marchands at Morbihan in Brittany. The association of the axe, the goddess and burial monuments is entirely normal: the goddess was presumably regarded as the bringer of life and death.

Pictorial representations of the goddess of the megaliths are not common, even in France, but there is enough evidence to make the connections. The earlier statues of the goddess were fairly realistic: eyes, nose, necklace, breasts, arms, hands, legs and feet are all recognizable on these menhirs, as on the statue-menhir from St Sernin in Guyenne. There are even some horizontal lines on the cheeks which may represent face-painting. Later these representations became more stylized and abstract, until they were little more than simple rectangles with a few details added: circles for breasts, a horseshoe for the necklace and a small dome for the head.

Now we can see that another of the Stonehenge carvings was intended to be the goddess. The strange, almost unrecognizable carving on the trilithon to the north of the Great Trilithon, that is, opposite the dagger and axe, is a squat coffin shape. Pecked into the hard sarsen of stone 57, it is quite large, almost 1 m square and difficult to see. Rising out of the upper edge of the image it is possible to make out a faint semicircle: this represents the goddess's head (Figure 81). The carving had been known about long before 1953, but it was only when Atkinson had discovered the dagger and axe carvings that he realized that the rectangle or 'Box Symbol' might be part of a decipherable bronze age ritual vocabulary, as indeed it is. Newall made a rubbing of the rectangle in 1953 and discovered the all-important, though very faint, knob on top, leading to its identification with the Breton mother-goddess carvings.[36]

The significance is now obvious. The carvings are not just graffiti casually carved by bronze age tourists, but added at the behest of the Stonehenge priests, ritual signs that helped the Stonehenge people, and can still help us today, to understand the purpose and majesty of the monument. There is no way of knowing how exclusive a cult centre this inner sanctum was, but as the worshippers or priests approached the Great Trilithon they would have seen to their left the weapon-symbols of the mother-goddess. To their right, and symmetrical with the weapon carvings, was the image of the goddess as a box with a semicircular head; and between them they would have seen the Altar Stone itself, a pillar rising to more than twice the height of the worshipper, an idol, a representation, a dwelling-place, perhaps even a manifestation, of the goddess herself.

8

THE MEANING OF
STONEHENGE

So very little is known for certain about the place that what I say is mainly conjecture, and it is to be hoped that future excavations will be able to throw more light upon it than I have done.

Colonel Hawley's final report on his Stonehenge excavations, 1928

Coming to the end of the most extensive excavations ever undertaken at Stonehenge, William Hawley gave vent to the despairing words which head this chapter.[1] All archaeological evidence is incomplete and there has of necessity to be some uncertainty about its interpretation, but in most people's minds an unnecessary amount of mystery surrounds Stonehenge. This is partly because much of the popular literature emphasizes Stonehenge's uniqueness; sometimes this unique status is accorded out of enthusiasm – one of the best of motives – but it tends to isolate it from rational explanation.[2] If we can see Stonehenge as part of a regional tradition, we stand a better chance of understanding it, simply because we can apply knowledge and insights acquired at other comparable sites: then it may be possible to make better sense of the monument's peculiarities – and deduce its meaning.

THE WIDER TRADITION

The large roundhouse which formed part of the Stonehenge I design was a regular component of the 'public' architecture of late neolithic Wessex, and some have been found further afield. Roundhouses are known to have existed at The Sanctuary, Marden, Mount Pleasant and at nearby Durrington Walls. The northern roundhouse at Durrington was very similar in size to the one built at Stonehenge.

Elements in the design were replaced, sometimes repeatedly, most conspicuously the roundhouse which was replaced by three successive stone circles (Figure 72).[3] This replacement practice goes back to the very beginning. The differing dates for the two dated mesolithic totem poles suggest that they were raised one after the other, the later one apparently replacing

185

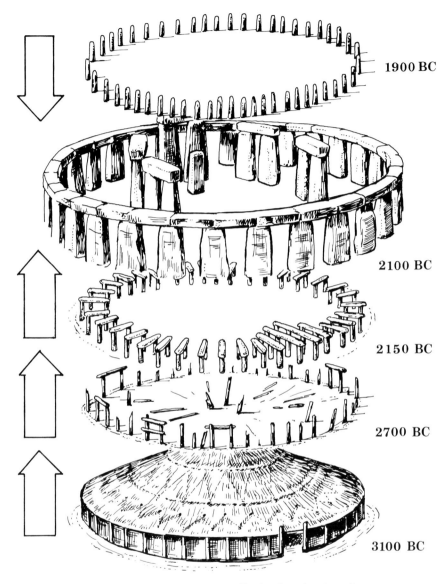

1900 BC

2100 BC

2150 BC

2700 BC

3100 BC

Figure 72 The roundhouse theme as repeatedly developed at Stonehenge.

the earlier; they were, in a functional sense, replaced by the earth circle and four monoliths of Stonehenge I nearby and later replaced again by the stone monuments of Stonehenges II and III, with the Altar Stone perhaps a reference back to the initial totem pole. This repetition and commemoration in wood and stone finds echoes at many other sites. At the Sanctuary, a thatched roundhouse was built in about 2800 BC,[4] replaced by another slightly bigger roundhouse in around 2600 BC, then by a stone setting in about 2400 BC.[5] The timber roundhouse at Mount Pleasant near Dorchester was replaced in about 2000 BC by a stone setting, a central cove and outlying marker stones indicating the outer ends of three of the four main corridors.[6] When the Longstone at Roche in Cornwall was moved from its original site on Longstone Downs to make way for china clay quarrying, it was found that the 3.2 m high slab had been raised in antiquity to replace an earlier stone and that this in turn had taken the place of a wooden post.[7]

The main feature of Stonehenge I was an earth circle, which puts Stonehenge into a very large family of monuments. Earth circles were created at many other places, either as causewayed enclosures with interrupted ditches in rather irregular arcs or as henges, which were more nearly circular and usually had just one or two entrances.[8] They were widespread in southern England with several examples nearby: Coneybury henge with its single entrance to the north-east, Woodhenge with a single entrance to the north-east and a precinct filled by its roundhouse, Robin Hood's Ball, an older causewayed enclosure also with its entrance to the north-east, and Durrington Walls, a gigantic irregular henge with two entrances. Each of these earth circles is unique, so we must not attach too much significance to any unusual features that Stonehenge may have: the others have unusual features too.

The Stonehenge ditch is unusual in being almost exactly circular, like a henge ditch, yet made of many coalescing round or oval pits, like a causewayed enclosure ditch. It is also unusual in being circular with a small number of entrances, typical henge features, but with the ditch outside the bank, which is more typical of the causewayed enclosures. The Stonehenge earthwork was a hybrid perhaps even consciously designed to combine the characteristics of both families of earth circles. The layout of the entrances is also unusual for a henge. Henges with two entrances normally have them diametrically opposite, like Durrington Walls,[9] yet the two known entrances at Stonehenge are placed asymmetrically, to north-east and south; the form of the ditch and bank suggests that there may have been a third, to the north-west, but this has yet to be proved by excavation.[10]

Stonehenge was in use for a very long time and its long life as a cult centre seems to mark it out as exceptional. There is positive evidence that at least one other major cult centre was in use for a long time, across what are often regarded as major cultural boundaries. At about the time the earth circle was laid out at Stonehenge, Cairnpapple in Lothian had an arc of seven small pits, which were probably dug as stone-sockets: then a cove was added; in about 2000 BC a two-entrance henge was laid out with an egg-shaped arrangement of twenty-four standing stones. Later, in about 1800 BC, a small cairn was raised over two rock-cut graves and enlarged in around 1500 BC; the site was still being used in the first century AD, when four people were buried there in full-length rectangular graves. Cairnpapple was therefore a ritual focus continually – possibly continuously – for at least three thousand years, but it is almost alone in British archaeology in offering evidence of long-sustained religious observance at a particular spot. The evidence from radiocarbon dating shows that Stonehenge was in use in 8000–7000, 3100, 2150, 2100, 1500 and 1100 BC – twice as long as Cairnpapple.

The origin of Stonehenge back in the mesolithic is a startling and fairly new idea, but it is not inconsistent with what we are learning about British cultural development. Instead of seeing the neolithic people as entirely 'new people' pioneering an untouched wilderness, we can now see them either as the descendants of the people who were there before, adding neolithic techniques to the old mesolithic way of life, or as a handful of incoming farmers forming alliances on well-established lines.[11] The contents of the Coneybury pit show that a middle stone age way of life was still being lived by some people in the Stonehenge territory as late as 3800 BC.[12] If the cultural development of the area is seen as continuous from the mesolithic to the neolithic, then it is less surprising to find a mesolithic cult centre still being used in the neolithic. We can apply this to the Stonehenge totem poles: we can similarly apply it to the Coneybury pit, dug as a repository for the debris from an early neolithic ritual hunting feast. The cache of bones half-filled the pit, but a hollow 0.5 m deep must still have been visible in 2750 BC when the Coneybury henge was laid out right beside it.[13] The location of the later neolithic henge side by side with the early ritual pit may have been coincidental, but it is at least equally likely that a 1,100-year-old trysting place was being reconsecrated. Much the same reinforcement went on at Stonehenge again and again.

The orientation of Stonehenge towards the midsummer sunrise may seem to mark it out as unique, but other monuments too were pointed towards the sun. The orientation of the entrance passages and 'roof-boxes' of Newgrange and Maes Howe towards the midwinter sunrise and sunset respectively is well known (Figure 73).[14]

The stone circle, in many people's minds virtually equated with Stonehenge, is also quite common. Over nine hundred stone circles or stone circle sites are known in the British Isles and there may originally have been twice as many: stone circles were a regular feature of the late neolithic and bronze age landscape, especially in the hard rock areas of the west and north. The existence of a stone circle at Stonehenge is not in itself exceptional, nor even its combination with a henge: the Ring of Brodgar, Cairnpapple and Avebury all consisted of stone circles set within earthworks.

Even the stone horseshoe can be seen elsewhere, if in slightly different forms. The arrangement of the trilithons round three sides of a rectangle is reminiscent of the 'cove' arrangement of three large stones at Avebury.[15] The trilithon idea itself is perhaps the most distinctive and individual feature of Stonehenge: it has not been found at any other site. There is a possible

Plate 30 Stonehenge trilithon 57–58 with two stones of the Bluestone Circle, 69 and 70, in front.

Figure 73 The entrance to the Newgrange passage grave as it probably looked when newly built in 3100 BC, although not as reconstructed in about AD 1970. The roofbox and its decorated lintel, discovered only in 1963, are clearly visible above the doorway. Like Stonehenge, Newgrange saluted a solstice sunrise.

parallel at the Arminghall henge in Norfolk. Within a ditched and banked enclosure a horseshoe setting of eight massive oak posts rose out of sockets 2 m deep. They were raised in 3050 BC, at about the same time as Stonehenge I. Possibly the uprights were topped by logs over 4 m long to make four huge trixylons, or wooden trilithons, but the uprights may equally well have been freestanding.[16] There is no evidence that any British monument other than Stonehenge had trilithons. Perhaps the nearest parallel is the T-shaped taulas of Minorca. The taula typically consists of a rectangular lintel stone tapering in towards its base, and looking very much like a Stonehenge trilithon lintel, hoisted 4 m into the air atop a single broad stone slab. The taula is surrounded by a ring of standing stones. The great taula of Talati is similar in design but with the addition of a strange diagonal stone which seems to hold up one end of the lintel like a crutch.[17] This is the closest we get to a parallel to a freestanding Stonehenge trilithon, and it is not known whether there is any significance in the similarity between these widely separated monuments.

As far as we can tell (though we have to remember that most stone circles are in a ruinous state) no stone circle other than the Great Sarsen Circle at Stonehenge had running lintels, so that sky-borne ring of stones may be seen as a unique creation. Yet there is every likelihood that all kinds of exotic structures were made of wood and that, wood being perishable, they have simply not survived. The post-holes of a timber circle, for instance, have recently been discovered at Welshpool in Powys: it would have been roughly the same size as the sarsen ring at Stonehenge, if less massive; Stonehenge is visible to us simply because there the form was translated from timber into stone.[18]

In its particular combination of features Stonehenge *was* unique, but most other monuments have idiosyncrasies that make them unique too. Stonehenge draws on a repertoire of architectural and symbolic gestures that were in use across a surprisingly large area, from Orkney to Brittany, Spain and Portugal. The fact that many of the components of Stonehenge can be found in varying combinations at other ritual centres is a cause for optimism: it increases our chances of understanding the monument. Stonehenge is, after all, not a Phaistos Disc.[19]

THE MEANING OF THE AVENUE

In trying to unravel the meaning of Stonehenge, we can approach it as a middle bronze age pilgrim may have done, from the River Avon along the sweep of linear earthworks leading to the north-east entrance. Since the Avenue was made in two stages at two different times we have to interpret the two stages separately. The first stage, laid out in about 2100 BC, is dead straight and leads from the monument's ceremonial entrance towards the midsummer sunrise: it was designed to reinforce the midsummer orientation of the monument's main axis. It may have had a secondary purpose which today, given the degraded state of the earthworks, we might easily overlook – to ensure the privacy of the sacred precinct inside the earth circle. The circle bank was originally 2 m high, high enough to stop people outside the circle from seeing the ceremonies being performed inside.[20] The broad gap in the bank on the north-east side would have been a weak point, where the curious and the uninitiated could peer in; the Avenue banks, probably also 2 m high when built, would have ensured secrecy whilst keeping the wide entrance gap open.

The Avenue was probably intended principally as a ceremonial way along which the sun-god himself, in his high-summer aspect, might approach the holy of holies.[21] It could have been used as a processional way by ordinary mortals instead or as well – there is, I think, no way of knowing now – but the idea of marking out a spirit path would be quite in harmony with the archaic beliefs of the late neolithic and early bronze age.

The geophysical survey evidence shows that the Avenue was given emphasis by paired stones standing on the banks, just as Roger Gale reminded William Stukeley in 1740.[22] If, in imagination, we reinstate the stones, there seems to be a resemblance between the Stonehenge Avenue and the West Kennet Avenue at Avebury: a restored section of the West Kennet Avenue gives an idea of what the Stonehenge Avenue may have looked like, but the parallel with Avebury is not close. The West Kennet Avenue was rather irregular: far from straight, it had a very deliberate kink close to the south entrance of the henge, and it was not ditched or embanked. Avebury had a second stone avenue, the Beckhampton Avenue, leading away from its west entrance, whereas Stonehenge had only one. There is a closer parallel to Stonehenge at Stanton Drew, where two of the stone circles have straight, though very short, stone avenues leading away a few metres to the north-east.

All the examples quoted so far could have been used as processional ways by mortal men and women but other contemporary and later monuments include single rows of stones and double rows set very close together, for instance at Merrivale and Drizzlecombe on Dartmoor.[23] Plainly, these could not have been used as processional ways by mere mortals.

The straightness of the Stonehenge Avenue must in itself be significant. So many neolithic and bronze age structures are geometrically imprecise in shape, like the West Kennet Avenue, that a dead-straight alignment must have had a specific purpose. Some monuments are arranged along otherwise unmarked lines. The three Thornborough henges, Nunwick henge and the three standing stones known as the Devil's Arrows lie on a straight line 17 km long in Yorkshire. Another alignment, 8 km long, runs from the Devil's Arrows through Cana henge, a barrow and Hutton Moor henge. The four Priddy Circles in Somerset lie on a much shorter straight line. Many of the barrow cemeteries in Wessex are also arranged in straight lines, often guided by the long axis of a neolithic long barrow, the oldest in the cemetery.[24] It is even possible that Stonehenge itself may have formed part of a line of monuments. The Coneybury henge to the south-east has been mentioned (Chapter 4), and there were two more very small henges away to the north, the Fargo and Winterbourne Stoke mini-henges.[25] Stonehenge, the two mini-henges and Coneybury henge form a straight line. Interestingly, the enclosed western ends of the Great Cursus and Lesser Cursus also lie very close to the line. Whether a linear arrangement was intentional is open to question: I suspect that it was chance in this instance.

It is tempting to draw comparisons with other cultures, other places, other times, and there are features of the neolithic and bronze age belief system which seem almost oriental in flavour. The alignment of the Altar Stone and Great Trilithon towards the midsummer sunrise framed by portal stones, for instance, finds a parallel in Japan. On the seashore at Futamigaura there was a shrine of adoration oriented towards the dawn; as the sun rose over the mountains on the far shore it was seen to be framed between two gigantic rocks rising from the sea as natural portals. The customary prayers and offerings were made in that direction and the observation point was marked by a ceremonial gateway, a kind of wooden trilithon, placed immediately behind an altar. The parallels between the Japanese ritual site and

Stonehenge vividly show how similar impulses, beliefs and trains of thought can produce similar ceremonial structures.[26]

The concept of alignment also crops up in oriental belief systems. The art of Feng Shui, still practised in China and Japan, concerns itself with aligning the homes and work-places of the living with the resting-places of the dead in a way that will harmonize with local currents of the cosmic breath.[27] It may be that a similar kind of earth-magic was practised in ancient Wessex. Marking out special places with magic circles is a part of this approach. Alignments connected with some kind of geomancy could explain the stone rows, avenues, cursus monuments and lines of henges and barrows. For some reason – and the explanation is probably supra-rational – certain points, directions and lines were regarded as favourable and attracted building work that emphasized them. For example, it is almost certainly not accidental that many of the monuments in the Stonehenge complex were built so that they faced towards the east or north-east: six of the long barrows, both the cursus monuments and the main entrances of Robin Hood's Ball, Stonehenge I, Coneybury henge, Woodhenge, Stonehenge II and Stonehenge III (Figure 74). With this pattern in mind, we can see that it may not be accidental that the line marked by the northern ditch of the Great Cursus continued eastwards passes through the Cuckoo Stone, probably a later standing stone, and then through the site of Woodhenge. The Cuckoo Stone can be found lying on its back in the middle of a field of peas halfway between Strangways Wood and Woodhenge (Plate 37): its upper surface is so deeply weathered that it is hard to tell if it was ever dressed to shape, but it seems likely that it once stood on its bluntly pointed eastern end.[28] The site of Woodhenge seems to have been consciously chosen because it lay on the cursus line, so the Cuckoo Stone was probably raised to indicate to people looking out from Woodhenge in which direction precisely the cursus line ran: this would have been necessary because the low rise west of Woodhenge rendered the cursus terminal invisible. The fact that different components of an alignment were created at different times emphasizes how deeply rooted in the prehistoric belief system these geomantic ideas must have been.

This is also clearly seen in the way the barrow cemeteries developed, over the course of hundreds of years, along lines dictated by the long axes of long barrows. Here the barrow-builders were apparently trying to bring the sepulchral landscape into harmony with spirit forces, although it is difficult to be sure how these were perceived. It may have been that the builders wanted to concentrate the benevolent spirits of ancestors and harness them to some good cause such as the well-being of the living community, or they may have intended to direct potentially harmful ghosts along the territorial boundaries and so minimize their effect, or even make use of their destructiveness to ward off strangers: a kind of spiritual barbed-wire. It is not possible to tell from the archaeological evidence whether the Stonehenge

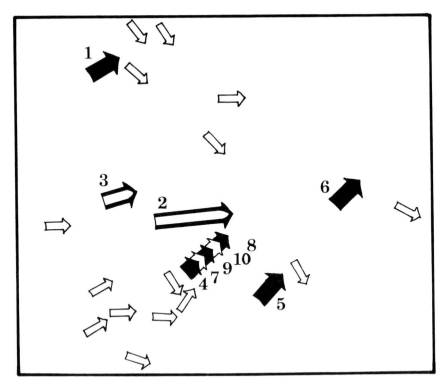

Figure 74 Monument-orientation in the Stonehenge area (same area and scale as Figures 11, 16, etc.). 1: Robin Hood's Ball. 2: Great Cursus. 3: Lesser Cursus. 4: Stonehenge I. 5: Coneybury henge. 6: Woodhenge. 7: Stonehenge II. 8: Avenue. 9: Stonehenge IIIa. 10: Stonehenge IIIc. Unnumbered arrows represent long barrows.

people honoured and loved their ancestors, or surrounded them with mumbo-jumbo and taboo because they feared them: perhaps it was something of each.

The traditional cultures of the North American Indians provide some useful parallels. Around the time of Christ, the Hopewell Indians of Ohio were building earthworks that had several features in common with Stonehenge and other British neolithic and bronze age monuments.[29] At Newark in Ohio there are two big circular earthworks, each with single entrances to the north-east and earthen avenues. The parallels between the Hopewell Indians and the Stonehenge people are significant: the Hopewell Indians built earth mounds as well as earth circles and avenues. At Hopeton a large circular earthwork 320 m in diameter with a 2 m high bank has three entrances and a fine earth avenue 730 m long leading away south-westwards to a point where it breaks off abruptly at a 10 m high bluff at the edge of the Scioto River's floodplain (Figure 75). This marks another parallel between

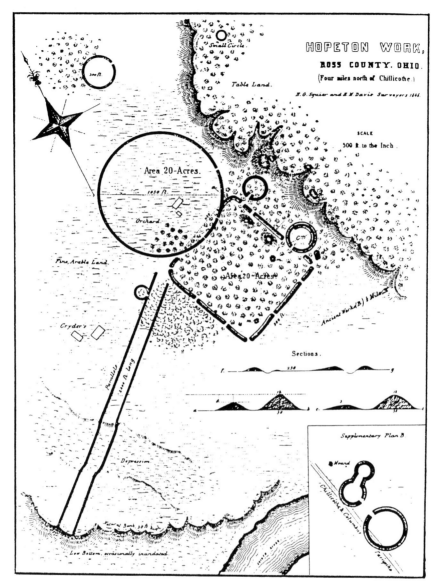

Figure 75 The Hopeton earthworks in Ohio. *Source*: Squier and Davis 1848.

Hopewell and Stonehenge: the English avenues often lead to streams or floodplains, as at Rudston, Stanton Drew and Stonehenge itself, at least in the second stage.

The lines on the Bolivian altiplano often cut straight across plains, ridges and valleys with surprising accuracy. Some of the shorter ones, simply made by sweeping aside the dark, oxidized surface layer of pebbles, link churches with shrines on nearby 'holy hills'. Sometimes mudbrick shrines or cairns are dotted along the lines. These Bolivian lines belong to a world of folk memory, a limbo between Christianity and the pre-Columbian religion. The Stonehenge Avenue in a similar way links the temple of Stonehenge with the natural abode of deities or spirits, in this case not hills but water. As recently as 1985, Bolivian Indians were seen walking along a line, making music as they went, praying and making offerings when they reached the top of the hill.[30]

When the makers of Stonehenge constructed the second stage of the Avenue they were tying the midsummer sunrise section of the processional way to the River Avon. They may have done this for a variety of reasons. The Avon was used for communication – the concentration of imported materials and goods along its valley proves that it was a trade route – and it may be that the completed Avenue was designed to shepherd river-borne visitors unfamiliar with the area's geography across to the monument. A second possibility is that the 2.4 km long curving sweep was marked out to commemorate the path followed by the sledges hauling the bluestones up from the river bank. The Stonehenge builders had long memories and they would have needed them as it had been a thousand years since the bluestones passed that way. An easier gradient lies a little to the east of the Avenue, one that would have avoided the fairly steep haul up from the river bank. The time-lag was long and the folk memory, though true in substance, had perhaps become slightly distorted by 1100 BC.

A third possibility is a purely spiritual explanation. The final stage of the Avenue links Stonehenge to the living river, acting as a siphon to draw up whatever magical elixir the Stonehenge people believed dwelt in the Avon. It is possible that two or even all three of these purposes were in the builders' minds. As we have already seen, the monument evolved so slowly that a great deal of thought, purpose and symbolic gesture could be invested in it. It is also a sobering thought that the intellectual capacity of these people was every bit as great as ours and that they had far fewer outlets for their intellectual creativity: in a situation like this, multiple purpose and multiple symbolism are likely to occur.

THE MAGIC CIRCLE

The earth circle created in 3100 BC stands at the watershed of two traditions. The older tradition, the causewayed enclosures with their ditches outside and banks within, had its beginning around 4000 BC. One of the earliest known was built at Abingdon in Oxfordshire in about 3900 BC. It may be significant that the Abingdon enclosure was built on the site of a mesolithic settlement that had been occupied a thousand years before. Once the ditches had been cut they began to fill and at some enclosures this silting was allowed to go on uninterrupted, whilst at others it was actually hastened by people shovelling bank material back into the ditch: at Abingdon the ditches were cleaned out repeatedly over a period of seven hundred years.

Some of the causewayed enclosures initially consisted of a single ditch and bank: extra rings were added later, perhaps as the sites grew in importance. This happened at Windmill Hill near Avebury, where work was begun around 3350 BC. The Windmill Hill site was replaced by the Avebury henge shortly afterwards: the charcoal beneath Avebury's henge bank has given calibrated radiocarbon dates as early as 3370 and 3040 BC, with the primary fill of the ditch dating to 2900 BC. New work on Windmill Hill suggests that the outer rings may have been built very soon after the inner, and presumably before work began on the Avebury henge bank. Since the circuits of ditch and bank at Avebury are fairly irregular some structures must already have been standing within the precinct in 3200–3050 BC, presumably the Obelisk and the North and South Circles, and these may have been raised straight after the completion of Windmill Hill, perhaps in around 3300 BC. Here again we stumble on an implied early parallel with Stonehenge, which was either abandoned or de-emphasized between 2600 and 2250 BC while the Durrington Walls superhenge was created. In fact this kind of supplanting was common.[31] What is unusual about Stonehenge is that after being abandoned, neglected or decommissioned for four centuries the builders returned to redevelop it, although it may be that the Obelisk was raised on the Avebury site *before* work began on the Windmill Hill causewayed enclosure, in which case Avebury too may have been redeveloped after an interval; really insufficient is known about the sequence of events at Avebury to draw close parallels.

Finds from the causewayed enclosures help to build an impression of the purpose behind these early earth circles. The ultimate question about Stonehenge is, after all, 'What was it for?' Some of the earth circles, especially those on defensive hilltop sites, seem to have been thorough-going settlements, like Hembury in Devon, built in about 4000 BC, and Whitehawk in Sussex, constructed in around 3450 BC: Whitehawk was a major fortified settlement with wooden gates and fences along its banks. Crickley Hill, another hilltop site, was clearly defensive, as can be seen from the archaeological evidence of an armed attack on its entrances.[32]

These enclosures were nevertheless more than villages. At Crickley Hill there is ample evidence that elaborate ceremonies took place. From about 2700 BC there was a sacred shrine area with a cult-house; in about 2300 BC a stone circle and cairn were built in the ritual area, and the cairn was later extended to make a long mound with a totem pole and a forecourt at one end. Like Stonehenge, Crickley Hill went through complex changes.

Some of the enclosures were definitely not defensive. Briar Hill in Northamptonshire was laid out on a gentle slope below a hill and probably functioned as a tribal meeting-place and livestock corral. Yet it too had its ritual aspect, with a substantial timber cove built in about 2600 BC near the centre: both the cove and the enclosure's main axis were oriented towards the north-north-east.[33] At Hambledon Hill in Dorset the enclosure ditches were repeatedly used around 3500 BC for the burial of human bones. This strongly suggests that the enclosure was used for the exposure of human bodies immediately after death; when the flesh had gone and the skeletons had begun to fall apart, bundles of bones were placed on the floor of the surrounding ditch and part of the bank pushed in to cover them. So this enclosure and probably some others too, such as Offham in Sussex, are thought to have been used as burial grounds.[34]

Many of the early enclosures had mixed uses. Etton in Cambridgeshire had one half devoted to funerary rites, the other half to non-funerary uses, the two areas separated by a fence. There were also offerings placed on the ditch floors close to the entrances: these were the simple offerings that we would expect from a poor, archaic community living close to the land – a carefully cut square of birch bark, a pile of butchered animal bones, a length of string, a pot on a birch bark mat.[35] These carefully placed offerings and the very similar offerings found at other sites will give us some useful clues when we come to examine and interpret the contents of the Stonehenge ditch.

The early enclosures with interrupted ditches had a range of uses, but they all had in common a role as a centre, a place where the scattered rural family groups of an area might meet for important gatherings. What these gatherings were we can only guess: they may have been calendar feasts, rites of passage such as weddings and initiation ceremonies, moots, livestock fairs and culls, acts of worship and propitiation and even, possibly, a 'counting' like Aunt Ada Doom's annual census of the Starkadder clan at Cold Comfort Farm.[36]

Henge-building was a later but overlapping tradition: the Llandegai henges in Gwynedd are among the earliest to have been dated, at 3600–3500 BC. In a henge the positions of bank and ditch were switched, so that the bank was outside. The plan was usually a simple circle, oval or egg shape and the number of entrances was reduced to one or two: some very large henges, such as Mount Pleasant and Avebury, had four, but this was exceptional. The plan was in effect simplified and reduced to an almost continuous double circle of bank and ditch; it is as if the design had come into sharp focus as a magic circle, just before the time when Stonehenge I was built as a kind of compromise between causewayed enclosure and henge.

Stonehenge was among the very earliest true magic circles. The idea of magical protection by a ritually drawn ring is a very ancient one, and we can see in these early earth circles the start of a long European tradition that lingers on even to the present day. Jung describes the case of a disturbed 7-year-old boy who drew a whole series of elaborate circle drawings to place round his bed; he called them his 'loves' and could not sleep without their protection. For that twentieth-century boy the power of the protective

Plate 31 North-east entrance to Stonehenge through the Bluestone Circle, stone 31 in shadow to the left, 49 in half-shadow to the right. Beyond is the centre of the temple.

Figure 76 Sixteenth-century magic circle. People dance a ceremonial round dance safely within the confines of their double circle. Note that the Devil is (just) excluded from the circle but waits patiently for them outside.

magic circle was still a real and living force, and there are many other cases like his.[37] The medieval magician withdrew into the safety of his carefully drawn circle, secure in the knowledge that hostile demons could not enter (Figure 76). 'The Key of Solomon', a medieval sorcerer's handbook, insists that no activity involving contact with the spirit world can succeed without the consecration of a magic circle. The magician must perform elaborate ceremonies of purification and dedication before he draws the circle, and he must choose a suitable place for it too.[38] He draws a circle on the earth with the Knife of the Art and a rope 9 ft long: a second circle with a radius of 8 ft is drawn concentric with the first – a distant parallel with the layout and method of construction of the bank and ditch of Stonehenge I.

The gap between the medieval earth-cut circles was used for writing the Names of Power, but that may be a late addition to the exercise. After the preliminary rituals, when only a small entrance gap is left in the magic circle, the magician enters. If he has disciples, the magician ushers them into the protection of the sacred precinct and closes the circle. Safely inside, he falls to his knees and recites the consecration of the circle: 'O Earth! I conjure thee by the holiest name ASHER EHEIEH, with this arc made by my own hand! May God bless this place with all the heavenly virtues. May no defiling spirit be able to enter this Circle or cause discomfort to anyone within it. Give us safety as thou art the Everlasting Ruler!'

After this, spirits might safely be conjured and sent on their way. This is but one form which the magic circle and its rite took. In some cults it shrank to a metal ring, which of itself conjured genii, whilst in others, especially in the late middle ages, magicians prudently carried folding paper circles about with them. All this may seem a far cry from neolithic Wessex, but the underlying principles seem to have been similar. A liturgy for the Circle of Protection was scratched on Sumerian clay tablets as early as 2000 BC, when the sarsen circle was newly completed. A continuous tradition of magic circle beliefs and rituals can be traced back almost to the time of the earth circle, and certainly to the time of Stonehenge III.

Why was Stonehenge drawn again and again as a circle rather than a square, triangle or some other shape? We can find a parallel in the Aboriginal Australian treatment of sacred sites. Within the last few centuries Aborigines have made earth circles, stone lines and avenues, even raised standing stones; they often made their *bora* or ceremonial ground in the form of an earth circle, although frustratingly the present-day Aborigines cannot remember why they were made that shape.[39] The circle was at least easily drawn with a rope and a stake, and well within the limitations of neolithic technology. Was there more to it than that? The moon was occasionally circular, but it changed and was as often a half-circle or crescent. Only the sun always appeared as a perfect circle, so it is possible that Stonehenge I was made circular in imitation of the sun on whose warmth food, health and comfort depended. The circle has always been a symbol of unity, of wholeness, of safety, and of the world. Jung saw the circle as an unusually potent image, a symbol of centrality and totality, one with an immediate *a priori* emotional value, a numen or spiritual value all its own. St Bonaventure used this archetype in his attempt to describe God: 'God is a circle whose centre is everywhere and the circumference nowhere.'

The crests of the 2 m high surrounding bank, well above the eye level of the average neolithic adult,[40] brought the far horizon in close and shrank the world disc to the size of the sacred precinct. This effect turned the enclosure into a microcosm, a universe in miniature where beneficent forces could be gathered and focused, especially along the Avenue as the sun rose on midsummer morning. Priests might then send out these gathered forces like the fertilizing rays of the sun itself into the surrounding fields and forests, stimulating them into fruition. It may be that the magic circle was conceived as a kind of power station.

MIDSUMMER DOORWAYS

The Heel Stones were raised as an outer doorway, a ceremonial entrance: significantly, the south entrance was not marked in this special way.[41]

Someone standing at the centre of Stonehenge would have looked through it as through a window-frame towards the north-eastern horizon, towards the point where the sun floated free of the horizon on midsummer morning in around 3100 BC. The surviving right-hand pillar may have been intended to mark the moonrise at midswing; the missing left-hand pillar may have emphasized or replaced the southernmost of the lunar A posts. The Heel Stones contained salutations to both sun and moon.

The inner portal stones reinforced Stonehenge's midsummer sunrise axis.[42] Seen from the centre of Stonehenge, the Slaughter Stone and its partner created an outer frame, adding drama and perspective to the sunrise spectacle. Neolithic people gathering at Stonehenge in 3000 BC to see the sunrise at midsummer probably felt that they were observing a mythic event rather than an astronomical one.[43] It is a mistake to attribute modern values and preoccupations to the people of an archaic community which saw the world very differently. We take for granted that the sun sets in the west and rises in the east because we think of the earth as an orb spinning on its own axis once in twenty-four hours, turning each place on its surface alternately towards and away from the sun: but in the archaic mind things happen differently. As the sun sets, the sun-god is shut in a chest for the perilous night sea journey from west to east through the waters of death that are under the earth; during this journey he is threatened by all manner of dangers such as being ensnared or swallowed by a monster.[44] This theme can be traced in the myths of one ancient culture after another, from Polynesia to India and Europe. In the Germanic myth of Siegfried, Sieglinde is commanded to hasten to the east where she will give birth to Siegfried, the sun-hero.[45] The same theme recurs in North American Indian mythology and even survives in Longfellow's *Hiawatha*:

All night long he sailed upon it,
Sailed upon the sluggish water,
Covered with its mould of ages,
Black with rotting water-rushes,
Rank with flags and leaves of lilies,
Stagnant, lifeless, dreary, dismal,
Lighted by the shimmering moonlight
And by the will-o'-the-wisps illumined,
Fires by ghosts of dead men kindled
In their weary night encampments.

The prehistoric worshippers at Stonehenge will have thought of the sun's nightly journey in these or similar terms. They will have devised similarly elaborate stories, perhaps even epic poems, to explain the sun-god's reduced power in winter, his increasing strength during the summer, his changing rising and setting places and the effects of all these changes on the seasons and the human economy. A master of ceremonies of a Pueblo tribe once explained, pointing at the sun, 'He who goes there, that is our Father. We must help him daily to rise over the horizon and to walk across the Heavens. And we don't do it for ourselves alone: we do it for America, we do it for the whole world.'[46] Perhaps marking the rising and setting places helped to make these events happen. The summer solstice, the longest day, when the sun climbs highest in the sky, was and still is a calendar landmark, one that tells us that cereals should be ripening and that harvest time is not far off. I have suggested elsewhere that the Wilmington Giant, the huge chalk hill figure in Sussex, is an icon of a prehistoric sun-god in his high-summer aspect, flying in through ceremonial portals just like those at Stonehenge to preside over the harvest.[47]

THE DOUBLE BLUESTONE CIRCLE

With the sacred site marked out and protected by an earthen bank and ditch, it is not immediately obvious why a stone circle should have been added. Surely it was gilding the lily to add the stones? Once again, a look at the regional context helps us to understand. The earth circles represent the earlier tradition, and these were relatively easy to make in the lowland and low-hill country of the south and east of Britain, where the soil is deep and the rock soft. In the highlands, where soils are thin and the rocks are hard, a substitute form of magic circle had to be devised: people used loose boulders prised up from the bedrock to mark out a ring with earth-fast slabs.[48] The two traditions developed side by side. Then the idea exported from lowland to highland was reimported: this happened especially in the 'border country' where the two traditions overlapped, and this is where Stonehenge lies.[49]

One effect of adding stones to an earth circle was that they reinforced it. This may have been prompted by the same motive that made the earlier causewayed enclosure builders add extra rings of banks and ditches: it was a way of emphasizing the perimeter. The bluestones that were brought in to build the stone circle had the extra quality of exoticism. They were fetched from Wales, from mountains that were possibly themselves regarded as sacred: possibly part of the magic lay in the series of expeditions to Wales to collect the stones. It may also be that the undertaking was a display of power, a demonstration of organizational ability, diplomacy and tech-nology. The motives are more likely to lie in these areas than in any architectural consideration: symbolic acts were all.

The bluestones were pillar-like and about the same size, when erected, as people. It may be that they were intended as idols or abodes for deities. Although this may seem an unwarranted speculation, some of the later standing stones, especially on mainland Europe, became recognizably hu-manoid: they were given sculpted facial features and other details making it clear that they were idols.[50] Perhaps the ring of stones was intended as a perpetual ceremonial dance in honour of a deity. At dusk at Avebury, I once

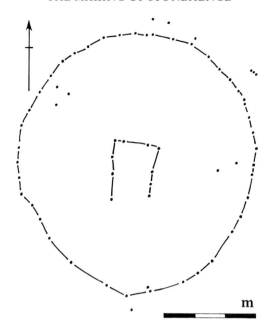

Figure 77 Amesbury 31. This round barrow 300 m south of the Lesser Cursus contains the remains of a post-circle and a small three-sided, cove-like mortuary house. The design is reminiscent of the horseshoe of trilithons and the sarsen circle of Stonehenge IIIa: a deliberate cross-reference may have been intended.

had the impression that the stones were not quite inanimate, that they were ready to break into a lumbering, elephantine dance: they stand still as if for a two-minute silence at some megalithic Cenotaph, but for four thousand years and more.

The question of the lintels for the Double Bluestone Circle is not resolved: there is no way of knowing how many lintels were actually made. The radial pattern, though unusual, would have been entirely consistent with what is known of the culture. The rayed lintels would have created a large sun-burst symbol similar to the small rayed motifs carved on many another megalithic monument (Figure 54). The design clearly symbolized the sun and confirms for us what we have already long suspected, that Stonehenge was a sun-temple.

THE SARSEN MONUMENT

Looking very much like great heavy doorways, the sarsen trilithons may well have been a deliberate architectural reference to the entrances of megalithic tombs. Tomb entrances were built in much the same way in Britain, Brittany and Spain. Even the ceremonial doorways of the Maltese

Figure 78 A megalithic tomb chamber (St Lythans, Glamorgan), showing the origin of the symbolic three-stone arrangements. Without the capstone it becomes a cove, without the backstone a trilithon.

temples, dating from the time of Stonehenges II and IIIa at the latest, were made in this way, from three colossal stones.

Two American writers have proposed that the five trilithons at Stonehenge represent the five early bronze age cemeteries in Wessex: Lambourn, Avebury, Oakley Downs on Cranborne Chase, the South Dorset Downs and the cluster round Stonehenge itself. The trilithons are seen as symbolic tomb entrances, each representing many barrow-burials but united by family and territorial ties. The entrances that in the cemeteries themselves lead to the mortal grave and the underworld open at Stonehenge onto the blood-lines of the chieftain families that interwove to make Stonehenge the metropolitan centre for the whole of Wessex. It was natural that one trilithon, the central one, should be significantly larger, to represent the central, dominant territory and its overking.[51]

Unfortunately, this neat and attractive idea cannot be substantiated. Stonehenge may have been a cult centre for a larger area than the territory immediately round the monument, but there is insufficient archaeological evidence to identify the extent of that larger area. It may be, given the spacing of the later neolithic and early bronze age centres (Figure 31), that the Stonehenge territory was no larger than about 30 km across from north to south. There were really four major chalkland territories in Wessex, focusing on Avebury, Stonehenge/Durrington, Knowlton and Mount Pleasant: there seems little justification for raising Lambourn with its thirty-three round and long barrows to the level of these high-status centres. Nor is it by any means certain that the centres Stover and Kraig list were actually under the rule of the Stonehenge chieftain: in fact it seems more likely that they were not.

The Great Sarsen Circle is easier to understand. With its running lintels it made a continuous ring of stone: as such it would have been seen as more powerful than a circle made of widely separated slabs. The ring of stones raised to the sky suggests a dedication to the sky gods and ties in well with the obsession with sun and moon we saw at the north-east entrance. The ring of Aubrey Holes with their offerings suggests a similar dedication to the earth deities, an acknowledgement that the earth receives the bodies of the dead and is also the mother of life. The components of Stonehenge thus contain the germs of a rudimentary mythology: an earth-mother or underworld-goddess who is visited annually and impregnated by a high-summer sun-god and visited irregularly by a lunar deity of some kind with a much more complicated cycle. The 'astronomical' orientations, midwinter sunset and northerly moonrises, were incorporated into the Stonehenge design specifically to honour these mythic events and confirm the builders' faith in them. There would also be a practical reason for interest in the passage of the seasons: in a farming, fishing and hunting community the seasons are often life and death, and always periods of alternate plenty and shortage.

The horseshoe of trilithons, as we have already seen, is an elaborate variant of the cove idea and as such symbolizes the tomb's heart. The arrangement of the trilithons round an open central space is reminiscent of the arrangement of some chambered tomb interiors. The internal plans of Hetty Pegler's Tump in Gloucestershire or the West Kennet Long Barrow in Wiltshire consist of an entrance passage leading to a central chamber with two chambers opening from each side and a fifth at the end (Figures 79 and 80). Huge though the trilithons are, the stones are set so close together that the 'doorways' are very constricted, just like real tomb chamber entrances (Plates 38 and 39). The narrowest part of each trilithon doorway measures only 28–31 cm: it is possible for a person to squeeze through them, but only just. It is as if the builders were emphasizing the difficulty of passing from world to world, the physical and emotional difficulties surrounding birth and death. The same ordeal of the rite of passage is emphasized in other belief systems too: ideas like the narrow way and the eye of the needle. The references to neolithic tomb architecture are clearly intentional and the builders would have expected prehistoric visitors to have recognized and understood them.[52]

Similar architectural references were made elsewhere. At the other end of Britain, the Orkney chamber tombs known as stalled cairns contained deliberate references to domestic architecture: in fact the megalithic tomb was perhaps as much a symbolic stone dwelling as the earthen long barrow

206

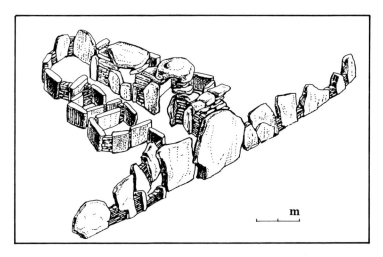

Figure 79 West Kennet Long Barrow: the 'horseshoe' arrangement of the five tomb chambers. The megalithic facade was added to mark the end of the monument's use for burial.

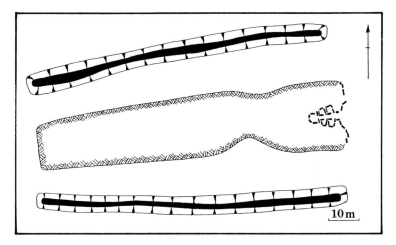

Figure 80 Plan of the West Kennet Long Barrow. The five tomb chambers can be seen at the eastern end of the mound.

was a symbolic wooden longhouse. Neolithic people entering a stalled chamber with lamps or torches would have seen the ghostly shapes of stone doorways materializing in the gloom. In the simpler chambers, they would have seen three pairs of doorjambs one after another and a sort of passage or

207

progression is suggested. This idea of a journey is even more evident in the exceptionally long chamber of Midhowe on Rousay, where visitors had to pass through twelve stone doorways one after another, each flickering into existence only as the fearful celebrants ventured deeper into the tomb.[53] House doors, tomb doors and free-standing trilithons were all part of a web of references and metaphors with which neolithic and bronze age people would have been very familiar. This is not to say that Stonehenge was dedicated to death. Like many major religious symbols it was ambivalent: in one and the same structure or image two opposites may be contained, just as the Latin word '*altus*' can mean both 'high' and 'deep'. In many cultures gods who brought fertility were also thought of as bringing destruction; the life-giving sun is represented in the zodiac by a lion. In the world of myth, death often in some mysterious way brings about birth. Just as Christ's death is celebrated by Christians as heralding life eternal, and the symbol of the cross is taken by them as a symbol of that life, so the death references in Stonehenge should be read equally as life references.[54]

When the stones of the monument are considered all together, the sarsen circle, sarsen trilithons, bluestone circle and bluestone horseshoe, something more emerges, a larger and more comprehensive image still, the image of a roundhouse in decay. As the large round communal dwellings fell into decay after centuries of use, the flimsy thatch disintegrated first, then the light radial rafters, but the stout uprights and horizontal ring beams endured for much longer. Their cracked and weathering timbers became a potent romantic image of the community's history, a symbol of the past, of the inheritance left behind by the ancestors, of the tribe's collective identity.

At any time from 2400 BC onwards there was probably always one roundhouse at Durrington Walls in that state, while others were built nearby to replace those that collapsed. We know from the archaeological evidence that they were not dismantled: they were just left to fall apart.[55] There had been a roundhouse at Stonehenge itself as part of the phase I design and part of the sequence of structures at the centre of the monument (Figure 72). What could be more natural than to replicate in stone the early wooden rotunda or one of the communal roundhouses as part of the final, climactic design? In order to understand the final design, an awareness is needed of the Stonehenge people's tribal consciousness and their love of metaphor, symbol and layered allusion. Once Stonehenge is seen in this way, the greater part of its multiple meaning becomes clear. The final design was one which forty or more generations of the tribe had groped their way towards, instinctually and empirically, drawn on by a powerful sense of collective identity and territorial bond.

The makers of Stonehenge were trying to find a symbol of their selfhood, faith and aspirations. Their remote ancestors had established squatters' rights to live, hunt, fish and farm there and, as in many another neolithic territory, a monument had to be raised to declare that link with the ancestors. The final symbol, final and overwhelming, the unique cipher of the Stonehenge people, was the image of *home*, the nostalgic and sentimental image of the communal ancestral home not quite complete, not yet quite fallen apart through decay. The Stonehenge builders created something close in spirit to the Gothick follies built by English squires in the eighteenth and nineteenth centuries. These later follies too were built to be conspicuous landmarks, as visual foci in the landscape: they were also built deliberately incomplete – fake ruins – as reminders of past times and the passage of time.[56] An important difference is that the Georgian and Victorian land-owners were merely decorating the boundaries of their estates, improving the views from their mansions, whereas the makers of Stonehenge were raising a temple as a centre-piece. Stonehenge was built as a focal display of power and status, whereas the English squires tended to invest most of that in their mansions.

Today we have grown accustomed to seeing Stonehenge as a ruin, but we tend to assume that it is ruinous because it is old. Yet, even when the sarsen and bluestone structure was new it was a ruin, or at least an idealization of a ruin. And now, after four thousand years, it has become all the world's image of the ancestral past, exactly as its makers intended.

THE CARVINGS

The early bronze age carvings at Stonehenge remove any possible remaining doubt that the building was a prehistoric temple. Rather surprisingly, the existence of the carvings was not noticed in modern times until July 1953, when Richard Atkinson was preparing to photograph a seventeenth-century inscription on stone 53, one of the trilithon uprights.[57] While he was looking at a row of capitals reading 'IOH: LUD: DEFERRE',[58] Atkinson noticed two blurred carvings underneath, a little below eye level. One was a dagger with a hilt, point downwards, and the other was an axe, haft downwards. The discovery of more prehistoric carvings soon followed.[59] A few days later, David Booth, then aged 10, discovered the first carvings in another group on stone 4.

In the same season, Robert Newall made a rubbing of a vague shape marked on the upper (now inner) face of stone 57. It had been softened and blurred by the hob-nailed boots of schoolboys sliding down the sloping stone before it was restored to its upright position, but it shows clearly in his rubbing as an irregular rectangle with a horizontal top and bottom and the sides elbowed outwards: there is a bump or pimple on top. The image on Newall's rubbing looks disconcertingly like a brimming tankard of beer. Newall saw at once that the shape was similar to those that had been found on standing stones and more revealingly inside chamber tombs in Brittany.[60]

On the strength of a vague similarity between the Stonehenge dagger and those found at Mycenae, an attempt was made to link Stonehenge with

Mycenean architects. Many archaeologists were still reluctant in the 1950s to believe that Stonehenge had been built by native Britons, and this evidence that sophisticated, culturally advanced visitors from the Aegean had come to the site opened up the possibility that these foreigners had built the monument.[61] In fact local English metal-workers of the Wessex Culture were making hilted daggers between 2000 and 1500 BC,[62] and it is much more likely that the carvings show locally made symbols of power and were added to the sarsen monument rather earlier than the flowering of the Mycenean civilization.[63]

English Heritage was kind enough to allow me to make new rubbings of the goddess carving in July 1992. Although the original of the large rubbing seemed to show little, in photo-reduction an image did appear, and a significantly different one from the Newall image (Figure 81). Whereas Newall's image looks like a tankard, mine looks like a giantess's shopping bag. The base of the figure is higher than Newall's, although the elbowed right (north-east) side is still there. Nigel Rose has kindly produced vu-foils for me of the two images at the same scale. Superimposing these reveals where the modern base line should run across Newall's rubbing, but without this aid it is impossible to detect; this is strange because today the base line as shown in Figure 81 is as clear, both to the eye and to the touch, as the sharply defined right-hand edge, and yet Newall's rubbing misses it. The bump at the top turns out to be the beginning of a faint, roughly semicircular channel: there are also two more ill-defined curving lines immediately to the left (south-west). The left-hand edge of the image is hard to follow, because it seems to run down the very edge of the stone and the line immediately inside it is a natural fissure. Within the rectangle there are no prehistoric man-made features. The lower edge of the image is exactly horizontal, suggesting that it was carved once the stone had been erected. This is a little surprising, as even the lower edge is too high to be carved from ground level: the carving must have been sculpted using a ladder or platform. Below the lower edge and parallel with it are two more straight, horizontal lines, one 29 cm below, the other 29 cm below that. The distance is in effect the 'Short Foot' of $11^{1}/_{2}$ in. that Cunnington thought was used in laying out the plan of Woodhenge. These lines peter out to the right, so it is not clear whether they were part of the box image above: the measurements imply that they were. If so they may, by comparison with the Breton images, represent a skirt and possibly a belt as well. The torso was ground out a few millimetres below the general surface and the bounding lines are the edges of a shallow trough; the two parallel lines are no more than grooves in the surface so, if they were intended to be part of a larger goddess image, perhaps the work was unfinished. We may be looking at an incomplete goddess in a skirt, 1.6 m tall. Alternatively, the lines may be part of a second, smaller, separate goddess image. Newall's rubbing and a recent photograph (in Atkinson 1987, p. 14) nevertheless both show the right-hand edge reaching down as

Plate 32 Meini-gwyr: adjacent bluestones of contrasting shapes. The right-hand stone is even more markedly triangular when viewed from the circle centre, that is, to the right. The avenue led away to the left.

Plate 33 Stonehenge bluestones 62 (rectangular) and 63 (tapered). Axe and dagger carvings are dimly discernible in the shadows to the right.

211

Figure 81 The Stonehenge goddess on stone 57 (rubbing).

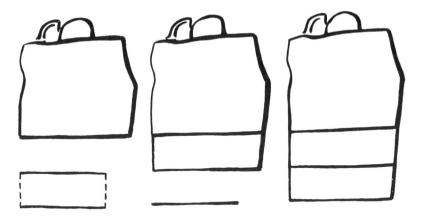

Figure 82 The Stonehenge goddess: three possible interpretations.

far as the upper line and making a clear corner with it, so that line at least would seem to be part of the main image.

The meaning of the carvings is of vital importance in reaching an understanding of Stonehenge. The large, more or less featureless, square carving may look unpromising, and by itself it cannot be made to mean anything at all. Like so much else at Stonehenge, it can only be understood by looking at

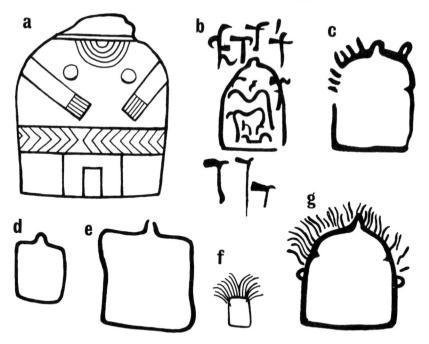

Figure 83 Images of the goddess in France. a: the Mas d'Asais statue-menhir at Montlaur in Aveyron. b: Mané-er-Hroeck, Locmariaquer (with axes and bows). c: Manio, Carnac. d: Mané Lud, Locmariaquer. e & f: Ile Longue, Morbihan. g: Barnenez, Finistère.

parallels and variants at other prehistoric sites. For some reason, English monuments are rather poor when it comes to carvings, and it may be that they were decorated instead with images in perishable materials: wood, cloth, feathers and paint, perhaps. There are nevertheless helpful parallels to the 'box' carving in megalithic contexts in France, and this confirms the cross-Channel contacts we noted in relation to the style of the rich burials (see Chapter 5). The same rectangular shape, about the same size, is carved on a passage upright in the Mané Bras chamber tomb at Erdeven.

The overall rectangular shape is shared by the Mané Rutual image, which is over 3 m high. The Stonehenge image slopes in towards the top and there is a projection from the top: the Mané Rutual image has curving shoulders with a similar projection on top. It is just possible to see the Mané Rutual shape as a massively exaggerated human form with the round projection as the head, the curving shoulders literally as shoulders and the two small 'dimples' as arms. On a wallstone in an Ile Longue chamber tomb there is another icon, almost exactly the same in shape but with what seems to be long hair streaming from the head and shoulders (Figure 83g). This may be a clue to the meaning of the two arcs immediately beside the Stonehenge

213

goddess's head: they may have been intended to represent the goddess's long, flowing hair. The Mas d'Asais statue-menhir has the same overall shape again, which tells us that it is fundamentally the same icon, but with significantly more detail; immediately below the semicircular head projection there are arcs to indicate a necklace and below these are two breasts: coming in diagonally from the shoulders are two crudely drawn arms with unmistakable hands at their ends. This figure even has legs and a decorative belt: it is clearly a goddess (Figure 83a).

By looking at these and other contemporary variations on the theme, we can see that even the simpler box shapes without any detail at all (Figure 83d) are intended to represent a humanoid figure. Whilst we are a long way from the modern idea of a portrait sculpture, we are unquestionably looking at the image of a goddess – the goddess whose worshippers built Stonehenge.

Carvings of weapons too are common at French megalithic sites. One of the upright slabs at the highly decorated Gavrinis tomb has about seventeen relief carvings of teardrop-shaped axe-heads, recognizably the non-functional type often made of jadeite, usually highly polished, and clearly high-value, high-status objects. The actual objects themselves are often found as burial offerings, and it seems very natural to find them carved on the walls of neolithic tombs. Similar axe carvings are to be seen in several tombs in northern France. One of the most significant sites of all is a hypogeum, an underground tomb cut out of the chalk at Coizard. The tomb chamber has a beautifully made doorway with a lintel and squared door-jambs projecting into the chamber, a white trilithon carved out of the living rock; to left and right, again carved in relief, are axes, one on each side as if guarding the doorway (Figure 84).

At another French site, the Prajou-Menhir gallery grave at Trébeurden in Brittany, there is a cluster of carvings on the stone slabs that make up the tomb's terminal cell. There is an antechamber that opens gradually into a 9 m long corridor-like chamber: there are no carvings here at all. At the end of the chamber, however, is a terminal cell separated off as a special place by a cross slab. Inside are carvings. There are stylized breasts, daggers and a necklace on one upright stone, and a square goddess carving on the upright next to it: as at Stonehenge the goddess carving is on the visitor's right hand. Opposite is a design made up of two pairs of breasts, while on the slab separating the terminal cell from the main chamber are two daggers and two more square goddess carvings: as at Stonehenge they mark the monument's main axis.[64]

Again and again, in Brittany and in Ireland too, the monument-builders decorated stones at the heart of the tomb, often putting the largest concentrations of carved symbols on the stones closest to the innermost point.[65] These non-Wessex sites all contain clues to the meaning of the carvings at Stonehenge. A mortal or immortal visitor to Stonehenge in 2000 BC arriving through the ceremonial north-east entrance would have come face to face

Figure 84 A rock-cut hypogeum at Coizard. Hafted axes carved out of solid chalk flank a carved 'trilithon' tomb entrance. The Stonehenge people were using an 'international' vocabulary.

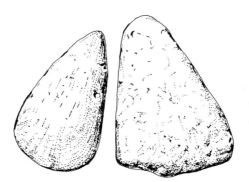

Figure 85 Miniature chalk axes from Woodhenge.

with the great monolith of the Altar Stone standing in front of the Great Trilithon. There, immediately to the right of the Altar Stone, on the face of stone 57 and very close to the edge nearest to the Altar Stone, was the image of the goddess, and there, on the trilithon to the left, on stone 53, were the goddess's symbols – her dagger, her axe.

215

In the Mané-er-Hroeck tomb at Locmariaquer in Brittany, the goddess and her symbolic axes were brought together. The goddess is shown in simplified form, a beehive shape with a tiny pimple for a head. Floating above her are four hafted axes (Figure 83b). In the Table des Marchands, also at Locmariaquer, the slab at the back of the tomb facing the chamber entrance is carved into a goddess shape covered with crooks (of unknown meaning), its sides fringed with loops representing her streaming hair. The tip of the backstone, the goddess's head, holds aloft one corner of the 50 tonne capstone, which carries a huge carved image of a hafted axe, the handle pointing down towards the goddess.

This association between axe and goddess in neolithic and bronze age France and Britain is reminiscent of a similar association between goddess and double-axe in bronze age Crete. There, in the Minoan temple-palaces that were in use from about 1900 to 1380 BC the goddess was sometimes shown with a double-axe, and sometimes the double-axe was shown as a substitute for the goddess, in much the same way that Christ is often represented by the cross alone rather than by a crucifixion.[66] At Stonehenge the goddess is represented equally by her stylized portrait – the box shape – and by her symbolic weapons.

There are other axe and goddess carvings at Stonehenge and it may be that to understand them fully we need to look at Stonehenge in plan. When their positions are plotted on a plan an interesting pattern emerges.[67] The goddess drawing lies to the west of the monument's centre, the dagger and axes on stone 53 to the south: in other words, they mark cardinal compass points.[68] The carvings on the stones in the sarsen circle fall into the same pattern. Axes carved on the outer faces of stones 3, 4 and 5 mark the east. The small goddess symbol, which would have been very hard to see against the sky, cut into the underside of circle lintel stone 120, was originally placed in the gap between the two uprights on the west side of the circle. Now that the lintel lies on its back on the ground, the goddess symbol is visible as a rectangular, 1 cm deep rebate cut right across the width of the stone. One side is dead straight, the other is disturbed by a natural pit which made the carvers place the head to one side, but the projection representing the head is plainly recognizable (Figure 86). Here, once more, we come face to face with the goddess whose temple this was.

Three cardinal compass directions were signed by the carvings – east, south and west – though not the north, and that was presumably because neither the sun nor the moon ever appears in the northern sky (Figure 87).

The association between the Stonehenge carvings and the goddess carvings found in Breton tombs is significant in proving a cultural link not only across the Channel but also across to sepulchral architecture. The icons that are found at the centre of Stonehenge are also found at the centres of tombs. The architecture of Stonehenge contains clear encoded references to tomb architecture and this leads on to the suggestion that the Altar Stone is itself

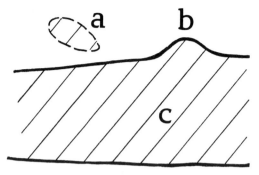

Figure 86 Goddess carving on stone 120 at Stonehenge. a: natural hollow. b: bump representing goddess's head. c: rectangular rebate representing goddess's body. Traced from a stone rubbing. (See plate 40.)

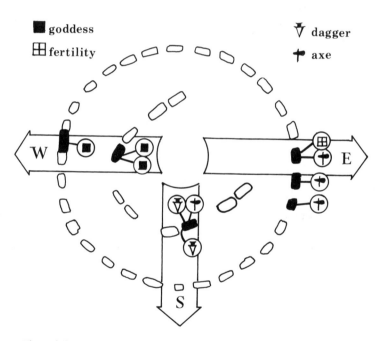

Figure 87 Plan of the Stonehenge sarsen monument: location of carved symbols.

an aniconic symbol of the goddess, presiding over her sanctuary and the spirits of the dead, and awaiting her Sacred Marriage, the annual impregnation by the sky- or sun-god who would come to her at dawn for just a week each midsummer.

TEMPLE OFFERINGS

Most of the offerings which worshippers left at Stonehenge have vanished. Like a prehistoric Parthenon, Stonehenge may have been equipped with all kinds of trappings invisible on the site today.[69] Archaeology can tell us only a fraction of what happened anywhere, since most human actions leave no trace whatever and others leave traces that are perishable. It is surprising that after four or five thousand years any of the temple offerings left at Stonehenge have survived: those that we find were deliberately buried in the bank or ditch or in the Aubrey Holes. Given that patterns emerged from the positions of the axe and goddess carvings, it may be that there was significance in the placing of offerings too. It is difficult to be certain about this, because a long section of the ditch on the northern and western side has yet to be opened, but a pattern is emerging.

The cremated remains of several people were buried close to the ditch end at the north-east entrance, on the right hand of the visitor we imagined approaching up the Avenue, and another cluster of cremations was buried in the bank close to the south entrance, again on its right-hand side.[70] An old stone-hole, which the builders intercepted when they dug out the ditch, was used as an improvised grave-pit for 'the bones of a very young person about the age of 8 or 9'.[71]

Between the two entrances a major cluster of cremations with a fine stone mace-head was deposited in the enclosure bank.[72] This point on the circumference, 142° from True North, marks the position of the major southern moonrise. A couple more cremations folded into the bank mark the equinoctial sunrise to the east. The north-east entrance was guarded by an adult and child burial – a child of 5, Hawley tells us – lying on its right-hand side. The south entrance was guarded by another adult and child, yet again on its right-hand side: the repetition of this 'right-handedness' must have been significant in some way. A third adult and child burial was deposited on the east-south-east; it is not clear what the significance of this might have been, but it was placed exactly halfway between the other two. We may be seeing only part of an overall symmetry: perhaps when the rest of the ditch is excavated it will emerge that there were six adult and child burials in all, equally spaced round the circle (Figure 88).

Some of the Aubrey Holes were used to deposit cremated human bones, but it would be unwise to read too much in the way of orientation into these. It looks as if the Stonehenge people began filling them in a fairly methodical way, starting at the all-important north-east entrance at Aubrey Hole 3 and working clockwise round the circle: they became less systematic as they approached the south entrance. The Aubrey Hole nearest the centre of the north-east entrance, Aubrey Hole 55, was honoured with a deposit of antlers. Another, close to the south entrance, Aubrey Hole 21, was marked with a deposit of antlers and a chalk ball, possibly a sun symbol.[73]

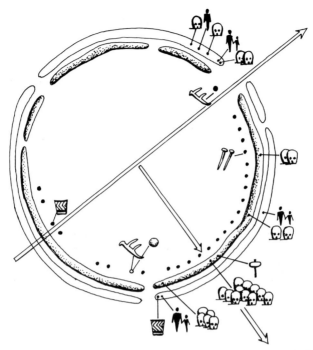

Figure 88 Stonehenge offerings. The distribution of cremations (skull symbol), adult-and-child burials, antlers, bone pins, pottery and mace-heads. The directions of the midsummer sunrise (top right) and southernmost moonrise (bottom right) are also shown.

The offerings were deliberately and purposefully placed round Stonehenge: very similar things happened at other ritual centres, like the recently discovered henge at Shepperton in Surrey. The Shepperton henge was probably created at the same time as Stonehenge I, around 3000 BC, and like Stonehenge it was but one component in a large ceremonial complex. The north-east entrance at Shepperton was oriented towards the midsummer sunrise and guarded, again on its right-hand side, by a crouched human burial. A woman's torso was buried 10 m to the west of the midsummer entrance and a deformed dog's head 10 m to the east.[74]

Deer antlers were deposited in random order, yet apparently with deliberation, along the floor of the Shepperton ditch, just as they were in the Little Cursus ditch near Stonehenge.[75] Lumps of red ochre were laid in the ditch at the point marking the most southerly moonrise, the position honoured by offerings of a valuable mace-head and a cremation cluster at Stonehenge.

The orientations have to be seen as meaningful when they are repeated at widely separated sites of the same period.[76] The people who made the Shepperton henge created an avenue of pits possibly originally 600 m long, leading to the River Ash; it was clearly not a random event or a piece of purely local thinking that led the Stonehenge people to extend their Avenue all the way to the River Avon.

The meaning of the cremations at Stonehenge is not immediately obvious. To argue from them that Stonehenge was a charnel-house or mortuary seems unwise.[77] The architectural references, and the shape and arrangement of the trilithons in particular, suggest that the temple was dedicated to a religion in which death played a major part. On the other hand, death was common among the Stonehenge people: average life expectancy was perhaps as low as 30, and it would be quite natural for people expecting to die young to be preoccupied with death. We would expect them to seek to explain and come to terms with death through their religion. An understandable preoccupation with human mortality was easily dovetailed into a myth that linked the rising and waning fortunes of man and landscape with the seasonal journeys of sun and moon deities. Like man, the sun-god went into decline and died, perhaps nightly, certainly every winter: but there was hope for the dying Stonehenge people if their gods could die and yet be reborn.

It was comparisons, images, analogues and metaphors that made the prehistoric mythology that hovers unseen behind Stonehenge. As the temple of the sun-god and earth-goddess – and who knows what other deities of the moon and sky – Stonehenge was a natural choice of place at which to offer up the remains of the dead, perhaps in the hope that they might be reborn, perhaps as a way of embedding the community in the monument and cementing that relationship.

Maybe not all of those who were buried at Stonehenge died naturally. We saw how the young archer killed there in about 2130 BC was very likely a refoundation sacrifice. When the same community built Woodhenge two hundred years earlier a 3-year-old girl was brutally killed as a foundation sacrifice. The cluster of nine cremations near Aubrey Hole 14, marking the southerly moonrise, may represent nine children sacrificed to the moon-goddess.[78] The adult and child burials and other human remains may represent sacrifices too.

It is easy to understand why offerings of antlers were made. Antlers are annually shed, annually regrown, and so symbolize the annual cycle of regeneration. They may have been seen as particularly suitable as foundation offerings because, unlike other annual produce, they are hard and enduring. Probably the Stonehenge people saw them in another way too, as part of the wildwood that they regularly took, trimmed and turned to their advantage. At some sites there are offerings, side by side, of unshaped antlers and trimmed antler picks; it is as if they are saying, 'This is what we found: this is what we made'.[79] The neolithic people were conscious that their made world was differentiated from the world of nature, yet utterly dependent on it: the two worlds existed side by side, interacting, and the offerings at Stonehenge were a way of affirming that this was so.

Figure 89 Stonehenge complete. The appearance of the temple from the centre looking towards the south-west, reconstructed in true perspective from photographs.

The sarsen–bluestone monument (Stonehenge IIIa–c) actually embodies this idea. Unfortunately it is no longer possible for most visitors to experience Stonehenge from the centre: rope barriers ensure that the view is, on the whole, from as far away as the ditch, and that view is of the outer faces of the circle stones. The architectural impression from the centre is significantly different, and for several reasons. In the first instance, the inner faces of the stones are dressed, smoothed and in some cases polished, so that there is a far greater impression of finish, of the stone-masons' craft, of modern architecture. The inner face of sarsen circle stone 30, for instance, has been ground to a flat surface as smooth as a sawn ashlar; the inner face of bluestone 70 has been given a convex, polished surface that is impossible not to stroke (see Plates 30 and 33). There is another contrast between outside and inside, and that is the height of the stones. The trilithons are much higher than the circle stones, so they are far more overpowering and awe-inspiring when viewed from the centre. This is partly because they are closer, but also partly because their soaring vertical lines are not cut across by the sarsen circle lintels: when they were all in place the architecture of the trilithon horseshoe would have been quite difficult to read from outside. Seen from inside, all is clear. The clean vertical lines of the trilithons are accented rather than interrupted by the pillars of the bluestone horseshoe, and the horizontal supplied by the running lintels of the sarsen circle would have created a perfect foil, like the level line of the plain's horizon accentuating an isolated clump of trees.

To explore this effect, I took a sequence of overlapping photographs from the centre of Stonehenge to make a continuous montage and transferred the outlines of the stones to tracing paper: I then raised fallen stones and replaced those that are missing. The result is two panoramic drawings, one centring on the Great Trilithon and the other looking back in the opposite direction towards the midsummer sunrise (Figures 89 and 90). Responses to architecture are subjective, of course, but it seems to me that these 'peeled back' panoramas show that in both conception and execution the Stonehenge III design was full of nobility, power and majesty. To stand alone at the centre of Stonehenge is to have the same sort of feeling as when standing in the choir of a great cathedral: the same screened, semi-enclosed

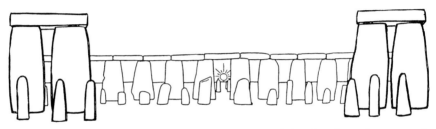

Figure 90 A reconstruction, based on photographs, of the view from the centre of Stonehenge towards the north-east in 1800 BC.

apse shape is there, the sense of an ambulatory running round behind it, the sense of stone verticals soaring up towards a vault. Stonehenge is not so much unvaulted as referring to a cosmic vault that is infinitely high and ever-changing in mood and colour, just as looking back towards the north-east the axis is seen to refer to the rising solstice sun. What we are seeing here is an interplay, without doubt a conscious interplay, between an architectural idea and the reality of nature, the one fixed, the other changing: the one doomed to eventual disintegration, the other endlessly self-renewing. This pairing of ideas is all of a piece with the late neolithic preoccupation with putting the wild and the tame side by side.

Even the bones scattered across the site of Woodhenge contain this polarity (Figure 91). Denizens of the wilderness – wild animals and the ghosts of dead ancestors – were kept outside the roundhouse by being confined to the ditch. Pigs were allowed to forage in the woodlands, so their (half-wild) bones are common at the edge of Woodhenge and become rarer

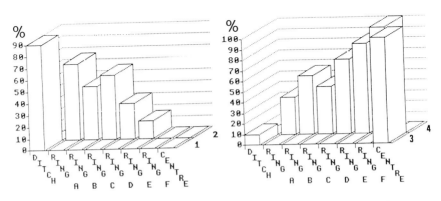

Figure 91 Distribution of bones at Woodhenge. 1: wild animals. 2: pigs. 3: humans. 4: cattle. The distinction between wild (left) and tame (right) is plain to see.

222

towards the centre. Cattle were completely domesticated and moreover grazed man-made pasture, so their bones become commoner towards the centre. At the centre was a single human burial; presumably exempt from exclusion because it was hallowed by the act of sacrifice, the offering of the little girl represented the ultimate in human control. The Woodhenge people were not just taming their young but were also ready under exceptional circumstances to tame their strongest feelings – and offer their young in sacrifice. How far the curious bone pattern at Woodhenge was consciously created cannot be known: it may have been deliberate or the by-product of several separate activities that happened to result in differentiation. Nevertheless, however it happened, the pattern of bones does show that the people living at Durrington Walls in 2300–2000 BC, the builders of Stonehenges II and III, were making statements about the difference between home and wilderness.[80]

Perhaps this same differentiation was being expressed on a much larger scale when the Great Cursus was laid out a thousand years earlier. South of the cursus was an east–west swathe of landscape that was a hive of activity, with dwellings, flintworking sites, pastures and garden plots; north of the cursus there were expanses of pasture but very little settlement, only the old enclosure on the hill. The Great Cursus may have been built partly to express the separation, the difference between the new, domesticated landscape in the centre of which Stonehenge would be built and the old, exotic, distant, marginal landscape to the north.[81]

Stonehenge is a complex monument: it has many parts, it was modified many times, and its builders expressed many of their ideas in its structure. Any short and simple explanation of Stonehenge is going to be very wrong, or at best very incomplete, because it took something like eighty generations to build and had to meet the changing needs of an evolving society. Some beliefs were very persistent through that time, and it seems extraordinary that the final major structure, the sarsen–bluestone building, should be a reworking of the idea of the timber roundhouse that had stood there a thousand years before: even more extraordinary, that this development should be resumed after several centuries of relative neglect during which the existence of the roundhouse might easily have been forgotten. Yet it was not forgotten. It seems as if nothing was forgotten, as if Stonehenge was there to make sure people remembered, like those monolithic First World War memorials with 'Lest we forget' inscribed on their plinths.

Stonehenge was a stone mnemonic encapsulating the community's belief system, its collective identity, its communal pride, its status (or at least self-perceived status), its faith, its history, its tryst with the gods and tribal ancestors, its technology, its ego, its self-esteem. Built in an age before books, Stonehenge was itself a book. It was built by no barbarians (in the worst sense), but by the sophisticated and subtle citizens of a nearby township that seems somehow to have been ahead of its time. At least until around 2200 BC they were content to express their power in an anonymously communal project: only after that were their chiefs given grandiose burials, and then began the slide into the pursuit of personal wealth and personal status.

Plate 34 The underside of bluestone 36 at Stonehenge, showing the seating for the uprights and marks of wear through rocking.

Plate 35 Two fallen stones from the Bluestone Circle at Stonehenge, 32 (left) and 150 (right). A mortice is visible at the centre of the picture.

9

STONEHENGE IN DECLINE

The magic of Stonehenge is never more powerfully felt than during the wild tempestuous autumnal gales . . . Thoughts rise suddenly of the many tragedies, feasts, sacrifices, mysterious rites that must have been enacted here in far-off, bygone days.

Lady Antrobus, *A Sentimental and Practical Guide to Amesbury and Stonehenge*, 1900

Y AND Z HOLES

After a time of uncertainties, we come to a firmly dated phase, when ragged rings of pits known as Y and Z holes were added round the outside of the sarsen monument as an afterthought. This phase, Stonehenge IIId, is dated to around 1500 BC.[1] Two hundred years before the golden age of Mycenae, yet Stonehenge was already in decline. It stood now in an open, cleared landscape with apparently unfenced pasture immediately round it: further off were clusters of small fenced fields marking the locations of farmsteads and villages. Here and there, long winding ditches stretched across the plain to mark the ranch boundaries; one of these approaching from the west curved slightly to avoid Stonehenge: it also avoided crossing the initial, straight stretch of the Avenue. Stonehenge, then, was still respected.

The rather informal pattern of pits, already described in Chapter 6, was the last component to be added to Stonehenge's magic circles. The holes closest to the north-east entrance were treated in a special way. Z29 contained a deposit of antlers and Z30, immediately outside the entrance to the Great Sarsen Circle and beside the midsummer sunrise axis, held a small stone sun-disc. Several metres further out towards the Heel Stone, Y30 in the outer pit-ring held a clutch of five antlers. These offerings confirm that the Y and Z holes were probably dug for the same purpose as the Aubrey Holes which had been dug over a thousand years earlier.[2] The pits, which are now filled in and invisible, were too shallow ever to have been intended as sockets for bluestones. It has often been assumed that the Y and Z holes were created as sockets for an alternative bluestone setting, but there is no pressing reason to go along with this idea.[3] An ingenious alternative, that each radial pair is in some way connected with the mechanism for raising a sarsen stone, is disqualified by the later radiocarbon date.[4] They have more the character of offering pits. In the archaic world, offerings were frequently made in this way to please the spirits of the underworld and enlist their support.[5]

THE LAST GESTURE

It may be that towards the end beliefs and values altered. Four hundred years on from the creation of the desultory offering pits, one hundred years after the Trojan War had ended with the destruction of the city of Troy, the Stonehenge people made one last gesture.[6] It was in the decades around 1100 BC that the Avenue leading north-east towards the midsummer sunrise was lengthened by another 2 km, eastwards over the hill and then south-east to descend to the River Avon.[7] It looks impressive on the map, but it was no great undertaking; the two not-quite-parallel ditches were cut into rough v-shapes and the upcast thrown inwards to form banks.[8] It has long since disappeared as a landscape feature, but can be spotted on air photographs as a cropmark, and sometimes shows up well when there is a light dusting of snow. Long before this last section of the earthwork was traced, William Stukeley had a hunch that the Avenue must have connected Stonehenge with the river 'at an ancient ford of the River Avon'; he had in mind Ratfyn, 1 km upstream from the place where the Avenue actually reaches the Avon floodplain.

Atkinson says that the last 200 m of the Avenue have not been found and there is general agreement that it petered out just north of West Amesbury House.[9] Certainly its termination on the river bank remains to be discovered, but there may be an intermediate section of the Avenue in the paddock immediately to the south of the main street in West Amesbury: two low, sub-parallel banks show in the pasture, about 38–40 m apart. Although this is an unexpected find, and it may yet prove that the banks date from the wrong period, it is clear that they are in the right place to be a continuation of the Avenue. The distance between them suggests that the Avenue goes on widening towards the Avon: it is 23 m wide overall near Stonehenge, broadening to 34 m at its last known position 100 m or so to the north. Unfortunately it is virtually impossible to follow the Avenue the last 100 m to the Avon as a dense, waterlogged woodland covers the Avon's northern bank (Plate 16).

O. G. S. Crawford, the founder-editor of the journal *Antiquity*, felt that since the Avenue curved it could not have been orientated towards the rising sun, or indeed anything else, and was relieved to be able to prove it.[10] In fact the first section to be built, back in 2150–2100 BC, *was* straight and, moreover, aligned on the midsummer sunrise. It was only the extension

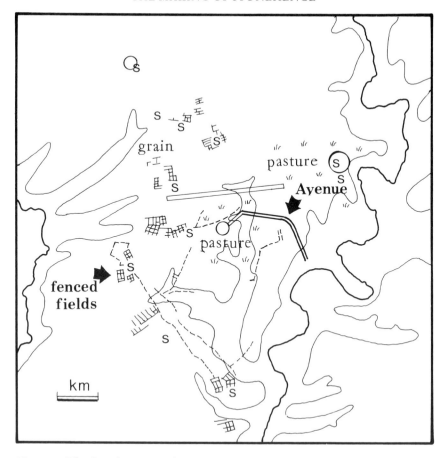

Figure 92 The Stonehenge area in 1100 BC.

added a thousand years afterwards that was curved. It may be that the extension to the Avon was a nostalgic backward glance to the time when the bluestones first arrived at Stonehenge. The stones were perhaps intended to arrive, like the midsummer sun they were destined to celebrate, through the ceremonial north-east entrance. If so, the long slow arc marked out by the Avenue's twin ditches and banks may mark where they followed up from the river bank as a kind of Via Sacra.

There may be another, additional or alternative, explanation. In the later bronze age water cults became conspicuous. Valuable objects such as rapiers made of bronze were thrown into rivers as offerings, and it may be that the Avenue was lengthened in order to link Stonehenge with water for cult reasons.[11] The need to do this speaks of a change in religious values, in that the original focus was well above and well away from any surface water. It was a time of general cultural change and Stonehenge and other major cult

228

centres of the neolithic and early bronze age may have been on the wane. The stone rows leading away from the stone circle at Callanish far away on the Isle of Lewis were left unfinished – just as Stonehenge's Avenue seems to have been. Had the tendency to federate and centralize gone into reverse? It may be that Europe as a whole underwent a period of trauma and instability at about this time, resulting in devolution and fragmentation into smaller chiefdoms. There are signs of political disturbances right across Europe and beyond. The Knossos Labyrinth was abandoned in 1380 BC. The Trojan War and the fall of Troy are believed to have happened around 1250 BC. Rameses III fought to keep Libyans out of the Nile Delta around 1200 BC. By 1200, famine was raging in the Hittite lands (i.e., Turkey) and many of the administrative centres on the Greek mainland were being attacked and destroyed: Mycenae was sacked in 1200 and finally destroyed in 1100 BC. The population of Britain swelled to a maximum, perhaps as high as $1^1/_2$ million, the Domesday figure, in about 1300 BC and collapsed to half that figure between 1300 and 1100 BC.[12] Disorientating evidence has emerged that the British hillforts we used to assume were iron age in date are in many cases late bronze age. At Dinorben in Wales, for instance, the first stout wooden box ramparts were built in about 1010 BC; similar forts in the Peak District were built from 1450 BC onwards.[13] Sure signs of unrest.

Something had gone badly wrong. What produced these catastrophic effects we cannot tell. It may have been population growth, warfare among the paramount chiefs, economic collapse, plague, or some combination of factors. A background problem at this time was certainly a continent-wide, long-term deterioration in climate, which must have made food production more difficult in every region. I would not be the first to propose that ceremonial monuments were built in an attempt to maintain soil fertility by supernatural means.[14] It is significant that the first earth circles and long barrows appeared shortly after the first farmers saw the harmful effects of forest clearance on the quality of the soil. It may be possible to see in the increasing elaborateness of the Stonehenge design an expression of anxiety, perhaps even of despair.[15] Was the sarsen monument an extravagant appeal to the gods to stop the soil erosion? There is widespread evidence that the environment of southern England was deteriorating in the late neolithic and bronze age.[16] The Y holes are filled with a wind-blown silt that speaks all too eloquently of an open, exposed and poorly managed prairie where bronze age farmers were gradually losing their soil to a winnowing wind.[17] In south-east England generally people drifted onto the new lands of the major river valleys and coastal plains, developing metal-working centres well away from the old Wessex heartlands: this demographic and economic shift may also help to explain the decline of a key Wessex monument.

The hasty extension of the Avenue towards the life-giving, rejuvenating river can be seen as a desperate, last-ditch attempt to siphon new life into the old religious centre, to give the old, marginalized temple a transfusion of water magic, and new life to the fields round it. Yet the will even to do that petered out.

A PREHISTORIC WESTMINSTER ABBEY

From its misty sunrise as a band meeting-place in 8000 or 7000 BC to its zenith in 2100 BC and on into the late bronze age twilight, Stonehenge underwent some remarkable changes of design. The middle to late bronze age phase was certainly a period of decline, contraction and waning ambition, yet Stonehenge remained, and that it remained meant that it drew some response from the people who lived nearby. It remained a focal point but, like a great Romanesque cathedral stranded in a twenty-first-century city, a focal point of a rather different kind. It remained a religious cult centre, although not exclusively that. It was probably still an object of civic pride, although it seems that it was no longer developed significantly as an organic part of the cultural fabric.

Even so, we should not rule out the possibility that, like Chichester Cathedral with its John Piper tapestry, bronze age Stonehenge was elaborately decorated with multi-coloured textile hangings and pennants, or fitted with painted wooden furnishings, or even cult objects of precious metal. Any or all of these embellishments could have been added to the monument and removed again without leaving any archaeological trace. Absence of evidence is not evidence of absence. At the same time, it must be admitted that nothing of the kind has survived.

It looks as if, all the way through, Stonehenge was connected with the key polarity of life and death. The Aubrey Holes from Stonehenge I contained, among other things, cloth bags of cremated human bones. The foundation of Stonehenge II was marked by the sacrifice of a young man who was then buried hastily in the enclosure ditch. By Stonehenge III the barrow cemeteries were being established – dense clusters of high-status burials – in the area round Stonehenge. By 1100 BC, it had become a small burial-free island surrounded by an incoming tide of bronze age round barrows. The landscape round Stonehenge had become as cluttered with the burials of chieftains, warrior-heroes and possibly warrior-queens as Westminster Abbey. Like the abbey, it had become a tradition fossil.

Two mysteries remain. It is known that Stonehenge cost a great deal: the total of all the labour invested in the successive building stages was not less than $2^{1}/_{2}$ million man-hours (see Appendix B). What is not known is how large an area and how many communities contributed to that cost. The larger the area, the more manageable the project would have been, in the sense that more people would have shared the cost, but that is not in itself a proof that Stonehenge was the metropolitan centre for a very large region. The sequence of maps (Figures 14, 31, 46, 93) implies rather the contrary, that the Stonehenge/Durrington Walls territory was one, albeit a very important one, of about half a dozen Wessex territories. It may be that from about 2100 BC onwards the Stonehenge people dominated and controlled Wessex, but there is no hard scientific evidence for it. Whether we believe the labour for Stonehenge was supplied locally, within, say, a 5–10 km radius, or from a medium-sized territory of 500 sq. km, or from a much larger province encompassing the whole of Wessex and perhaps more lands beyond will inevitably be determined by our assumptions about the nature of, in particular, early bronze age society. My own preference is for the smaller territory of 10–100 sq. km for the early and middle neolithic and medium-sized for the late neolithic and early bronze age, since I believe that we habitually underestimate the potential for achievement of small but highly motivated and committed groups of people. Even Stonehenge IIIa could have been built by a community with a population total as low as between two thousand and five thousand, one that today we would think of as a village, although it would have stretched its resources to the limit. When the sarsen monument was being built there may have been as few as fifty people actually working on the site – a far cry from the epic 'cast of thousands' most people have envisaged. It is worth recalling Geoffrey of Monmouth's remark about the dismantling of the Giants' Dance: was it built just as it was dismantled, 'more easily than you could ever believe'?

The other abiding mystery of Stonehenge is that it did not lead on to anything else. We take for granted that it should have developed as it did, as far as it did, then stopped: but the sequence of events was by no means inevitable. Given the dynamism of the culture that produced Stonehenges I, II and III and the high levels of organization involved in the creation not only of Stonehenge but also of Durrington Walls, we may wonder why a full-scale bronze age civilization did not emerge to rival those of the eastern Mediterranean: Egypt of the pharaohs, Minoan Crete and Mycenean Greece. All the preconditions for civilization seem to have existed. The great days of the sarsen monument and the rich chieftain burials might have prepared the way for a flowering of fully fledged urban life, with craft specialism, monarchy, writing, and the rapid accumulation of knowledge that follows from writing. A civilization as strong and original as the great Mediterranean civilizations might have emerged in Wiltshire between 2000 and 1500 BC and yet, the evidence tells us, it did not happen; the stage was set, yet the curtains stayed closed.

The political map of Wessex changed significantly (Figure 93), with the four large superterritories of the Hampshire Basin and Marlborough Downs fragmenting into nine. Why this retrogression happened will probably never be known. It is possible that the environmental disaster that flowed from forest clearance and poor land management finally caught up with the Wessex communities: perhaps economic decline and socio-political fragmentation together prevented the proto-civilization from taking off.

Possibly, as has already been hinted at, the elaboration of Stonehenge was

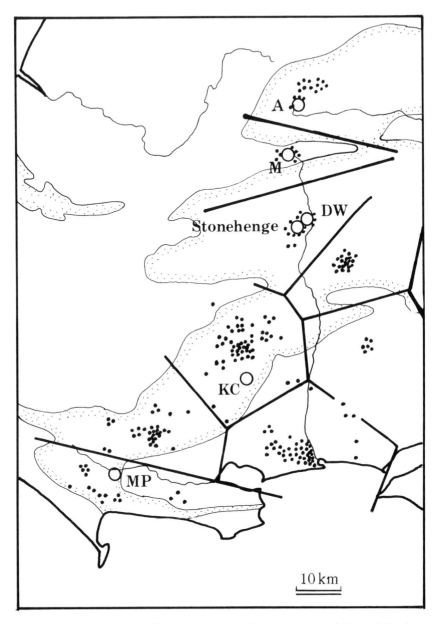

Figure 93 Late bronze age Wessex territories. Concentrations of Deverel-Rimbury cremation urns suggests nine territorial centres with 'frontiers' midway between them. A: Avebury. M: Marden. DW: Durrington Walls. KC: Knowlton Circles. MP: Mount Pleasant. Note that Christchurch seems to have become as important as any of the inland centres.

actually stimulated by economic challenges and setbacks, the successive building phases representing ever more extravagant appeals to the wayward gods. Britain's climate gradually deteriorated after 2000 BC, with summers becoming cooler and wetter. In the uplands, peat bogs began to grow and many of the early bronze age farmers had to abandon their steadings.[18] In the main the farmlands of southern England seem not to have been directly affected by the worsening climate, but the long-exploited Wessex chalklands had lost their resilience, become vulnerable. The number of settlement sites on the chalk was already quite considerable in the early neolithic and by the late neolithic that number had doubled: the land was probably approaching exhaustion.[19] The final small gesture, the extension of the Avenue around 1100 BC may have been prompted by a major economic crisis; it is known that a volcanic winter created by a dust veil from the 1159 BC eruption of Mount Hekla produced between ten and twenty years of very cool conditions, cloudy skies – and failed harvests.[20] Possibly other key stages in the development of the Stonehenge territory were also stimulated by large-scale volcanic eruptions. The 4400 BC Masaya eruption, for instance, may have nudged mesolithic hunters into adopting agricultural techniques as a more efficient method of food production; it may also have stimulated neolithic colonists to migrate and so indirectly caused the spread of new ideas.[21] The building of Stonehenge I (and indeed the Avebury henge) may have been prompted by another economic crisis created by the eruption in about 3195 BC of an as yet unidentified volcano. Some of the later stages in Stonehenge's development may similarly be linked to global events: the creation of the Y and Z holes, for instance, seems to have coincided with a cluster of large-scale volcanic eruptions (of Rabaul, Etna and Thera) which must have reduced temperatures in Britain (see Appendix D).

THE FALL OF THE STONES

A worse misfortune was to overtake Stonehenge. At some time after 1000 BC but before the documented period, Stonehenge was savagely vandalized and it is to this sad episode, the last in its prehistory, that we now turn. The destruction of Stonehenge can be viewed as the work of man or the work of nature. Some scholars believe that natural processes are mainly to blame.[22] Piecemeal stone robbing may account for the rest. That some stones have fallen down as they have become unsafe in modern times suggests that time and weather may be enough to explain all the damage. Stone 14, an upright on the south-west side of the Great Sarsen Circle, is known to have fallen inwards in AD 1750: it still lies where it fell. In 1797 an entire trilithon fell backwards across the sarsen circle: it has since been re-erected.[23] In 1963 stone 23, a circle stone close to the fallen trilithon, collapsed in a gale, probably after being disturbed during the re-erection of the trilithon just months earlier. If we extend this rate of collapse back in time to 1100 BC, it is possible to account for all the damage we can see. In support of this idea, much of the damage seems to be on the south-west side, the side that bears the brunt of the weather flung at Stonehenge by the prevailing wind. Gusting gale-force winds from the south-west could have rocked uprights in their sockets and dislodged lintels.[24]

It may also be that the weather has acted on a monument that was not sufficiently strongly built. The uprights of trilithon 57–58 were set in shallow pits, apparently so that the undersized stones could reach the same height as trilithon 53–54 opposite. With this shallow seating, 57 and 58 were in greater danger of collapsing, and collapse they did – on 3 January 1797.[25]

In a similar way the uprights of the Great Trilithon were of different lengths. Stone 56 was a very long stone indeed, so it was given an unusually deep socket, 2.5 m deep, to bring its top to a level 6.7 m above the ground (Plate 41). The builders of Stonehenge IIIa were apparently unable to find a stone to match it: the stone chosen to be its partner was quite a lot shorter and had to stand in a shallower pit. The builders evidently well understood the danger of instability and shaped its base into a broad foot: this lowered its centre of gravity and improved its chances of staying upright, but it fell at some time just the same. Stone 55 still lies where it fell, and the havoc that its falling caused can still be seen. It broke itself in two like a wafer as it fell across the Altar Stone, which it apparently knocked over, broke in two and now covers. The Altar Stone is hidden under stones 55 and 156, the Great Trilithon's lintel, which came crashing down at the same time (Plate 41). One of the bluestones was also felled: stone 67 was knocked sideways to the north; stone 66, the tongued bluestone, seems already to have been broken off when this disaster happened. So, perhaps Stonehenge was insecure from the very beginning. Some stones were shallow-seated and, pushed by gales, loosened by freeze-thaw, doomed to fall at some time. In such a dense cluster of uprights, one fall caused another. Just two or three unsafe stones acted like detonators with a timing device, or fifth columnists, destroying Stonehenge from within.

The case against time, weather and excessively shallow sockets seems a strong one, but there is also the possibility that Stonehenge was deliberately destroyed. In the seventeenth century, Inigo Jones believed there had once been a sixth trilithon and that it had been carried off by 'Violence of Time, and Injury of Weather' and by 'the Rage of Men likewise'.[26] He was wrong about the sixth trilithon – there never was one – but Stonehenge certainly suffered from the rage of men.

The bluestones would have been particularly easy to uproot, being smaller and lighter than the sarsens, and we can visualize builders or road-menders from nearby villages carting them off in pieces with little difficulty. Stukeley was complaining in 1740 about visitors breaking off pieces with 'great hammers' to test whether the stones were natural or made of some artificial cement, or just to take them away as souvenirs.[27] Aubrey wrote that 'the

Plate 36 Daggers carved on the Badbury Barrow slab.

Plate 37 The Cuckoo Stone.

Figure 94 Engraving of Stonehenge showing trilithon 57–58–158 just after it fell over in 1797.

inhabitants about the Amesburys have defaced this piece of antiquity since my remembrance' and even explained why they were doing it. 'It is generally averred hereabout, that pieces (or powder) of these stones put into their wells, do drive away the toads, with which their wells are much infested, and this course they use still.' Apparently this was because no toad (or snake or magpie for that matter) was ever seen at Stonehenge but, as Aubrey himself observed, that was only because the landscape was open and treeless.

It looks as if there is documentation of a sort for the theft of at least one stone. John Aubrey informs us that 'Philip, Earle of Pembroke did say, that an Altar-stone was found in the middle of the Area here: and that it was carried away to St James's (Westminster)'.[28] Members of the Wiltshire Archaeological Society, believing that this remark of Aubrey's must refer to the Court of St James's, wrote to the Clerk of Works there in 1868 in an attempt to trace the lost stone, but they were told that 'no such stone' existed there.[29] It looks as if some garbling of a real event took place, or that Aubrey himself simply misinterpreted Lord Pembroke's reference to 'St James'. Another of Aubrey's contacts, Mrs Trotman, told him that 'one large stone was taken away to make a Bridge by the inhabitants about the Amesburies'. It may be that this was the stone Lord Pembroke was talking about, and that it was taken to the hamlet of Berwick St James, just 6 km west of Stonehenge, and not to London at all.

In 1933 a Wiltshire man reported that two stones that had once lain across a stream had been set up in the middle of the hamlet.[30] This is surely Mrs Trotman's stone, stolen to make a bridge though now a bridge no longer, and the Earl of Pembroke's as well. The stones still stand there in the main street of Berwick St James, each bearing furrows worn by feet along its face.[31] They stand like negligent sentries at the turning into the byway to Steeple Langford. The south stone is immediately visible, standing 1.5 m high on the pavement near the corner of a house, as if waiting for a bus. It is 0.75 m wide and only 0.22 m thick, which makes it too slight a stone to have been any part of the sarsen monument. Its northern partner is shorter and hides among nettles. The two stones could, as Engleheart proposed in 1933, once have been part of a single long stone, similar in size and shape to the Altar Stone, but where this might have stood or when is not known: they are now worn so far from their original shape that it is impossible to tell. A more likely possibility is that they are Avenue stones. Although the phase II circle was made of bluestones, there is no reason why the Avenue could not have been made of sarsens, especially sarsens of bluestone size, like the Station Stones, which also belong to phase II. The Avenue stones have understandably been grubbed out or buried by farmers, just like their counterparts at Avebury, and might well have been reused in the way that the Berwick St James stones have (Plates 42 and 43).

The stumps of some bluestones have been discovered still in their sockets: the broken-off upper parts of at least nine bluestones have been removed.[32] In addition, possibly as many as eleven complete bluestones from the Bluestone Circle and eight of the Horseshoe bluestones have been taken away. It is easy to understand the piecemeal theft of bluestones, whether complete or in fragments, but it is surprising that anyone should have attempted to steal the sarsens: five complete uprights from the Great Sarsen Circle are nevertheless missing.[33] The main concentration of missing and fallen stones is on the south-west side. Of the original thirty sarsen lintels, twenty-two have been stolen: since they were only a quarter of the weight of the uprights, they were easier to take.

Whatever effects the weather has had in dislodging stones, pillaging has been a major factor in reducing the monument.[34] Some stones may have been collected after they fell as a result of natural processes; others have clearly been rooted out, and with some force – the broken bluestones, for instance. Twenty-nine bluestones have been taken from Stonehenge, and thirty-one sarsen stones, not counting the Avenue stones (probably a further thirty-four).[35]

THE RAGE OF MEN

However convincing the case against time and weather may be, we should consider the alternative – that a concerted and deliberate act of destruction was carried out. The iron age Britons who inhabited Salisbury Plain from about 500 BC onwards would never have thought of building a temple on such a grandiose scale as Stonehenge. For the most part they conducted their religious ceremonies in clearings in sacred groves. These ill-defined, dim, rural sanctuaries were regarded by the Romans, always eager to justify conquest, as evidence of the lowest state of barbarism.[36] In some places there were small rectangular temples built of timber, like the one discovered when Heathrow Airport was laid out: it was a modest 6 m square building surrounded by a palisade. There were also some ditched-and-banked circular shrines, and these show continuity with the neolithic/bronze age tradition.[37]

The ancient heritage was not altogether lost, but it had withered: a typical iron age shrine was only 6–12 m in diameter, with a single east-facing entrance. These round shrines were still in use in the sixth century AD in Ireland, where the native culture was allowed to go on developing uninterrupted by Roman invasion. King Diarmaid held the Feasts of Tara in a circular enclosure surrounded by a high wall. The rites performed inside this magic circle are unrecorded: the chronicles tantalizingly say that they were too obscene to describe, so we must assume that they included sexual fertility rites that may have been a direct inheritance from neolithic ritual.[38] This continuity with the remote and archaic past was broken by St Columba, who, with true missionary zeal, stalked round the barbarian enclosure cursing Tara and its pagan kings. After this, the Church fathers forbade any repetition of the Feasts of Tara.[39]

Bearing in mind this use of a circular sanctuary for their special rites, it is easy to imagine the Celtic priests' delight when they first caught sight of Stonehenge, then still intact. An impressive circular enclosure, ready-made, with a central sanctuary that was on about the same scale as their larger shrines, it would have been taken over with alacrity as a Celtic shrine.[40] As the only *stone* temple, unless other ancient stone circles such as Avebury were taken over in a similar way, Stonehenge would have gained an automatic pre-eminence among Celtic shrines because of its magnificent architecture – even if the Celtic priesthood had its power-base elsewhere, as seems to have been the case.

THE DRUIDS

Tacitus gives us a glimpse of the Druids, the Celtic priestly caste, besieged in their island-headquarters on Anglesey. He paints a vivid picture of the Druids gathered by the shores of the Menai Straits, raising their hands to heaven and howling ritual curses at the Roman troops who had come in flat-bottomed vessels to massacre them.[41] The Romans routed the resistance and destroyed the Druids' sanctuaries. It may be significant that there is still an unusual concentration of megalithic monuments close to that coast, and it is possible that the Druids chose to carry out their sacrifices and ceremonies close to ancient shrines to keep faith of a sort with the neolithic past.[42]

The best evidence, ambiguous though it is, comes from Hecateus of Abdera, who was writing in about 330 BC. Long before, in about 650 BC, a Greek traveller called Aristeas described reports collected in Romania of a distant race of people called the Hyperboreans, the dwellers beyond the north wind. Aristeas thought this legendary race lived away to the east, in the neighbourhood of present-day Afghanistan, but he was probably hearing garbled reports of the advanced civilization in China. By Hecateus's time, the Hyperboreans were nevertheless associated with Britain, so when Hecateus writes of the Hyperboreans, it is clear that he means the British.[43]

Hecateus's original text is lost, but fragments of it are quoted by Diodorus Siculus in the *Histories* he wrote in 50–30 BC. Britain, Hecateus tells us through Diodorus,

> is at least the size of Sicily, and lies opposite the land inhabited by the Celts (France) out in the Ocean. This is in the far north, and is inhabited by the people called Hyperboreans from their location beyond Boreas, the North Wind. The land is fertile and produces every sort of crop; it is remarkable for the excellent balance of its climate and each year it produces two harvests. Moreover, the following legend is told concerning it: Leto was born on this island, and for that reason Apollo is honoured among them above all other gods; and the inhabitants are looked upon as priests of Apollo, in a way, because they worship this god every day with continuous singing and hold him in exceptional honour.[44]
>
> And there is also on this island a magnificent precinct sacred to Apollo and a notable spherical temple which is decorated with many votive offerings. There is also a community sacred to this god, where many of the inhabitants are trained to play the lyre, and do so continuously in the temple. They worship the god with songs celebrating his deeds . . .
>
> They say also that from this island the moon appears to be but a short distance above the earth and that it has certain definite prominences on it, just like the earth, which are visible to the eye. It is said that the god returns to the island every 19 years, the period in which the return of the stars to the same place in the heavens is accomplished . . . At the time of the appearance, the god plays on the lyre and dances continuously by night from the spring equinox until the rising of the Pleiades, expressing his delight in his triumphs. The kings of this city and the supervisors of the sacred precinct are called Boreades, as they are descendants of Boreas and the succession to these positions is always a matter of birth.[45]

The passage is admittedly open to more than one interpretation, but there are several striking features that may throw light on the Stonehenge story.

Apollo is the sun-god and we can see from the way the temple was developed how its builders were obsessed with the sun and its movements; from 3100 through to 2000 BC and later the monument was oriented towards the midsummer sunrise. The reference to the moon and the celebration of its nineteen-year cycle recalls the lunar obsession that is also clearly recorded in the Stonehenge design; the stake-holes on the entrance causeway were made as people tracked the moon's movements and identified turning-points in the cycle.

The imposing precinct sacred to Apollo may be Avebury, or the larger ceremonial complex surrounding and including Stonehenge. The spherical temple is more problematic. The word 'spherical' seems a puzzling description at first, but it becomes clear when we remember that the word was sometimes used in antiquity as a synonym for 'astronomical'. The spherical temple is thus a reference to the incorporation of celestial sight-lines into Stonehenge's design, rather than to its circular shape as many have assumed. The sacred city of the Boreads may be a dim memory of Durrington Walls, which in Hecateus's day had long been abandoned. The golden age nostalgia inherent in Hecateus/Diodorus's description is also a hint that this is a window onto a distant past rather than a description of Britain as it actually was in 330 BC. A memory was being kept alive, and it may even be that the Druids themselves had somehow become the legatees of an ancient wisdom: something of the kind is implied by the survival into the middle ages of the oral tradition about the origin of the bluestones.

SUPPRESSION OF THE DRUIDS

An association with Druids may be enough in itself to explain why, how and when Stonehenge was destroyed. Suetonius tells us that Augustus first took steps to limit the spread of the Druids' religion by prohibiting Roman citizens from Druidism, and Pliny relates how under Tiberius the senate issued a decree against the Gaulish Druids. In AD 54, the emperor Claudius ordered the complete abolition of the 'barbarous and inhuman religion of the Druids in Gaul'. Tacitus, writing in AD 61, described the suppression of the Druids in Britain. Pliny too described Britain at about that time: 'At the present day, Britain is still obsessed by magic and performs its rites with so much ceremony that it almost seems as though it was she who imparted the cult to the Persians!' Then, as to later scholars, it seemed an impossible joke that Britain might actually have been the cradle of a powerful and original culture.[46]

Normally the Romans tolerated native religions, except when they were the cause of rebellion or civil unrest. They regarded Druidism as seditious and put it down with relentless ferocity. The Druids were suppressed because, quite simply, they opposed the Empire. Whether the Druids were using Stonehenge as a temple or not, the Romans evidently *thought* they were using it. Perhaps they remembered the Druidical cult centre at Sarmizegetusa in Romania, where they felt obliged to smash down the stone pillars of an astronomical circle with a superficial similarity to Stonehenge. It may be that the Romans came upon Stonehenge as a fully fledged 'adopted' Druidical temple, or they saw traces there of offerings or other superstitious acts; either way, it appears that during the blitzkrieg on Druidism in AD 61 the Romans descended on Stonehenge and set about dismantling it.

'AN ASYLUM IN TIMES OF DANGER'

Just over 2 km away to the east is a much larger earthwork than Stonehenge, which seems on the face of it to confirm the presence of the Romans in the area: but Vespasian's Camp is misleadingly named (Figure 95). The tree-covered hillfort was built by local iron age people around 500 BC and later reinforced as a refuge *against* the Roman invasion. John Aubrey was convinced that it was a Roman garrison fortress, 'without doubt the Camp of the Emperor Vespasian for it is a perfect Roman fortification.' There is nevertheless no question but that it was built by the native inhabitants of the area well before the Romans arrived.[47]

The camp covers some 15 ha and is marked out by a ditched-and-banked rampart that in places stands 6.5 m high. It occupies a strong defensive site on a ridge-crest at the southern end of a narrow spur and is surrounded on three sides by the River Avon, which makes a great loop round it. There was an entrance at the northern end, just where the A303 now brushes past it, and there was probably another at the south-east corner at Gallows Hill, where Stonehenge Road still crosses the fortification. In the eighteenth century the interior was romantically landscaped with woodland paths, and a Druid grotto called Gay's Cave on its eastern side. Sir Richard Colt Hoare nevertheless understood the true nature of the site: 'This was originally the stronghold of those numerous Britons who inhabited the plains around STONEHENGE, an asylum in times of danger, for their wives, children and cattle.'[48] In fact there is every reason to suppose that this was a settlement and gathering-place as well as a refuge for the iron age people of the Stonehenge area.

The camp has never been systematically or even partially excavated, but road-widening in 1964 on the Stonehenge Road threw up pieces of both early and late iron age pottery. This suggests that the site was laid out in about 500 BC and continued in use for several centuries. Pieces of very similar pottery have been found in the upper silts of the Y and Z holes, though none right at the centre of Stonehenge, within the stones.[49] This suggests that people using or even living in Vespasian's Camp visited Stonehenge but when they did they either kept clear of the centre because of some taboo or superstition or deliberately reserved the centre for special ceremonies – possibly even Druidical ceremonies.[50] This is a shadowy

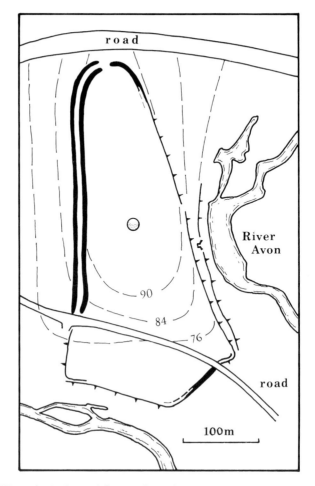

Figure 95 Vespasian's Camp. The numbers show contours in metres.

chapter in the Stonehenge story. The precise nature of the relationship between Stonehenge and the iron age fort may never emerge, although a major excavation of the fort may well fill out the picture.

A PLACE OF CURSES

The pattern of barrows and burials in the Stonehenge area shows that by the iron age times and values had changed, but the evidence is once more ambiguous. Round barrows were actually built inside the Great Cursus, implying that this monument at least was no longer regarded as sacrosanct, but that is understandable since it was built before Stonehenge I and its purpose may have been forgotten even by the time of Stonehenge III.

Plate 38 The needle's eye at Stonehenge: stones 51 and 52 seen between 7 and 6. This shows well how closely set the trilithon uprights are.

Plate 39 A resurrected trilithon at Stonehenge: stone 58 (left), 57 (right).

243

Figure 96 William Cunnington's drawing of himself and his daughter, *The Antiquary and his daughter carry home the Stonehenge urn May 1802.*

A fine bell barrow was built even closer to Stonehenge, only 90 m east of the stones. The mound contains bluestone chippings, showing that bluestones had been dressed nearby, although not necessarily at the time when the barrow was built. The late bronze and iron age people may still have respected the ring of stones, but were not averse to raising burial monuments in the ancient cordon sanitaire which had once existed immediately round it. There is a parallel here with the twentieth-century 'popular' approach to Stonehenge, which is to regard the stone rings as the ancient monument and everything round them as no more than countryside. Archaeologists – like the original builders – have always known that the monument-complex is much bigger.[51] The fact that late bronze and iron age burials were sprinkled amongst the older monuments does not mean that the stone circle at the centre was treated as anything other than a sacred site. One of the barrows 'produced the largest sepulchral urn we have ever found, it measures 15 inches [38 cm] in diameter at the top and is 22 inches [57 cm] high'.[52] There is a delightful contemporary sketch of William Cunnington, the excavator, riding home on his trap with his daughter holding the huge urn, which survived the journey and is now safely in Devizes Museum (Figure 96). The size of the urn may indicate a high-status burial.

The extended body of a man was buried close to Y hole 9, inside Stonehenge itself: the burial was later disturbed so it is difficult to interpret. The evidence for this period as a whole is ambiguous. It may be that the people living at Vespasian's Camp had their own contemporary sanctuaries that have so far gone undetected, or it may be that Stonehenge became once again a focus for religious ceremonies.

One piece of evidence, which was found and then lost again, points positively to Stonehenge as an iron age sanctuary. According to William Camden, 'In the time of King Henrie the Eighth, there was found neere this place a table of metall, as it had beene tinne and lead commixt, inscribed with many letters, but in so strange a Caracter, that neither Sir Thomas Eliot, nor master Lilye, Schoolemaster of Pauls, could read it, and therefore neglected it. Had it been preserved, somwhat happily might have been discovered as concerning *Stonehenge*, which now lieth obscured.'[53] Reading this account, John Aubrey rightly guessed that 'The Inscription on Lead found at Stonehenge wch Mr Lilly the Schoolmaster, and Sir Tho. Eliot could not read, might be made by the Druides.'[54] It is very unfortunate that the tablet itself has vanished without any record being made of its inscription. Now we shall never know what was written on it. 'Eternally to be lamented is the loss of that tablet of tin . . . inscribed with many letters.'[55] But perhaps something can be retrieved: it is known from other sites that in the Romano-British world curses or prayers were offered to gods and goddesses and that these were inscribed on metal tablets. These *defixiones* were made of lead and often demanded revenge from the gods against a wrongdoer.[56]

Stonehenge was still regarded as a place of sufficient sanctity in the first century BC for people to visit it and leave supplications to the gods there. We may, if we wish to see Stonehenge in the iron age as a deserted temple, dismiss this as an isolated incident, a lone vengeance-crazed man or woman hurrying to the overgrown stone circle as a desperate last remedy for wrong when all other forms of redress had failed. Or we may see it as evidence that Stonehenge was still regarded as a holy place, the dwelling place of a goddess.

THE ROMANS AT STONEHENGE

Where, then, does the balance of evidence lead? Wind, rain and frost have clearly played their part in the ruination of Stonehenge, and so have stone-pilferers and souvenir-hunting visitors. But the probability that the stones might fall down entirely of their own accord is far less than many have supposed.[57] Most of the stones are set in much deeper sockets than is normal in stone circles generally. We can, for example, draw useful comparisons with Avebury, where the stones are just as massive, and some of the big Avebury stones are perched in precariously shallow bowls barely 40 cm

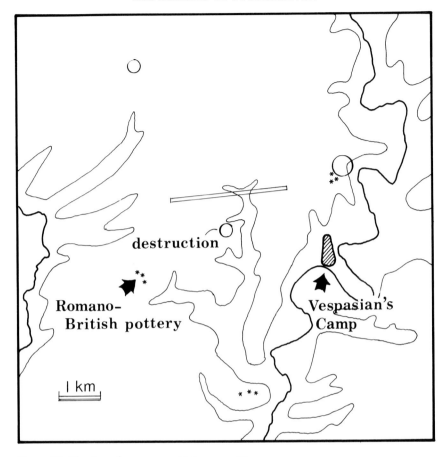

Figure 97 The Stonehenge area, 500 BC–AD 70.

deep. These stones are virtually balancing on the surface of the ground and yet they are still standing in spite of a systematic medieval campaign to destroy them. At Stonehenge, stones that were embedded far more securely 1 m or more into the chalk lie fallen. At Stonehenge there is no evidence of medieval destruction but there is circumstantial evidence of a systematic Roman destruction. The Romans might well have perceived Stonehenge as a symbolic threat to imperial authority, giving them a powerful motive for destroying it. But is there proof positive?

The filling of the Y and Z holes is very telling here. These holes were dug in around 1500 BC and then left to silt up naturally. At the bottom there are a few bluestone chips which probably represent the dressing of the bluestones for the earlier phase IIIc: the debris would still have been loose on the ground surface in phase IIId. Above that bluestone lining the filling is relatively clean soil, which fits in with the late bronze and iron age picture

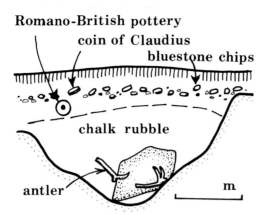

Figure 98 Section through socket E at Stonehenge, next to the Slaughter Stone. The slab in the bottom of the pit may have been broken off when a stone was uprooted in antiquity: the arrangement of posts and stones at the entrance was changed several times (after Hawley).

that we have seen so far: very low-level activity overall or ritual activity that yielded no archaeological deposit.

Towards the middle and top of the filling, something very significant happens: the number of bluestone chips increases again. This can only be explained in terms of the destruction of some of the bluestones: we know from the remaining stumps that some bluestones were broken on the site. There is more evidence still: the numbers of fragments of Roman pottery increase towards the top of the filling as well. In fact, the distribution of stone chips is so strikingly matched by the distribution of Roman pottery that they must be contemporary with one another. The potsherds and the stone chips are of about the same size, which means that they will have been disturbed and buried by earthworms at the same rate: they must have been deposited on the land surface at the same time. The inference is clear. The stones were broken up during the period of the Roman occupation, not before, and by people using Roman pottery – a Roman military force.[58]

The scatter of stone chips across the whole site seems very uniform. It tends to be denser near the centre and thin out towards the edge of the site, but it reaches right out beyond the enclosure ditch. This may be explained as a way of emphasizing that the slighting of Stonehenge was a purposeful act of desecration. At the end of the operation, only a few stones of the barbarian temple had been overturned – it was probably heavier work than the Romans had expected, but the debris was deliberately brushed or kicked about across the whole site. There were tens of thousands of small pieces of broken stone, though their total mass is only equivalent to three stones of bluestone size.[59]

The Romans overturned what they saw as the most important parts of Stonehenge, and toppling the Great Trilithon and the Altar Stone was clearly essential to achieve that. They wrenched stone 56 over, but it resisted their efforts: seated in its 2.5 m deep socket, it was far more secure than they expected. They left it leaning slightly and hauled its partner, stone 55, over instead.[60] As stone 55 crashed in towards the centre it knocked over a bluestone, felled, broke and buried the Altar Stone, and of course brought down its own lintel. Whether at the outset the Romans intended to pull down the entire monument we can probably never know, but it looks as if they found the sarsen uprights far more secure in the ground than they anticipated; possibly they rooted out bluestones and pulled off lintels when they found the sarsen uprights virtually immovable. A complete demolition job would have taken a long time and it seems they contented themselves with a slighting, a level of damage that would be irreparable and be seen by the natives as a sacrilege that would render the monument unusable.

The most likely date for the destruction is the black year of AD 61, the peak of the Druid purge when Paulinus's legionaries attacked and massacred the Druids on Anglesey.[61] From then on, Stonehenge seems to have become frozen in time. It exists now much as it existed then, inert and desecrated, while sixty generations of people have woven an ever-denser fabric of speculation and fantasy round it. It stands, like the castle in the fairy tale of the Sleeping Beauty, paralysed in its moment of trauma and waiting through the centuries for a reawakening that may never come.

The perceptions, values, gods and goddesses of the people who made Stonehenge were different from ours though we share with them a common race, mortality and bond with the earth's limited resources. They seem to have known something was wrong when their tree-felling and cultivation led on to the impoverishment of the soil and waning food production, and they responded by building and elaborating monuments to appease and control the cosmic forces that gave (or withheld) rain, sunshine and harvest. Reaching a new millennium, as we step warily from century to century, we too are becoming acutely aware, collectively aware as never before, of the destruction that we have wrought on our environment. As we struggle to come to terms with this, it is appropriate that a door should open onto the remote past to show that the people of an earlier age went through a similar rite of passage.

We know that we risk damaging the atmosphere by burning fossil fuels in power stations and motor vehicles; we know that by releasing CFCs and puncturing the ozone layer we are exposing ourselves to higher rates of skin cancers and cataracts, and that by warming the atmosphere we risk raising the sea level, possibly flooding coastal cities and losing fertile, food-producing lowlands. But the lavish self-blame popular among journalists on our behalf may be misplaced. Environmental changes are not entirely due to

Plate 40 Goddess carved on stone 120 at Stonehenge. Compare Figure 86.

Plate 41 The wreckage of the Great Trilithon at Stonehenge: fallen upright 55 (left), fallen lintel 156 (right), Altar Stone (underneath), bluestone 68 (behind 156) and the unmistakable stone 56 with its well-preserved tenon. The rectangle in the background is an English Heritage goon-post, aptly nicknamed 'Tardis' after Dr Who's time-travel machine by the guards.

human action. The eruption of Mount Pinatubo in June and July 1991 was a timely reminder that natural processes can produce measurable changes on a global scale. Pinatubo ejected 19 million tonnes of sulphur dioxide into the atmosphere, where it turned into millions of droplets of sulphuric acid, and the effect of this may be to screen sunlight and reduce global temperature by 0.5° Celsius and so partly offset the greenhouse effect. This event and the known result of the El Chichon eruption of 1982 – a fall in global temperature of 0.3° Celsius lasting three years, and noticeable within two months of the eruption – should make us reconsider the relative roles of man and nature in environmental disasters of the past.

In the neolithic and bronze age, people certainly played their part in altering the landscape, clearing forests and depleting the soil, but nature played its part too and after El Chichon and Pinatubo the likely effects of much larger volcanic eruptions in prehistory should be considered. Masaya, Long Island, Mount St Helens, Aniakchak, Rabaul, Etna, Hekla and Thera all erupted on a grand scale during the time when Stonehenge was being made.[62] With their global fall-out effects, they must all have had an impact on the lives and well-being of the people living round Stonehenge. It may not be a coincidence that building work on Stonehenge I began immediately after a very large unidentified eruption: raising the monument may have been a distressed response to the famines of a twenty-year long volcanic winter. Stonehenge IIIa may similarly have been a response to the hardship following a huge eruption in Melanesia in about 2050 BC.

The polarities of birth and death, of summer and winter, of plenty and famine, of sun and moon, of male and female are familiar enough in the making of Stonehenge. Now a new polarity, a more ambiguous one, emerges. We cannot be sure whether Stonehenge was elaborated in a mood of triumph or one of despair. Put differently, were the makers of Stonehenge not waving but drowning?

Either way, the Stonehenge people built Stonehenge III with the intention that it should stand for ever. It was to represent a passing phase in a wooden building's collapse turned to stone for all time, and yet one cannot help feeling that the subsequent fall and destruction of some of the stones has accentuated, actually improved, the sense of ruin. If their ghosts still haunt the empty plain, maybe the makers of Stonehenge accept with equanimity the slow-motion collapse of the loosened stones, imitating as it does on a different time-scale the fall of the roundhouse. The roundhouse may have stood as a rotting, ivy-grown ruin for a century or two before disintegrating into the earth, while the stones will take ten thousand years to fall, until global cooling turns the plain back into an arctic tundra once more. The Stonehenge people cannot have visualized it in this way – their archaic sense of time and history will have been very different from our own – yet they made this place special with timber, earth and stone from the very beginning of the interglacial. It looks as if the place will stay marked out as a special place, a place of creative incubation, a place like no other, with rings of earth and stone until the snow and ice return and the land is empty of people once more.[63]

APPENDIX A

THE CHRONOLOGY OF STONEHENGE

Stonehenge	Stonehenge area	Date BC
'Stonehenge O': totem poles	Pine–hazel woodland	8000–7000
	Beginning of farming	4500
	Robin Hood's Ball enclosure	3900
	Coneybury feast pit	3850
	Long barrows; Great Cursus	3500
	Great Cursus ditch enlarged	3400
	Lesser Cursus	3400
	Lesser Cursus extended: extension immediately filled	3350
	Durrington Walls site cleared and settled	3300
	Normanton Down mortuary enclosure	3250
Lunar observations began	Volcanic eruption caused twenty-year volcanic winter	3200
Lunar observations completed: causeway posts, A posts, **Stonehenge Ia** earth circle and Heel Stones	Durrington Walls continued	3100
Roundhouse? **Stonehenge Ib** Aubrey Holes	Durrington Walls: domestic midden	2910
Stonehenge I ditch silted up	Coneybury henge built	2750
Stonehenge I abandoned/ low-level activity phase began	Lesser Cursus (W half) decommissioned; Durrington Walls superhenge earthworks laid out	2550

Stonehenge	*Stonehenge area*	*Date* BC
	Durrington Walls: southern roundhouse first built	2460
Neglect, encroachment by vegetation continued	Durrington Walls: northern roundhouse first built	2440
	Durrington Walls: southern roundhouse rebuilt	2330
	Durrington Walls: Woodhenge built, sacrifice of girl	2300
Stonehenge II: bluestones brought from Wales, made into Double Bluestone Circle; Avenue		2150
Young archer sacrificed		2130
Stonehenge IIIa: sarsens brought from Avebury to build Great Sarsen Circle and Trilithon Horseshoe: bluestones removed		2100
Carvings added	'Bluestonehenge' (**Stonehenge IIIb**) built at unknown site	2000
	Woodhenge fell into disuse	1900
Stonehenge IIIc: bluestones brought back and added as Bluestone Circle and Bluestone Horseshoe to sarsen monument	Several large-scale volcanic eruptions at about this time could have produced a severe volcanic winter	1800
	Wilsford Shaft	1640
Stonehenge IIId: Y and Z holes		1500
	Major eruption of Hekla in Iceland caused twenty-year volcanic winter	1159
Stonehenge IV: Avenue extended to River Avon		1100
Stonehenge possibly visited for religious worship	Vespasian's Camp: early iron age fort built	500
'Curse-tablet' left at Stonehenge		100
Stonehenge slighted by Roman troops		AD 61

APPENDIX B

THE COST OF BUILDING THE STONEHENGE COMPLEX

A standard formula has been used to calculate how long it would have taken to create earthworks in chalk country, based on the volume of chalk shifted and the mean distances vertically and horizontally that it had to be moved. The figures arrived at here for transporting and raising the stones are lower than those normally quoted because I am assuming oxen were used for pulling. The figure for sarsen lintel raising is based on the Atkinson method, not the Pavel method. The convention of using the term 'man-hours' is used, although most of the work would probably have been done by young teenagers: 'child–hours' would be nearer the truth.

Robin Hood's Ball	175,000 man-hours
Coneybury feast pit	70
Long barrows (17 barrows, 5,000 per barrow)	85,000
Great Cursus	1,250,000
Lesser Cursus	68,000
Stonehenge I (+ 4 sarsens from Avebury)	100,000
Coneybury henge	45,000
Durrington Walls superhenge	880,000
Durrington Walls 4 roundhouses	20,000
Woodhenge	5,000
Stonehenge II Double Bluestone Circle	840,000
Stonchenge II Avenue (+ 17 pairs of stones)	110,000
Stonehenge IIIa transporting stones	380,000
making stone-holes	20,000
felling and shaping timber	5,000
sledges, back-up	15,000
shaping the stones	700,000
raising the uprights	100,000
raising the lintels	180,000
Stonehenge IIIa total work	1,500,000
Stonehenge IIIb	10,000
Stonehenge IIIc	10,000

(Coneybury henge through Woodhenge bracketed together: 950,000)

Stonehenge IIId (Y and Z holes)	5,000
Stonehenge IV	100,000
Round barrows (240 barrows, 1,000 each)	240,000
Total work on Stonehenge I–IV	*2,675,000*
Total work on monuments excluding Stonehenge	*2,768,000*
Total work: all monuments in 100 km²	*5,443,000*

Interesting and unexpected results emerge from these new calculations. The spectacular Stonehenge IIIa design took a comparable amount of labour as building the Great Cursus and thus, by implication, could have been built by a community of comparable size. Stonehenge certainly absorbed an enormous amount of labour, but not nearly as much as is conventionally assumed. The total figure arrived at (admittedly a minimum figure) is less than a tenth of the 30 million man-hours often quoted, partly because the use of sledges and oxen is assumed. Even so, by the end (i.e., around 1100 BC) Stonehenge had absorbed thirty times as much labour as Stonehenge I.

At the other end of the time-scale, it is clear that the causewayed enclosure required a large amount of work, and represents a significant community effort as early as 3900 BC. This background context of large communal work projects is vital to any understanding of Stonehenge. Even though Stonehenge took a large amount of labour it still, incredibly, represents only half the work that was invested in ritual monuments in that (100 sq.km) area, the clearest possible indication of ceremonial hyperactivity.

Plate 42 Berwick St James: the southern stone.

Plate 43 Berwick St James: the northern stone.

APPENDIX C

RADIOCARBON DATES

The Table gives two sets of calibrated dates, the first using the Arizona-Pennsylvania calibration curve dating from the 1970s*, the second using calibration curves devised by Pearson and Stuiver in 1986 †. In the text the calibrated dates are based on the latter, the closest we can get at the moment to calendar dates. Note that the calibrated dates may be in error by ± 50–150 years.

	raw date bc	*calibrated** BC	*calibrated*† BC
Car park post-hole	7180±180	[8000?]	[8000?]
Car park post-hole	6140±140	[7000?]	[7040?]
Coneybury feast pit	3100±100	3850	3880–3820
Lesser Cursus	2690±100	3400	3370
Lesser Cursus	2600±100	3350	3350
Durrington Walls early settlement	2634±80	3350	3360
Durrington Walls early settlement	2625±50	3350	3355
Normanton mortuary enclosure	2550±120	3250	3300–3110
Durrington Walls early settlement	2450±150	3150	3040
Stonehenge I (30 cm above ditch floor)	2460±60	3150	3040
Stonehenge I (base of ditch)	2440±60	3120	3030–2940
Coneybury henge (bone from pit inside henge)	2420±90	3100	3020–2930
Durrington Walls midden	2320±95	3000	2910
Coneybury henge (primary ditch fill, dating henge building)	2250±110	2900	2880–2710
Stonehenge I (ditch fill)	2180±105	2800	2860–2660
Great Cursus (antler in intrusive ditch = later than Cursus)	2150±90	2750	2860–2620
Lesser Cursus ditch fill (dates decommission)	2050±120	2600	2560–2500
Durrington Walls henge ditch	2015±90	2500	2480

Durrington Walls southern roundhouse phase 1	2000–90	2500	2460
Durrington Walls northern roundhouse	1955±110	2450	2440
Durrington Walls southern roundhouse phase 2	1900±100	2350	2330
Woodhenge (antler on ditch floor)	1867±74	2300	2300
Aubrey Hole cremation (thought to be unreliable)	1848	2300	2250
Stonehenge II SE Avenue ditch	1770±100	2200	2160
Stonehenge II NW Avenue ditch	1728±68	2150	2070
Stonehenge IIIa erection ramp	1720±150	2150	2060
Stonehenge II antler	1620±110	2050	1930
Stonehenge Y Hole antler	1240±105	1550	1480
Stonehenge IV Avenue ditch near Amesbury	1070±80	1350	1300
Stonehenge IV Avenue ditch near road	800±100	1000	900

APPENDIX D

LARGE VOLCANIC ERUPTIONS AND STONEHENGE: A POSSIBLE CONNECTION?

Known, located large-scale eruptions (approx. dates BC)		Known, dated environmental effects (dates BC)	Significant cultural changes (dates BC)
73,000	Toba (Sumatra)	Onset of glaciation	–
9000	Laacher See (Europe)	Severe cooling	–
8600	Mt Katla (Iceland)	Ashfall, NW Europe	–
7100	Karkar (Melanesia)	–	–
	Fisher (US)	–	–
	Grimsvatn (Iceland)	Ashfall, British Isles	Totem pole raised: Stonehenge 0
6200	Kurile Lake (Kamch.)	–	–
5400	Mt Mazama (US)	–	–
4400	Masaya (C America)	4400 acidity layer, Greenland ice sheet	Development of farming
		4375 low growth (Ireland)	
3195	unidentified	3195 acidity peak	
		3150 low growth (Ireland)	3100 Stonehenge Ia
2690	unidentified	2690 acidity peak	2700 Aubrey Holes: Stonehenge Ib
		2345 low growth (Ireland)	
2050	Long Is (Melanesia)	2035 frost damage, California	2050 Stonehenge IIIa
1860	Mt St Helens (US) 'Yn' eruption	–	–
1850		Massif Central (Europe) –	–
1800	Aniakchak (Alaska)	Climate deteriorates	1800 Stonehenge IIIc
1650	Vesuvius (Europe) 'Avellino' eruption	1645 acidity peak	–
1628	unidentified	1628 low growth (Ireland)	–
1525	Thera (Europe)?	–	
1500	Etna (Europe) Rabaul (Melanesia)	–	1500 Y & Z holes dug: Stonehenge IIId
1159	Hekla-3 (Iceland)	1159 low growth (Ireland), Scottish Highland farms abandoned	
		1120 acidity peak	1100 Stonehenge IV: Avenue extended to R. Avon

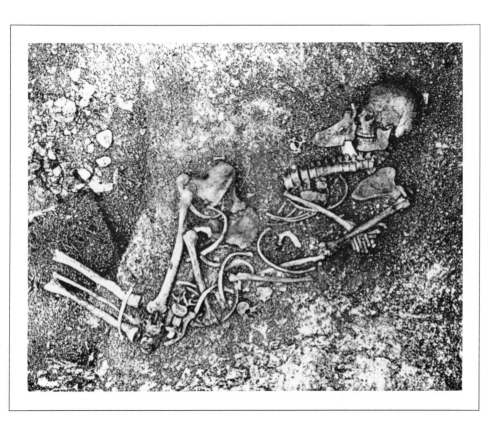

Plate 44 Murder at Stonehenge. The remains of the archer who died in about 2130 BC.

NOTES

1 INTRODUCTION

1 Castleden 1987, pp. 5–6.
2 Castleden 1992.
3 Thomas 1991.
4 Hartley 1953 *The Go-Between*, p. 2.
5 Thomas 1991, p. 13; Hodder 1990. The British neolithic ran from about 4700 until about 2100 BC.
6 Hawley 1928.
7 Chippindale 1983. Burl 1987; Richards 1990 and 1991.
8 Atkinson 1956, revised 1979; Burl 1987; Richards 1990 and 1991.
9 Sir Michael Tippett wrote of Tess at Stonehenge in his Foreword to the 1988 rev. pbk edn of R. Castleden 1987 *The Stonehenge People*, London: Routledge, pp. xi–xii.
10 Stukeley 1740.

2 'BEYOND ALL HISTORICAL RECALL'

1 I leave until later a discussion of the dagger, axe and goddess carvings. See Chapter 8.
2 The only missing stones that have been positively identified are the two fragments of sarsen found in the village of Berwick St James. See Chapter 9.
3 Reported in a letter from Dr Maton dated 30 May 1797 and published in Legg 1986, p. 112.
4 Stonehenge is often mentioned, if fleetingly, on page 1 of British school history textbooks. The treatment is often cursory and uninformative, not much more than forelock-touching to Britain's prehistory.
5 Chippindale 1983 is excellent on this social history.
6 In the 1980s I was approached by a magazine editor for a piece about access to Stonehenge. This was at a time when there was a lot of popular feeling that Druids at least should have access. I think the editor in question must have been surprised when I took the opposite view. In fact abuse of Stonehenge by subsequent solstice visitors has been a good deal worse: the back of stone 57 has been badly scored by a New Age hob-nailed boot.
7 Thomas Arnold (ed.) 1879 *Henrici Archidiaconi Huntendunensis Historia Anglorum*, Rolls Series, pp. 11–12. The other wonders of Britain are the huge caves at 'Chederhole' (Cheddar Gorge) and the cave in a mountain called 'Pec'

NOTES

from which powerful winds gust: this is presumably the cave in the Peak District known as The Devil's Arse.

8 Acton Griscom (ed.) 1929 Geoffrey of Monmouth: *Historia Regium Britanniae* [1135], Longman, trans. Lewis Thorpe 1966 *The History of the Kings of Britain*, Penguin.

9 The medieval idea that Stonehenge had evolved through more than one stage of development in antiquity and was the scene of more than one type of ceremony is an interesting one, and closer to the prehistoric reality than many later interpretations.

10 Gerald of Wales tells how a Welsh bard informed Henry II that Arthur was buried at a particular spot at Glastonbury. Henry communicated the news to the Abbot who, after a delay, excavated and found the royal grave in about 1190. See Giraldus Cambrensis (1861–91); Ashe 1977, pp. 93–6.

11 Long 1876, pp. 36–7, 39, 237.

12 Jones 1655. An omnibus edition of 1725 includes Walter Charleton's 1663 *Chorea Giganteum* and John Webb's 1665 *Vindication* of Jones's 1655 book: this was reprinted by Gregg International in 1971.

13 Chippindale 1983, p. 48.

14 Daniele Barbaro (ed.) 1567 *I Dieci Libri dell'Architettura di M. Vitruvio*.

15 Inigo Jones's copy of this is in the Chatsworth library, and it is rather surprising that Jones's notes in it make no reference to Stonehenge.

16 Corpus Christi College MS 194, folio 57r.

17 C. E. Wright and R. C. Wright 1966 *The Diary of Humfrey Wanley*, Bibliographical Society. John Conyer's diary, unpublished, British Library MS Sloane 937, folio 179r.

18 Charleton 1663.

19 William Mathews (ed.) 1967 *Charles II's Escape from Worcester*, University of California Press, p. 68.

20 John Dryden *Epistle to Charleton*.

21 Aubrey [1665] 1982.

22 Piggott 1950; Stukeley 1724 *Itinerarium Curiosum*.

23 Aubrey *An essay towards the description of the northen division of Wiltshire*, quoted in Hunter 1975.

24 Revd Henry Rowlands 1723 *Mona Antiqua Restaurata*, Dublin.

25 ibid., p. 281.

26 Piggott 1950, pp. 44, 53–7.

27 *The Annals and History of C. Cornelius Tacitus*, 1698, vol. 2, pp. 354–5.

28 Diodorus Siculus *Histories* Book V, 31.

29 Pliny *Natural History* XVI, 44. Translated in 1601 as *The Historie of the World*.

30 Piggott 1974, pp. 122–57.

31 Hunter 1975, p. 159.

32 Burke [1756] 1958.

33 Wordsworth *Guilt and Sorrow, or incidents upon Salisbury Plain*.

34 Duke 1846.

35 Lockyer and Penrose, 1906.

36 Lockyer took the main axis to be the centre line of the Avenue, which seems to me to be quite right, at least for Stonehenges II and III.

37 Hawkins 1963 'Stonehenge decoded', *Nature* 26 October; 1965 *Stonehenge Decoded*, New York: Doubleday and 1966, London: Souvenir Press.

38 Hawkins 1966, p. 178.

39 Atkinson 1966a.

40 Atkinson 1966b.

41 Burl 1987.
42 Hoyle 1966a; 1966b.
43 Sadler 1966; Colton and Martin 1967.
44 Thom 1962; 1964; 1977a.
45 Thom 1955; 1961; 1967.
46 Thom 1951; 1967; 1971; 1974; 1977b.
47 Thom 1967, in *Hoyle on Stonehenge: Some Comments*, Ant. 41, 95–6.
48 Thom, Thom and Thom 1974; Thom and Thom 1978.
49 Thom and Thom 1978, pp. 149–62.
50 Atkinson 1975.
51 For example, Renfrew 1970 'The tree-ring calibration of radiocarbon: an archaeo-logical evaluation', *PPS* 36, 280–311. Renfrew vividly outlines the effect on European prehistory of 'ageing' radiocarbon dates: he shows Europe separated from Egypt and the Near East by a chronological 'fault line'. Developments in Europe turn out to be significantly earlier than previously thought.
52 Castleden 1987, pp. 204–20.
53 ibid., pp. 246–53.
54 For example, the elegantly simple scheme involving just two or three posts and a length of rope proposed by Cowan 1970.
55 See, for example, Porteous 1973. These ideas on body-units are to a great extent a revival of earlier and saner thoughts on the subject, such as Lewis 1895, who proposed that a spear-length could have been used, and this in its turn would have varied significantly from person to person.
56 Hawkins 1966, pp. 178–80; G. Van den Bergh 1954 *Eclipses, -1600 to -1207*, Holland: Tjeenk, Willink and Zoon.
57 The controversy between steady state and big bang theories of the universe was in full swing.

3 THE FIRST STONEHENGE

1 Stonehenge has been only partially excavated, so it is still possible that new and as yet unsuspected construction phases and extra details of the known phases may yet come to light.
2 RCHM 1979, p. ix. Even Stonehenge I was undoubtedly built in an area that was *already* notable for its high density of monuments. In 3150 BC, when Stonehenge I was laid out, the two cursuses and the causewayed enclosure of Robin Hood's Ball were already built. There were also seventeen long barrows in the 100 sq. km centring on Stonehenge, eleven of them within 3 km.
3 Vatcher and Vatcher 1973. If visualizing the distance (253 m) is difficult, it is approximately the overall length riverbank to riverbank of London's Tower Bridge.
4 MacKie 1977a. Euan MacKie proposes Stonehenge I or SI (old SI), SII (old SII and old SIIIa, because they were continuous). SIII (old Y and Z Holes, SIIIb and SIIIc). Obviously other alternatives suggest themselves, such as SI for the meso-lithic phase, SII for old SI, SIII for old SII, SIV for old SIIIa, SV for old SIIIb, SVI for old SIIIc, SVII for SIIId, SVIII for old SIV.
5 For example the roundhouses at Durrington Walls. Increasingly we find conti-nuity of customs across what were once seen as major cultural divides.
6 The raw radiocarbon dates are 7180±180 bc and 6140±140 bc (7040 BC).
7 RCHM 1979, p. 33.
8 The evidence for the features shown on Figure 12 comes from a large number of palaeoclimatic and palaeoecological studies. Note that the colder conditions were

associated with a sea level 20–30 m lower than today: this meant that the coastlines were further out and also that Britain was still connected to mainland Europe by a wide land-bridge. As the climate warmed up, the sea rose and flooded the southern North Sea area, making Britain an island in about 6500 BC.

9 Julian Richards 1991, p. 73, however, faces up to them admirably.
10 Vatcher and Vatcher 1973.
11 Newham 1972, pp. 23–5.
12 Thom and Thom 1978, p. 160.
13 Chippindale 1983, pp. 233, 265.
14 Burl 1979, p. 65; 1987, p. 144.
15 A mesolithic axe was dropped about 200 m south of the posts, a collection of Portland chert flakes, blades and an axe 1000 m to the east-south-east and a stone pick 1500 m away to the north-east. See Wymer 1977.
16 Richards 1991, pp. 70–3.
17 Palmer 1977, p. 214.
18 Drewett 1992.
19 Pequart et al. 1937.
20 Compare Thomas 1991, p. 31.
21 For an account of the forest clearance and beginning of agriculture in Britain see Castleden 1987, pp. 13–31.
22 Evidence for land use comes from pollen contained in the silt lining the ditches of the monuments raised at this time: the causewayed enclosure, long barrows and the slightly later cursus monuments.
23 Thomas 1964.
24 A selection of examples of neolithic false-cresting: Whiteleaf Barrow, Bucks.; Wor Barrow, Dorset; Old Winchester Hill Long Barrow, Hants; Cliffe Hill Long Barrow, E. Sussex; Giant's Grave Long Barrow, E. Sussex; Windover Long Mound, E. Sussex; Bury Hill Enclosure, W. Sussex; Corton Long Barrow, Wilts.; Giant's Grave Long Barrow, Wilts.; Windmill Hill Causewayed Enclosure, Wilts.; Great Ayton Round Barrow, N. Yorks.; Staney Hill Standing Stone, Orkney. See Castleden 1992.
25 Hoare 1812.
26 Richards 1990, pp. 61–5, 233–4; 1991, pp. 73–4.
27 The calibrated radiocarbon dates from the animal bones are 3640–3370 BC and 3361–3039 BC. See Richards 1990, p. 61.
28 Richards 1990, pp. 233–4.
29 Gabbroic ware from The Lizard peninsula was apparently shipped along the south coast to Weymouth Bay and Christchurch Harbour: from there it could easily have been taken up the Avon to the Stonehenge territory.
30 3850 BC is a calibrated radiocarbon date (OxA 1402) from a bone sample with a raw date of 5050 bp. See Richards 1990, pp. 40–61 for details about the pit, which he calls the 'Coneybury Anomaly'.
31 The neolithic enclosure on Hambledon Hill had a great many human remains buried in its ditches.
32 There was a large ditched and banked enclosure on Normanton Down. It was rectangular, 37 m by 20 m, with its long axis oriented towards the south-east, where the entrance was situated. Just inside this entrance were two bedding trenches for posts, perhaps to make a ceremonial gateway, perhaps simply to stop the bank material slipping and blocking the entrance. The mortuary enclosure has been dated to 2560 bc (3250 BC), just before Stonehenge I was built.
33 Case 1962; Ashbee 1970.
34 Morgan 1959; Vatcher 1961. The raw radiocarbon date for Nutbane is 2730± 150 bc.

35 The figures are given in Burl 1987, pp. 126–7.

36 Many long barrows are actually called Giant's Grave. Some of the early excavators convinced themselves that they had discovered the very large bones of giants within the barrows but significantly none of these relics seem to have survived.

37 This is inferred from the family likeness detected among the bones from some of the long barrows, such as Lanhill near Avebury. Keiller and Piggott 1938.

38 Castleden 1987, pp. 210–11.

39 e.g. Ashbee 1978a, pp. 75–82; Burgess 1980, pp. 234–6; Drewett 1992.

40 The combined length of the cathedrals at Bristol, Canterbury, Chester, Chichester, Ely, Exeter, Gloucester, Hereford, Lichfield, Lincoln, London, Norwich, Oxford, Peterborough, Rochester, St Albans, Salisbury, Southwark, Southwell, Wells, Winchester and Worcester is 2,800 m, the same as the overall length of the Great Cursus (Clifton-Taylor 1986, pp. 264–76). This gives a very clear idea of the ambitious scale of the Stonehenge monuments. Alternative comparators might be the length of 42nd Street in New York, or the distance between the Arc de Triomphe and the Louvre.

41 RCHM 1979, p. 14. The cross bank was first noticed by Stukeley: it was rediscovered by excavation when the woodland was cleared, but is not visible now as it is covered by tansy and knee-high grass.

42 The barrow is known as Amesbury 42.

43 Other cursus monuments are also believed to have been deliberately oriented towards long barrows. The Dorset Cursus, the longest one of all, was lengthened at least once during its period of use (just like the Lesser Cursus) and it is plain that both earlier and later phases were 'pointed', north-eastwards, towards long barrows.

44 The Great Cursus has unfortunately yet to be radiocarbon dated, but it is likely to have been built round about 3500–3300 BC, just before or just after the Lesser Cursus.

45 The Parthenon is 69 m long and 30 m wide.

46 Details of this very revealing excavation are in Richards 1990, pp. 72–96.

47 The Phase 1 ditch of the Lesser Cursus was 0.75 m wide and 0.4 m deep. The Phase 2 ditch was 1.5 m wide and 0.7 m deep, a significant enlargement.

48 The raw radiocarbon date (OxA 1405) is 2690±100 bc.

49 It is difficult to give a precise date for Stonehenge I. Because of a 'ripple' in the radiocarbon date conversion graph, raw dates at about this time can be equated to three corrected dates: Stonehenge I could have been built at any time between 3250 and 3000 BC. Using the mathematically derived smoothing line I use elsewhere in this book, a single date of 3150 BC is produced.

50 Pollen from the lower layers of the ditch fill suggests that Stonehenge I was built on a cleared, open site. Nevertheless the survival of fragile folds produced by freezing and thawing in the ice age just a few centimetres below the surface suggests that the site of Stonehenge itself had not been tilled at the time when the henge was laid out – and indeed has never been ploughed.

51 Burl 1987, pp. 50–1, suggests that a sharpened stick was used to cut two continuous circles into the turf, but circles made in this way would have healed quickly and there is every reason, given the small scale of the communities involved, to suppose that they took several seasons to dig out the ditch. Circles of pegs would be easier to create: they would also remain visible in the turf, if need be, for several years.

52 Wooden spades of the type that might have been used for this purpose have been

found at a neolithic settlement site at Ehenside Tarn in Cumbria. See Castleden 1987, pp. 92–3.

53 A different attitude to time is strongly implied by the very long time-scale involved in Stonehenge's development. Stonehenge evolved with a slowness that is almost inconceivable to a modern western mind.

54 All this can be inferred from the detailed form of the ditch. It is a typical early-middle neolithic 'beaded' ditch, each bead or bulge in the ditch representing a work-stint or quarry pit.

55 The builders of Thornborough Circles in N. Yorks. coated the darker stones of the henge banks with crystals of white gypsum in an attempt to whiten them. The Newgrange passage grave was at least partly covered with white quartz cobbles which were not, incidentally, obtained locally.

56 The Stonehenge I ditch varies between 1.4 and 2.1 m in depth and its flat floor is 3–4 m wide.

57 This calculation is based on Burl 1987, pp. 51.

58 The antlers produced raw radiocarbon dates of 2180, 2440 and 2460 bc, which are corrected to 2800, 3150 and 3150 BC.

59 The entrance, 10.7 m wide, was at first obstructed by the maze of stakes. When they were taken out, the Heel Stones and A posts were put in; the activity involved suggests that a relationship between the circle and the sun and moon deities was being organized here, rather than access for mortals.

60 Burl 1987, p. 53.

61 Hawley 1926.

62 Newham 1972, pp. 15–17.

63 Hedges 1984, pp. 175–89; Castleden 1987, pp. 197–9. The death rate in neolithic Britain was probably about forty per thousand per year, compared with only fourteen in western Europe today. The very high death rate is similar to that of many Third World countries. Life expectancy at birth was only about 25 for women, 30 for men. At the same time there were rare individuals who lived to be 60 or 70: these 'elders' must have seemed immortals.

64 Hawley 1924; Newham 1972; Heggie 1981, p. 202; Wood 1978, p. 101; Atkinson, in Heggie 1982, pp. 107–16; Burl 1987, p. 68.

65 Wood 1978.

66 Thomas 1991, p. 151, is wrong to suggest that the Heel Stone was raised in the early bronze age. Early bronze age beaker fragments were found in the side of the stone-hole as he says, but both Stone 1958, p. 77 and Atkinson 1979, p. 70 make it clear that the fragments are in the side fill: they fell into the socket when the Heel stone canted over, possibly, as Stone proposes, as a result of the anti-friction stakes on the south-west side rotting away and leaving the stone unsupported. The late pottery therefore does not date the erection of the stone.

67 Many a popular image of Stonehenge shows the sun rising directly over the Heel Stone and the stone framed by the uprights of the sarsen circle as if it lay on the main axis of the monument, even, ironically, the cover photograph for the 1979 Pelican edition of Atkinson's *Stonehenge*! Much depends on the camera angle, but the Heel Stone is just to the south of the axis and the sun rose well to the north of it on the summer solstice.

68 Hoyle 1977; Atkinson 1979, p. 29.

69 Burl 1987, p. 75.

70 Burl 1991a.

71 Stukeley 1740, p. 35.

72 ibid., p. 56.

73 Wood 1747, pp. 81–2.

74 Smith 1771, p. 63.
75 Stone 1924, p. 130.
76 Atkinson 1979, p. 30.
77 Burl 1991.
78 Pitts 1982.
79 Castleden 1987, pp. 129–30.
80 Brunaux 1987, p. 27.
81 1725 omnibus edition including Jones 1655 and Webb 1665, reprinted Gregg International 1971, pp. 38 and 141; Aubrey [1665] 1982, vol. I, p. 80; Stukeley 1740, p. 33.
82 Mayburgh in Cumbria had a four-post stone portal of this kind. One of the entrances at Whitehawk in Sussex had a timber gateway of some kind, built round two pairs of wooden posts.
83 Seven of my steps are approximately 5 m.
84 e.g. Hawkins 1966; Hoyle 1966a.
85 Hawley 1922. Questions from the Revd G. Engleheart and Reginald Smith imply that they and Hawley were all assuming that the Aubrey Holes were early sockets for the bluestones. In 1928 (*Antiq. Journal* 8, pp. 149–76), following the discovery of Woodhenge, Hawley began to speculate that the sockets were for posts instead.
86 Castleden 1989, pp. 79–80, Plate 1; 1990, Plate 18.
87 *Odyssey* Book XI.
88 *Aeneid* Book VI, ll. 248–63.
89 Atkinson 1979, p. 27.
90 Burl 1987, pp. 47, 97.
91 This is inferred from comparisons with other neolithic sites in Wessex.
92 Burl 1987, p. 98.
93 For more on post-circles, see Cunnington 1929; Piggott 1939; Musson 1971.
94 As at the Sanctuary near Avebury and Mount Pleasant near Dorchester.
95 Hawley 1926, p. 15.
96 Atkinson 1979, p. 61.
97 There seems to me to be very little evidence of a palisade or surrounding wall beyond this. Burl 1987, pp. 54–5 mentions three or four possible posts of a palisade, but they (e.g., the two holes associated with Z hole 13) do not lie on a circle concentric with the roundhouse. The evidence for the roundhouse wall itself is much stronger.
98 Burl 1987, p. 53. Hawley, who discovered the post-passage in 1924, described the post-holes as 15–23 in. (38–58 cm) in width and up to 28 in. (71 cm) deep. He also said, significantly, that they were identical in type and appearance to the post-holes he had found on the north-east entrance causeway. This may imply that they belong to the same cultural phase; the causeway posts date from early in the Stonehenge story, and this fits well with the proposed date for the roundhouse and post-passage.
99 This processional corridor reminds me of the so-called 'Banqueting Hall' on the Hill of Tara. This slightly sunken strip 200 m long and 30 m wide runs between two parallel banks towards the main group of monuments on the hilltop: at this larger scale it has more the appearance of a cursus, which is what it may in effect be. In Irish myth, the boy Conaire is advised by a bird-man to go naked to Tara. As he approaches the hill he is met by three kings who dress him in royal robes and conduct him in a chariot to install him as High King. This suggests that the ceremonial ways, at Tara and Stonehenge alike, may have been used in important rites of passage. See Crampton 1968.

4 STONEHENGE ABANDONED?

1 For example Chippindale 1983, p. 267, where Stonehenge I is dated 3100–2300 BC and Stonehenge II 2150–2000 BC; Atkinson 1980, p. 7: 'Stonehenge seems to have remained in use as a place of neolithic worship and burial for about seven centuries [meaning 2800–2100 BC]. Then, in Period II, it was altered by the addition of the Avenue and the bluestones, about 2100 BC.' Ideas have developed since Stone (1924, p. 2) wrote, 'The present structure of Stonehenge, as we now see it, is all of one period. The erection of the sarsens is contemporaneous with that of the bluestones, the work having been continuous.'

2 Hawley 1923.

3 Evans 1984; Richards 1991, p. 68. Richards says the site, if not the area round it, became 'much overgrown'.

4 Hawley 1923.

5 Evans 1984.

6 Lehmann 1977, p. 191.

7 Castleden 1987, pp. 16–31.

8 The Coneybury henge was known to exist beforehand from air photographs, but not excavated until 1980. It is radiocarbon dated (calibrated) to about 2750 BC. It is clearly not by chance that Robin Hood's Ball, Stonehenge I and Coneybury are all oriented to the north-east; the lesser Cursus and Great Cursus are oriented to the east-north-east. The first leg of the Dorset Cursus, although in a different territory away to the south, was also oriented to the north-east.

9 It is possible that even quite large monuments were made and left in this way. A survival of this practice is described by Athenaeus; he refers to an iron age chieftain called Loernius, who ordered the creation of a huge enclosure for a single feast. After the feast, Loernius distributed largesse from his chariot, leaving the enclosure as a permanent memorial to a single grand ceremonial occasion. See Tierney 1960.

10 The raw radiocarbon date is 2630 bc.

11 Wainwright and Longworth 1971; RCHM 1979.

12 For example Burl 1987, p. 92.

13 For example, Mount Pleasant in Dorset, Meldon Bridge in Borders and Forteviot in Tayside: all were palisaded enclosures.

14 Burl 1987, p. 92.

15 For example Thornborough Circles in North Yorkshire and Milfield Henges in Northumberland.

16 The association of henge and water is seen at several other important neolithic ritual enclosures such as Stanton Drew in Somerset and Waulud's Bank in Hertfordshire.

17 The patterns of movement can be deduced by carefully mapping the density of imported objects, such as Cornish greenstone axes: numbers of these have been found along the Avon valley, with concentrations round Christchurch Harbour and Stonehenge. At least one was taken into the southern roundhouse at Durrington Walls. Another was dropped into the Altar Stone's socket as a foundation offering.

18 Organic remains from the bottom of the enclosure ditch gave raw radiocarbon dates of 2050, 2015 and 1977 bc, which may be corrected to 2600, 2500 and 2450 BC in calendar years.

19 Wainwright and Longworth 1971.

20 It was Piggott 1939 who first proposed that the post-circles were best interpreted as the remains of roofed buildings.

21 The raw radiocarbon dates are 3950 and 3850 bc, corrected to 2500 and 2350 BC.

22 This date is based on a raw radiocarbon date of 2320 bc for the midden material.

23 Bowls with a relief pattern imitating a string net were found nearby, at Woodhenge. The remains of their dogs have been found too: they were rather like fox terriers.

24 Cunnington 1929; RCHM 1979.

25 Antler and bone found on the Woodhenge ditch floor were radiocarbon dated to 1867 and 1805 bc, implying that the ditch was dug in 2300 BC or very shortly before that date.

26 Hadrian's Pantheon is also, coincidentally, the oldest important building in the world to have retained its roof to the present day, and it seems to represent a major rediscovery of the rotunda idea in architecture. Like Woodhenge, the Pantheon was lit by a large central hole in the roof 10 m across. Large wooden round houses were still being built in iron age northern Europe, to judge from the writings of Posidonius, who was deeply impressed by great, thatch-domed, single-storey rotundas that he saw. See Tierney 1960, p. 268.

27 Castleden 1992, pp. 246–8.

28 Burl 1987, p. 124; Castleden 1992, pp. 95–6. The circular timber building at Mount Pleasant also had rings of posts that imply a counting base of four: from the outer edge inwards the rings contained fifty-two, forty-eight, thirty-six, twenty-four and sixteen posts: three of these numbers recur as diameters in Beaker Yards at Woodhenge.

29 Thomas 1991, pp. 48–51.

30 Because the site lies in the floor of the coombe it is covered by up to 1 m of soil; this means that the footings of this structure have probably been preserved well and would repay excavation.

31 For example, a 40 m long Late Bandkeramik longhouse at Cuiry-les-Chaudardes excavated in 1972–81, an example 32 m long at Sittard in Holland, examples 30 and 35 m long at Langweiler near Köln in Germany. See Scarre 1987, p. 27; Whittle 1985, pp. 84, 194.

32 Castleden 1987, p. 44.

33 MacKie 1977a.

34 This is Euan MacKie's view, not my own: there is little evidence that people had specialist occupations in the neolithic.

35 Thomas 1991, pp. 149–50. Marine shells have been found in pits at Woodlands, Larkhill and Ratfyn.

36 The middle neolithic open settlement has been dated to 3300 BC, the construction of Stonehenge I to 3150 BC, and the start of lunar observations at Stonehenge to about 3250 BC.

37 Castleden 1987, p. 150–1.

38 ibid., p. 41.

5 STONES FROM AFAR: THE BLUESTONE ENIGMA

1 Castleden 1989, p. 1.

2 Burl 1987, pp. 105–7.

3 The Stonehenge people were great importers. They used at least three different styles of pottery, one of them imported in quantities from Cornwall. They also imported greenstone axes from Cornwall and smaller numbers of stone axes from Wales and Cumbria. Marine shells at Durrington Walls show trade with the coast. Later concentrations of amber objects indicate trade with Denmark.

4 Atkinson 1979, pp. 175–6 outlines the arguments for believing the Preselis were

sacred hills; see also Lynch 1975 on the magic of Carnmenyn.

5 Bushell 1911; Burl 1976, pp. 255–7.

6 e.g. Grimes 1938 on Meini-gwyr.

7 Thorpe et al. 1991 are mistaken. There is a preference shown for spotted dolerite in megalithic monuments close to Carnmenyn. It is used at the Gors Fawr stone circle (twelve out of seventeen stones) and the ruined Meini-gwyr circle, where it accounts for at least two out of the surviving three stones: Thorpe and his colleagues seem not to have noticed the huge upright thrown down and incorporated into the adjacent field wall at Meini-gwyr, and two more recycled as gateposts close to the site of Stukeley's cove in spite of the evidence that they have recently been tested with geological hammers and found to be spotted dolerite. Olwen Williams-Thorpe seriously misrepresented the situation in her 1991 lecture to the Royal Society, in which she stated that only one megalithic monuments in the Preselis was made of spotted dolerite: four monuments include a proportion of spotted dolerite.

8 Beck and Shennan 1991.

9 Burl 1976, p. 256.

10 This idea was proposed by Clarke 1970, p. 224. It may be relevant that two of the Preseli circles have similar dimensions to the bluestone circle raised at Stonehenge.

11 Bushell 1911.

12 Castleden 1987, pp. 76–7, 106, 208, 217–18.

13 Eighty-five uprights were needed for the Stonehenge II design: if the whole structure was topped by stone lintels a total of 125 stones would have been needed.

14 Acton Griscom (ed.) 1929 Geoffrey of Monmouth: *Historia Regium Britanniae* [1135], Longman, Penguin. trans. L. Thorpe 1966, *The History of the Kings of Britain.*

15 The connection between Ireland and south-west Wales may be closer still. Leslie Grinsell 1975 tells us that Carnmenyn was settled by an Irish tribe called the Deisi, from Leinster, from about AD 250 onwards. So, in the early middle ages, south-west Wales would have had very strong Irish associations. I cannot vouch for the truth of this story.

16 Thomas 1923.

17 Piggott 1941.

18 Burl 1985 takes the opposite view to the one I am developing here; Piggott 1941; Ashbee 1978a, p. 107.

19 Giraldus Cambrensis [1861–91] 1982, p. 51.

20 Burl 1987.

21 It is also possible that very large bluestones existed. Some substantial dolerite monoliths were raised in the bluestone source area. Examples at Efailwen and Cwm-garw must weigh 10 tonnes, more than twice the weight of the bluestones transported to Stonehenge.

22 Aubrey [1665] 1982, vol. I, pp. 89–90.

23 Stone 1924; Piggott 1941; Burl 1985.

24 Thomas 1923.

25 The builders of Gors Fawr used only small boulders, about 0.3–0.4 m high, when larger boulders were available on the site: it seems very odd that they should have selected small stones in preference.

26 Atkinson 1979, p. 49. Atkinson identifies the *un*spotted dolerite at Stonehenge as another Preseli rock.

27 ibid., p. 57.

28 Kellaway 1971; Thorpe et al. 1991 and Burl 1987 support the Kellaway glacial scenario. Richard Atkinson, Julian Richards and I believe the evidence points to people bringing the stones from Wales.

29 W. Judd 1903 *WAM* 33, pp. 47–64.

30 Thorpe et al. 1991.

31 See, for example, Shotton 1978, pp. 233, 234, 238; Keene 1984.

32 M. E. Cunnington 1935.

33 Thorpe et al. 1991 argue that trails of erratics often have gaps in them, to explain the absence of further bluestones on Salisbury Plain. It seems unwise to argue from absence of evidence. As with the mysterious 'north Welsh erratic', on which so much has been made to depend, the lack of evidence critically weakens their case. De Luc referred specifically to *Midland* counties, not Wiltshire.

34 Similar spreads of sandstone-derived muds and gravels may be seen in front of the greensand escarpment at Sevenoaks Weald in Kent. See Robinson and Williams 1984, pp. 17–20, 22.

35 Green 1973.

36 M. E. Cunnington 1935.

37 The stone circles that we know of close to Carnmenyn are Meini-gwyr and Gors Fawr, but Cwm-garw and Efailwen are the likely sites of two more stone circles in the area.

38 The Gelli launching-place, which I think has not been proposed before, is 7 km upstream from Blackpool Mill.

39 The Gambian pirogue is amazingly strong and seaworthy: it can ride ocean waves that one would have thought would swamp a mere dug-out.

40 There is archaeological evidence that neolithic builders made and used planks for various purposes at many sites. The mortuary house inside the Haddenham Long Barrow near Cambridge was made of oak boards up to 1.3 m wide and 4 m long: under waterlogged conditions in the Fens, these have survived almost intact to the present day, but this is rare. (See Hodder and Shand 1988.) Planks were used to build the trackways of the Somerset Levels (Godwin 1960) and a house at Drumkelin in County Donegal. The earliest known British dug-out canoe, now lost, was found at Friarton in Tayside and may have been made as early as 4000 BC (Coles et al. 1978); several other prehistoric dug-outs have been recovered, but most are undated. The earliest known dug-out in Europe is the one found at Pesse in the Netherlands, which has been radiocarbon dated to 6315 bc or about 7000 BC (Johnstone 1980).

41 A recent discovery confirms that there may have been some sort of ferry crossing from Caldicot. The remains of an oaken plank-boat, perhaps originally 15 m long, were found in 1990 at Caldicot Castle. The boat probably dates to between 3000 and 2000 BC and possibly functioned as a regular ferry across the Severn estuary in much the same way as the North Ferriby boats served as ferries across the Humber estuary. The Caldicot find nevertheless does not prove that the bluestones passed this way. See *The Times* 11 September 1990.

42 Atkinson 1979, p. 110.

43 The late neolithic foci in Wessex that we know of are Priddy, Stanton Drew, Avebury, Marden, Durrington, Knowlton and Mount Pleasant.

44 Atkinson 1979, p. 110.

45 Although the 30 km run from Caldey Island to Lundy might seem too far for an early bronze age crew to navigate across open sea, we should remember that they were travelling in a straight line, due south, and could easily have navigated by the sun. Lundy is also a steeply cliffed island rising to a height of 144 m and as a result is visible from the Welsh coast on clear days as an unmistakable seamark. The

voyagers may have rested on their paddles in the 5 km of sheltered water on the leeward side of Lundy, Lundy Roads, possibly even going ashore near the southern tip. The second leg of the voyage, the 19 km of open water before Hartland Point came up on the port bow, was easier, and after that it was a matter of following the cliffed Cornish coast as far as Crackington Haven.

46 The rock carvings are in the Rocky Valley between the villages of Bossiney and Trethevy; a footpath runs down the ravine from the point where the road crosses it, and the carvings are to be seen on the east side about halfway down to the sea. The folklore and interpretation of St Nectan's Kieve are developed in Seddon 1990, pp. 6–7, 164–5.

47 The Mount's Bay axe factory in west Cornwall is thought to have begun operations in about 2500 BC, exporting axes along the south coast to Wessex, East Anglia and Yorkshire (Smith 1974). There is a high concentration of these Cornish axes all the way up the Avon valley and in the Stonehenge and Avebury heartlands. See Cummins 1980. Gabbroic pottery from The Lizard was similarly shipped along the Channel coast to Christchurch Harbour and up the Avon.

48 Christchurch Bay and the Blackwater estuary are still excellent natural harbours. Pevensey Bay *was* a large harbour protected from the open sea by a shingle spit in the neolithic. It is now totally silted up, with the spit forming the shingle headland of Langney Point. Cumbrian axes were traded similarly long distances. See Fell 1964; Manby 1965; Cummins 1980.

49 Stone 1941, p. 114; Burl 1987, pp. 193–4.
50 Stone 1958, p. 49.
51 Darvill 1986.
52 Palmer 1977, p. 211.
53 Bradley 1984.
54 Ashbee 1978a, p. 126.
55 Stone 1958, pp. 113–14; Scarre 1987, p. 301.
56 Cunliffe 1987.
57 Burl 1991b gives as one of his 'six good reasons' for not believing that people transported bluestones from the Preselis the unnavigability of the Avon at Amesbury. In fact the modern Avon is 12–15 m wide and 0.6 m deep in summer at the end of the Avenue, certainly broad and deep enough for rafting or for poling a composite log-boat. Atkinson's 1954 experiment showed that it is possible for a boat of this type laden with a bluestone to draw as little as 23 cm (9 in.). See Atkinson 1979, p. 113.
58 Evans 1984. The bones and other finds from this important excavation are on display in Salisbury Museum.
59 Evans 1984 specifically draws attention to this detail of the man's physique: it was also possible to discern from the asymmetric development of the arms that he was right-handed.
60 Cunnington 1929; Anon, 1936 *PPS* 2, pp. 1–51; Burl 1987, p. 125.
61 The north-east entrance of the Shepperton henge in the Thames valley was 'guarded' by a male skeleton (Castleden 1992, p. 176) in much the same way as the Stonehenge entrance. The burial of a 14-year-old girl in a stone-hole at the Sanctuary near Avebury suggests another human sacrifice as a foundation rite: her body was buried immediately before the stone was hauled upright over it (ibid., p. 225). At Duggleby Howe in North Yorkshire the burial of each high-status elder was followed by the burial of a boy and then of a very young child, both pole-axed (ibid., p. 249). The 5-year-old girl buried in a Folkton round barrow with beautiful chalk drums may have been a sacrificial victim too.
62 This operation, called trepanning, was not uncommon. Its purpose is unknown,

but we do know that some victims survived: some neolithic skulls have well-healed holes in them.

63 Castleden 1992, p. 208.

64 Gibson 1992.

65 The sockets are difficult to 'read' because they are close to and overlapped by the sockets of the later (Stonehenge IIIc) bluestone circle. It was Hawley's excavation of 1926 that first exposed traces of the earlier circle: Hawley opened up a rectangle on the main axis just inside the bluestone circle and found the inner ends of five radial trenches. Each trench seemed to be associated with a bluestone but the alignment was not quite true, so the trench had to belong to an earlier stone setting. Hawley, as elsewhere in his excavations, was unable to make sense of this important find, even though it was his final season at Stonehenge (Hawley 1928). Excavation of the next section of the bluestone circle in 1954, between stones 32 and 33, revealed the sockets of five extra stones of the late bluestone circle and also the dumb-bell-shaped sockets of five pairs of stones of the earlier double circle. Atkinson 1979, pp. 58–61 summarizes his own deductions about the Q and R holes.

66 Vyner 1988.

67 The axis of Stonehenge I and Stonehenge II is oriented to 49° 54'. Burl 1987, p. 140 argues, using the mid-point of the SI causeway and its cluster of stake-holes, that the SI axis was oriented to 46° 33' – 3 degrees difference – but the SI axis should be seen as passing halfway between the portal stones, 96 and 97, and the SII axis almost exactly coincides with this.

68 Hawley 1924, p. 30). The causeway was thereby widened from 11 m to 18.5 m.

69 The chalk filling the ditch set so hard that it was probably both dug and deposited when saturated with water: perhaps this part of Stonehenge was made in the rain. See Hawley 1924, p. 30.

70 The Avenue's banks and ditches were still plainly visible in the eighteenth century. Stukeley 1722–4 and 1740 commented that 'the two ditches that formed the outside of it are very visible the whole length.'

71 Grimes 1938. The Meini-gwyr avenue banks had a middle bronze age hearth on them as well as a scatter of middle bronze age pottery, implying that by then the ceremonial sanctity of the avenue (and possibly the circle as well) had been lost.

72 Castleden 1992, pp. 328, 378.

73 Stukeley 1722–4.

74 *Proceedings of the Society of Antiquaries of London* 7, 1877, pp. 268–71.

75 Pitts 1982. Two different kinds of survey were undertaken, resistivity and magnetometer; the first revealed the positions of four stone-sockets (my numbers 1b, 2a, 3a and 5a on Figure 53), the second the positions of five more (my numbers 3b, 4b, 5b, 6a, 6b). When I superimposed the plans I derived from the two surveys a pattern emerged: there are three pairs of stone-sockets (3, 5 and 6) and two further sockets that are unpaired. The spacing seems very suggestive, with the distance 28.5 m cropping up no less than five times. Careful scrutiny of Pitts's data shows that sockets may have existed at 7a, 7b, 8a and 8b, and this introduces two more occurrences of the distance 28.5 m. The Heel Stone and its partner were raised 28.5 m outside the inner edge of the Stonehenge I ditch and the first pair of Avenue stones, the presumed 1a and 1b, lay 28.5 m beyond the Heel stones. It must be significant that this measurement repeats again and again, and I tentatively propose that the Avenue was, with a few hiccups, laid out with pairs of stones 28.5 m apart. This measurement corresponds to 34.3 of Thom's Megalithic Yards, and more significantly to 4.99 of the 'Phoenician' units of 5.71 m that Sir Flinders Petrie identified in the Stonehenge earthworks.

76 The Q and R lettering is based on the 'Quaere' notes that John Aubrey often wrote to remind himself to follow up some line of enquiry.

77 The ring of R holes had a diameter of 22 m: this is exactly 30 Beaker Yards. The round number suggests that the Beaker Yard was used in laying out the Stonehenge II design. The slightly rougher circle of Q holes had a diameter of 35 Beaker Yards. The inner ring (R holes) is the more regular and more nearly circular of the two, which means that it was probably the first to be laid out: probably the Q holes were measured radially outwards from the R holes, and may even have been positioned by eye.

78 Burl 1987, p. 148.

79 The West Kennet double palisade enclosure has been radiocarbon dated to 3810 bp and 3620 bp, which calibrate to a mean date of 2125 BC.

6 CULMINATION: THE SARSEN MONUMENT

1 The major barrow cemeteries near Stonehenge are the Stonehenge Down Group (12 barrows), Normanton Down Barrows (26), Winterbourne Stoke Barrows (39 in two groups), Cursus Barrows (20), Old and New King Barrows (16), Lesser Cursus Barrows (13), Durrington Down Barrows (20) and Lake Barrows (20). A little further off are the Lake Down Barrows (16) and Wilsford South Barrows (17).

2 Burl 1987, p. 170.

3 Petrie 1880, p. 26.

4 Castleden 1987, pp. 208–9.

5 Castleden 1992, pp. 249–50, 321. In the Quanterness chamber tomb on Orkney the first burial was that of a 30–40-year-old man, who was complete, curled up on his left side in the main chamber. His was different from the later burials in that he had been buried immediately after he died, and not exposed first. Apparently it was his death that prompted the Quanterness people to raise the tomb in 3420 BC: it went on being used as a communal tomb for some nine hundred years. The round barrow of Duggleby Howe in North Yorkshire tells a similar story. At the centre of the huge barrow the Duggleby people dug a cube-shaped grave-pit 3 m across for the body of a strongly built man. Close to his body, which was contained in a small wooden mortuary house, were grave-goods. Duggleby is different from Quanterness in that other, later, bigman burials were added, each accompanied by human sacrifices.

6 Pierpoint 1980; Castleden 1987, p. 218.

7 In some ancient societies women were able to attain very high status, for example Boudicca, queen of the Iceni at the time of the Roman occupation, and the priestesses of Minoan Crete, 1900–1400 BC. Some of the high-status Wessex Culture burials at Stonehenge are of women, and it is possible that they were queens, rulers in their own right.

8 The Bush Barrow was partially excavated in July 1808 by William Cunnington. He returned in August to complete the dig without his patron, Sir Richard Colt Hoare, who had a migraine, and made the most spectacular discovery of his career. As a migraine sufferer, I can guess how Sir Richard must have felt.

9 Hoare 1812, pp. 202–5; *WAM* 10, 1867, p. 86; R. H. Cunnington 1935, p. 130.

10 Castleden 1990, pp. 98–9.

11 Opinions differ about the bone zig-zags: it may be that they were not after all mounted on the mace shaft but on some other object(s).

12 Hoare 1812, p. 202.

13 Others before me have suggested this, including Aubrey Burl 1987, p. 157, and

Dominic Flessati in 'Who built Stonehenge?', *Horizon*, BBC TV, 1986.

14 Renfrew, speaking in Flessati's 'Who built Stonehenge?', 1986.

15 The royal standard idea has been suggested by Ashbee and ApSimon in *WAM* 55, 1954, pp. 326–9.

16 One burial that *has* turned up the right date is the Amesbury Bowl Barrow. This stands beside the Avenue to the west of the New King Barrows and looks across to Stonehenge, which stands about 900 m away. There was a fire, perhaps a funeral pyre, on the early bronze age land surface. The grave-goods included the remains of clothing, shale beads and a shale button. The burial dates from 2100 BC, the time when Stonehenge IIIa was built. The building date for SIIIa comes from an antler found on the ramp down which stone 56 slid into its socket: this yielded a radiocarbon date of 1720 bc (2080 BC).

17 This idea is developed in Clarke et al. 1985.

18 Coles and Harding 1979, p. 239. Patton 1993, pp. 126, 174, 184–96.

19 Burl 1987, p. 175.

20 Atkinson 1979, p. 116.

21 Castleden 1991, p. 27.

22 It is known from occupation debris dated to 1610 bc (1920 BC) that Durrington Walls was still inhabited at the time when Stonehenge IIIa was being built.

23 Looked at on the 'Wessex' scale, both Avebury and Stonehenge lie at the heart of a cluster of long barrows, and this implies that their territories were established back in the middle neolithic. Marden does *not* have a readily identifiable heartland of this kind: nor does it have later round barrows clustering round it as Avebury and Stonehenge do. This suggests that Marden was weaker as a territorial focus than either of the neighbouring superhenges.

24 The Sanctuary overlooks the site of three more post-circles, recently discovered at West Kennet farm. Traces of another post-circle have been found in the north-east quadrant of Avebury itself.

25 The status of the Beckhampton Avenue has been in doubt for some time, as only one of the stones, Eve, is still standing and no fallen stones can be seen. William Stukeley nevertheless believed that such an avenue once existed and a recent resistivity survey in Longstones Field to the north-east of Beckhampton Cove has revealed at least eleven avenue stone-sockets, four of them clearly arranged in pairs about 10 m apart. See Ucko et al. 1991.

26 Atkinson 1979, pp. 118–9.

27 A monolith stands at Gore Cross: the Robbers' Stone bears a plaque commemorating the occasion in 1839 when 'Mr Dean of Imber was Attacked and Robbed by Four Highwaymen'. There is no reason to suppose that the monolith is ancient, although it stands in just the right spot to commemorate the major prehistoric achievement of hauling the sarsens up the escarpment.

28 A territory of 500 sq. km, which Stonehenge III may have commanded, may have had a population of only 5,000: see Castleden 1987, p. 259, for population density estimates. Of these about half would probably have been of working age and condition, between the ages of 10 and 30; therefore the 1,200 children and young adults needed to drag the sarsens would have taken almost half the entire work force of the region, which is scarcely credible. The use of oxen instead seems very likely.

29 Atkinson 1979, p. 122.

30 Castleden 1987, p. 107.

31 *WAM* 42, 1924, pp. 593–4.

32 Hawley 1925.

33 For example, the upper/outer face of the fallen stone 59, and the lower part of the

outer face of stone 54.

34 An average upright in the sarsen circle measures 4.1 by 2.1 by 1.1 m.
35 The original 'orange-peel' texture is only preserved underground and therefore cannot normally be seen. Nevertheless, a large flake from the base of the deeply socketed stone 56 was found broken off when the stone was pulled upright in 1901. This flake, which preserved its original surface texture, is now in Devizes Museum.
36 Atkinson 1979, p. 126.
37 Thom 1974.
38 The word 'trilithon' was coined by Stukeley in 1740.
39 The Lion Gate is a simple trilithon doorway with a 3 m clearance. It is 4 m high to the upper surface of its lintel, 6 m including the triangular sculpture with lions and Minoan pillar on top. See Mylonas 1983.
40 Burl 1987, pp. 174–5.
41 The club foot idea may have been borrowed from the standing stones at Cwm-garw near Carnmenyn; these natural boulders of spotted dolerite were apparently selected because in each case the jointing created a swelling at one end of the stone: used as a base, this lowered the centre of gravity and gave greater stability. This may be further evidence of contact between Wessex and Preseli (Plate 10).
42 Stone 1924.
43 Atkinson 1979, p. 133, suggests that a 26 tonne circle stone might be raised by 180 people. The trilithon uprights are taller, but I allow for the fact that oxen are nine times stronger than people, so 25 oxen would have been sufficient to haul stone 56 upright – not such a great undertaking as most people have imagined.
44 ibid., p. 133.
45 Burl 1987, p. 180.
46 Leaving a couple of circle stones unraised would have left a broad gap to provide access to the centre of the circle for the five lintel stones and the equipment needed to mount them.
47 The Tarxien Temple near Valletta, for example, has been radiocarbon dated to 3000 BC, the time of Stonehenge I. By the time Stonehenge IIIa was being built, the megalithic temple culture had come to an end.
48 Atkinson 1979, p. 134.
49 The method outlined here is the one proposed by Atkinson 1979, p. 135.
50 Pavel 1992. Although this seems incredible, Pavel took photographs of his concrete trilithon during construction to prove that it can be done.
51 Hawley 1922 shows how the disintegration of stone 30 was narrowly averted as it was being raised by planting lots of posts in the socket when a large crack (still visible) developed (Figure 63, Plate 25).
52 T. S. Eliot *The Waste Land*.
53 Newall 1928 and 1955.

7 STONEHENGE COMPLETED: THE RETURN OF THE BLUESTONES

1 Discovered by Hawley in 1923–4. See Hawley 1925.
2 Stones 36 and 150. Stone 150 lies with its mortices exposed for visitors to see, but stone 36 lies with its mortices buried: it was raised and photographed in 1954. Stone 67 has a worn-down tenon on its exposed end: although hard to see it is possible to detect it by touch. Stone 70 has a more clearly visible tenon, but you cannot see this from the ground, only from a ladder. Stone 69 is alleged to have a

battered-down tenon, but close inspection shows that its top is dead flat: nevertheless its ridged edge suggests a seating for a lintel.

3 Meaden 1992, p. 173, says 'it is hard to imagine such a sacred circle, once re-erected, willingly being removed afterwards', yet changes of mind of just this kind did occur: the Double Bluestone Circle itself was removed.

4 Ashbee 1978b.

5 Stone 1958, p. 100 mentions 'the possibility of another bluestone structure at the western end of the Cursus'.

6 Burl 1987, p. 198.

7 There were thirty of each in the *plan*, although in the event Z8 was left undug.

8 Atkinson 1979, p. 81.

9 Atkinson 1987, p. 13.

10 This is the hypothesis put forward by Atkinson 1979, p. 81.

11 Chippindale 1983, p. 271, has already proposed that the Y and Z holes were made later: a radiocarbon date confirms this.

12 Stone 1958, p. 100; Atkinson 1979, p. 82. The evidence for the oval consists of just three holes (J, K and L) which seem not to belong to the IIIc Bluestone Horseshoe design because of their spacing.

13 Atkinson 1979, p. 83.

14 Burgess 1980, p. 334.

15 Atkinson 1979, p. 81.

16 Burl 1987, p. 198.

17 The raw radiocarbon date is 1240 bc. The antler came from Y30.

18 The coarse pottery is known among archaeologists as Deverel-Rimbury and was not in use at the time when the sarsen structure was built.

19 Compare Colin Richards' views in Sharples and Sheridan 1992, p. 73.

20 Charrière 1961.

21 Atkinson 1979, pp. 49–50.

22 Burl 1987, p. 201.

23 The upright stones are 31, 33, 34, 46, 47, 49; the leaning stones are 32, 37, 38, 39, 48; the fallen stones are 36, 40, 41, 42, 43, 44, 45, 150; 35, 32C, 32D, 32E, 33F, 40C, 40G, 41D, 42C are broken stumps, all except 35 invisible under the soil.

24 Brunaux 1987, pp. 13–16.

25 Atkinson 1987 shows five stones in the gap, but it is not clear whether his estimate is based on found sockets or inferred from the spacing of stones elsewhere.

26 If the sarsen monument was erected in the years around 2100 BC, the bluestones must have been taken offsite at that time. The wear on lintel 36 shows that 'Bluestonehenge' (IIIb) must have been standing for up to a century or more, so 2000 BC is the earliest possible date when the bluestones could have returned. If the Y and Z holes were designed as alternative sockets for the bluestones, and they had been dug by 1500 BC, 1550 BC is the latest possible date for the building of the Bluestone Circle (Stonehenge IIIc).

27 Atkinson 1979, pp. 53, 97.

28 Burl 1987, p. 209.

29 Castleden 1989, pp. 48, 105–18, 119; 1990, pp. 134–6.

30 Burl 1987, p. 209, suggests that the Stonehenge goddess was the death-goddess, but there are no grounds for making such a specific identification: her attributes were probably wider-ranging than that.

31 Atkinson was photographing the seventeenth-century inscription on stone 53 on 10 July 1953. He waited until late afternoon to take his photograph, knowing that the low-angle sunlight would give greater depth to the image of the carving; it was

then that he saw the dagger and four axes below it.

32 Burgess 1980, pp. 334–6, still believes that the Stonehenge carvings show Mycenean daggers.

33 e.g. Atkinson *PPS* 18, pp. 236–7; Crawford *Antiquity* 28, pp. 25–31.

34 This rethinking is part and parcel of the 'radiocarbon revolution'. The calibration (i.e., ageing) of British prehistory has put a new perspective on the prehistory of north-west Europe, where it can now be seen that all sorts of cultural innovations occurred independently of developments in the Mediterranean.

35 Now in the British Museum.

36 Atkinson 1979, pp. 44–5, 179.

8 THE MEANING OF STONEHENGE

1 Hawley 1928.

2 Even Stone 1958, p. 95 made the mistake of overemphasizing Stonehenge's uniqueness: 'Such a unique object postulates a unique event, and I feel sure that we must look to the literate civilizations of the Mediterranean for the inspiration and indeed for the actual execution.'

3 The Double Bluestone Circle (Stonehenge II), Great Sarsen Circle (Stonehenge IIIa) and Bluestone Circle (Stonehenge IIIc).

4 Thatch is inferred from the shells of damp-loving snails found on the site: these could have been brought to what is now a rather dry chalk hillside location in bundles of rushes gathered from the Kennet valley floor.

5 Castleden 1992, p. 225.

6 ibid., pp. 95–6.

7 ibid., p. 41.

8 Case 1962; Burl 1969; Smith 1971; Catherall 1972; Wilson 1975; Ashbee 1978a.

9 Many henges have only one entrance: e.g., Mayburgh, Condicote, Arminghall, Gorsey Bigbury, Priddy Circles, Woodhenge, Stenness, Meini-gwyr. This may be why many writers have been content to see Stonehenge as a single-entrance henge, but the archaeological evidence clearly shows that there was a south entrance as well. Other two-entrance henges include King Arthur's Round Table, Knowlton Central Circle, Balfarg, Brodgar, Thornborough.

10 Even three entrances would not be unique. The recently discovered Shepperton henge had three – to north-east, south-east and west-south-west.

11 Bradley 1984, pp. 12, notes that the major neolithic pottery styles are distributed over much the same areas as the social territories of the late mesolithic.

12 Richards 1990, pp. 42, 43.

13 The henge was built just 9 m away from the pit, and on its south side.

14 See, for example, Spence 1894; Patrick 1974; Burl 1981, pp. 82–7, 124–6. The specially crafted 'letterbox' above the Newgrange closing stone is well known, but Burl reminds us that the doorstone at Maes Howe, when pivoted out into its closed position, is 40 cm short: in other words it too was made with the intention of letting sunlight into the chamber even when the door was shut.

15 Only two of these stones survive at Avebury today, the backstone and one of the pillar-like flankers. The socket of the other flanker has nevertheless been revealed by a resistivity survey. It was demolished before 1713, when Stukeley visited the site.

16 Clark 1936.

17 Service and Bradbery 1981, pp. 133–42.

18 Gibson 1992.

19 The Phaistos Disc is a small terracotta disc with spirals of pictograms printed on

both sides. It was found among Linear A tablets in the ruins of the Minoan palace-temple of Phaistos on Crete, and is thought to have been made in about 1700 BC. All attempts to decipher the pictograms have failed, largely because of the dearth of comparable texts.

20 The original height of the bank is inferred from the width and depth of the ditch, which is where the bank material came from.

21 This idea that the sun-god had different aspects and attributes according to the season of the year is developed in Castleden 1983, pp. 144–8, 174–94.

22 Pitts 1981 (and see Chapter 4 in this book).

23 At Drizzlecombe a single row of stones runs south-west from a barrow for 150 m, ending at a standing stone; a second stone row runs 84 m to a monolith 4.3 m high. At Merrivale two double rows of stones run parallel to each other from west to east, one 180 m long, the other 264 m.

24 The Winterbourne Stoke Crossroads barrow cemetery not far from Stonehenge is a good example of this linear layout.

25 Stone 1938; Green and Rollo-Smith 1984.

26 Gowland 1902.

27 Feng Shui means 'wind-water'. The universal energy it seeks to manage is called Qi (or Ch'i) in China and Ki in Japan, and the energy is channelled along lung mei, or dragon lines.

28 The Cuckoo Stone is a slab roughly 2 m long, 1.3 m wide and 0.5 m thick. It lies on private land.

29 Squier and Davis 1848; Pennick and Devereux 1989, pp. 165–71.

30 Pennick and Devereux 1989, p. 189.

31 The Dorchester complex is similar. Maiden Castle causewayed enclosure was created around 3500 BC, though parts of the ditch seem to have been dug out as early as 3900 BC. It was abandoned in about 3100 BC: after that a string of new monuments was laid out on lower ground to the north-east – Greyhound Yard (2750 BC), Flagstones and Conquer Barrow (2600 BC), Mount Pleasant (2500 BC) and Maumbury Rings (2150 BC).

32 Castleden 1992, pp. 106–8. The attack is indicated by the distribution of flint arrowheads along the bank-palisade, clustering at the entrances and petering out along the 'streets' inside the settlement.

33 ibid., pp. 145–6.

34 Drewett 1977 argues that Offham was used in this way from the overall cleanness of the site: a few human bones were found.

35 Castleden 1992, pp. 20–1.

36 Gibbons 1938, pp. 177–8. Seth explains: 'Tes the record of th' family that Grandmother holds every year. See – we'm violent folk, we Starkadders. Some on us pushes others down wells. Some on us dies in childerbirth. There's others as die o' drink or goes mad . . . Tes difficult to keep count on us. So once a year Grandmother she holds a gatherin', called the Counting, and she counts us all, to see how many on us 'as died in th' year.'

37 Jung 1968, vol. 9, part 1, p. 376.

38 Shah 1957.

39 Flood 1989.

40 Neolithic eye level would have been no higher than 1.5 m. See Atkinson, in Hawkins, Atkinson, Thom and Newham 1967, pp. 91–8.

41 By the Heel Stones I mean stones 96 and 97.

42 The inner portals were the Slaughter Stone and its neighbour, the missing stone from socket E.

43 Having said this, astronomy as we recognize it today began surprisingly early.

When Alexander the Great conquered Babylon, taking it from the Medes and Persians in 344 BC, he was presented with the Babylonian astronomical records, and these were found to date back to 2230 BC. But even this does not prove that astronomical records were kept at Stonehenge.

44 Frobenius 1904; Jung 1956.
45 For example in Wagner's *Die Walküre*, 11 1782–94.
46 Jung 1968, vol. 18, p. 274.
47 Castleden 1983, pp. 123–8, 174–96.
48 Burl 1976, p. 26.
49 ibid., pp. 27–8.
50 The earliest menhirs and circle stones may fall into a class of aniconic (non-representational) idol not unlike the sacred pillars of the Minoan civilization or even Old Testament Palestine. In Genesis 28 we hear that after dreaming of the ladder to heaven Jacob 'took the stone that he had put for his pillows and set it up as a pillar and poured upon the top of it . . . And Jacob took a vow, saying, If God will be with me . . . then shall the Lord be my God and this stone which I have set for a pillar shall be God's house.' This tells us what was probably in the minds of the megalith-builders.
51 Stover and Kraig 1978, pp. 170–2.
52 Newall 1928.
53 Richards 1992.
54 Compare Jung, vol. 18, p. 443.
55 Pieces of the posts were found in the sockets when they were excavated, which would not be the case if the buildings had been dismantled.
56 For instance, Mow Cop in Cheshire, which was built in 1754 to be seen from Rose Hall.
57 It is just possible that an eccentric lady made this discovery in the 1890s. A letter from G. E. Dartnell dated August 1893 mentions her claim 'to be able to take rubbings from invisible picture carvings on the stones, which reveal their true identity.' Dartnell felt that this indicated 'lack of mental balance somewhere'. See Rogers 1991.
58 The signature of an unknown visitor called perhaps Jean Louis de Ferre or, as Burl (1987, p. 160) suggests, Lucas de Heere, the Dutch artist who drew Stonehenge.
59 The carvings soon became the currency of popular entertainment. Jacques Tourneur's horror film *Night of the Demon* is a free adaptation of M. R. James's story *The Casting of the Runes*. Sinister film footage of Stonehenge is used to establish a supernatural atmosphere while the leading man discovers runes carved on the back of trilithon 53–54. Perhaps it is a coincidence that it was on the front of the same trilithon that Atkinson discovered the real axe and dagger carvings in 1953. Perhaps not: the film was released in 1957.
60 Atkinson 1979, pp. 44–5, 179. The Newall rubbings are in the Alexander Keiller Museum at Avebury.
61 Stone 1958, for instance. Stone speculated that there was a Mycenean trading post on the River Avon near Amesbury and that this was the direct cause of the building of the sarsen monument.
62 Several hilted daggers have been found in the burial mounds of the local chieftains.
63 It is just possible that carvings could have been added by Mycenean visitors in, say, 1600 BC, long after the sarsens were raised although still just within the Wessex Culture period. There is nevertheless no pressing reason to introduce Greek tourists or architects when there is plenty of evidence that the local people

were quite capable of building and elaborating the monument as a whole and in detail. See Renfrew 1968; Branigan 1970; McKerrell 1972.

64 Bender 1986, pp. 74–5.

65 e.g. Loughcrew Cairn T. See Thomas 1992, p. 151.

66 Castleden 1990, pp. 134–6. For the significance of the stone axe in the bronze age, see Maher 1973.

67 Burl 1987, pp. 186–7.

68 The goddess carving may have been positioned so that it would face the sunrise at the equinoxes, which in effect means that it is oriented to the east. On the other hand, in practice stone 4 would have prevented the first rays of the rising equinoctial sun reaching the carving, so the interpretation is uncertain.

69 There is no trace on the Acropolis today of the huge ivory and gold statue of Athena Parthenos made by Pheidias, or the bright colours with which the Parthenon was painted.

70 The important goddess image on stone 57 was also on the right hand of the visitor. What the significance of this 'right-handedness' may be we can only guess.

71 Hawley 1924, p. 32–3.

72 The mace-head is made of hornblende-gneiss and probably came from Brittany. There are enough cultural parallels, in addition to this mace, to suggest that the Stonehenge people of the early bronze age had at least trading links, and probably closer links, with the megalith-builders of Brittany.

73 Burl 1987, pp. 197–101.

74 Castleden 1992, pp. 176–7. Other monuments near the Shepperton henge include the large Yeoveny causewayed enclosure and the Stanwell Cursus. An extensive ceremonial complex developed at a natural meeting-place, where the Colne and Wey valleys joined the Thames valley.

75 Richards 1991, p. 87.

76 'Significant' placing of offerings of bones persisted at later sacred sites too. The rectangular ditch of the iron age enclosure at Gournay-sur-Aronde in France shows very definite and symmetrical arrangements of bones: an ox skull on each side of the entrance, sheep and pig bones along the sides, and human bones at the corners. Gournay also had offering pits very like the Aubrey Holes, but rather larger. See Brunaux 1987, pp. 8–9, 28–9.

77 Burl 1987, pp. 48, 59, 63, 71, 75, etc. Burl himself admits that very few people were buried at Stonehenge.

78 ibid., p. 103, suggests that the cremations may have been placed there by the native people reasserting their right to use the enclosure, a reference to the monument's early use as a moon-temple and its supposed conversion to a sun-temple. My reading of the evidence is that both sun and moon were honoured at Stonehenge in both early and late periods: there is no clear evidence for a major divide in beliefs.

79 For example, in shaft 10 at Maumbury Rings in Dorset people left a deposit of used and unused antler. Maumbury Rings was created in about 2150 BC (see Bradley 1976). Unfortunately, it is not usually clear from the archaeological reports whether the antlers found at Stonehenge were used or unused: the excavators did not realise that it might be significant.

80 Hodder 1990 discusses the neolithic concepts of home and wilderness, or domus and agrios as he likes to call them. Thomas 1991, pp. 71–3: the treatment of human remains is particularly interesting, implying that in the late neolithic and early bronze age the spirits of the dead were regarded as belonging to the wilderness. This finding harmonizes well with the idea that long barrows were

generally built on or near territorial boundaries, that is, as far from home as possible.
81 Thomas 1991, p. 146. This inference is really not very well substantiated, because there are actually concentrations of artefacts that imply at least five farmsteads or occupation sites *north* of the Great Cursus.

9 STONEHENGE IN DECLINE

1 An antler found in the bottom of Y30 has yielded a radiocarbon date of 1240 bc (1470 BC).
2 This link underlines the recurring theme of the book – continuity of ritual and beliefs, implicitly continuity of religious worship.
3 e.g. in Stone 1958, p. 100.
4 Stevens 1938, p. 23.
5 Homer *Odyssey* Book XI.
6 The Trojan War is believed to have ended around 1250 BC.
7 Sections of the Avenue have been radiocarbon dated to 800 bc (900 BC) and 1070 bc (1290 BC), that is, an average date of around 1100 BC.
8 The v-shaped cross-section of the ditches in itself represents a break with the older tradition.
9 Atkinson 1979, p. 67.
10 Crawford *Illustrated London News* 18 August 1923, pp. 302–3.
11 Burl 1987, p. 220.
12 Burgess 1985, p. 213; Burgess 1989.
13 Harding 1970; Savory 1971; Pierpoint 1982.
14 Ashbee 1978a.
15 'Time of Darkness', *Horizon*, BBC TV, 23 March 1992.
16 Drewett 1992.
17 Evans 1971.
18 Burgess 1989.
19 Barrett 1980. There are many other studies of palaeoecological and palaeoeconomic collapse at this time, but the main problem is the incompleteness of the evidence. We do not know the complete settlement pattern for any of these prehistoric periods, for instance, because some sites have been destroyed by later farming, others by quarrying or road-building; others lie under later settlements or under natural sediments. One neolithic site was found recently under 7 m of later sediments.
20 'Time of Darkness', *Horizon*, BBC TV, 23 March 1992.
21 Burgess 1989, pp. 325–9.
22 Burl 1987, p. 221. Burl points out that frost may have loosened the stones in their sockets and that the pushing effect of the wind is considerable. A 20 mph wind exerts a pressure of 10 kg per sq. m, and storm winds may have been strong enough to push the stones over.
23 The trilithon that fell in 1797 was the one with the goddess carving on its inner face, stones 57, 58 and 158. It was not the Great Trilithon, stones 55, 56 and 156, as Richards 1991, p. 61 mistakenly says: the lintel and one upright of the Great trilithon fell down, or were pulled down, at an unrecorded date in antiquity.
24 But the mortice-and-tenon joints were well crafted and a very considerable force would have been needed to dislodge a well-seated lintel.
25 Stones 57 and 58 were re-erected and set in concrete in 1958.
26 Jones 1655.
27 Stukeley 1740, p. 5.
28 Aubrey [1665] 1982, pp. 93–5.

29 *WAM* 11, 1869, p. 395.

30 Engleheart 1933a, pp 395–7.

31 Engleheart rightly identifies the stones as sarsens. Burl 1987, p. 139 rather implies that they are bluestones.

32 The broken stumps have been numbered 32C, 32D, 32E, 32F, 40C, 40G, 41D, 42C and 66.

33 The missing sarsen uprights are stones 13, 17, 18, 20, 24.

34 Burl 1987, p. 218, believes that weather and stone-robbing are enough to explain the present state of Stonehenge.

35 Where all this large quantity of stone is now is a matter for speculation. If only it could be brought back!

36 Tacitus *Agricola* 11 and 13; Caesar *Gallic Wars* V, 14; Strabo IV, 4–5. These are examples of Roman contempt for Britons, especially for their custom of worshipping in the open air.

37 A shrine at Winchester consisted of a simple four-post structure 4 m across within a circular ditch 11 m in diameter. A circular ditched temple at Brigstock in Northants was 13 m in diameter. See Harding 1974, pp. 106–11.

38 Giraldus Cambrensis (1861–91) implies that at his inauguration rite the king mated with a white mare. There are many stories in Irish mythology in which the inaugurated king copulates with a bride who represents his territory and/or the goddess Medhbh, 'The Intoxicating One'. There was a stone phallus on the Hill of Tara, Lia Fail, which cried out when it was touched by the true king. See McCana 1970, pp.117, 120–1.

39 McCana 1970, pp. 117–21; Burl 1981, pp. 229–33.

40 e.g. Hayling Island, a square enclosure with an eastern entrance, is 23 m across.

41 Tacitus *Annals* Book XIV, 29–30.

42 Among the megalithic sites are Barclodiad y Gawres, Bodowyr, Bryn-Celli-Ddu, Bryn Gwyn, Bryn yr Hen Bobl, Castell Bryn Gwyn and Plas Newydd.

43 The ancient sources can be found in Piggott 1968.

44 Leto was the mother of Apollo and Artemis: Zeus was their father.

45 Diodorus Siculus *Histories* Book II.

46 Piggot 1968.

47 RCHM 1979, pp. 20–2; Aubrey [1665] 1982, vol. I, p. 293.

48 Hoare 1812, vol. I, p. 126.

49 Burl 1987, p. 218.

50 Burl interprets the evidence differently. He thinks that the occupants of Vespasian's Camp did not use Stonehenge and that Stonehenge was completely abandoned some time between 1250 and 500 BC. The Avenue extension nevertheless suggests to me that Stonehenge was still in use in 1100 BC, and the iron age pottery fragments at Stonehenge itself imply that some, possibly low-level and intermittent, religious worship was still going on there in the centuries leading up to the Roman invasion.

51 This is why, at the time of writing, there is a move to close the A344, which runs clean across the centre of the Stonehenge complex. We must hope that this closure comes to pass and that in the near future a similar move will be made to divert the traffic passing through the centre of Avebury.

52 This was Amesbury 3. Hoare 1812, vol. I, p. 126.

53 Camden 1637, p. 254.

54 Aubrey [1665] 1982, vol. I, p. 92.

55 Stukeley 1740, p. 31.

56 'Defixio' is a gloss on the word 'defigo' normally meaning 'to fasten down' or 'fix', but it also has a religious sense, meaning 'to bewitch or curse'. A lead *defixio*

was found at Bath: it invoked Sulis, the healing goddess presiding over the water sanctuary.

57 Atkinson 1979, pp. 85–6.

58 ibid., p. 99.

59 ibid., pp. 65, 86, 99–100. Some of the stone chips were actually made of sarsen, not bluestone: this comparison is made merely to give an idea of the total volume of stone involved.

60 Stone 56's angle of tilt was exaggerated by wind and weather during the next 1,800 years. Stone 55, in a much shallower socket, was much easier to push over.

61 Tacitus *Annals* Book XIV; Stover and Kraig 1978, p. 80. Stover and Kraig believe Stonehenge was 'reinvested' during the Roman conquest by a Druid-led rebellion, asserting that the Romans based at Old Sarum were interested in the grain Salisbury Plain could supply; Stonehenge, standing in the midst of the wheatfields, was appropriated by the Druids as a gathering-place for rebels. It may be so, but it is pure speculation.

62 Masaya in Central America erupted in 4400 BC, Long Island caldera in Melanesia in 2050 BC, Mount St Helens in 1860 BC, the huge Aniakchak caldera in 1800 BC, Etna and the very large eruption of Rabaul in about 1500 BC, Hekla-3 in 1159 BC; two unidentified volcanoes erupted on a very large scale in 3195 and 2690 BC. The Minoan eruption of Thera may have occurred in 1628 BC or a century later.

63 According to a recent computer-model projection of climatic change, the ice is expected to return to Britain in three thousand years' time. This allows for a delay in the onset of the cold stage by man-enhanced greenhouse effect.

BIBLIOGRAPHY

ABBREVIATIONS

Ant   *Antiquity*
Ant J   *Antiquaries Journal*
Arch J   *Archaeological Journal*
BAR   British Archaeological Report
CBA   Council for British Archaeology
Curr Arch *Current Archaeology*
HMSO   Her Majesty's Stationery Office
PPS   *Proceedings of the Prehistoric Society*
RCHM   Royal Commission on Historical Monuments
WAM   *Wiltshire Archaeological Magazine*
WANHM   *Wiltshire Archaeological and Natural History Magazine*

Angell, I. O. (1976) 'Stone Circles: megalithic mathematics or neolithic nonsense?', *Mathematical Gazette* 60, 189–93.
Anon. (1954) 'Daggers and axes at Stonehenge', *WAM* 55, 289.
Antrobus, Lady F. (1904) *A Sentimental and Practical Guide to Amesbury and Stonehenge*, Amesbury.
Ashbee, P. (1966) 'The Fussell's Lodge Long Barrow', *Archaeologia* 100, 1–80.
—— (1970) *The Earthen Long Barrow in Britain*, Norwich: Geo Abstracts.
—— (1978a) *The Ancient British*, Norwich: Geo Abstracts.
—— (1978b) 'Amesbury Barrow 51: Excavation 1960', *WAM* 70–1, 1–60.
—— (1981) 'Amesbury Barrow 39: Excavations 1960', *WAM* 74–5, 3–34.
—— (1985) 'The excavation of Amesbury Barrows 58, 61a, 61, 72', *WAM* 79, 39–91.
Ashe, G. (1977) *King Arthur's Avalon*, London: Fontana.
Atkinson, R. J. C. (1954) 'Stonehenge in the light of recent research,' *Nature* 176, 474–5.
—— (1956) *Stonehenge*, London: Hamish Hamilton.
—— (1959) *Stonehenge and Avebury*, London: HMSO.
—— (1961) 'Neolithic engineering', *Ant* 35, 292–9.
—— (1962) *What is Stonehenge?* London: HMSO.
—— (1966a) 'Moonshine on Stonehenge', *Ant* 40, 212–6.
—— (1966b) 'Decoder misled', *Nature* 210, 1302.
—— (1967) 'Hoyle on Stonehenge: some comments', *Ant* 41, 92–5.
—— (1975) 'Megalithic astronomy – a prehistorian's comments', *Journal for the History of Astronomy* 6, 42–52.
—— (1976a) *Stonehenge and Avebury*, London: HMSO.

—— (1976b) 'The Station Stones', *Journal for the History of Astronomy* 7, 142–4.
—— (1977) 'Interpreting Stonehenge', *Nature* 265, 11.
—— (1987a) *Stonehenge and Neighbouring Monuments*, London: HMSO.
—— (1978b) 'Some new measurements on Stonehenge', *Nature* 275, 50–2.
—— (1979) *Stonehenge*, Harmondsworth: Penguin.
—— (1980) *The Prehistoric Temples of Stonehenge and Avebury*, London: Pitkin Pictorials.
—— (1987) *Stonehenge and Neighbouring Monuments*, London: English Heritage.
Atkinson, R. J. C. and Evans, J. G. (1978) 'Recent excavations at Stonehenge', *Ant* 52, 235–6.
Atkinson, R. J. C., Piggott, S. and Stone, J. F. S. (1952) 'The excavation of two additional holes at Stonehenge, and new evidence for the date of the monument', *Ant J* 32, 14–20.
Atkinson, R. J. C., Vatcher, F. and Vatcher, L. (1976) 'Radiocarbon dates for the Stonehenge Avenue', *Ant* 50, 239–40.
Aubrey, J. [1665] (1982) *Monumenta Britannica*, 2 vols, Sherborne: Dorset Publishing. From 1665–93 MSS in the Bodleian Library, Oxford.
Barclay, E. (1895) *Stonehenge and its Earthworks*, London: D. Nutt.
—— (1911) *The Ruined Temple Stonehenge*, London: St Catherine Press.
Barrett, J. (1980) 'Evolution of the late bronze age settlement', in J. Barrett and R. Bradley (eds) *Settlement and Society in the British Late Bronze Age*, BAR 83.
Barton, R. N. E. and Bergman, C. (1982) 'Hunters at Hengistbury: some evidence from experimental archaeology', *World Archaeology* 14, 237–48.
Beach, A. D. (1977) 'Stonehenge I and lunar dynamics', *Nature* 265, 17–21.
Beck, C. and Shennan, S. (1991) *Amber in Prehistoric Britain*, Oxford: Oxbow Press.
Bender, B. (1986) *The Archaeology of Brittany, Normandy and the Channel Islands*, London and Boston: Faber and Faber.
Bergström, T. and Vatcher, L. (1974) *Stonehenge*, London: Bergstrom and Boyle.
Bolton, E. (1624) *Nero Caesar or Monarchie Depraved*, published anonymously.
Bond, D. (1983) 'An excavation at Stonehenge, 1981', *WAM* 77, 39–44.
Booth, A. and Stone, J. F. S. (1952) 'A trial flint mine at Durrington, Wiltshire', *WAM* 54, 381–8.
Bowden, M., Bradley, R., Gaffney, V. and Mepham, L. (1983) 'The date of the Dorset Cursus', *PPS* 49, 376–80.
Bowen, H. C. and Smith, I. F. (1977) 'Sarsen stones in Wessex', *Ant J* 57, 185–96.
Bradley, R. (1976) 'Maumbury Rings, Dorchester: The excavations of 1903–1913', *Archaeologia* 105, 1–98.
—— (1984) *The Social Foundations of Prehistoric Britain*, London: Longman.
Bradley, R. and Ellison, A. (1976) 'Rams Hill', *Curr Arch* 36, 8–9.
Branigan, K. (1970) 'Wessex and Mycenae: some evidence reviewed', *WAM* 65, 89–107.
Brentnall, H. C. (1946) 'Sarsens', *WAM* 51, 419–39.
Brinckerhoff, R. F. (1976) 'Astronomically-oriented markings on Stonehenge', *Nature* 263, 465–9.
Brunaux, J. L. (1987) *The Celtic Gauls: Gods, Rites and Sanctuaries*, London: Seaby.
Burgess, C. (1980) *The Age of Stonehenge*, London: Dent.
—— (1985) *Population, Climate and Upland Settlement*, BAR 143.
—— (1989) Volcanoes, catastrophe and the global crisis of the late second millennium BC, *Curr Arch* 117, 325–9.
Burke, E. [1756] (1958) *A Philosophical Enquiry into the Origin of our Ideas of the Sublime and the Beautiful*, ed, J. T. Boulton, London: Routledge.
Burl, A. (1969) 'Henges: internal features and regional groups', *Arch J* 126, 1–28.

—— (1976) *The Stone Circles of the British Isles*, New Haven and London: Yale University Press.

—— (1979) *Rings of Stone*, London: Dent.

—— (1981) *Rites of the Gods*, London: Dent.

—— (1985) 'Geoffrey of Monmouth and the Stonehenge Bluestones', *WAM* 79, 178–83.

—— (1987) *The Stonehenge People*, London: Dent.

—— (1991a) 'The Heel Stone, Stonehenge: a study in misfortunes', *WANHM* 84, 1–10.

—— (1991b) 'The Bluestones again', *Curr Arch* 125, 238–9.

Burleigh, R., Longworth, I. H. and Wainwright, G. J. (1972) 'Relative and absolute dating of four late neolithic enclosures', *PPS* 38, 389–407.

Bushell, W. D. (1911) 'Amongst the Prescelly Circles', *Archaeologia Cambrensis* 11, 287–333.

Butler, J. J. (1963) 'Bronze Age connections across the North Sea', *Palaeohistoria*, 9, 1–286.

Camden, W. (1637) *Britannia*, 2nd edn in English, translated by Philemon Holland.

Campbell Smith, W. (1963) 'Jade axes from sites in the British Isles', *PPS* 29, 133–72.

Case, H. J. (1962) 'Long barrows and causewayed camps', *Ant* 36, 212–6.

Castleden, R. (1983) *The Wilmington Giant: the Quest for a Lost Myth*, Wellingborough: Turnstone Press.

—— (1987) *The Stonehenge People: Life in Neolithic Britain, 4700–2000 BC*, London and New York: Routledge.

—— (1989) *The Knossos Labyrinth: a New View of the 'Palace of Minos' at Knossos*, London and New York: Routledge.

—— (1990) *Minoans: Life in Bronze Age Crete*, London and New York: Routledge.

—— (1991) *Book of British Dates*, Bromley: Harrap.

—— (1992) *Neolithic Britain: New Stone Age Sites of England, Scotland and Wales*, London and New York: Routledge.

Catherall, P. D. (1972) 'Henges in perspective', *Arch J* 128, 147–53.

Charleton, W. (1663) *Chorea Gigantum, or, The most Famous Antiquity of Great Britain, Vulgarly called Stone-Heng, Standing on Salisbury Plain, Restored to the Danes*, London: Henry Henigman.

Charrière, G. (1961) 'Stonehenge: rythmes architecturaux et orientation', *Bulletin Société Préhistorique Française* 58, 276–9.

Chippindale, C. (1983) *Stonehenge Complete*, London: Thames & Hudson.

Christie, P. M. (1963) 'The Stonehenge Cursus', *WAM* 58, 370–82.

Clark, G. (1966) 'The invasion hypothesis in British archaeology', *Ant* 40, 165–71.

Clark, J. G. D. (1936) 'The timber monument at Arminghall and its affinities', *PPS* 2, 32–58.

Clarke, D. L. (1970) *Beaker Pottery of Great Britain and Ireland*, Cambridge: Cambridge University Press.

Clarke, D. V., Cowie, T. G. and Foxon, A. (1985) *Symbols of Power*, Edinburgh: National Museum of Antiquities of Scotland and HMSO.

Clay, R. C. C. (1927) 'Stonehenge Avenue', *Ant* 1, 342–4.

Clifton-Taylor, A. (1986) *The Cathedrals of England*, London: Thames & Hudson.

Coles, J. M. and Harding, A. F. (1979) *The Bronze Age in Europe*, London: Methuen.

Coles, J. M., Heal, S. V. E. and Orme, B. J. (1978) 'The use and character of wood in prehistoric Britain and Ireland', *PPS* 44, 1–45.

Coles, J. and Taylor, J. (1971) 'The Wessex Culture: a minimal view', *Ant* 45, 6–14.

Colton, R. and Martin, R. L. (1967) 'Eclipse cycles and eclipses at Stonehenge', *Nature* 213, 476–8.

—— (1969) 'Eclipse prediction at Stonehenge', *Nature* 221, 1011–2.

Cowan, T. M. (1970) 'Megalithic rings: their design construction', *Science* 168, 321–5.

Crampton, P. (1968) *Stonehenge of the Kings*, New York: John Day.

Crawford, O. G. S. (1924) 'The Stonehenge Avenue, *Ant J* 4, 57–8.

—— (1929) 'Durrington Walls', *Ant* 3, 49–59.

—— (1954) 'The symbols carved at Stonehenge', *Ant* 28, 25–31.

Cummins, W. A. (1974) 'The neolithic stone axe trade in Britain', *Ant* 48, 201–5.

—— (1980) 'Stone axes as a guide to neolithic communications and boundaries in England and Wales', *PPS* 46, 45–60.

Cunliffe, B. (1987) *Hengistbury Head, Dorset: 1, The Prehistoric and Roman Settlement, 3500 BC–AD 500*, Oxford: Oxford University Committee for Archaeology.

Cunnington, M. E. (1929) *Woodhenge*, Devizes: George Simpson.

—— (1931) 'The "Sanctuary" on Overton Hill, near Avebury', *WAM* 45, 300–35.

—— (1935) 'The Blue Stone from Boles Barrow', *WAM* 47, 267.

Cunnington, R. H. (1935) *Stonehenge and its Date*, London: Methuen.

Darvill, T. (1986) *The Archaeology of the uplands: a Rapid Assessment of Archaeological Knowledge and Practice*, RCHM (England) and CBA.

Dawson, A. G. (1992) *Ice Age Earth*, London and New York: Routledge.

Decker, R. (1990) 'How often does a Minoan eruption occur?', in D. A. Hardy (ed.), *Thera and the Aegean World III Vol. 2 Earth Sciences*, London: Thera Foundation.

de Luc, J. A. (1811) *Geological Travels Vol. 3: Travels in England*, London: F. and J. Rivington.

Dibble, W. E. (1976) 'A possible Pythagorean triangle at Stonehenge', *Journal for the History of Astronomy* 7, 141–2.

Drewett, P. L. (1977 'The excavation of a neolithic causewayed enclosure on Offham Hill, East Sussex', *PPS* 43, 201–41.

—— (1992) 'Destruction of the South Downs: an Environmental Holocaust 5000–3000 BC', Lecture given to Sussex Archaeological Society at Lancing College.

Duke, Revd E. (1846) *The Druidical Temples of the County of Wiltshire*, London.

Engleheart, G. H. (1925–6) 'The story of Stonehenge: fact and fiction', *Wiltshire Gazette*, 5, 12, 19, 26 November 3, 10 December (1925), 11, 18, 25 February (1926).

—— (1933a) 'A second Stonehenge Altar Stone?', *WAM* 46, 395–7.

—— (1933b) 'Iron or Bronze?', *Wiltshire Gazette* 24 June, 6, 13, 20, 27 July.

Evans, A. J. (1889) 'Stonehenge', *Archaeological Review* 2, 312–30.

Evans, J. G. (1971) 'The pre-henge environment', in G. J. Wainwright and I. H. Longworth (eds), *Durrington Walls: Excavations 1966–1968*, London: Society of Antiquaries.

—— (1984) 'Stonehenge: the environment in the late neolithic and early bronze age and a Beaker age burial', *WAM* 78, 7–30.

Farrer, P. (1918) 'Durrington Walls or Long Walls', *WAM* 40, 95–103.

Fell, C. I. (1964) 'The Cumbrian type of polished stone axe and its distribution in Britain', *PPS* 30, 39–55.

Fergusson, J. (1872) *Rude Stone Monuments*, London: John Murray.

Fleming, A. (1969) 'The myth of the Mother Goddess', *World Archaeology* 1, 247–61.

—— (1971) 'Territorial patterns in bronze age Wessex', *PPS* 37, 138–66.

Flood, J. (1989) *Archaeology of the Dreamtime*, Sydney: Collins Publishers.

Frobenius, L. (1904) *Das Zeitalter des Sonnengöttes*, Berlin.

Gay, R. (1660) 'A fool's bolt soon shott at Stonage', in T. Hearne (ed.), *Langtoft's*

Chronicle, published in 1725.

Gibbons, S. (1938) *Cold Comfort Farm*, London: Longman.

Gibson, A. (1992) 'The timber circle at Sarn-y-Bryn-Caled, Welshpool, Powys: ritual and sacrifice in bronze age mid-Wales', *Ant* 66, 84–90.

Gingell, C. J. (1988) 'Twelve Wiltshire round barrows: excavations in 1959 and 1961 by F. de M. and H. L. Vatcher', *WAM* 82, 19–76.

Giraldus Cambrensis [1861–91] (1982) *Giraldi Cambrensis, Opera*, ed. J. S. Brewer, London.

Godwin, H. (1960) 'Prehistoric wooden trackways of the Somerset Levels: their construction, age and relation to climatic change', *PPS* 26, 1–36.

Gowland, W. (1902) 'Recent excavations at Stonehenge', *Archaeologia* 58, 37–105.

Green, C. P. (1973) 'Pleistocene river gravels and the Stonehenge problem', *Nature* 243, 214.

Green, C. and Rollo-Smith, S. (1984) 'The excavation of eighteen round barrows near Shrewton, Wiltshire', *PPS* 50, 255–318.

Grimes, W. F. (1938) 'Excavations at Meini-gwyr, Carmarthen', *PPS* 4, 324–5.

Grinsell, L. V. (1958) *The Archaeology of Wessex*, London: Methuen.

—— (1975) *Legendary History and Folklore of Stonehenge*, Guernsey: Toucan Press.

—— (1978a) *The Druids and Stonehenge*, Guernsey: Toucan Press.

—— (1978b) *The Stonehenge Barrow Groups*, Salisbury: Salisbury and South Wiltshire Museum.

Harding, D. (1970) 'The "new" iron age', *Curr Arch* 20, 233–40.

—— (1974) *The Iron Age of Lowland Britain*, London: Routledge & Kegan Paul.

Harris, J. R. (1932) *The Builders of Stonehenge*, Cambridge: W. Heffer.

Harrison, W. J. (1901) 'A bibliography of the Great Stone Monuments of Wiltshire Stonehenge and Avebury', *WAM* 32, 1–169 (947 entries).

Harvey, C. (1923) *The Ancient Temple of Avebury and its Gods*, London: Watts.

Hawes, L. (1975) *Constable's Stonehenge*, London: HMSO.

Hawke-Smith, C. (1982) 'Land use, burial practice and territories in the Peak District *c.* 2000–1000 bc', in G. Barker (ed.), *Prehistoric Communities in Northern England*, Sheffield: Sheffield University.

Hawkins, G. S. (1966) *Stonehenge Decoded*, London: Souvenir Press.

Hawkins, G. S., Atkinson, R. J. C., Thom, A. and Newham, C. A. (1967) 'Hoyle on Stonehenge: some comments', *Ant* 41, 91–8.

Hawley, W. (1921) 'Stonehenge: interim report on the exploration', *Ant J* 1, 19–39.

—— (1922) 'Second report on the excavations at Stonehenge', *Ant J* 2, 36–51.

—— (1923) 'Third report on the excavations at Stonehenge', *Ant J* 3, 13–20.

—— (1924) 'Fourth report on the excavations at Stonehenge', *Ant J* 4, 30–9.

—— (1925) 'Report on the excavations at Stonehenge during the season of 1923', *Ant J* 5, 21–50.

—— (1926) 'Report on the excavations at Stonehenge during the season of 1924', *Ant J* 6, 1–25.

—— (1928) 'Report on the excavations at Stonehenge during 1925 and 1926', *Ant J* 8, 149–76.

Hedges, J. W. (1984) *Tomb of the Eagles: a Window on Stone Age Tribal Britain*, London: John Murray.

Heggie, D. C. (1981) *Megalithic Science*, London: Thames & Hudson.

—— (1982) *Archaeoastronomy in the Old World*, Cambridge: Cambridge University Press.

Herbert, A. (1849) *Cyclops Christianus; or an argument to disprove the supposed antiquity of Stonehenge and other megalithic erections in England and Brittany*, London.

Hoare, R. C. (1812) *The Ancient History of South Wiltshire*, London: William Millar.

Hodder, I. (1990) *The Domestication of Europe*, Oxford: Basil Blackwell.

Hodder, I. and Shand, P. (1988) 'The Haddenham long barrow: an interim statement', *Ant* 62, 349–53.

Holgate, R. (1988) 'A review of neolithic domestic activity in southern Britain', in J. C. Barrett and I. A. Kinnes (eds), *The Archaeology of Context in the Neolithic and Bronze Age*, Sheffield: Department of Archaeology, University of Sheffield.

Hoyle, F. (1966a) 'Stonehenge: an eclipse predictor', *Nature* 211, 454–6.

—— (1966b) 'Speculations on Stonehenge', *Ant* 40, 272–6.

—— (1972) *From Stonehenge to Modern Cosmology*, San Francisco: W. H. Freeman.

—— (1977) *On Stonehenge*, London: Heinemann.

Hunter, M. (1975) *John Aubrey and the Realm of Learning*, London: Duckworth.

Ivimy, J. (1975) *The Sphinx and the Megaliths*, Wellingborough: Turnstone Press.

James, Col. Sir H. (1867) *Plans and Photographs of Stonehenge, and of Turusachan in the Island of Lewis*, Southampton: Ordnance Survey.

Johnstone, P. (1980) *The Sea-craft of Prehistory*, London and New York: Routledge.

Jones, I. (1655) *The Most Notable Antiquity of Great Britain, Vulgarly Called Stone-Heng, on Salisbury Plain, Restored, by Inigo Jones, Esquire, Architect-General to the Late King*, London: D. Browne.

Jung, C. G. (1956) *Symbols of Transformation*, London: Routledge & Kegan Paul.

—— (1968–79) *The Collected Works*, trans, R. F. C. Hull, London: Routledge & Kegan Paul.

Keene, P. (1984) *Classic Landforms of the North Devon Coast*, Sheffield: Geographical Association.

Keiller, A. and Piggott, S. (1938) 'Excavations of an untouched chamber in the Lanhill long barrow', *PPS* 4, 122–50.

Kellaway, G. A. (1971) 'Glaciation and the stones of Stonehenge', *Nature* 233, 30–35.

Kendrick, T. D. (1927) *The Druids, A Study in Keltic Prehistory*, London: Methuen.

King, A. N. (1970) 'Two "new" class 1 henges in south Wiltshire', *WAM* 65, 190.

Laidler, B. and Young, W. E. V. (1938) 'A surface flint industry from a site near Stonehenge', *WAM* 48, 151–60.

Legg, R. (1986) *Stonehenge Antiquaries*, Sherborne: Dorset Publishing.

Lehmann, J. (1977) *The Hittites: People of a Thousand Gods*, London: Collins.

Lewis, A. L. (1895) 'Prehistoric remains in Cornwall', *Journal of the Anthropology Institute* 25, 15.

Lockyer, Sir N. and Penrose, F. C. (1901) 'An attempt to ascertain the date of the original construction of Stonehenge', *Proceedings of the Royal Society of London* 69, 137–47.

—— (1906) *Stonehenge and Other British Monuments Astronomically Considered*, London: Macmillan.

Long, W. (1876) 'Stonehenge and its barrows', *WAM* 16, 1–244.

Lukis, W. C. (1864) 'Danish cromlechs and burial customs', *WAM* 8, 145–69.

Lynch, F. (1975) 'The impact of landscape on prehistoric man', in J. G. Evans, S. Limbrey and H. Cleere (eds), *The Effect of Man on the Landscape of the Highland Zone*, CBA Research Report No. 11.

—— (1986) 'The bronze age (2000–800 BC)', in T. Darvill (ed.), *The Archaeology of the Uplands: A Rapid Assessment of Archaeological Knowledge and Practice*, RCHM (England) and CBA.

McCana, P. (1970) *Celtic Mythology*, London: Hamlyn.

Mackenzie, Sir K. (1928) 'Who built Stonehenge and when?', *The Referee* 7 April.

McKerrell, H. (1972) 'On the origins of British faience beads and some aspects of the

Wessex–Mycenae relationship, *PPS* 38, 286–301.

MacKie, E. (1977a) *Science and Society in Prehistoric Britain*, London: Elek.

—— (1977b) *The Megalith Builders*, London: Phaidon Press.

Maher, J. P. (1973) 'HAEKMON: "Stone Axe" and "Sky" in Indo-European/Battle Axe Culture', *Journal of Indo-European Studies* 1, 51–4.

Malone, C. (1989) *Avebury*, London: Batsford and English Heritage.

Manby, T. G. (1965) 'The distribution of rough-cut "Cumbrian" axes and related axes of Lake District origin in northern England', *Transactions of the Cumberland and Westmorland Antiquarian and Archaeological Society* 65, 1–37.

Maskelyne, N. S. (1878) 'Stonehenge – the petrology of its stones', *WAM* 17, 147–60.

May, V. J. (1966) 'A preliminary study of recent coastal change and sea defences in south-east England', *Southampton Research Series in Geography* 3, 3–24.

Meaden, G. T. (1992) *The Stonehenge Solution: Sacred Marriage and the Goddess*, London: Souvenir Press.

Moir, G. (1979) 'Hoyle on Stonehenge', *Ant* 53, 124–9.

Moore, C. N. (1966) 'A possible Beaker burial from Larkhill, Durrington', *WAM* 41, 92.

Morgan, F. de M. (1959) 'The excavation of a long barrow at Nutbane, Hampshire', *PPS* 25, 15–51.

Musson, C. R. (1971) 'A study of possible building forms at Durrington Walls, Woodhenge and the Sanctuary', in G. J. Wainwright and I. H. Longworth, *Durrington Walls: Excavations, 1966–8*, London: Society of Antiquaries.

Mylonas, G. (1983) *Mycenae Rich in Gold*, Athens: Ekdotike Athenon.

Newall, R. S. (1928) 'Stonehenge: the recent excavations', *WAM* 44, 348–59.

—— (1929) 'Stonehenge', *Ant* 3, 75–88.

—— (1931) 'Barrow 85, Amesbury', *WAM* 45, 253–61.

—— (1955) *Stonehenge*, London: HMSO.

—— (1966) 'Megaliths once near Stonehenge', *WAM* 61, 93.

Newham, C. A. (1964) *The Enigma of Stonehenge*, Leeds: John Blackburn.

—— (1966) 'Stonehenge – a neolithic observatory', *Nature* 211, 456–68.

—— (1972) *The Astronomical Significance of Stonehenge*, Leeds: Blackburn.

Newton, R. R. and Jenkins, R. E. (1972) 'Possible use of Stonehenge', *Nature* 239, 511–12.

Palmer, S. (1977) *Mesolithic Cultures of Britain*, Poole: Dolphin Press.

Passmore, A. D. (1940) 'A disc barrow containing curious flints near Stonehenge', *WAM* 49, 238.

Patrick, J. (1974) 'Midwinter sunrise at Newgrange', *Nature* 249, 517–19.

Patton, M. (1993) *Statements in Stone: Monuments and Society in Neolithic Brittany*, London: Routledge.

Pavel, P. (1992) 'Raising the Stonehenge lintels in Czechoslovakia', *Ant* 66, 389-91.

Pearson, G. W., Pilcher, J. R., Baillie, M., Corbett, D., F, (1986) High precision 14$_C$ measurement of Irish oaks to show the natural 14$_C$ variations from AD 1840 to 5210 BC,' *Radiocarbon* 28, 911–34.

Pearson, G. W. and Stuiver, M. (1986) 'High precision calibration of the radiocarbon time-scale, 500–2500 BC', *Radiocarbon* 28, 839–62.

Pennick, N. and Devereux, P. (1989) *Lines on the Landscape: Leys and Linear Enigmas*, London: Robert Hale.

Pennington, M. (1974) *The History of British Vegetation*, London: English Universities Press.

Pequart, M. and Pequart, S. J. (1937) 'Téviec, station-nécropole mesolithique du Morbihan', *Archives de l'Institut de Palaeontologie Humaine* 18.

Peterson, F. (1972) 'Traditions of multiple burial in later neolithic and early bronze age England', *Arch J* 129, 22–40.

Petrie, Sir W. M. F. (1880) *Stonehenge: Plans, Description, and Theories*, London: Edward Stanford.

Pierpoint, S. (1980) *Social Patterns in Yorkshire Prehistory 3500–750 BC*, BAR 74.

—— (1982) 'Land settlement and society in the Yorkshire bronze age', in G. Barker (ed.), *Prehistoric Communities in Northern England*, Sheffield: Sheffield University.

Piggott, S. (1938) 'The early bronze age in Wessex', *PPS* 4, 52–106.

—— (1939) 'Timber circles: a re-examination', *Arch J* 96, 193–222.

—— (1941) 'The sources of Geoffrey of Monmouth. II. The Stonehenge story', *Ant* 15, 305–19.

—— (1948) 'The excavations at Cairnpapple Hill, West Lothian', *Proceedings of the Society of Antiquaries of Scotland* 82, 68–123.

—— (1950) *William Stukeley*, Oxford: Clarendon Press.

—— (1954) 'Recent work at Stonehenge', *Ant* 28, 221–4.

—— (1956) 'Architecture and ritual in megalithic monuments', *Journal of the Royal Institute of British Architects* 63, 175.

—— (1958) 'Stonehenge restored', *Ant* 33, 50–1.

—— (1968) *The Druids*, London: Thames & Hudson.

—— (1964) 'Excavations at Avebury, 1960', *WAM* 59, 28–9.

—— (1974) *The Druids*, Harmondsworth: Penguin.

Pitts, M. W. (1979–80) 'On two barrows near Stonehenge', *WAM* 74–5, 181–4.

—— (1982) 'On the road to Stonehenge: report on the investigations beside the A344 in 1968, 1979 and 1980', *PPS* 48, 75–132.

Porteous, H. (1973) 'Megalithic yard or megalithic myth?', *Journal for the History of Astronomy* 4, 22–4.

Pryor, F. (1987) 'Etton 1986: neolithic metamorphoses', *Ant* 61, 78–9.

—— (1989) 'Earlier neolithic organized landscapes and ceremonial in lowland Britain', in J. C. Barrett and I. A. Kinnes (eds), *The Archaeology of Context in the Neolithic and Bronze Age*, Sheffield: Department of Archaeology, University of Sheffield.

Rankine, W. F. (1955) 'Mesolithic finds in Wiltshire', *WAM* 56, 149.

RCHM (1970) *An Inventory of Historical Monuments in the County of Dorset, II: South-East*, London.

—— (1979) *Stonehenge and its Environs*, Edinburgh: Edinburgh University Press.

Renfrew, A. C. (1968) 'Wessex without Mycenae', *Annual of the British School of Archaeology at Athens* 63, 277–85.

—— (1973a) *Before Civilization*, London: Jonathan Cape.

—— (1973b) 'Wessex as a social question', *Ant* 47, 221–4.

—— (1973c) *The Explanation of Culture Change: Models in Prehistory*, Pittsburgh: University of Pittsburgh Press.

Richards, C. (1992) 'Doorways into another world: the Orkney-Cromarty chambered tombs', in N. Sharples and A. Sheridan (eds), *Vessels for the Ancestors: Essays on the Neolithic of Britain and Ireland in Honour of Audrey Henshall*, Edinburgh: Edinburgh University Press.

Richards, C. and Thomas, J. (1984) 'Ritual activity and deposition in later Neolithic Wessex', in R. Bradley and J. Gardiner (eds), *Neolithic Studies*, BAR 133.

Richards, J. C. (1985) *Beyond Stonehenge*, Salisbury: Trust for Wessex Archaeology.

—— (1990) *The Stonehenge Environs Project*, English Heritage Archaeological Report No. 16.

—— (1991) *Stonehenge*, London: Batsford and English Heritage.

Robinson, D. A. and Williams, R. B. G. (1984) *Classic Landforms of the Weald*, Sheffield: Geographical Association.

Robinson, J. H. (1907) 'Sunrise and moonrise at Stonehenge', *Nature* 225, 1236–7.

Rogers, N. (1991) 'Earlier evidence for Stonehenge carvings?' *WAM* 84, 116.

Ruddle, C. S. (1901) 'Notes on Durrington', *WAM* 31, 331–42.

Sadler, D. H. (1966) 'Prediction of eclipses', *Nature* 211, 1119.

Savory, H. N. (1971) 'A Welsh bronze age hillfort', *Ant* 45, 251–61.

Scarre, C. (1987) *Ancient France, 6000–2000 BC*, Edinburgh: Edinburgh University Press.'

Seddon, R. (1990) *The Mystery of Arthur at Tintagel*, London: Rudolf Steiner Press.

Service, A. and Bradbery, J. (1981) *A Guide to the Megaliths of Europe*, St Albans: Granada Publishing.

Shah, I. (1957) *The Secret Lore of Magic: Books of the Sorcerers*, London: Frederick Muller.

Shakley, M. (1978) 'How the megaliths were moved', *Country Life* 26 October, 1305.

Sharples, N. and Sheridan, A. (eds) (1992) *Vessels for the Ancestors: Essays on the Neolithic of Britain and Ireland in Honour of Audrey Henshall*, Edinburgh: Edinburgh University Press.

Sherratt, A. G. (1972) 'Socio-economic and demographic models for the neolithic and bronze ages of Europe', in D. L. Clarke (ed.), *Models in Archaeology*, London: Methuen.

Shortt, H. de S. (1946) 'Bronze Age beakers from Larkhill and Bulford', *WAM*, 51, 381–3.

Shotton, F. W. (1978) *British Quaternary Studies: Recent Advances*, Oxford: Clarendon Press.

Smith, A. G. (1970) 'The influence of mesolithic and neolithic man on the British vegetation: a discussion', in D. Walker and R. G. West (eds), *Studies in the Vegetational History of the British Isles*, Cambridge :Cambridge University Press.

Smith, G. (1973) 'Excavation of the Stonehenge Avenue at West Amesbury, Wiltshire', *WAM* 68, 42–56.

—— (1979–80) 'Excavations in Stonehenge car park', *WAM* 74–5, 181.

Smith, I. F. (1971) 'Causewayed enclosures', in D. D. A. Simpson (ed.), *Economy and Settlement in Neolithic and Early Bronze Age Britain and Europe*, Leicester: Leicester University Press.

—— (1974) 'The neolithic', in A. C. Renfrew (ed.), *British Prehistory*, London: Duckworth.

Smith, J. (1771) *Choir Gaur; the Grand Orrery of the Ancient Druids, Commonly called Stonehenge*, Salisbury.

Somerville, B. (1923) 'Orientation in prehistoric monuments of the British Isles,' *Archaeologia* 73.

Spence, M. (1894) *Standing Stones and Maeshowe of Stenness*, Paisley: Rilko.

Squier, E. G. and Davis, E. H. (1848) *Ancient Monuments of the Mississippi Valley*, Boston: Smithsonian Institution.

Stevens, F. (1919) 'Skeleton found at Fargo', *WAM* 40, 359.

—— (1938) *Stonehenge Today and Yesterday*, London: HMSO.

Stone, E. H. (1924) *The Stones of Stonehenge*, London: Robert Scott.

—— (1925–6) 'The story of Stonehenge', *Wiltshire Gazette*, 17, 24 Sept. 1, 8, 15 Oct. 17, 24, 31 Dec. (1925) 7, 14, 21, 28 Jan. (1926).

Stone, J. F. S. (1933) 'A middle bronze age urnfield on Easton Down, Winterslow, *WAM* 46, 218–24.

—— (1935) 'Some discoveries at Ratfyn, Amesbury and their bearing on the date of Woodhenge', *WAM* 47, 55–67.

—— (1938) 'An early bronze age grave in Fargo Plantation near Stonehenge', *WAM* 48, 357–70.

—— (1941) 'The Deverel-Rimbury settlement on Thorny Down, Winterbourne Gunner, S Wilts', *PPS* 7, 114–33.

—— (1947) 'The Stonehenge Cursus and its affinities', *Arch J* 104, 7–19.

—— (1949) 'Some Grooved Ware pottery from the Woodhenge area', *PPS* 15, 122–7.

—— (1958) *Wessex Before the Celts*, London: Thames & Hudson.

Stone, J. F. S., Piggott, S. and Booth, A. (1954) 'Durrington Walls, Wiltshire: recent excavations at a ceremonial site of the early second millennium BC' *Ant J* 34, 155–77.

Stone, J. F. S. and Young, W. E. V. (1948) 'Two pits of Grooved Ware date near Woodhenge', *WAM* 52, 287–306.

Stover, L. E. and Kraig, B. (1978) *Stonehenge: the Indo-European Heritage*, Chicago: Nelson-Hall.

Stukeley, W. (1722–4) 'The History of the Temples of the Ancient Celts', Bodleian Library MS Eng. Misc. c. 323.

—— (1740) *Stonehenge: A Temple Restor'd to the British Druids*, London.

Switsur, V. R. (1973) 'The radio-carbon calendar recalibrated', *Ant* 47, 131–7.

Tarkhanov, A. and Kavtaradze, S. (1992) *Stalinist Architecture*, London: Laurence King.

Taylor, C. and Tratman, E. K. (1957) 'The Priddy Circles', *Proceedings of the University of Bristol Speleological Society* 7, 7.

Thatcher, A. R. (1975) 'The Station Stones of Stonehenge', *Ant* 49, 144–6.

Thom, A. (1951) 'The solar observations of megalithic man', *Journal of the British Astronomical Association* 64, 396–404.

—— (1955) 'A statistical examination of the megalithic sites in Britain', *Journal of the Royal Statistical Society* A 118, 275–95.

—— (1961) 'The geometry of megalithic man', *Mathematics Gazette* 45, 83–92

—— (1962) 'The megalithic unit of length', *Journal of the Royal Statistical Society* A 125, 243–51.

—— (1964) 'The larger units of length of megalithic man', *Journal of the Royal Statistical Society* A 127, 527–33

—— (1967) *Megalithic Sites in Britain*, Oxford: Clarendon Press.

—— (1971) *Megalithic Lunar Observatories*, Oxford: Clarendon Press.

—— (1974) 'Astronomical significance of prehistoric monuments in western Europe', *Philosophical Transactions of the Royal Society of London* A 276, 149–56.

—— (1975) 'Stonehenge as a possible lunar observatory', *Journal for the History of Astronomy* 6, 19–30.

—— (1977a) 'The Megalithic Yard', *Measurement and Control* 10, 488–92.

—— (1977b) 'Megalithic astronomy', *Journal of Navigation* 30, 1–14.

Thom, A. and Thom, A. S. (1978) *Megalithic Remains in Britain and Brittany*, Oxford: Oxford University Press.

Thom, A., Thom, A. S. and Thom, A. S. (1974) 'Stonehenge', *Journal for the History of Astronomy* 5, 71–90.

Thomas, H. H. (1923) 'The source of the foreign stones of Stonehenge', *WAM* 42 325–44 (and also *Ant J* 3, 239–60).

Thomas, J. (1991) *Rethinking the Neolithic*, Cambridge: Cambridge University press.

—— (1992) 'Monuments, movement and the context of megalithic art,' in N. Sharples and A. Sheridan (eds), *Vessels for the Ancestors: Essays on the Neolithic of Britain and Ireland in Honour of Audrey Henshall*, Edinburgh: Edinburgh University Press.

Thomas, J. and Whittle, A. (1986) 'Anatomy of a tomb – West Kennet revisited *Oxford Journal of Archaeology* 5, 129–56.

Thomas, N. (1964) 'The neolithic causewayed camp at Robin Hood's Ball, Shrewton', *WAM* 59, 1–27.

Thorpe, R. S. and Williams-Thorpe, O. (1991) 'The myth of long-distance megalith transport', *Ant* 65, 64–73.

Thorpe, R. S., Williams-Thorpe, O., Jenkins, D. and Watson, J. S. (1991) 'The geological sources and transport of the Bluestones of Stonehenge, Wiltshire, UK', *PPS* 57, 103–57.

Thurnam, J. (1870) 'On Ancient British barrows', *Archaeologia* 43, 285–552.

Tierney, J. J. (1960) 'The Celtic ethnography of Posidonius', *Proceedings of the Royal Irish Academy* 60, 189–275.

Twohig, E. S. (1981) *The Megalithic Art of Western Europe*, Oxford: Clarendon Press.

Ucko, P. J., Hunter, M., Clark, A. J. and David, A. (1991) *Avebury Reconsidered: From the 1660s to the 1990s*, London: Unwin Hyman.

Vatcher, F. de M. (1961) 'The excavation of the long mortuary enclosure on Normanton Down, Wiltshire', *PPS* 27, 160–73.

—— (1969) 'Two incised chalk plaques near Stonehenge Bottom', *Ant* 43, 310–11.

Vatcher, L. and Vatcher, F. de M. (1973) 'Excavation of three post-holes in Stonehenge car park', *WAM* 48, 57–63.

Vayson de Pradenne, A. (1937) *The Use of Wood in Megalithic Structures*, reviewed anonymously in *Ant* 11, 87–92.

Vyner, B. E. (1988) 'The Street House Wossit: the excavation of a late neolithic and early bronze age palisaded ritual monument at Street House, Loftus, Cleveland', *PPS* 54, 173–202.

Wainwright, G. J. (1969) 'A review of henge monuments in the light of recent research', *PPS* 35, 112–33.

—— (1971) 'The excavation of a late neolithic enclosure at Marden, Wiltshire', *Ant J* 51, 177–239.

Wainwright, G. J., Donaldson, P., Longworth, I. H. and Swan, V. (1971) 'The excavation of prehistoric and Romano-British settlements near Durrington Walls, Wiltshire, 1970', *WAM* 66, 76–128.

Wainwright, G. J. and Longworth, I. H. (eds) (1971) *Durrington Walls: Excavations 1966–1968*, London: Society of Antiquaries.

Webb, J. (1665) *A Vindication of Stone-Heng Restored*, London: R. Davenport.

Wheeler, F. (1966) 'Stonehenge: further software', *New Scientist* August, 251–3.

Whittle, A. (1977) *The Earlier Neolithic of Southern England and its Continental Background*, *BAR* S35.

—— (1985) *Neolithic Europe: a Survey*, Cambridge: Cambridge University Press.

Whittle, P. J. (1978) 'Resources and population in the British Neolithic', *Ant* 52, 34–42.

Wilson, D. R. (1975) 'Causewayed camps and interrupted ditch systems', *Ant* 49, 178–86.

Wood, J. (1740) *Descriptions of Stanton Drew and Stonehenge*, British Library, Harleian MS 7354/5.

—— (1747) *Choir Gaure*, Oxford.

Wood, J. E. (1978) *Sun, Moon and Standing Stones*, Oxford: Oxford University Press.

Worm, O. (1643) *Danicorum Monumentorum Libri Sex*, Copenhagen.

Wrigley, C. C. (1989) 'Stonehenge from without', *Ant* 63, 746–52.

Wymer, J. J. (1977) *Gazetteer of Mesolithic Sites in England and Wates*, Norwich: Geo Abstracts.

INDEX